American Empire in Global History

This book shows how the predominantly national focus that characterises studies of the United States after 1783 can be integrated with global trends, as viewed from the perspective of imperial history. The book also argues that historians of European empires have much to gain by considering the United States after 1783 as a newly-decolonised country that acquired overseas territorial possessions in 1898 and remained a member of the Western 'imperial club' until the mid-twentieth century.

The wide-ranging synthesis by A. G. Hopkins, *American Empire: A Global History* (2018), provides the starting point for contributions that appraise its main theme and take it in new directions. The first three chapters identify fresh approaches to U.S. history between the Revolution and the Civil War, suggesting ways in which the United States can be considered as a newly-decolonised country, examining shifting meanings of the term 'empire', and reassessing the character of continental expansion. The second group deals with initiatives and responses in the Philippines and Cuba, reconsidering the character of nationalism in two of the most important overseas territories that were either ruled directly or controlled indirectly by the United States, and placing it in an international context. The third group examines the exercise of U.S. power in the twentieth century, identifying aspects of international law that have been overlooked and reviewing the extensive literature on the controversial themes of the Cold War and informal empire after 1945.

The ten chapters in this edited volume bring together noted specialists on the history of international relations, the United States, and the insular empire it ruled in the twentieth century. The chapters were originally published as articles in a special issue of *The Journal of Imperial and Commonwealth History*.

Shigeru Akita is Professor of Global History, Osaka University, Japan. His major publications include *From Empires to Development Aid* (2017, in Japanese); (ed. with G. Krozewski); *The Transformation of the International Order of Asia: Decolonization, the Cold War, and the Colombo Plan* (London: Routledge, 2015).

American Empire in Global History

Edited by
Shigeru Akita

LONDON AND NEW YORK

First published 2022
by Routledge
2 Park Square, Milton Park, Abingdon, Oxon, OX14 4RN

and by Routledge
605 Third Avenue, New York, NY 10158

Routledge is an imprint of the Taylor & Francis Group, an informa business

Chapters 1, 2 and 4–10 © 2022 Taylor & Francis
Chapter 3 © 2021 Max M. Edling. Originally published as Open Access.

With the exception of Chapter 3, no part of this book may be reprinted or reproduced or utilised in any form or by any electronic, mechanical, or other means, now known or hereafter invented, including photocopying and recording, or in any information storage or retrieval system, without permission in writing from the publishers. For details on the rights for Chapter 3, please see the chapter's Open Access footnote.

Trademark notice: Product or corporate names may be trademarks or registered trademarks, and are used only for identification and explanation without intent to infringe.

British Library Cataloguing in Publication Data
A catalogue record for this book is available from the British Library

ISBN13: 978-1-032-18668-9 (hbk)
ISBN13: 978-1-032-18669-6 (pbk)
ISBN13: 978-1-003-25564-2 (ebk)

DOI: 10.4324/9781003255642

Typeset in Minion Pro
by Newgen Publishing UK

Publisher's Note
The publisher accepts responsibility for any inconsistencies that may have arisen during the conversion of this book from journal articles to book chapters, namely the inclusion of journal terminology.

Disclaimer
Every effort has been made to contact copyright holders for their permission to reprint material in this book. The publishers would be grateful to hear from any copyright holder who is not here acknowledged and will undertake to rectify any errors or omissions in future editions of this book.

Contents

Citation Information   vii
Notes on Contributors   ix

Part I: Introduction

1   American Empire in Global History   3
      Shigeru Akita

Part II: The American Revolution and The Post-Colonial Order

2   Imperial Confusion: America's Post-colonial and Post-revolutionary Empire   19
      Patrick Griffin

3   United States Expansion and Incorporation in the Long Nineteenth-Century   36
      Max M. Edling

4   The British Empire after A.G. Hopkins's American Empire   64
      Jay Sexton

Part III: Insular Perspectives on Empire

5   Cuba: Context and Consequences for the American Empire   89
      William A. Morgan

6   The Road to 1898: On American Empire and the Philippine Revolution   113
      Reynaldo C. Ileto

7   Restoring Asia to the Global Moment of 1898   135
      Nicole CuUnjieng Aboitiz

Part IV: The Empire in the Twentieth Century

8   Law Against Empire, or Law for Empire? – American Imagination and the International Legal Order in the Twentieth Century   163
Seiko Mimaki

9   Informal Empire and the Cold War   186
Hideki Kan

Part V: Response

10   Imperial Puzzles   219
A. G. Hopkins

Index   238

Citation Information

The chapters in this book were originally published in *The Journal of Imperial and Commonwealth History*, volume 49, issue 3 (2021). When citing this material, please use the original page numbering for each article, as follows:

Chapter 1
American Empire in Global History
Shigeru Akita
The Journal of Imperial and Commonwealth History, volume 49, issue 3 (2021) pp. 401–413

Chapter 2
Imperial Confusion: America's Post-colonial and Post-revolutionary Empire
Patrick Griffin
The Journal of Imperial and Commonwealth History, volume 49, issue 3 (2021) pp. 414–430

Chapter 3
United States Expansion and Incorporation in the Long Nineteenth-century
Max M. Edling
The Journal of Imperial and Commonwealth History, volume 49, issue 3 (2021) pp. 431–458

Chapter 4
The British Empire after A.G. Hopkins's American Empire
Jay Sexton
The Journal of Imperial and Commonwealth History, volume 49, issue 3 (2021) pp. 459–480

Chapter 5
Cuba: Context and Consequences for the American Empire
William A. Morgan
The Journal of Imperial and Commonwealth History, volume 49, issue 3 (2021) pp. 481–504

Chapter 6

The Road to 1898: On American Empire and the Philippine Revolution
Reynaldo C. Ileto
The Journal of Imperial and Commonwealth History, volume 49, issue 3 (2021) pp. 505–526

Chapter 7

Restoring Asia to the Global Moment of 1898
Nicole CuUnjieng Aboitiz
The Journal of Imperial and Commonwealth History, volume 49, issue 3 (2021) pp. 527–552

Chapter 8

Law Against Empire, or Law for Empire? – American Imagination and the International Legal Order in the Twentieth Century
Seiko Mimaki
The Journal of Imperial and Commonwealth History, volume 49, issue 3 (2021) pp. 553–575

Chapter 9

Informal Empire and the Cold War
Hideki Kan
The Journal of Imperial and Commonwealth History, volume 49, issue 3 (2021) pp. 576–606

Chapter 10

Response: Imperial Puzzles
A. G. Hopkins
The Journal of Imperial and Commonwealth History, volume 49, issue 3 (2021) pp. 607–625

For any permission-related enquiries please visit:
www.tandfonline.com/page/help/permissions

Notes on Contributors

Nicole CuUnjieng Aboitiz is Research Fellow at Clare Hall, University of Cambridge, UK. She most recently authored *Asian Place, Filipino Nation: A Global Intellectual History of the Philippine Revolution, 1887–1912* (2020).

Shigeru Akita is Professor of British Imperial History and Global History, and Head of the Division of Global History Studies, Institute for Open and Transdisciplinary Research Initiatives, Osaka University, Japan. His major publications include *From Empires to Development Aid* (2017, in Japanese); (ed. with G. Krozewski) *The Transformation of the International Order of Asia: Decolonization, the Cold War, and the Colombo Plan* (London: Routledge, 2015); *The History of the British Empire from Asian Perspectives* (2012, in Japanese); and *The British Empire and the International Order of Asia* (2003, in Japanese).

Max M. Edling is Reader in Early American History at King's College London. An expert on the American founding and the early federal government, he is the author of *A Revolution in Favor of Government: Origins of the U.S. Constitution and the Making of the American State* (2003); *A Hercules in the Cradle: War, Money, and the American State, 1783–1867* (2014); and *Perfecting the Union: National and State Authority in the U.S. Constitution* (2021).

Patrick Griffin is Madden-Hennebry Professor of History at the University of Notre Dame. His most recently published book is *The Townshend Moment: The Making of Empire and Revolution in the Eighteenth Century* (2017).

A. G. Hopkins is Emeritus Smuts Professor of Commonwealth History in the University of Cambridge. Besides *American Empire: A Global History* (2018), he is the author of *An Economic History of West Africa* (London: Routledge, 2nd ed., 2019); *Africa, Empire and World Disorder: Historical Essays* (London: Routledge, 2020); and with P. J. Cain, *British Imperialism, 1688–2015* (London: Routledge, 3rd ed., 2016).

Reynaldo C. Ileto is Honorary Professor in the College of Asia and the Pacific at the Australian National University. He also lectures on history and politics in the Rajaratnam School of International Studies at the Nanyang Technological University, Singapore. He is the author of *Knowledge and Pacification: On the U.S. Conquest and the Writing of Philippine History* (2017).

Hideki Kan is Emeritus Professor of U.S. Diplomatic History at Kyushu University and Visiting Professor at Osaka University, Japan. His major publications include *American Policy toward Asia in the Cold War Years: The Transformation of the 'Liberal International Order' and 'Japan-U.S. Cooperation'* (2019 in Japanese); *The Cold War and the 'American Century': 'An Informal Empire's Order-Making in Asia* (2016 in Japanese); and *U.S. Global Strategy* (2008 in Japanese).

Seiko Mimaki is Associate Professor at Takasaki City University of Economics. She has published *The Era of the Outlawry of War Movement* (2014, in Japanese); contributed to *The Palgrave Handbook of State-Sponsored History After 1945* (London: Routledge, 2018); *Modern Japanese Political Thought and International Relations* (2018); and *Asia-Pacific between Conflict and Reconciliation* (2016).

William A. Morgan is Professor of History at Lone Star College, U.S. His work appears in *Tabaco y Esclavos en los Imperios Ibéricos* (2015), edited by Santiago de Luxán, João Figueirôa-Rêgo and Vicent Sanz, and in the journals, *Slavery & Abolition* (2016); *Colonial Latin American Review* (2020); and *Agricultural History* (2020). His forthcoming manuscript: *A Different Kind of Servitude: Cuban Tobacco in the Age of Atlantic Slavery* is under contract.

Jay Sexton is the Rich and Nancy Kinder Chair of Constitutional Democracy at the University of Missouri. His most recent publications include *A Nation Forged by Crisis: A New American History* (2018); and two co-edited volumes, with Kristin Hoganson, *Crossing Empires: Taking U.S. History into Transimperial Terrain* (2020) and *The Cambridge History of America in the World*, Volume 2, general editor Mark Bradley, (forthcoming 2021).

Part I
Introduction

American Empire in Global History

Shigeru Akita

This special issue on 'American Empire in Global History' is the result of a joint-research project at the Global History Division, the Institute for Open and Transdisciplinary Research Initiatives (OTRI)[1], Osaka University, to celebrate the 70th Anniversary Annual Congress of Japanese Association of Western History, in May 2020 at Osaka University, Japan. We originally planned to have an international workshop followed by a symposium on '**"American Empire" in the context of Global History'**. The symposium aimed at reconsidering the presence of the United States (US) in the twentieth century by combining recent historiographical developments in studies of the American empire in Europe and the US, with work on international relations and comparative studies of empires by East Asian and Japanese scholars set in the wider context of global history.

The OTRI of Osaka University is conducting a series of joint research projects that are related to the historical origins of the contemporary economic resurgence of East Asia, or 'the East Asian Miracle' (as named in a World Bank report in 1993). We tried to reveal the close links between the development and transformation of 'intra-Asian trade', the emergence of 'open-regionalism' in the Asia-Pacific, and the formation of 'developmental states' and the progress of 'developmentalism' as the driving forces behind the economic resurgence of East Asia. This subject aims to investigate the modern and contemporary international economic order of Asia through collaboration with scholars from the United Kingdoms (UK) and the US as well as Asian scholars from Korea, China, and India. Relevant research areas include the role of hegemonic states in transforming the international order, and the comparative study of empires from the early modern period to the twentieth century.

Based on this experience, we decided to start our project by examining a provocative book, *American Empire: A Global History*, written by Antony Hopkins. We have eight contributors to this special issue from the US, the UK, the Philippines, Australia, and Japan. Some are well-established senior scholars; others are young and spirited historians. Due to the Covid-19 pandemic, we organised four intensive Zoom meetings in 2020 as substitutes for the Congress.

American Empire and Globalisation

Given that *American Empire* is a large, wide-ranging book that covers three centuries, readers might find a compass and map helpful in guiding them through the detailed essays in this volume. The book approaches U.S. history from an external perspective to reappraise events that have usually been considered within a domestic frame of reference. The central hypothesis holds that important and familiar developments can be fitted into the history of globalisation, which encompassed most of the Western world from at least the eighteenth century onwards and spread throughout the globe in the nineteenth and twentieth centuries. The Osaka group's complementary approach covered the history of globalisation from the Mongolian World Empire in the thirteenth century to the present.[2] It paid close attention to the role of empires, which contributed to the development and transformation of globalisation, not only in early-modern Asia on the Eurasian continent but also in the modern and contemporary world. The so-called 'American Empire', or the global-scale American hegemony in the twentieth century, known as the 'Pax Americana', can be included in this wider range of empire studies. By utilising Hopkins's *American Empire*, we aim to locate and interpret familiar features of US history as crucial components of global history.

American Empire conceives of globalisation not as a general, undifferentiated process that simply became bigger over time, but as three overlapping but still distinct phases – proto, modern, and post-colonial – each with distinguishing characteristics. The book then argues that empires were the most powerful agents of globalisation during this period. The transformation of one phase into another was driven by a dialectic that elevated a particular social formation to the point where countervailing forces arose to challenge its supremacy. These propositions are expanded to show how each phase applied first to the mainland colonies and then to the US, which retained close ties with Europe and, in particular, the UK. The book brings economic considerations into focus, while also linking them to political and cultural developments to avoid charges of determinism and monocausality. The discussion of post-colonial globalisation in the final part of the *American Empire* differs from previous chapters. Its purpose is not to produce a comparably detailed account but to identify the main features of the emerging post-colonial order, which represents a fundamental departure from the conditions that had defined the great age of Western territorial empires. Post-colonial, it is worth noting, is not synonymous with post-imperial. Imperialism can survive the end of formal colonial rule.

Proto-globalisation was the product of pre-industrial, predominantly agricultural economies and dynastic states under the control of landowners. Although the reach of these societies extended to distant parts of the world, their ability to penetrate societies beyond Europe was limited by technological constraints. Improvements in the technology of destruction, however, were sufficient to transform military power and led to increased warfare among European states during the eighteenth century. The result was a rapid growth in public debt and a mounting financial crisis that eventually brought down many of Europe's dynastic states. The UK survived partly because its financial system was superior to those of continental European states. Moreover, it used the empire to offset the costs of war and avert domestic discontent. India served the purpose for a time but soon became a costly commitment. At that point, the government in London turned to the mainland colonies as a source of taxation that would help reduce the national debt. The move proved to be counter-productive; it played a key role in the American Revolution and the consequent creation of the US in 1783. Independence, however, was formal rather than effective. The US remained dependent on the British connection through continuing bonds spanning the economy, politics, culture, and defence. Any established historiography that treats 1783 as a great divide underestimates the long lines of continuity that survived the constitutional break, as they did in other countries where decolonisation remained incomplete.

Modern globalisation was characterised by the development of industrialisation and the rise of nation-states, which eroded predominantly agricultural societies and displaced or modified dynastic polities. The upheaval brought by the revolutions of the late eighteenth century continued throughout the nineteenth century and was manifested in a political struggle between conservatives and progressives, typically representing land and town, an economic contest between established agricultural interests and expanding urban manufacturing centres, and a developing conflict between capital and labour. The strains imposed by these structural changes stimulated a range of responses, one of them being the assertive imperialism that was a common feature of the late nineteenth century.

Similar trends affected the US and can be seen in the rivalries that led to the Civil War, the displacement of Southern plantation owners, the demise of slavery, the bonding of a nation-state, and the expansion of modern manufacturing from the 1870s. By the 1890s, these developments had induced rapid social changes, alienated key rural and urban interests, and heightened the political contest to control the federal government. These manifestations of a society caught in the middle of immense structural changes were reproduced throughout Europe. Similarly, the participation of the US in the assertive imperialism that marked the end of the century and the creation of an insular empire was neither a coincidence nor an aberration but a consequence of these developments.

Post-colonial globalisation, which gathered pace after the Second World War, was marked by the rise of mass anti-colonial movements, changes in the structure as well as the orientation of world trade and finance, and the promotion of concepts of human rights through the agency of supra-national organisations, notably the United Nations (UN).[3] These influences were consequences of the further development of the advanced economies, the global spread of industrialisation, and mass opposition to colonial rule, all of which reduced the value of colonies while increasing the cost of holding them. The US fitted into these broad trends, as it had done in the past. It acquired its formal, territorial empire in 1898, at the high point of the scramble for colonies, and unscrambled it after 1945, when the European empires were also being dissolved. Between these dates, the US managed its empire the same way as the European empires and with similar results.

The first three articles in this special issue cover the eighteenth and nineteenth centuries as well as dealing with features of US history that arose from its proto-global phase, when the economy was dominated by agriculture, landed interests (large and small), and slavery. The next three articles illustrate aspects of imperialism during the early phase of modern globalisation. Each represents a historiograpical trend that highlights the role of the recipients of imperialism, or the periphery, whether in opposition or as associates. The two final articles deal with the formation of policies in the twentieth century that either underpinned the empire or sought to perpetuate it after the demise of formal rule.

Decolonisation, Settler Colonialism and Intra-imperial Relationship

Based on these grand outlines of the history of globalisation, as the subtitle of the book indicates, *American Empire* covers the history of US expansion from the eighteenth century to the present. Part I 'Decolonization and Dependence, 1756-1865' (Chapters 2-5) and Part II 'Modernity and Imperialism, 1865-1914' (Chapters, 6-9) occupy about 60 per cent of the text. The main focus of US activities overseas is on the territorial empire from the Spanish-American War of 1898 to the incorporation of Hawai'i as the 50th state in 1959. It is worth emphasising this feature of the book because it deals with four sites in the Caribbean and Pacific (Cuba, Puerto Rico, Hawai'i and the Philippines) that have rarely been given the visibility they deserve in general studies of Western empire-building and management. However, there are two reasons why the book begins in the eighteenth century and covers the nineteenth century down to 1898. The first is obvious: until 1783 the US was itself a colony, or rather a set of colonies under British rule. Durng this period. American Empire meant the British Empire in North America. The second reason is not immediately apparent and follows from the proposition that formal independence in 1783 was not immediately followed by effective sovereignty. On the contrary, during the period down to the Civil War decolonisation was incomplete and the United States remained subject to Britain's informal influence.

The articles by **Griffin, Edling, and Sexton** are concerned with the 'long nineteenth century' in the US. They examine the enduring links between the US and the former colonial power and its implications for the new republic's aim of creating a continental-scale sovereign nation-state. One of the most provocative arguments of *American Empire* is its claim that the US remained dependent on the British connection through continuing bonds spanning the economy (trade, migration, and finance), politics, culture, and defence (through the agency of the Royal Navy). These kinds of dependence on multiple British influences can be related to the famous controversy on 'informal empire' or 'the imperialism of free trade' advanced by Gallagher and Robinson in 1953. *American Empire* underlines the need to consider the historical process of 'decolonisation' in a long perspective. Formal indpendence can be dated to the day and hour; effective independence is the work of decades.

Griffin re-examines the familiar story of westward expansion after 1783 to see whether it fits the defnition of empire and, if so, in what sense. Territorial acquisition, through wars and treaties with indigenous Americans were undoubtedly imperialist in intent and they have regularly been seen as resulting in the creation of an empire through the ultimate incorporation of Territories into the federal Union. The expansionary process was promoted and accelerated by a huge influx of white settlers and migrants from Europe, who are often gathered together under the heading 'settler colonialism'.[4] Drawing a distinction between post-colonial and post-revolution, Griffin argues that the US was constructing an empire in the eighteenth-century sense of an extensive sovereign state. Jefferson and his successors faced the conundrum of managing a potentially anarchic and radicalised mass of new immigrants. The solution was to appropriate the resources of indigenous Americans to allow the liberty of white Americans to flourish while keeping them within the post-revolutionary state. The strategy did not create an empire in the sense that was to gain currency as the nineteenth century progressed because the constitutent states of the federal Union enjoyed constitutional equality and, unlike colonies, were not subjected to commands from an authoritarian centre. Griffin's central argument not only supports the position taken in *American Empire* but also offers a challenge to specialists to re-think customary approaches to the period by pursing the paradox that the United States acquiesced in continuing dependence on the former colonial power as a means of preserving liberty through territorial expansion.

By concindence rather than planning, **Edling** follows Griffin's lead and carries it through most of the nineteenth century. In a perceptive and thorough review of westward expansion, he, too, concludes that the term 'empire' is applicable only in the eighteenth-century sense. His reasoning, however, adds considerably to our understanding of the acquisition of territory on the continent. It had two distinctive features: reublicanism and federalism. The former installed civic equality; the latter ensured constitutional parity within a federal system. Morewover, they were bound together by one overriding consideration: equality and parity applied to white settlers only. Edling contrasts these conditions, which emphasised homogeneity, with those characterising empires, which relied heavily on their ability to manage, not erase, ethnic, religious, and linguistic diversity. He demonstrates the importance of the racial qualification by tracing the various stages of incorporation of the designated Territories into constituent states of the Union. His interpretation should ensure that westward expansion is seen in a new light that adds to our understanding of the formation of the US state. It should also contribute to the appraisal of the slippery term 'empire' and the wider literature that treats it as a common currency.

Sexton is in sympathy with Hopkins's broad interpretation of the continuing dependence of the US on informal influences stemming from Britain, and contributes some telling examples of the relationship after 1783. He then proceeds to consider the obverse side of the story, namely the ways in which co-existence in the British orbit allowed the US to transmit its own influences to Britain and its empire during the mid-Victorian period. Informal integration was a mutual process, though not an equal one. It was mediated by Anglo-American networks spanning commerce, banking, and socio-political issues. The immense importance of the economic connection gave both parties a stake in upholding it. Liberal ideas stemming from the US model of republican federalism were shipped across the Atlantic. Anti-British diasporic communities, such as the Irish Fenians, and colonial exiles, like the Ghadar Party in California, were among the most fervent advocates of political reform.[5] Britain's imperial policy learned the lesson of 1776 and became willing to devolve sovereignty to the colonies that became dominions. Darker influences were also operating: American attitudes helped to harden opinion in Britain toward racial issues. Relations in foreign affairs were characterised by 'collaborative competition' as in the cases of Latin America and East Asia. In these ways, Sexton's contribution is a valuable reminder that national studies often underplay mutual interactions within empires and elements of co-operation between competing imperial states.

Peripheral Approaches, 'Regions', and Area Studies

The articles by **Morgan, Ileto, and CuUnjieng Aboitiz** analyse peripheries within the formal US insular empire, specifically the Cuba Protectorate and the Philippines, the influences coming from the metropole, and the interactions among them. This approach has become known as the 'peripheral theory' or 'thesis' since the development of Area Studies in the 1960s. The practitioners of the 'peripheral approach' emphasise the causal role of forces on the periphery in both repelling and inviting imperialist influences. Some formulations posit a dichotomy between the centre or core and the periphery and have placed variations of the model in a hierarchical order. Osaka scholars in global history have taken a different position, named the 'four-layers approach' that characterises interactions at different levels: local history, national history, regional history and global history.[6] National history has been a standard unit of analysis for historical studies since the nineteenth century. The Osaka approach is more spacious and not only incorporates research on different perhiperies but also includes perspectives that extend beyond the nation, such as Benedict Anderson's concept of 'imagined communities'.

As an alternative framework of analysis, we propose the 'four-layers approach'. We considered the idea of 'region', which is a key concept in Area Studies, to be a flexible and dynamic unit of analysis. 'Local history' is a common term for a small village or town in the countryside as well as a micro-community. The typical cases of 'region' are applied not only in East Asian Studies, European Union (EU) Studies, and Asia-Pacific Studies but also in Ancient Central-Eurasian Studies (such as the Silk-Road) and Maritime Asian Studies, which can include many states and empires. These can be called 'mega-regional' studies, which try to locate nation-states and other polities in a larger historical framework. Based on these regional perspectives, we can place the American insular empire in the Asia-Pacific, more specifically, in the context of East and Southeast Asian history. We can also connect these mega-regional histories to global history, within which liberal-capitalism and US hegemony functioned, especially during the Cold War. This 'four-layers approach' to global history is useful in avoiding a simple dichotomy between internal and external forces as well as allowing a more flexible understanding of the multiple interactions occurring within and beyond an insular empire.

Morgan shows how Cuba's nationalists created a self-conscious non-racial ideology to counter Spain's insistence on racial hierarchy and applied it successfully through armed resistance that began in 1868 and culminated in 1898, when Spanish rule was brought to an end and replaced by the US. His interpretation is a powerful statement of the 'peripheral thesis' and invites readers to consider how local causes fit with the broader perspective presented in *American Empire*. Although Morgan does not apply the 'four-layers approach', he shows that it is possible to identify themes for comparative study arising from the movement that led both to the end of Spanish rule and the advent of American dominance. One dominant theme, the abolition of slavery, formed the key ideology of the Cuban multi-racial army of liberation. It had a common purpose, based on ideas of racial equality, that resonated widely far beyond Cuba, the Atlantic, and the US. At the same time, the means of escaping slavery differed: in Cuba it took the form of armed struggle; circumstances in the US determined that ending segregation and attaining racial equality would be by protest and court action and would take many decades. A second theme, the attainment of independence, also prompts comparison with the US. In both cases, there were ideological similarities, burdensome taxes, loss of political representation, censorship and arbitrary political decisions that were followed by successful armed resistance. The irony is that, in carrying the ideals and success of the American Revolution into the nineteenth and twentieth centuries, the US also managed to make them appear compatible with creating an empire of its own.

Ileto provides a complementary account of the nationalist movement in the Philippines, while also relating it to causal influences transmitted from Spain. His detailed analysis provides a fresh understanding of the three much-discussed heroes of the nationalist movement: José Rizal, Andrés Bonifacio, and Emilio Aguinaldo. Ileto peels away layers of historiography produced by American rule and subsequent US influences and offers an alternative interpretation based on a forensic examination of the personal history of the three leaders and the rapidly changing circumstances that surrounded them during the 1890s. His analysis includes the role of the Catholic Church and its friar representatives, the importance of Manila as a commercial, educational and political centre, and the role of Hispanised Catholic ***pueblo***, representing local communities outside the capital. This approach identifies the historical and cultural influences spread by Spanish rule and the Spanish Catholic ordering of society. Building on his own research, Ileto proposes a reclassification of the three leaders. [7] Rizal can be seen as a liberal moderate; Bonifacio as a radical who was ill-equipped for leadership; Aguinaldo emerges from the many ambiguities that have accompanied him as both a radical and a local town-mayor who had collaborated with the friars. The final political compromise made by Aguinaldo paved the way for local elites to strengthen their political and social influence under the American rule during the twentieth century. The complex context of resistance to and collaboration with imperialism identifies the ambivalent position of 'collaborators' in the framework of national history and is clearly expressed in the case of the Philippines.[8]

CuUnjieng Aboitiz complements Ileto's analysis by showing that there was an Asian as well as a Western context for understanding Filipino nationalism. She shows how the transformation of the Asian regional order following the Sino-Japanese War (1894-95) and the Russo-Japanese War (1904-05) influenced the American Empire in the Pacific. The Philippines had long-standing connections with the Malay peninsular and with China, especially through commerce and migration from the latter. The large Chinese community in Manila constituted a considerable socio-economic force in the Philippines under both Spanish and American colonial rule. She shows how the rise of the Pan-Asianism influenced Filipino nationalists at the turn of the century, and how in return Filipino opposition to Spain and the US affected nationalist movements in Asia.[9] Southern parts of the Philippines are a part of the Malay-Islamic world and belong to 'Maritime Asia'.[10] By way of these economic-cultural networks and intra-Asian trade, major port-cities in Asia, such as Hong Kong, Singapore, Shanghai, Guangzhou, Yokohama and Kobe, were connected with Manila.[11] These transregional or transnational relationships in the Asia-

Pacific can be seen as intermediate and middle-level channels connecting the Spanish and US insular empire with the emerging Japanese empire to create a form of 'trans-imperial history'.[12]

Informal Empire, 'Open-door Imperialism', and Collaborators

The articles covering the eighteenth and nineteenth centuries lead to Part III of *American Empire*, 'Empires and International Disorder, 1914-1959' and Part IV 'The Outcome: Postcolonial Globalization', which deal with the twentieth-century world order. **Mimaki** and **Kan** examine the growth of US influence and the formation of the 'Pax Americana' in the twentieth century, though they do so in different ways: Mimaki by considering the role of international law; Kan by reassessing the Cold War. Both, however, are primarily concerned with US informal influence rather than with its formal territorial empire. In this regard, they follow the principal path taken by studies of US 'empire' in the twentieth century. Travellers received both direction and impetus from the 'Wisconsin School', which was led in the 1950s and 1960s by William A. Williams, who viewed overseas expansion as 'Open-Door imperialism'. Since then, members of the 'Wisconsin School' have published numerous books and articles on US informal influence in East Asia, while also neglecting the 'formal empire' of insular colonies.[13] As they suggested, to understand the US presence fully, emphasis should also be placed on American informal or indirect influences in East Asia and the Asia-Pacific through trade, finance, and cultural diplomacy.

Mimaki's article fills a gap in *American Empire* by considering the relationship between international law and the growth of US influence overseas.[14] She shows that international law, though apparently objective, functioned as a means of maintaining US economic and strategic interests. These interests were present at the outset of the century, when Secretary of State Elihu Root formulated a way of using international agreements to suit US interests. They were present, too, in Article 10 of the Covenant of the League of Nations (1919), the 'Washington System' following the Washington Conference and the conclusion of the Nine Powers Treaty in 1922-23, and the Pact of Paris (1928), all of which prepared the way for thespread of US 'informal' influence during the inter-war period.[15] Mimaki goes on to argue that, during the second half of the twentieth century, the attitude of the US changed. Following decolonisation, independent states increased their presence in the United Nations and associated international orgnisations. As international law lost its value as an agent of US interests, Washington responded by withdrawing from organisations that might threaten its own sovereignty and by taking unilateral action to achieve its goals.

Kan's article undertakes a detailed examination of US informal influence after the Second World War. His central argument holds that US empire-building transformed itself into a fully-fledged 'informal empire' during the Cold War era, when policy-makers in Washington tried to manage the foreign policies of other countries by establishing collaborative ties with ruling elites in other countries. Kan's application of 'collaboration theory' identifies four categories: acceptance, cooperation, adaptation, and resistance. His analysis covers the Cold War regimes of Chiang-Kai shek in Taiwan, Ngo Din Diem in South Vietnam, Shigeru Yoshida in Japan, Pakistan from 1954 to 1965, Jawaharlal Nehru in India, Rhee Syngman and Park Chun-hee in South Korea, and Suharto in Indonesia.[16] He provides a committed defence of standard accounts of the period, which also emphasise the extent of US informal influence. This position contrasts with that presented in *American Empire*, which takes a sceptical view of claims that informal influence can be equated with informal empire during this period. However, given that assessments of informal influence rely heavily on different emphases being placed on similar facts, Kan's account suggests the advantage of integrating the interpretation in *American Empire* with the rich results of research in Asian Area Studies and other accounts of international relations that have examined the role of collaborators in post-colonial globalisation.

Studies of US informal influence provide a reminder of the need to consider the mutual nature of the relationship between formal and informal techniques of overseas expansion. More concretely, as a prominent Japanese economic historian, Yuzo Yamamoto, has pointed out, both concepts can be used concurrently to explore both US and British overseas influence.[17] In other words, even after the end of the formal US empire in 1959, it remains important to apply the most accurate terms to describe the US international presence during the period of post-colonial globalisation. In this regard, *American Empire* presents a useful conceptual distinction between 'informal empire' and 'hegemony' (aspiring or effective) that invites us to pause before applying the term 'empire' indiscriminately to large, powerful states.

The Way Ahead

Taken together, the eight articles presented here offer new ways of looking at the concept of 'empire' and its history under or, in some cases, besides the American flag. The first three articles underline the benefits of considering the US as a newly decolonised state after 1783 that was beset with practical problems of making formal independence effective. This perspective suggests that standard approaches, which take a predominantly insular approach to the period, fail to capture crucial features of the new republic arising from its continuing and predominantly dependent relationship with the UK. The next three articles, which deal with Cuba and the Philippines, introduce readers to some of the detailed research undertaken on the territorial empire that was acquired after the US had become fully independent and began to advertise its claim to be a world power. The history of the insular empire has long escaped the attention of US historians. The studies presented here detailing local resistance to and collaboration with US incursions and the character of the nationalist movements should not only inform future work on US imperialism but also add to the list of comparative examples of Western empire-building. The two final essays, which deal with the twentieth century, make contrasting contributions: one illuminates a neglected feature of imperial history, namely the changing role of international law; the other gives new life to an old debate by restating, in contrast to the interpretation advanced in *American Empire*, the view that the informal influence of the US after 1945 qualified it for imperial status.

Valuable though they are, the articles in this collection are necessarily selective. As always, much more could be said on a subject that is constantly expanding, even if empires themselves are not. There is space here to mention just two of the themes that are not represented prominently here but deserve further discussion. First, *American Empire* uses the conceptual framework provided by globalisation to add a prominent economic theme to the analysis. Given that economic history has been out of favour for some time and is only now experiencing a revival, the book ought to alert readers to the explanatory value of this approach. To avoid charges of economic determinism, *American Empire* also explores the relationship between this theme and political and cultural influences. Next, although the symposium was unable to cover all the major important topics discussed in *American Empire*, the omissions leave room for contributions from other scholars. Examples include: the reassessment of the Civil War, the revisionist analysis of US imperialism in the late nineteenth century, the review of the record of US colonial rule in the twentieth century, and the account given of the decolonisation of the territorial empire after the Second World War. The main message of the book and this symposium, however, is that fresh thinking on these topics and US history in general will benefit from setting familiar themes in a much larger international and imperial context. Put another way, it can be said that a globalised world requires a global history.

Notes

1. https://en.globalhistoryonline.org/
2. Akita, ed., *Groubaru-ka no Sekaishi [World History of Globalisation]*.
3. Hopkins, "Globalisation and Decolonisation," 275–89.
4. Hechter, *Internal Colonialism: the Celtic fringe in British national development, 1536-1966, 2nd ed*. Recent additions to the literature on settler colonialism are given in the articles by Griffin and Edling that follow.
5. See also, Burton, *The Trouble with Empire*.
6. Akita and Momoki, eds., *Rekishigaku no Frontier [Frontiers of Historical Studies]*, Introduction ; Akita and Momoki, eds., *Global History to Teikoku [Global History and Empire]*.

7. Ileto, *Pasyon and Revolution*
8. Robinson, "Non-European Foundation of European Imperialism," 117–42.
9. For recent comprehensive studies of Pan-Asianism, see Matsumura, ed., *Ajia-Shugi wa Nanio Katarunoka [What Said Pan-Asianism? : Memory, Power and Values]*.
10. As for comprehensive historiography of "Maritime Asian History," please see Momoki, ed., *Kaiiki-Ajiashi Kenkyu Nyumon [Introduction of Maritime Asian History]*; Haneda and Oka, eds., *A Maritime History of East Asia*.
11. As for the formation and development of intra-Asian trade, Sugihara, *Ajiakan-Boeki no Keisei to Kouzou [Formation and structure of Intra-Asian Trade]* .
12. Hedinger and Heé, "Transimperial History," 429–52.
13. Williams, *The Tragedy of American Diplomacy*; LaFeber, *The New Empire* ; McCormick, *China Market*.
14. *Mimaki, Senso-Ihouka Undou no Jidai* [*The era of the Outlawry of War Movement: the Development of International Political Thought during the "Twenty Years' Crisis" in the United States*].
15. Iriye, *After Imperialism; Iriye, The Globalizing of America, 1913-1945*.
16. Kan, *Reisen to America no Seiki: Ajia ni okeru 'Hi-Koushiki Teikou' no Chitsujyo Keisei [The Cold War and the 'American Century': An Informal Empire's Order-making in Asia]*.
17. Yamamoto, "Teikoku towa Nanika" [What are Empires], 3–30. See also, Doyle, *Empires*.

Disclosure Statement

No potential conflict of interest was reported by the author(s).

Funding

Four-times online-zoom meetings in 2020 were financially supported by the Global History Division, the Institute for Open and Transdisciplinary Research Initiatives (OTRI), Osaka University, Japan.

References

Akita, Shigeru and Momoki Shiro, eds. *Rekishigaku no Frontier [Frontiers of Historical Studies]*. Osaka: Osaka University Press, 2008.

Akita, Shigeru and Momoki Shiro, eds. *Global History to Teikoku [Global History and Empire]*. Osaka: Osaka University Press, 2013.

Akita, Shigeru, ed. *Guroubaru-ka no Sekaishi [World History of Globalisation]*. Vol. 2 of Minerva World History Series. Kyoto: Minerva-shobo, 2019.

Burton, Antoinette. *The Trouble with Empire: Challenges to Modern British Imperialism*. New York: Oxford University Press, 2015.

Doyle, Michael. W. *Empires*. Ithaca and London: Cornell University Press, 1986.

Haneda, Masashi and Mihoko Oka, eds. *A Maritime History of East Asia*. Kyoto and Melbourne: Kyoto University Press and Trans Pacific Press, 2019.

Hechter, Michael. *Internal Colonialism: the Celtic Fringe in British National Development, 1536-1966*. Berkeley: University of California Press, 1975. 2nd ed., 1999.

Hedinger, Daniel and Nadi.n Heé. "Transimperial History: Connectivity, Cooperation and Competition." *Journal of Modern European History* 16, no. 4 (2018): 429–452.

Hopkins, Antony G. "Globalisation and Decolonisation." In *Africa, Empire and World Disorder: Historical Essays*, 275–289. London and New York: Routledge, 2021.

Ileto, Reynaldo Clemena. *Pasyon and Revolution: Popular Movements in the Philippines, 1840-1910*. Quezon City: Ateneo de Manila University Press. 1979.

Iriye, Akira. *After Imperialism: the Search for a new Order in the Far East, 1921-1931*. Cambridge, Mass: Harvard University Press, 1965.

Iriye, Akira. *The Globalizing of America, 1913-1945*. Cambridge: Cambridge University Press, 2013.

Kan, Hideki. *Reisen to America no Seiki: Ajia ni Okeru 'Hi-Koushiki Teikoku' no Chitsujyo Keisei [The Cold War and the 'American Century': An Informal Empire's Order-Making in Asia]*. Tokyo: Iwanami-Shoten, 2016.

LaFeber, Walter. *The New Empire: an Interpretation of American Expansion, 1860-1898*. Ithaca: Cornell University Press, 1963.

Matsuura, Masataka, ed. *Ajia-Shugi wa Nanio Katarunoka [What Said Pan-Asianism?: Memory, Power and Values]*. Kyoto: Mineruva-shobo, 2013.

McCormick, Thomas. *China Market: America's Quest for Informal Empire, 1893-1901*. Chicago: Qaudrangle Books, 1967.

Mimaki, Seiko. *Senso-Ihoka Undou no Jidai: 'Kiki no Nijyunen' no Amerika Kokusaikannkei Shiso [The era of the Outlawry of War Movement: the Development of International Political Thought During the "Twenty Years' Crisis" in the United States]*. Nagoya: Nagoya University Press, 2014.

Momoki, Shiro. *Kaiiki-Ajiashi Kenkyu Nyumon [Introduction of Maritime Asian History]*. Tokyo: Iwanami-shoten, 2008.

Robinson, Ronald. "Non-European Foundation of European Imperialism: Sketch for a Theory of Collaboration." In *Studies in the Theory of Imperialism*, edited by Roger Owen, and Bob Sutcliffe, 117–142. London: Longman, 1972.

Sugihara, Kaoru. *Ajiakan-Boeki no Keisei to Kouzou [Formation and Structure of Intra-Asian Trade]*. Kyoto: Mineruva-shobo, 2003.

Williams, William Appleman. *The Tragedy of American Diplomacy*. Cleveland: World Pub., 1959, 2nd ed., 1972.

Yamamoto, Yuzo. "Teikoku Towa Nanika." [What are Empires?.] In ed, *Teikoku no Kenkyu [Studies of Empires]*, edited by Yamamoto Yuzo, 3–30. Nagoya: Nagoya University Press, 2003.

Part II
The American Revolution and The Post-Colonial Order

Imperial Confusion: America's Post-colonial and Post-revolutionary Empire

Patrick Griffin

ABSTRACT
This essay explores the question of whether we should consider the newly-independent United States an 'empire.' It does so by discussing emerging schools of thought that have suggested that the post-revolutionary state was more powerful than we had previously reckoned, as well as those that argue that the new state, though efficacious, is best considered post-colonial in its international standing and in its fit in a global political economy. To reconcile these positions, to tie the post-revolutionary to the post-colonial, we would be wise to look around the Atlantic and consider how what was happening in the United States was not exceptional during the broader Age of Revolution. The United States, like others, had to be an expansive state – even if the word 'empire' does not fit its case perfectly – to address its continuing colonial status stemming from independence and the dilemmas created by revolution.

Introduction

I am confused. Let me try to explain why. In a recent edition of the flagship journal in colonial American history, the *William and Mary Quarterly*, Gautham Rao wrote a long essay on 'the New Historiography of the Early Federal Government.' In it, Rao discusses how the early American polity was, in fact, 'an imperial state.' The story he presents is not novel. For some time, historians have been telling us as much.[1] For ages we thought that the state was weak. Conventional wisdom suggested that weakness stemmed from a revolutionary inheritance. The Revolution inclined men and women to fear power. Think here of Bernard Bailyn's *Ideological Origins of the American Revolution* and how he encouraged us to see how the fight between liberty and power transfixed Americans. Because power was always in tension with liberty, they erred in the direction of attenuated sovereignty.[2] Rao shows how this simple balancing act does not get at the ways in which the founders and others embraced power. Even if citizens of the United States proved proverbial amateurs compared to 'real' imperial powers, like all those in Europe with their fiscal-military states, Rao compiles much of the work done lately to demonstrate what anyone in the field now knows: far from weak, the state wielded considerable power. Of course, the debate centres on just how considerable we should consider considerable, and what made it so. Nonetheless, as Rao argues, we have witnessed a sea change when it comes to appreciating the efficacy of a state we usually think tipped the balance to legitimacy just after revolution came to a close. This is what we have come to know as 'the new history of the state.' This has become a new and exciting orthodoxy.

Now, here is the source of my confusion. Lately, I picked up a book by a British imperial expert named A.G. Hopkins. His name, of course, is synonymous with studies of British empire and lately with global history. In a bold book simply called *American Empire: A Global History*, Hopkins argues that all this talk about American empire is overwrought.[3] America, he believes, did not have an empire – or a proper one – until the Spanish-American War. At that point, America left the kid's table of global power politics to join the adults. That is when unambiguously the United States could stand 'among the powers of the earth.' Before this? Well, Hopkins thinks that America was still dependent on Britain. As a quasi-colonial appendage of what we call 'informal empire,' how imperial could the United States really be? To be sure, he acknowledges that Americans pressed themselves across the Continent, but this did not add up to real empire, but a version of 'internal colonialism,'[4] or what we would more fashionably these days call 'settler colonialism.'[5] The weakness of the state, not its power, allowed this to be. As an accomplished comparativist, Hopkins knows how to persuasively place early America in a broader context. And once he does so, all of our talk about imperial America, at least before the twentieth century, seems overblown. After the Revolution, America still functioned as a colony.

What to make of my confusion? We could address these questions centring on the imperial nature of the state in a number of ways. The most obvious would be to consider the word 'empire.' How could we or should we define empire? Of course, the answers lie in the eye of the beholder. Or, if I can mix my metaphors, should we think of empire like a duck or like pornography? We would, I wager, know it when we saw it, or heard it when it quacked. But as Hopkins suggests, once we go down the rabbit hole of definitions, everything 'frays at the edges.'[6] He is right. Definitions of this sort prove devilishly difficult; in fact, trying to fasten on one at the expense of other plausible definitions would not address my confusion and only add to yours.

So, let's think of another way. I would like to bring us to different words, ones stressed by Rao and Hopkins respectively: 'revolution' and 'colonial.' For once we understand that these dynamics and the ways they were related, more than anything else, transfixed Americans, we gain a greater appreciation of how they thought power should work in their society. Revolution did not only revolve around ideas, as someone like Bailyn suggests, but process and a colonial past. As part of the revolutionary process, Americans also had to address their colonial inheritance, not only their continuing dependence on a great power but the many twisted legacies of their history. More to the point, the post-revolutionary and post-colonial were entangled. The end result was this: Americans had to reckon with power in ways that made them uncomfortable. They had to if they wanted to bring revolution to a close. Doing so entailed confronting their own colonial ghosts and then using these very same ghosts to end revolution and to impose a new colonial regime of their own. Ultimately, they had to imagine and then create, to invoke Jefferson's evocative phrase, 'an empire of liberty.' Was this an empire that imperialists would recognise as such? Maybe. Maybe not. But it certainly functioned like one.

We can, I think, only appreciate this phrase if we use a broad comparative approach, but one that differs a bit from Hopkins and from those cited by Rao. For the answer to the question posed by American empire does not only lie in comparing its emergence to other former colonies of empire, or of seeing America as an exceptionally expansive place with a frontier, but of also seeing it within a broader age of revolution. Employing this formulation to address my confusion is not a novel move. Since the time of R.R. Palmer and Jacques Godechot, and in a more pronounced way since the birth of the 'new' Atlantic history, the Atlantic revolution framework has enjoyed great appeal.[7] Through recent work especially, we now appreciate that experience in the age was defined by the ways the local and particular were bound to the broad and general. This essay takes this tack. Doing so allows us to reconcile the two approaches that have confused me so much. The new United States cohered to broader sets of revolutionary and imperial rules, but in ways that spoke to its distinctive colonial history and nature of its revolutionary experience. It offered a variation on a common set of themes. Hopkins, I think, usefully asks to consider America after its revolution a 'post-colonial' society. This is something that most of the new-history-of-the-state people miss. What he does not suggest, I think, and what many of the people Rao lionises take for granted, is the fact the America was 'post-revolutionary' state. In fact, as I shall argue, the newly independent Americans used the post-colonial to address the post-revolutionary, an entangling which helps us appreciate the nature of the early American state.

The Case Against Empire

As I say above, Hopkins is a first-rate comparativist, who views American power through the prism of other imperial stories.[8] Before revolution, as he suggests, America was a colonial outpost of a broader British empire, and the story of independence has less to do with ideals of liberty than with the tensions of managing empire in a competitive world. In doing so, Hopkins places the history of the colonies and their break with the mother country within a broader British narrative of a global imperial age. When it comes to independence, and thinking of the first chapters of the American Revolution as a crisis of British empire, he is not alone. As the late great American historian John Murrin put it, the American Revolution 'was a crisis of political *integration* that the British state could not handle.'[9] Indeed, many of the latest works on the period and on the origins of the American Revolution situate America in exactly this context. Think here of Eliga Gould, Stephen Conway, Brendan McConville, Steven Pincus, and Andrew O'Shaughnessy, not to mention Jack Greene, T.H. Breen, and Fred Anderson. For these scholars, changes in the British Atlantic spurred centralising reform, which in turn led to a civil war within the empire. Revolution began as an imperial secession crisis.[10]

These historians offer the latest versions of a running series of interpretations that looked and continue to look across to Britain and its historians for inspiration. Every generation hopes to 'revise' the ways we study eighteenth-century America in light of the latest trends in Britain. We used to call these borrowers part of the 'imperial school' or 'new' Atlanticists. Now they are everyone who is doing good work on revolutionary origins. Americans were an imperial people – 'far-west Britons,' we could call them – and the experience of engaging with debates over empire in the years after the Seven Years' War – even if peripherally – pointed out the fact that the idea of empire structured the ways they understood power. They both dreaded unregulated power and gloried in being part of a greater imperial whole. To put it another way, and I think Hopkins would have no truck with this characterisation, empire was the template for how Americans, and by extension all Atlantic peoples, appreciated power. Sovereignty was inextricably bound to empire. As such, Americans were both colonists and an imperial people, who would go to war with empire.[11]

Given how Hopkins casts the pre-independence period, we would expect that the Revolution would prove a watershed. Some of those who agree with his pre-independence interpretation of Americans as an imperial people argue that the revolution made them even more imperially-oriented, albeit as imperialists. The Revolution, therefore, loomed large in American sense of self and understandings of sovereignty.[12] For Hopkins, it does not. In truth, Hopkins does not spend much time on the event. In his 700-page book – which incidentally covers nearly everything else; it is an extraordinary piece of work – the Revolution does not merit much of a mention. To be fair, the internal workings of early America do not interest him. And why should they? His interpretation stems from his comparative imperial approach. But if we are interested in understanding how and why the new United States wielded power, we can and should pose the following question: Did America change through revolution? I think he would say not fundamentally.[13]

Hopkins presents us with a tale of 'colonial continuities.'[14] A colonial people on the periphery of a global empire became a post-colonial people still on the global margins of an imperial world. Britain left the period not humbled but reinvigorated, and with new understandings of trade coupled with older ideas about sovereignty, the British empire stood poised for a new period of growth and development. The new United States were – as opposed to was – still bound to this empire, albeit informally. Though technically independent, Americans did not have a state powerful enough to remain independent of Britain's mediating influence around the globe. They could not even control their own borders and frontiers.[15] Culturally, they remained British.[16] They traded within the parameters of the new Pax Britannica. As Hopkins argues, the new nation slotted itself into the global economy in the ways most colonies did in a mercantilist political economy: its farmers produced goods destined for metropoles in exchange for finished products and capital investment. The Royal Navy 'shielded' the newly independent nation; British capital paved the way for expansion. Any development was dependent.[17]

Again, given his argument and its thrust, this characterisation would seem, as Jefferson would say, self-evident. It is important to stress, however, that early American historians rarely – if ever – use the term 'post-colonial' to define the state of the new United States. From this point, as a rule, historians now fast-forward to the tensions and issues of the nineteenth century and what they would mean for American nationhood. Post-coloniality does not fit into interpretations of a society that would with time become a behemoth. As a rule, when we think about the Revolution and what its legacies would be we have a difficult time conceding that the new United States was struggling with the same sorts of issues that would confound other 'post-colonial' societies in the nineteenth and twentieth centuries still in the thrall of more powerful imperial regimes. I use the term literally and conventionally. We do not need to strike a post-modern pose to appreciate that a post-revolutionary society faced the arduous task of negotiating the end of colonial rule and what that rule entailed for society and culture, never mind economy. The end result? Independence represented more aspiration than fact. Hopkins is able to characterise things this way, in part, because of how he views the Revolution as an imperial event and because of his comparative/globalist perspective.

In approaching post-revolutionary America in this way, Hopkins gives us some terrific food for thought. The sorts of issues that would bedevil others who would fight for independence also haunted Americans, and the world they inherited also was defined by the frameworks their former colonial masters had imposed and the global world of sovereign competition they had to navigate. In this story of continuities, it stands to reason that the Revolution did not matter all that much and therefore does not feature in Hopkins' treatment. To understand Americans in the 1780s and 90s means appreciating what made them tick in the 1750s and 60s; sovereign status changed but condition did not. Hopkins work points us to the conclusion that 'empire of liberty' amounted to a myth. It allowed Americans to conceive of themselves as exceptional and to learn to live with the galling aspects of their subservient status in an imperial world. Americans employed the term – well, Jefferson did – but it papered over the reality of what they had become and what they aspired to be. It was not fact. They did not differ from others who had been colonised. The real story, Hopkins suggests, lies elsewhere.

The Case for Empire

Not so for those trained as Americanists, certainly those writing recently. They encourage us to pay attention on a different 'post' experience. And if anything, they are transfixed with Jefferson's phrase. It explains a great deal once we unpack it. As a rule, scholars of 'new history of the state' focus on the revolution and what it did to American society to understand the politics and culture of the new state. For them, the new United States was – not were – a 'post-revolutionary' society. The best historian on this point is Peter Onuf. Onuf argues that Americans struggled with the implications of mass mobilisation in the wake of the Revolution. To prosecute a war against Britain meant unleashing America's human capacity. Men and women had to be mobilised for the war effort, and the elites of the early republic inherited a society that was caught in the throes of revolutionary ferment. All were playing roles they had previously been unaccustomed to. Leaders had to manage this dynamic with the tools at hand. For Onuf and for others who subscribe to his views, fighting a war and dealing with a democratised people meant that the state, which had already augmented its capacity through war-making, would be compelled to amplify it further still.[18]

According to these historians, the independent United States faced a 'post-revolutionary' dilemma. Americans had experience negotiating the tensions Onuf lays out. As provincials in an empire, they had encountered a similar dilemma earlier. In the years before the Revolution, local elites had to decide if they were willing to run the risk of social revolution – the threat from below – to confront the threat from without – a reforming and assertive British empire. They made a decision that they could manage this dilemma, that they could hold onto the autonomy that had defined colonial American life throughout the eighteenth century. They could resist imperial demands that impinged on their freedom to engage the Atlantic as they saw fit while ensuring that any resulting social tensions unleashed by imperial destabilisation did not overwhelm them.[19] After the war, and now independent, elites confronted a similar concern: could they put the genie of mobilisation back into the bottle? Of course, they could not revert to a pre-war understanding of deference. Popular sovereignty, after all, had become animating fact. The new national elite, though, had to see to it that the Furies of revolution could be consigned to oblivion, and doing so entailed muting and channelling the voice of the people. Only the state could play this role. Its powers had to grow alongside democratic impulses if Americans were to be able to leave a revolutionary world. The result was an efficacious state with enriched capacity through war-making to manage space and manage a politicised people.[20]

The American genius was to obscure the powers of this new state, as Brian Balogh suggests.[21] And throughout the early part of the nineteenth century, this is how American power functioned. Part of this functioning was imperial in scope. The federal arrangement allowed a virus-like replication of powerful quasi-sovereign entities, the states, to expand across space. They captured, domesticated, and also critically harnessed the energies of mobilised (and politicised) men and women. Officials came to see that the West could serve as a safety valve for politicisation so long as the federal arrangement held and news states could be added to the old. They would be brought in on exactly the same footing as older states. In this way, the states within the state were premised and primed for expansion. 'Imperium in imperio,' previously considered a political heresy, became an article of faith for a post-revolutionary people. This proved the only way that popular sovereignty could serve the purposes of sovereignty and not act against it. Did empire result? Well, this did: an embryonic nation-state built on multiple layers of shared power and imperialist expansion, much of which was accomplished by subjecting indigenous peoples and harnessing slave labour.[22]

The so-called 'empire of liberty,' maybe not fully operating as conventional empires would in the nineteenth century, was an internally-focused entity that was designed to grow outward. Even as the United States looked to carve out a niche in a world of imperial nation-states, the 'emperor of liberty' and others were as consumed with internal dynamics as they were with dominating regions beyond the frontier. And Jefferson above all others served as architect for the symbiótic relationship between sovereign power and popular domestication that would sustain America's lurch across the West. He would, fittingly, be the first president to imagine a western American domain, but one meant to preserve what had been achieved in the East. In making this point, scholars like Onuf, Frank Cogliano, and most significantly Max Edling demonstrate the sinews of an American expansionist state were made of such stuff. This new nation could with time control and police its borders, allowing it to stand 'among the nations of the earth,' as Eliga Gould suggests. It could, Edling argues, accomplish all of this inconspicuously.[23]

This interpretation, more importantly, comports with our standard view about what the broader American Revolution meant and means for American sense of self. The 'empire of liberty' said just as much, if not more, about how Americans had to deal with the energies unleashed by popular revolution as it did about asserting itself as a player on an international stage on which empires or expansive states still played the leading roles. Empire of Liberty, then, was not a phrase made up of hollow words. It reflected both the distinctive promise of American nationhood and the non-distinctive ways Americans conceived of sovereignty. With the exception of Gordon Wood, who does not to portray the ideal of 'liberty' in any sort of paradoxical fashion, nearly all political historians would agree with this formulation.[24] Those who see paradox configure the period as one in which the fundamental characteristics of American nationhood, its libertarian ethos and its fascination with power, were laid out. The Revolution may not have been an event driven by ideals – though Wood would argue otherwise – but it was a watershed that left a Janus-faced inheritance. Discussions of post-coloniality? They do not feature. Post-revolution? It is the only game in town.

In this regard, the story of the United States that the new-history-of-the-state school posits is hardly exceptional. The history of France in this period, of course, follows this pattern. Those mobilised had to smell the whiff of grapeshot from time to time, as Napoleon said, if revolution was to end. And throughout these years, in the streets of Paris and in battlefields far from France, men and women had become political creatures. Arguably, this is the story of the whole age. Even those who did not experience revolution – like the Prussians, the Austrians, and especially the British – also contended with similar pressures. To keep pace with the French, as war became entangled with revolutionary energies, meant doing what the French had done to get men into the field. Though all did not have to resort to a levee en masse, the need for men was felt acutely by all throughout the age, even those untouched by revolutionary ferment. These genies also had to find bottles, and states with increased capacity through a generation of war-making had the measure of them. Once, again, all was not coercion. Common men who mobilised for war were offered cultural currency or some share of political rights in exchange for becoming peaceable once more. British reform followed this script, but so too did Prussian nationalist discourse. The winners and losers of the age, those whose worlds had been turned upside down and those that remained secure had to address the same sorts of problems that compelled American elites to meet in the stuffy room in Philadelphia to draft a constitution, one that both recognised a politicised and mobilised people but that muted their voices in the same breath, and to imagine an American West that could disperse popular energies. All faced the same conundrum the United States did, even if the specific answers differed.[25]

A Post-colonial and Post-revolutionary State

Two persuasive interpretations, and two that place the United States in broader contexts in just the way that scholars have been encouraging us to do for the past generation. Moreover, two that eschew American exceptionalism, even if they help explain it. So which are we to subscribe to, without going down into the rabbit hole of definitions? Was the United States a post-colonial or post-revolutionary society? Well, we could argue it was both. And the best way to demonstrate as much is to place both its post-coloniality and its post-revolutionary status in a broader Atlantic context. North Americans, of course, were not the only people to deal with the sort of dilemmas that bedevilled their elites, and these binds that many others throughout the Atlantic had to contend with were both imperial and revolutionary. In fact, in some cases, the two were entangled. Before the age of revolution, all peoples living in colonies (or in Ireland's case, a kingdom-colony) throughout the Atlantic struggled with the provincial imperial dilemma that Americans confronted. All empires in the wake of the Seven Years' War reformed. All elites struggled to contain pressures from below as they pushed against metropolitan assertions of authority. Of course, North American creoles would only be the first to push back so hard that imperial sovereignty teetered and then collapsed. But they would not be the last. The Irish, all in Latin America, those in Saint-Domingue would encounter the sort of creole imperial dilemma that Americans had.[26]

Like those in Latin America, like the Irish and Haitians, American experiences would be complicated because the inheritors of British America lived in both an age of *independence* and an age of *revolution*. As a rule, creole rebellion, no matter where it happened, helped turn society upside down. In this broader age, empires first fractured along their peripheries in the places furthest removed from authority. They did so because imperial officials in metropoles had to manage their holdings and the people who lived on them in more thoroughgoing fashion to create fiscal military states that could compete in a world of heightened competition. As the era of revolution wore on, these pressures only grew. Because of these geo-political realities, provincial dilemmas, themselves a pretty straightforward push and pull between the metropole and colonies, became bound to revolutionary dilemmas. The sorts of tangled tensions persisted after independence, only now they were defined as *post*-colonial and *post*-revolutionary. Their intersection defined the lot of many throughout the Atlantic in these years.

All former colonists would also have to deal with the pressures and tensions that Americans like Jefferson had to address in the wake of revolutionary ferment. Independence simplified tensions, giving them a channel and vent. It also created vexing problems as those below could point to service against empire to buttress their claims, and all legitimacy was premised upon the anti-imperial. In this vein in particular, post-revolution could not be disentangled from post-colonial. The details may have differed – again premised on intellectual inheritance and on deep and more proximate history – but those who claimed independence in an era of revolution tended to respond in similar ways. They, too, as we shall see, were impelled to create their own 'empires of liberty,' even if their parameters differed.

Many peoples throughout the Atlantic in these years (or in the case of Latin America, a generation later) were 'post-colonial' and 'post-revolutionary' peoples. The Haitians, Colombians, Mexicans, all had to reckon with the costs of politicisation and mobilisation and with colonial hold-overs. Politicisation gripped each society in which sovereignty effectively collapsed, and each fell apart along the fault-lines that had been created in colonial periods. The competition to reconstitute legitimate political authority that ensued also cohered to colonial fault lines. Read any history of these places in these years, and the parallels are unsurprisingly evident. Here's how the stories go. Imperial sovereignty cracks, fault lines are exposed, competition ensues to reconstitute sovereignty, men and women are politicised, and violence results. In each place, moreover, elites have to try to manage the forces of mobilisation by acknowledging colonial pasts. All are not only involved in revolution but also in the wars that go hand-in-hand with them. To fight them means that more men from marginalised groups have to be put under arms, and armed men usually don't give up their weapons without some sort of assurances or unless leviathan can overawe them. To emerge from the period means that these fraught and fractured post-revolutionary societies have to re-enter an international order still defined by empire and an ideal of free trade in which they enjoy no competitive advantages. To survive and to bring internal order to their own societies, they have to look to suitors, like the British. Once again, this story is the same in each of these places, even for some – such as those in Haiti – who could not find post-revolutionary patrons. The American story, therefore, seems to be one of the broader age.[27]

How do we explain the 'success' North American revolutionaries achieved? Part of the answer stems from some exceptional circumstances. The empire of liberty could only be imagined or countenanced when one had at one's disposal space, a people who could be regarded as racially or culturally inferior, and a past that harkened back to both of these. In this vein, 'post-coloniality' matters a great deal. Americans had ample experience clearing the land of Indians. Indeed, at the time of the Revolution, they argued that independence could be conceivable because of a long history serving as the vanguard of colonisation. After all, they had cleared a 'wilderness.'[28] In this regard, Frederick Jackson Turner did and does have a point. We might not couch the frontier as 'a line' separating 'civilization and savagery,' but as he argued, the process of moving west did have implications for a democratic ethos, and it depended quite simply on having land that settlers construed as 'available,' as well as a past premised on appropriation. What we know now is the facilitating role the state played in all this. It was hardly an invisible hand, even if it was not as powerful as those of other sovereign powers.

What also made America's case distinctive, and I think Hopkins is right in this regard, is the fact that America could disperse revolutionary energies across space with the impunity that was supplied by British power. The United States needed both to work in tandem. And in this vein, Hopkins has given us a powerful means of addressing America's response to its post-revolutionary dilemma. Post-coloniality – combining their colonial past of appropriation with their neo-colonial status within informal empire – helped Americans solve their post-revolutionary conundrum. They could run roughshod over the continent.

The Treaty of Paris conferred space. The Louisiana Purchase would offer more. Yes, there were snags; 1812 comes to mind. Yet, under the veneer of the British imperial gaze, Americans could reject British notions of development across time to have the freedom to expand across space. Think here of Drew McCoy, who argued that Americans understood and feared how their society would develop through discrete stages with time, which could imperil republican virtue. Instead, they hoped to allow the nation-state to expand westward and so avoid the later stages of development that could kill the nation's republican ethos. His notion that America could forestall development over time by moving across space is only imaginable if the United States had freedom to move.[29] With the British gone as rulers but still present after the Revolution as patrons, the eastern woodlands were available to expansion. With the Napoleonic Wars, the rest of the continent lay open. And Britain was happy to let the United States have its way on land, so long as the new nation was beholden to the free trade empire of the seas. In fact, the City of London provided a great deal of the financing for the westward movement.[30] Ironically, Americans did much of what they did with British help to try to become fully free of British hegemony on the high seas. British protection proved the only reliable means to step outside of Britain's ample international shadow.[31]

The British role can help us explain why the United States differed from other societies in the New World which also struggled with their post-revolutionary and post-colonial conundrums. Without a doubt, that instability which dogged others contending with the post-revolutionary and post-colonial dilemmas did not stymie Americans. For Americans, the typical post-colonial struggles never emerged as such because Americans had the autonomy to expand while the other legatees of empire devoured themselves as they tried to put revolution to bed. The successor states of Spanish American empire, of course, are often seen as not following what should be the normative model. In fact, the United States proved the outlier. It had fertile land and the silent protection to use it to disperse the energies that crippled the new republics to the south. All creole societies had to try to reconcile home rule with rule at home in an age of independence and revolution. British informal empire gave the United States an advantage in doing so. This arrangement would hold until the years before the Civil War, when the fundamental issue not resolved by the Revolution – slavery – could not be displaced across space any longer. Then the post-colonial came back with a vengeance. Arguably, the British umbrella brought the new republic time that other creole revolutionaries were not granted by their unresolvable post-colonial status.

Perhaps America was exceptional in managing post-revolutionary and post-colonial pressures by resorting to imperial practices under the protection of empire. The end result was American empire, or something quite like it. A post-colonial federal state – one designed for colonial expansion – was the only way to manage a post-revolutionary society. Only a dependent empire could manage post-coloniality. In this way, Jefferson was an American Napoleon. Like those others who pressed the state outward to address internal tensions, such as Napoleon did across all of Europe and even to Egypt and Saint-Domingue, Jefferson also was the architect of post-revolutionary expansion, and perhaps its most articulate prophet. Think here, too, of Simon Bolivar, Jose de San Martin, and Toussaint Louverture. Each of these revolutionaries, people who weighed their own provincial dilemmas, all used expansive power to address the Furies. Nonetheless, none proved as successful as Jefferson.[32] Though he only uttered the phrase 'empire of liberty' twice, by using it he was capturing how this group of creole revolutionaries could address the complex relationship between revolution and empire in ways others could not, even if they aspired to. America was able to harness its colonial past to expand across space and to address its post-revolutionary present. The British afforded them the protection to do so. Others did not have this luxury.

Empire of and for Liberty?

The paradox Jefferson left us with, of course, centred on squaring liberty and power. It also was about squaring the varied inheritances of the Revolution. Americans could countenance expansive state power, so long as they could believe it was balanced by liberty. What they could not stomach was the fact that they were still dependent. That is the truth that dare not speak its name. But this is the silent feature of the age that underscored the balance Jefferson worked so hard to achieve.

Maybe what Americans created then, one final way to address my confusion, was an empire 'of and for' liberty.[33] Theirs was aspirational, but also reactive. The formulation cohered to the world they inherited, one in which they appeared as pygmies in a world of imperial giants. Hence they needed to bind themselves informally to a formal empire in order to manage the Hobbesian world of international rivalry and burgeoning free trade. Yet equally imperative was the need to address the very real pressures unleashed by revolution. Expanding, even if under a British umbrella of protection – or better, because of that umbrella – could only address this concern fundamental to internal stability. Jefferson's genius was, perhaps, binding these two together. America could act imperially because it was part of another empire. Nonetheless, to those Indians on the receiving end, these concerns were academic. The empire of and for liberty was aimed at them. Given the geographical position of the United States, and the fact that it had protection and an urgent need to expand, it could not be any other way. Or so thought America's Bonaparte and Bolivar, Thomas Jefferson.

Even though America's experience was not exceptional but was born through the pressures of the age, the empire of liberty would be distinctive. It represented a peculiarly American response, one rooted in its geography and its history of coercion and within empire, and it would be imperial. The American imperial state was, no doubt, more decentralised and less powerful than others, but it was the product of revolutionary inheritance. It was federal, volitional, and democratic, less driven by the centre, in a way that spoke to how revolutionary energies had been unleashed and had to be recognised. The new state did not so much animate but manage these tensions. And this was an estimable challenge, one a state with expanded capacity was up to. At the same time, Americans could not accept that they were creating something that resembled an empire. This represents part of their post-colonial inheritance. They were crafting a vision of sovereignty premised on the rejection of the very idea of empire. They had to believe they were building something vast that would sustain liberty. That necessarily, in this particular context, entailed expanding. If anything, this imperial 'Catch-22' determined the nature and shape of the early state.

So, let's end where we started, the sources of my confusion and definitions. Was Jefferson's 'empire of liberty' an empire after all? It was, without doubt, a sovereign expansive state. It was premised on a well-articulated understanding of how power should work, and its leaders deployed such power in a sophisticated and conscious fashion. That power was pointed at a group of people deemed culturally and/or racially inferior. The impulse to expand as a colonising state was bound up in the need to secure post-revolutionary stability for the whole, a not uncommon concern for other imperial powers. To put an end to my confusion, let's end with this. The United States was born in a colonial and revolutionary age. It also necessarily came into being in what would be an imperial and new colonial age. The new nation stood on the cusp as one merged into the other. It was bound to both. It was defined by both. The 'empire of and for liberty' could only have emerged in that liminal – and confusing – place-in-time.

Notes

1. Rao, "The New Historiography of the Early Federal Government," 97–128.
2. Bailyn, *Ideological Origins*.
3. Hopkins, *American Empire*.
4. I reckon the inspiration for the term is the old classic by Michael Hechter. See *Internal Colonialism*.
5. This is a very trendy topic. For the idea of settler colonsialism, see Ostler and Shoemaker, "Settler Colonialism in Early American History"; Wolfe, *Settler Colonialism and the Transformation of Anthropology*; Veracini, *Settler Colonialism*; Cavanaugh and Veracini, *The Routledge Handbook of the History of Settler Colonialism*; Hixson, *American Settler Colonialism*; Witgen, "A Nation of Settlers"; Ostler, "Locating Settler Colonialism in Early American History"; and Saler, *The Settlers' Empire Colonialism and State Formation in America's Old Northwest*. For a taste of some of the critiques of this approach, see Daniel Mandell's review of Dahl, *Empire of the People* in the *Journal of American History* 106 (2019): 429–30.
6. Hopkins, *American Empire*, 25.

7. Palmer, *The Age of Democratic Revolution*; and Godechot, *France and the Atlantic Revolution of the Eighteenth Century*. For just the latest examples, see Israel, *The Expanding Blaze*; and Polasky, *Revolutions without Borders*.
8. Hopkins, *American Empire*, 41.
9. Murrin, "1776: The Countercyclical Revolution," 67. Also see Hopkins, *American Empire*, 8.
10. Representative works of this generation of imperially-oriented histories are: Gould, *The Persistence of Empire*; Conway, *The British Isles and War of American Independence*; McConville, *The King's Three Faces*; Pincus, *The Heart of the Revolution*; O'Shaughnessy, *The Men Who Lost America*; Greene, *Evaluating Empire and Confronting Colonialism in Eighteenth-century Britain*; Breen, *The Marketplace of Revolution*; Anderson, *Crucible of War*; Griffin, *The Townshend Moment*.
11. For this, I am indebted to Trevor Burnard, "Continuity, Stability and Prosperity: Eighteenth-Century British History and Even More Revisions Needing Revising," unpublished manuscript; Breen, "Ideology and Nationalism on the Eve of the American Revolution"; Morgan, "The American Revolution"; Andrews, "On the Writing of Colonial History." On the imperial school, see Johnson, "Charles Maclean Andrews and the Invention of American Colonial History."
12. See, for instance, Griffin, "Imagining America's Imperial-Revolutionary Moment."
13. Hopkins, *American Empire*, 190.
14. Ibid., 126.
15. Taylor, *The Divided Ground*.
16. See, for instance, Yokota, *Unbecoming British*.
17. Hopkins, *American Empire*, 158–66, 192–96. For a different take, one which posits that the American tail wagged the British free-trade dog, see Fichter, *So Great a Profit*.
18. Onuf, "Imperial Peoples"; *Jefferson's Empire*; and "Introduction" to *Statehood and Union*.
19. I cover this in *The Townshend Moment*.
20. For a fuller explanation, see Griffin, *The Ties That Bind: On the Age of Revolution* (forthcoming, Yale University Press).
21. Balogh, *A Government out of Sight*.
22. See LaCroix, *The Ideological Origins of American Federalism*. I owe this formulation to Tony Hopkins.
23. Cogliano, The Emperor of Liberty; Edling, *A Revolution in Favor of Government*; Edling, *A Hercules in the Cradle*; Gould, *Among the Powers of the Earth*.
24. See John Brooke's review of Wood's, *Empire of Liberty* in *William and Mary Quarterly*, 3rd ser., 67 (2010): 549–57.
25. For a taste of this, see Cannadine, *Victorious Century*, 54, 74; Linch, *Britain and Wellington's Army*; Alan Forest, Karen Hagemann, and Michael Rowe, "Introduction: War, Demobilization and Memory in the Era of Atlantic Revolution"; Alan Forrest, "The French Revolution and the First Levée en masse"; Hagemann, *Revisiting Prussia's Wars against Napoleon*; Hagemann, "A Valorous Nation in a Holy War."
26. On creoles, see Paquette, *The European Seaborne Empires from the Thirty Years' War to the Age of Revolution*; Simon, *Ideology of Creole Revolution*.
27. Works that stress these themes include Lynch, *Spanish American Revolutions*; Hamnett, *End of Iberian Rule*; McFarlane, *War and Independence in Spanish America*; and Dubois, *Avengers of the New World*.
28. Yirush, *Settlers, Liberty, and Empire*.
29. McCoy, *The Elusive Republic*.

30. On Louisiana in a broader context, see Mikaberidze, *The Napoleonic Wars*.
31. I am obliged to Eliga Gould on this point. It will feature in his forthcoming book entitled *Crucible of Peace: The Turbulent History of America's Founding Treaty* (Oxford University Press).
32. On this, see Lynch, *Simón Bolívar*; Dubois, *Avengers of the New World*.
33. I owe this formulation to Peter Onuf.

Disclosure Statement

No potential conflict of interest was reported by the author(s).

References

Anderson, Fred. *Crucible of War: The Seven Years' War and the Fate of Empire in British North America*. New York: Alfred A. Knopf, 2001.

Andrews, Charles Maclean. "On the Writing of Colonial History." *William and Mary Quarterly*, 3rd series 1 (1944): 27–48.

Bailyn, Bernard. *The Ideological Origins of the American Revolution*. Cambridge, MA: Harvard University Press, 1968.

Balogh, Brian. *A Government out of Sight: The Mystery of National Authority in Nineteenth-Century America*. New York: Cambridge University Press, 2009.

Breen, T. H. "Ideology and Nationalism on the Eve of the American Revolution: Revisions Once More in Need of Revising." *Journal of American History* (1997): 13–39.

Breen, T. H. *The Marketplace of Revolution: How Consumer Politics Shaped American Independence*. New York: Oxford University Press, 2005.

Cannadine, David. *Victorious Century: The United Kingdom, 1800–1906*. London: Viking, 2017.

Cavanaugh, E., and Lorenzo Veracini. *The Routledge Handbook of the History of Settler Colonialism*. New York: Routledge, 2017.

Cogliano, Francis. *The Emperor of Liberty: Thomas Jefferson's Foreign Policy*. New Haven: Yale University Press, 2014.

Conway, Stephen. *The British Isles and War of American Independence*. Oxford: Oxford University Press, 2000.

Dahl, Adam. *Empire of the People: Settler-Colonialism and the Foundations of Modern Democratic Thought*. Lawrence, KS: University of Kansas Press, 2018.

Dubois, Laurent. *Avengers of the New World: The Story of the Haitian Revolution*. Cambridge, MA: Harvard University Press, 2004.

Edling, Max. *A Hercules in the Cradle: War, Money, and the American State, 1783–1867*. Chicago: University of Chicago Press, 2014.

Edling, Max. *A Revolution in Favor of Government: Origins of the U.S. Constitution and the Making of the American State*. New York: Oxford University Press, 2008.

Fichter, James. *So Great a Proffit: How the East Indies Trade Transformed Anglo-American Capitalism*. Cambridge, MA: Harvard University Press, 2010.

Forrest, Alan. "The French Revolution and the First Levée en masse." In *The People in Arms: Military Myth and National Mobilization Since the French Revolution*, edited by Daniel Moran and Arthur Waldron, 8–32. New York: Cambridge University Press, 2003.

Forest, Alan, Karen Hagemann, and Michael Rowe. "Introduction: War, Demobilization and Memory in the Era of Atlantic Revolution." In *War, Demobilization and Memory: The Legacy of War in the Era of Atlantic Revolutions*, edited by Alan Forrest, Karen Hagemann, and Michael Rowe, 3–29. New York: Palgrave Macmillan, 2016.

Godechot, Jacques. *France and the Atlantic Revolution of the Eighteenth Century, 1770–1799.* New York: The Free Press, 1965.

Gould, Eliga. *Among the Powers of the Earth: The American Revolution and the Making of a New World Empire.* Cambridge, MA: Harvard University Press, 2014.

Gould, Eliga. *The Persistence of Empire: British Political Culture in the Age of the American Revolution.* Chapel Hill: University of North Carolina Press, 2000.

Greene, Jack. *Evaluating Empire and Confronting Colonialism in Eighteenth-Century Britain.* New York: Cambridge University Press, 2013.

Griffin, Patrick. "Imagining America's Imperial-Revolutionary Moment." In *Experiencing Empire: Power, People, and Revolution in Early America*, edited by Patrick Griffin, 1–24. Charlottesville: University of Virginia Press, 2017.

Griffin, Patrick. *The Townshend Moment: The Making of Empire and Revolution in the Eighteenth Century.* New Haven: Yale University Press, 2017.

Hagemann, Karen. *Revisiting Prussia's Wars Against Napoleon: History, Culture, and Memory.* New York: Cambridge University Press, 2015.

Hagemann, Karen. "A Valorous Nation in a Holy War: War Mobilization, Religion and Political Culture in Prussia, 1807 to 1815." In *The Napoleonic Empire and the New European Political Culture*, edited by Michael Broers, Peter Hicks, and Agustín Guimerá Ravina, 186–198. Basingstoke: Palgrave Macmillan, 2012.

Hamnett, Brian. *The End of Iberian Rule, 1770–1830.* New York: Cambridge University Press, 2017.

Hechter, Michael. *Internal Colonialism: The Celtic Fringe in British National Development.* New York: Routledge, 1998.

Hixson, Walter. *American Settler Colonialism: A History.* New York: Palgrave Macmillan, 2013.

Hopkins, A. G. *American Empire: A Global History.* Princeton: Princeton University Press, 2018.

Israel, Jonathan. *The Expanding Blaze: How the American Revolution Ignited the World, 1775–1848.* Princeton: Princeton University Press, 2017.

Johnson, Richard. "Charles Maclean Andrews and the Invention of American Colonial History." *William and Mary Quarterly*, 3rd series 43 (1986): 519–541.

LaCroix, Alison. *The Ideological Origins of American Federalism.* Cambridge, MA: Harvard University Press, 2010.

Linch, Kevin. *Britain and Wellington's Army: Recruitment, Society, and Tradition, 1807–1815.* New York: Palgrave Macmillan, 2011.

Lynch, John. *Simón Bolívar: A Life.* New Haven: Yale University Press, 2006.

Lynch, John. *Spanish American Revolutions, 1808–1826.* New York: W.W. Norton, 1986.

McConville, Brendan. *The King's Three Faces: The Rise and Fall of Royal America, 1688–1776.* Chapel Hill: University of North Carolina Press, 2007.

McCoy, Drew. *The Elusive Republic: Political Economy in Jeffersonian America.* Chapel Hill: University of North Carolina Press, 1996.

McFarlane, Anthony. *War and Independence in Spanish America.* New York: Routledge, 2014.

Mikaberidze, Alexander. *The Napoleonic Wars: A Global History.* New York: Oxford University Press, 2020.

Morgan, Edmund. "The American Revolution: Revisions in Need of Revising." *William and Mary Quarterly*, 3rd series 14 (1957): 3–15.

Murrin, John. "1776: The Countercyclical Revolution." In *Revolutionary Currents: Nation Building in the Transatlantic World*, edited by Michael Morrison and Melinda Zook, 65–90. New York: Rowman & Littlefield, 2004.

Onuf, Peter. "Imperial Peoples: America, Ireland, and the Making of the Modern World." In *Ireland and America: Empire, Revolution, and Sovereignty*, edited by Patrick Griffin and Frank Cogliano, 301–321. Charlottesville: University of Virginia Press, 2021.

Onuf, Peter. *"Introduction" to Statehood and Union: A History of the Northwest Ordinance.* Notre Dame: University of Notre Dame Press, 2019.

Onuf, Peter. *Jefferson's Empire: The Language of American Nationhood.* Charlottesville: University of Virginia Press, 2000.

O'Shaughnessy, Andrew. *The Men Who Lost America: British Leadership, the American Revolution, and the Fate of Empire.* New Haven: Yale University Press, 2014.

Ostler, Jeffrey. "Locating Settler Colonialism in Early American History." *William and Mary Quarterly*, 3rd series 76 (2019): 443–450.

Ostler, Jeffrey and Nancy Shoemaker. "Settler Colonialism in Early American History: Introduction." *William and Mary Quarterly*, 3rd series 76 (2019): 361–368.

Palmer, R. R. *The Age of Democratic Revolution* (Two Volumes). Princeton: Princeton University Press, 1959–1964.

Paquette, Gabriel. *The European Seaborne Empires from the Thirty Years' War to the Age of Revolution.* New Haven: Yale University Press, 2019.

Pincus, Steven. *The Heart of the Revolution: The Founders' Case for an Activist Government.* New Haven: Yale University Press, 2016.

Polasky, Janet. *Revolutions Without Borders: The Call of Liberty in the Atlantic World.* New Haven: Yale University Press, 2015.

Rao, Gautham. "The New Historiography of the Early Federal Government: Institutions, Contexts, and the Imperial State." *William and Mary Quarterly*, 3rd series 77 (2020): 97–128.

Saler, Bethel. *The Settlers' Empire Colonialism and State Formation in America's Old Northwest.* Philadelphia: University of Pennsylvania Press, 2015.

Simon, Joshua. *Ideology of Creole Revolution: Imperialism and Independence in American and Latin American Political Thought.* New York: Cambridge University Press, 2017.

Taylor, Alan. *The Divided Ground: Indians, Settlers, and the Northern Borderland of the American Revolution.* New York: Alfred A. Knopf, 2007.

Veracini, Lorenzo. *Settler Colonialism: A Theoretical Overview.* New York: Palgrave Macmillan, 2010.

Witgen, Michael. "A Nation of Settlers: The Early American Republic and the Colonization of the Northwest Territory." *William and Mary Quarterly*, 3rd series 76 (2019): 391–398.

Wolfe, Patrick. *Settler Colonialism and the Transformation of Anthropology: The Politics and Poetics of an Ethnographic Event.* London: Continuum, 1999.

Wood, Gordon. *Empire of Liberty: A History of the Early Republic, 1789–1815.* New York: Oxford University Press, 2009.

Yirush, Craig. *Settlers, Liberty, and Empire: The Roots of Early American Political Theory, 1675–1775.* New York: Cambridge University Press, 2011.

Yokota, Kariann. *Unbecoming British: How Revolutionary America Became a Post-Colonial Nation.* New York: Oxford University Press, 2014.

United States Expansion and Incorporation in the Long Nineteenth-Century

Max M. Edling

ABSTRACT
Historians of the United States are making increasing use of the term *empire* to describe and analyse U.S. expansion in the nineteenth century. But this process is better captured by the term *incorporation*, which is used by Antony Hopkins in his *American Empire*. Nineteenth-century U.S. statesmen strove to people outlying territories with white settler-colonies that could be incorporated into the American federal union as sovereign and equal republics. They avoided acquiring territories with large non-white populations due to their belief that these were not fit for incorporation in the Union but had to be ruled as imperial dependencies. The American mode of territorial expansion was ultimately shaped by the organisation of the United States as a federal union of republics that rejected imperial rule. Neither republican government nor federal union were compatible with the jurisdictional and ethnic heterogeneity typical of empires. For this reason, American territorial expansion tried to reproduce on a continental scale the white republics of the Atlantic seaboard. The dispossession and exploitation of ethnic 'others' that characterised nineteenth-century territorial expansion therefore originated in American republicanism and American federalism, principles that can be traced back to the nation's point of origin, rather than in imperial legacies or borrowings.

Introduction

In *Boots and Saddles* Elizabeth Bacon Custer tells a spirited tale of the trials and tribulations of an officer's wife with the 7th U.S. Cavalry on the Northern Great Plains after the American Civil War. Custer accompanied her husband, Lieutenant-Colonel George Armstrong Custer, to Fort Abraham Lincoln in the Dakota Territory in the spring of 1873. Two years into his command, the colonel was granted leave and the couple returned to the East Coast. '[I]n the autumn we went into the States,' writes Custer, 'and spent most of the winter delightfully in New York'.[1] The idea of going from Dakota 'into the States,' as if crossing the border into another country, sounds strange to modern ears. Yet the juxtaposition of 'the territories' and 'the States,' which appears frequently in Custer's book, reminds us that nineteenth-century Americans saw their nation as divided into two very different kinds of political space. In popular literature, the territories were often portrayed as a place of adventure, as in Custer's *Boots and Saddles*, or as a refuge and a land of opportunity, as when the eponymous hero of Mark Twain's *Adventures of Huckleberry Finn* declares 'I reckon I got to light out for the Territory ahead of the rest, because Aunt Sally she's going to adopt me and sivilize [*sic*] me, and I can't stand it'.[2]

Colonel Custer went to the Dakota Territory to claim the Black Hills' gold deposits for the U.S. government and to drive away the resident Lakota Sioux. The colonel and most of his command met a violent end beside the Little Bighorn River, but the Lakota and their allies, the Arapaho and Cheyenne, soon succumbed to the army and were herded into reservations. Elizabeth Custer's presence in Dakota may seem more of a mystery. But she, too, had a role to play. In the Great Plains Wars, the United States did not just conquer space but 'civilized' it. Custer's story is full of examples of how in their crude and distant frontier post, the officers' wives staged the rituals of the refined life led by the middle and upper classes back in 'the States' or 'the East'.[3] Custer and her sisters-in-arms were America's *missionnaires civilisateurs* who ensured that when Huck reached the territories the likes of Aunt Sally would be there to meet him, working tirelessly to stop the frontier from backsliding into the kind of filthy, lawless, immoral and irreligious place where the Huck Finns of the world thrived.

When Custer and Twain published their books, the division of the United States into 'states' and 'territories' was a century old. In that century, 'territories' had metamorphosed into 'states' at often dizzying speed. The vast Northwest Territory, created in 1787, was the first territory organised by the federal government. In due course it would become no less than five states and contribute a sliver of land to a sixth. The first of the states to emerge was Ohio, admitted to the American union in 1803. Ohio was also the birthplace of George Custer. Born on the northern border in 1839, he was sent to school across the state line in Michigan, which had transitioned from territory to state only two years earlier. Here, in Monroe County, ten-year old George first laid eyes on Libby, three years his junior. Although Elizabeth Clift Bacon was born in Michigan Territory, her family was part of the great outmigration from New York State. Her grandfather, in turn, had gone to northern New York from Connecticut. George's family had a similar history of sojourning. Arriving from Germany in the late seventeenth century, the first three generations of the American Küster family remained in the vicinity of Philadelphia before George's grandfather upped sticks and crossed the Alleghany Mountains into western Maryland early in the nineteenth century. George's father moved on from Maryland to northern Ohio and later to southern Michigan.[4] When Elizabeth and George Custer set out for the Dakota Territory in 1873 – a territory formed out of the vast Louisiana Purchase of 1803 – the erstwhile frontier societies of Ohio and Michigan had become the thriving heartland of the Midwest, their relatively recent histories as federal territories now a distant memory.

The family trajectories of the Bacons and the Custers were caught up in three interrelated trends that profoundly shaped the United States in the nineteenth century: A fluid and constantly shifting political geography, an explosive population growth, and the westward surge of the resulting population surplus. Territorial and demographic expansion have always been central themes in American historiography. But whereas expansion was once seen as natural and inevitable – the 'manifest destiny' of the American nation – more recently historians have taken an interest in how a broad swathe of the North American Continent came to be part of the United States and what that process entailed. Frequently, such investigations are framed as stories of an expanding *empire*. Gordon Wood's synthetic *Empire of Liberty* takes its title from a celebratory term associated with Thomas Jefferson. More critical and analytical works addressing U.S. expansion are Fred Anderson and Andrew Cayton's *The Dominion of War: Empire and Liberty in North America, 1500-2000*, Carroll Smith-Rosenberg's *This Violent Empire*, Bethel Saler's *The Settlers' Empire*, Paul Frymer's *Building an American Empire*, and Stefan Heumann's dissertation on 'The Tutelary Empire'. Examples abound. Yet if the term is in frequent use, its meaning is rarely addressed. Scholars have turned to empire for rhetorical effect rather than analytical insight. The only real exception to this rule is the attempt to apply the concept and theory of *settler colonialism* to North American history.[5]

Given their new interest in the U.S. empire, historians of nineteenth-century America will turn eagerly to Antony Hopkins's magisterial *American Empire*. The timing is certainly right for Hopkins's call to American historians to engage with their nation's imperial past. But there is a risk that his call may fall on deaf ears. In his book, Hopkins refuses to see an American empire in the two periods that students of the U.S. have been accustomed to label *imperial*: The nineteenth-century conquest of the North American continent and the nation's global dominance after World War II. *American Empire* instead concerns itself with the *insular empire* that the United States acquired mostly in the Spanish-American War and lost in the same worldwide process of decolonisation that ended European empires,[6] the remnants of which are today known as the 'Territories of the United States'.

Faced with the disconnect between Hopkins's work and American historiography, it is tempting to say that his unwillingness to equate contiguous expansion with imperial domination is simply a mistake. As Linda Colley, another renowned historian of the British Empire has remarked, not only was U.S.

expansion coeval with the expansion of the Russian Empire in Siberia and Central Asia and with British expansion overseas, but the United States came out a winner because it was better 'than these rival powers in devising ways of cementing together diverse peoples over a huge geographical expanse'. Hopkins is perhaps guilty of the common failure to recognise how 'successful, overland empires can segue into apparently uncontroversial nation states'.[7]

But this would be the wrong conclusion. Hopkins is correct that American territorial expansion did not create an empire and we need to pay attention to the qualitative differences between American contiguous expansion and overseas empire if we are to move beyond rhetorical slogans to reach a real understanding of either of these manifestations of U.S. power. *Incorporation*, the seemingly innocuous term Hopkins uses for contiguous expansion, captures the essence of the process better than *empire*. It also allows us to see why nineteenth-century territorial expansion could not serve as a model for the twentieth-century American Empire. In the following pages, I aim to add nuance to Hopkins's interpretation by arguing that the distinctive form that U.S. incorporation took was shaped more by the nation's commitment to republicanism and federalism, than by imperialism.

In pursuing this line of inquiry, I also hope to highlight an important, if not necessarily intended, consequence of Hopkins's treatment of the American imperial past. As noted, in recent scholarship on the U.S., the term *empire* has served a rhetorical rather than analytical function. The term allows certain unpalatable features of the American past – its racially inscribed violence, its dispossession of American Indians, and its exploitation of captive Africans and African Americans – to be described as aberrations incompatible with the true identity of the United States as a federal union of republics. If only mistaken imperial ambitions can be shed, if only past imperial transgressions can be recognised and amends made, the United States may finally become true to its founding ideals. Such a reading of the American past and the American future has its uses and should not be dismissed out of hand. Yet we are forced to ask more searching and more pertinent questions about the identity of the American political project, and its possible maladies, once we accept that territorial expansion and the dispossession and exploitation of ethnic 'others' originated in American republicanism and American federalism, principles that can be traced back to the nation's point of origin, and not in imperial legacies or borrowings.

The Meaning of *Empire*

To Hopkins, the nineteenth-century United States falls short of an empire for reasons of definition. Imperialism, he explains, can have three different outcomes. *Formal empire* results when 'the dominant power annexes territory by force or negotiation and abolishes the constitutional independence of the polity concerned. Subordination enables the dominant power to manage the internal and external policies of the dependency to ensure, as far as possible, that they reflect its own priorities'. *Informal influence* or *informal empire* is an outcome 'whereby the constitutional independence of the satellite is untouched but the dominant power is able to diminish or reshape other elements of sovereignty, again within limits, to suit its own interests'. The third possibility is that imperialism results in a *unitary state* or *nation-state*, whereby 'imperialist actions lead to the incorporation of territory and the assimilation of its people on a basis of equality'.[8]

In *American Empire*, continental expansion is treated in the fifth chapter, 'Wars of Incorporation'. The chapter begins with a succinct and insightful analysis of Indian removal, white settler migration, and state formation set against the backdrop of the 'Anglo expansion' that has been the subject of recent books by James Belich and John Weaver.[9] But Hopkins soon turns to the U.S. wars against Britain (1812-1815) and Mexico (1846-1848), and to the American Civil War (1861-1865). In his reading, the significance of the period lies much less in continental conquest than in the defeat of the South's distinctive socio-economic formation, which broke America's 'neocolonial relationship' with Britain and prepared the ground for the realisation of the North's vision of a self-contained and sovereign American nation-state. Although these developments did not create the American Empire, they were necessary prerequisites for the process that began in 1898.[10]

At the close of the chapter, Hopkins explains why labelling U.S. rule over the North American continent *imperial* would be a mistake. Partly it is a question of scale. Although Hopkins certainly has sympathy with the plight of American Indians, they were simply too few in number for the history of their subjugation to define nineteenth-century United States in any meaningful way: 'Characterizations of the polity need to take account not only of intent but also of scale, and Native Americans represented only a tiny fraction of the population'.[11] But most of all it is a question of outcomes. Before 1898, the United States contained no subordinate polities with circumscribed independence. And operating in a world dominated by the British Empire, the federal government was too weak to exert much informal influence beyond the North American borderlands. In the nineteenth century, the United States was busy conquering, purchasing and annexing territory. But the aim was always territorial incorporation, never formal empire. Hopkins notes that 'expansion had the potential to create an independent territorial empire on the North American continent'. Yet, 'in practice, the resulting structure reproduced states with broadly equal rights under a federal system of government, even though statehood generally followed a period of administration directed by Washington'.[12] It would therefore be an error to equate 'imperialist expansion on the North American continent with the type of territorial empire discussed in this study'.[13]

Hopkins follows in the footsteps of scholars who have interpreted the Northwest Ordinance and its plan for the organisation of the trans-Appalachian West as a rejection of empire. Whereas before U.S. independence an imperial centre governed thirteen colonial dependencies, after independence a different principle would apply. In Belich's words, 'the template of American expansion was to be cloning rather than extension' of existing states.[14] Wood notes that the Northwest Ordinance put an end to 'permanent second-class colonies' and 'set forth the unprecedented principle that new states of the American empire settled in the West would enter the Union "on an equal footing with the original States, in all respects whatsoever"'.[15] Rejection of Britain's imperial organisation did not mean a rejection of the language of empire, however. To most Americans, and to many Britons, in the late eighteenth-century, the word *empire* meant nothing more precise than a geographically extensive and jurisdictionally composite polity.

As a historian of the British Empire, Hopkins is of course well aware that the meaning of *empire* has shifted over time. John Pocock writes that 'the word "empire," as used by English-speakers in the eighteenth century, did not primarily denote a hegemonic central power and its dependent colonies'.[16] Instead, *empire* was often used as a synonym of *confederation* or *federal republic*. Montesquieu's *Spirit of the Laws*, which more than any other work provided American state-builders with their vocabulary of federalism, is a case in point. Montesquieu treated the Dutch and Swiss republics alongside *l'Allemagne* – the Holy Roman Empire of the German Nation – in his discussion of European perpetual unions, or *républiques éternelles*. 'It seems,' Pocock comments, that *empire, confederation*, and *republic* could all 'be used to denote political systems of indefinite extent and multiple structure, and to denote very little more: to denote a plurality of political entities, held together by a *confederatio*, which is no more than the sum of the arrangements, or *foedera*, which exist between them, and to which each entity, if it is sovereign, stands committed by the exercise of its sovereign power'.[17]

The vague and elastic meaning of *empire* in early modern political discourse explains why American statesmen and political writers saw no incongruity in calling the United States an *empire* despite embracing republicanism and federalism. In 1779, the *United States Magazine* referred to the new American republics as the 'several states in the union of the empire'.[18] Eight years later, Alexander Hamilton commented in *The Federalist* that the adoption of the U.S. Constitution would determine 'the fate of an empire, in many respects, the most interesting in the world'.[19] Praising the adoption of this constitution, Francis Hopkinson's 'Ode for the 4th of July, 1788' invited listeners to 'Behold! behold! an empire rise!'[20] A few years later, Hamilton's nemesis Thomas Jefferson described the Louisiana Purchase as the foundation of an 'empire of liberty',[21] and in the 1830s Henry Clay said the public domain was large enough 'to found an empire.[22] Even as late as 1927, Oregon's official state song celebrated the 'Land of the Empire Builders, Land of the Golden West; Conquered and held by free men, Fairest and the best'.[23]

Such rhetorical flourishes did not amount to an endorsement of either formal or informal empire. Nor did it signal a continuity with the imperial past. Despite this language, the American Revolution created a polity in important respects different from the British composite empire. Above all, the United States was much less tolerant of jurisdictional and status diversity than the British Empire had been. When English monarchs claimed dominion over land in the Americas, they also claimed lordship over native peoples who were neither conquered nor incorporated into the English nation. English, later British, kings ruled, sometimes in name only, their American dominions by forming alliances and agreements with American Indian nations that were autonomous polities with recognised territorial rights. With time, the British Empire also came to rule over French- and Spanish-speaking Catholic settlers in Florida, Grenada, and Quebec, Dutch-speaking Calvinist settlers in the Hudson River Valley, and a large and diverse enslaved population of West African origin. Like the inhabitants of Britain and transplanted Englishmen around the Atlantic basin, these people were all *subjects* of the Crown, a political status that was both inclusive and shallow.[24] In colonial North America, imperial policy tried to juggle the interests of very different ethnic groups of American subjects alongside the military and economic priorities of the British government and merchant class. The outcome was not always support for the interests of the English-speaking colonists, as is evidenced by the so-called Proclamation Line, the territorial extension of Quebec Province, and, of course, the attempts to regulate and tax the American colonies after the Seven Years' War.

The United States was a different story. It was the common government of the thirteen colonies, which represented no one else. And it was organised as a federal union of republics. Both its republicanism and its federalism would profoundly shape the template of American territorial expansion by cloning.

A Federal Union of Republics

For present purposes, the outcome of the American Revolution can be summarised in three points. *Independence* turned thirteen British colonies on the North American mainland into sovereign states. All thirteen rejected monarchy and adopted a *republican form of government* that was founded on the principle of popular sovereignty and institutionalised relatively broad male suffrage, frequent elections, elective political offices, and rotation in office. Yet, despite such principles, an institutionalised racism made American republicanism *exclusive*. The British Empire could function, even thrive, with a multiethnic, multilingual, and multireligious subject population living in distinctive and distinctively different jurisdictions. The American federal union of republics could not.

Whereas monarchy and aristocracy are systems of rule based on the principle of social rank, republicanism is based on the principle of civic equality. In a republic, citizens partake in the adoption of the laws under which they live, and their law apply equally to all. It is a system of government that demands much from the citizenry and republican thinkers have always emphasized the need for the citizens of a republic to possess certain qualities in order to sustain their government, qualities often denominated *virtue*.[25] Nicholas Guyatt has traced American racial discrimination back to the Revolution's commitment to republican equality. Revolutionary North America was ethnically much more heterogenous than Britain. Guyatt argues that the American founders believed strongly in the equality of man but had an equally strong conviction that European men and their descendants in America were superior to Native American, African, and African American men. Such racial superiority was not perceived to be inherent but was rather seen as the function of social and cultural refinement. In principle, non-European Americans could therefore catch up with their betters, at which point they could be assimilated into the republic's body politic on terms of equality. However, when their uplift seemed hampered instead of promoted by cohabitation, American ideologues and policy makers concluded that successful assimilation was preconditioned on their removal from interaction with the 'white' population to surroundings where non-white peoples could develop at their own pace.[26] Less charitable readings of American founding principles are possible. But Guyatt is correct to argue that the refusal to incorporate non-whites as equal citizens in the American republics, in combination with the reluctance to turn these republics into societies of ranks, gave birth to the long-lived American dilemma of assimilation.

New work on the American founding has demonstrated how an American political identity was crafted by means of an aggressive othering of non-whites and non-Anglophones.[27] The craftmanship is on display already in the nation's organic laws. Below a veneer of universal rights talk and references to 'one People', the Declaration of Independence imposed a logic of exclusion. George III was accused of having 'excited domestic Insurrections amongst us' and having 'endeavoured to bring on the Inhabitants our Frontiers, the merciless Indian Savages whose known Rule of Warfare, is an undistinguished Destruction, of all Ages, Sexes and Conditions'. In one place, the document speaks of 'all Men' being 'created equal'. In the next, it pits enslaved African American insurrectionists against a European American 'us', and American Indians against 'the Inhabitants of our Frontiers'.[28] Similar to the Declaration, both the Articles of Confederation and the U.S. Constitution excluded Indians nations from the 'firm league of friendship' and 'more perfect Union' binding the thirteen republics together. The Northwest Ordinance detailed the creation of three to five new white settler states but was silent on the place and role of indigenous peoples in the United States. The Shawnee, Wyandot, Delaware,

Miami, Sauk, Chippewa and other nations were *in*, but not, *of* the United States. Once subjects of the British Empire, they were now expelled beyond what Barbara Young Welke calls the American republics' 'borders of belonging'.[29]

African Americans, too, found themselves in, but not, of the American body politic. The first U.S. naturalisation law defined the U.S. as a 'white' nation.[30] The Northwest Ordinance banned slavery north of Ohio River, but the Constitution delegated the definition and realisation of civic rights, and the question of the legality of slavery, to the states. After independence, the northern republics put slavery on the road to extinction. After a brief period of emancipation, the southern states in contrast perpetuated their 'peculiar institution'. In the late eighteenth century, it was widely recognised that slavery concentrated wealth and perverted the morality of slaveowners, and thus was not conducive to a republican system of government by equal and 'virtuous' citizens. But at least enslaved individuals were civically dead and thus outside the pale of the political community. Emancipated slaves were more troublesome. Once freed, the question arose whether African Americans could and should also be citizens. In the South, North and West, the answer was no. The preferred solution was to let emancipation be followed by expulsion from the state to the western borderlands, the Caribbean, Mesoamerica, or West Africa, a project known as 'colonization'.[31] Few African Americans showed any interest in exile, however. Instead, the American republics reluctantly turned into multiethnic societies of ranks in which 'whiteness' was a precondition for full citizenship. Racial separation remained. But rather than a continental or transcontinental vision it became a principle for the ordering of local society and everyday life.

The republics' corruption into societies of rank can be observed in the evolution of voting rights. A process that past historians were too keen to label *democratization* saw the expansion of white male suffrage in combination with the introduction of explicit race and gender restrictions on the right to vote. In 1790, ten of the thirteen states in the American union had property requirements for voting. By 1855, restrictions existed in only three of thirty-one states. In contrast, in 1790 only three states excluded non-whites from voting. By 1855, twenty-five states did. In 1790, there were a few states in which adult unmarried women could vote. By 1855, voting was everywhere explicitly reserved for men only.[32]

As the United States grew by cloning, the exclusion of American Indians from the nation and the discrimination against non-whites were faithfully copied and implemented in the new republics of the West. Had the United States thought of itself as an early modern empire, it could have existed as a multiethnic composite polity that combined white republics with non-white jurisdictions. It is at least conceivable that an organisation like the eighteenth-century British Empire could have functioned as a system of alliances between the British Crown and a conglomeration of largely self-governing white settler colonies, Indian nations and confederations, French- and Spanish-speaking conquered provinces, and even an African American Maroon state. Some U.S. 'colonization' projects included ideas about an African American self-governing polity in the western borderlands and the idea of an 'Indian state' was flouted on various occasions.[33] Yet American founding principles could ill cope with such diversity. The reason can be found in another commitment of the American founders. Not only did they turn colonies into republics, they also made their republics join together in a federal union.

As Pocock notes, early modern political taxonomists placed empires and federal unions in the same category of *républiques éternelles*. Federal union was a well-known institutional solution to external threat. American state-builders learnt about its benefits from Montesquieu's *Spirit of the Laws*. In the chapter 'How Republics Provide For Their Security', Montesquieu explained that, by joining in federal union, republics could combine 'all the internal advantages of a republican government' with 'the external force of monarchy'. Thanks to 'the force of the association', he continued, such 'a society of societies' had 'all the advantages of large monarchies' in its dealings with the outside world. In a federal union, the member-states delegated their powers over war, peace, and alliances to a common government to better secure their protection and independence. But if empires were compatible with heterogeneity in the forms of government of their composite parts, federal unions depended for their stability and longevity on the homogeneity of their member-states. For the union to be permanent and successful, it had to 'be composed of states of the same nature', Montesquieu wrote. This was true, 'above all' for 'republican states'. Because monarchies were prone to war and expansion it was against their spirit to confederate with others. Allowing monarchies to become part of a union was an invitation to disaster. Montesquieu warned that 'in Greece, all was lost when the Macedonian kings gained a place among the Amphictiones'.[34]

Union followed on independence by necessity. The American colonies were simply too small to survive on their own. The Articles of Confederation and Perpetual Union that created the first American union in 1781 were silent on the form of government of the confederating states. But when time came to form a more perfect union in 1787, the new Constitution stipulated that 'the United States shall guarantee to every State in this Union a Republican Form of Government' (Art. IV, §4). The Northwest Ordinance, adopted in the same year, said that all new states formed in the territories were to have a 'republican' constitution and a government that conformed 'to the principles contained in these articles' (Sect. 14, art. 5). The repeated sectional conflicts between slave states and free states in the antebellum era that culminated in the Civil War demonstrate how homogeneity of form remained an existential matter to the American union.

The American union expanded by incorporating additional republics. Homogeneity of form was a central question in this process. During Reconstruction, in the short window of opportunity when an alternative vision of the U.S. can be glimpsed, the concern with homogeneity served to banish race restrictions on citizenship from the constitutions of new and readmitted states. If civic rights were not equal and universal, American statesmen argued, that state did not have a republican form of government. In the words of Senator Charles Sumner, a constitution that restricted non-white suffrage 'is not republican, for the first principle of republican government is equality'.[35] But for most of the nineteenth century this logic was reversed. The belief in the superiority of whites and anglophones made U.S. politicians wary of incorporating racial 'others'. In 1811, some congressmen found Louisiana too 'foreign' to qualify as an American state. Its population had different 'habits, customs, manners, and language' from Americans and 'never have been, and ... never will be, citizens of the United States'.[36] Nine decades later, New Mexico was denied statehood because the 'great majority' of the population were of 'Spanish and mixed Spanish and Indian descent'. Only when the territory had acquired a sufficient number of white migrants could 'this mass of people unlike us in race, language, and social customs' be incorporated into the Union.[37] Homogeneity was not always about race. New states had to comply with American social and political norms. Although the population was white and therefore capable of self-government, the practice of polygamy, an alien church doctrine, and the political power of the priesthood kept the Mormons in Utah territory outside the American union for half a century.

Organising Expansion

Born in a violent uprising against Britain's attempt to create a formal empire in America, the Articles of Confederation and perpetual Union jealously guarded the sovereignty of the new American republics. But jealousy made the union too weak to effectively protect the independence and promote the interests of the states. Three problems plagued the American union once independence had been secured in the 1783 Peace of Paris: Congress's default on the public debt, its failure to protect American international commerce, and its slow progress in organising and settling the trans-Appalachian west.[38] Overcoming these challenges, most of all the third, was a prerequisite for the launch of U.S. continental expansion.

The peace treaty recognised the independence of the Atlantic seaboard states and granted them dominion over a vast region in the continental interior, from the Appalachian Mountains to the Mississippi River. Several of the states held overlapping claims in the area, which were derived from their colonial charters. These claims were ceded to Congress in the mid-1780s, resulting in the creation of a 260,000-square mile public domain north of the Ohio River. Fruitful soils made this a land of great potential. The successful incorporation of the West into the United States became possible only after a complete overhaul of the American union, however.[39] The Constitution of 1787 laid the foundations for a stronger central government that could raise taxes and an army and gave Congress the power to 'make all needful Rules and Regulations' respecting U.S. territories (Art. 3, sect. 3). The rules were spelled out in the Northwest Ordinance and the land ordinances preceding it. With occasional but relatively minor changes, the ordinance would serve as the blueprint for the incorporation of the territories that the United States conquered, annexed, and purchased over the century that followed.

Because the Constitution reconfirmed the Revolution's commitment to republican government and federal union, the expanding United States came to be organised as two distinctive jurisdictional spaces. In the East was the union of American republics and the federal district. In the West was a complex and growing marchland of federal territories, unorganised lands, and Indian Territory. From this marchland was carved the new republics that completed the process of territorial expansion by incorporation or cloning. The process had run its course by 1912, when Arizona and New Mexico were granted statehood. Hopkins's map of US territorial acquisitions and state-formation, found in chapter five, illustrates the political geography of continental expansion. Between 1783 and 1912, thirty-seven new states were added to the original thirteen on land acquired through seven cessions, purchases, and annexations ratified by international agreement.[40] A didactic tool typical of its kind, the map tries to capture a rapidly changing reality that is too complex for easy depiction, no matter the degree of cartographical detail.

Such maps invariably leave out American Indian land cessions. International agreements did not extinguish native land titles, which required an additional treaty. No official list of Indian Treaties exists but the National Archives holds 374 of these documents. Many but not all involved one or more territorial cessions. The Indigenous Digital Archives database of Indian Treaties records and maps a staggering 717 cessions by treaty between 1784 and 1894.[41] Nor did new states emerge organically out of geographically identical federal territories, as these maps typically suggest. The Northwest Ordinance stipulated the borders of three future states to be formed out of the Northwest Territory. But this practice was quickly abandoned. For much of the nineteenth century, the federal government instead organised territories of enormous extent: Indiana Territory (1800); the Territory of Louisiana (1805), which became the Missouri Territory (1812); the extended Michigan Territory (1834); Oregon Territory (1849); Utah Territory (1850); and New Mexico Territory (1850). These were subsequently carved up into smaller territories, which eventually became states. For a few years in the middle of the century, huge tracts of the national domain were simply left 'unorganized'. Internally, federal territories were often composite jurisdictions that included self-governing Indian nations with recognised territorial rights. In addition to such organic native polities, Congress created Indian Territory in 1824. It would exist in shifting geographic shapes to 1907 and serve as the receptor of American Indians forcibly removed from their homelands.[42]

All of this goes to show that incorporation was indeed a complicated affair. A semblance of order can be achieved by focusing on how early U.S. policy created two distinctive jurisdictional spaces in the western marches. When Congress adopted the Northwest Ordinance in the summer of 1787, successful incorporation of the West was anything but a certainty. U.S. surveyors had just laid out the so-called Seven Ranges, a six-mile-square pattern of townships west of the Ohio River. This land was to be sold in 640-acre plots, half plots or quarter plots to farming families migrating from the Atlantic states. The first inroad in the national domain, the Seven Ranges stretched a mere 42 miles into the vast Ohio country. Even so, surveying required army protection against Indian attack. In 1787, the only white residents north of the Ohio River were a few squatters, the sojourning surveyors, and a handful of miniscule army detachments. The organised West was no more than a prospect.[43]

Real power north of the Ohio River rested with an Indian confederacy of the Shawnee, Wyandot, Delaware, Miami and other nations. Further afield lived peoples like the Sauk and the Chippewa. From their homelands in upper New York, the Haudenosaunee Six Nations confederacy also had a long-standing interest in the region.[44] Remarkably, none of them were mentioned in the Northwest Ordinance. True, there were general stipulations regarding 'Indians'. There was the promise that future republics to be formed in the territory would treat resident American Indians with 'good faith' and the pledge that the United States would protect and preserve peace and friendship with them. The federal government would also guarantee 'their lands and property', which could only be alienated with the Indian nations' consent or following U.S. conquest 'in just and lawful wars authorized by Congress' (Section 14, article 3). Nevertheless, the most striking feature of the Northwest Ordinance is that the first U.S. plan for incorporating new territories did not outline a place for native peoples in the American union.

The Northwest Ordinance instead concentrated on the settler-migrant farming families from the Atlantic states that Congress hoped to attract to the region. The ordinance was both a form of government for the federal territories and a compact of union outlining the conditions territories had to fulfil to be incorporated into the United States. How a unilaterally adopted ordinance could be construed as a 'compact' between contracting parties is far from obvious. But it made sense if the act of settling in the territory could be interpreted as a tacit agreement to the compact. In any event, the 'articles of compact' were to 'forever remain unalterable' and thereby significantly shaped the states that would emerge from the Northwest Territory. Unbridled settler sovereignty was never in the cards.

The ordinance stipulated that territories would initially be governed directly by Congress without popular participation. The territorial government would consist of a governor, a secretary, and three judges, who were all appointed by and answerable to Congress. This unelected government would give law to the inhabitants by adopting 'laws of the original States', subject to congressional approval. It also had the power to lay out townships and counties, and to appoint all local government officials. As a form of government, it was far removed from republican self-government. In fact, the first governor of the Northwest Territory referred to his province as a 'dependent colony' and insisted that migrants to the territory left behind their status as citizens in their home states to become 'subjects of the United States' in the territories.[45] An element of self-government was introduced as soon as the number of 'free male inhabitants of full age' reached 5,000, who were then allowed to elect a legislative assembly. The territorial assembly could send a delegate to Congress who had the right to debate but not to vote. But the federal government would continue to appoint the executive and the judiciary, and the governor had the right to veto legislation.[46]

The second stage in the incorporation process began when a 'state' in the territory had reached 60,000 free 'inhabitants'. The settlers could now write a constitution, form a government, and apply to join the American union as a sovereign state 'on an equal footing with the original States in all respects whatever' (Art. 5). Despite these words, settler sovereignty continued to be circumscribed in important ways. The transition from territory to state could only be initiated after Congress had passed an enabling act,[47] which meant that settler colonists had no absolute right to statehood and an end to their dependent status. Furthermore, the ordinance's 'articles of compact' meant that the constitution and form of government of new states had to conform to rules laid down by the federal government.

In the most literal sense, Congress shaped future states by determining their borders. The fifth article of the Northwest Ordinance specified the territorial borders of three states to be formed out of the Northwest Territory and left room for the creation of an additional two states. This provision was abandoned in 1800 and never resurrected. But the principle that the federal government rather than the settlers would decide the borders of new states remained. The article also required that the constitution and government of new states had to 'be republican' and conform to 'the principles contained in these articles'. The 'principles' referred to guaranteed to the citizens of the new republics rights that were considered integral to American republican government, for example freedom of religion, the right to habeas corpus and to jury and common law trials, and proportional representation in the legislature. Other principles guarded the sanctity of contracts, declared navigable rivers public highways, and banned slavery from the Northwest Territory. The third article obliged new states to encourage 'religion, morality, and knowledge' and to treat American Indians with good faith. The fourth article's stipulation for perpetual union proscribed secession. It also made unsold public lands federal property exempt from state taxation. Finally, the fifth article of the ordinance gave Congress discretion to award statehood to a territory before it reached the threshold of 60,000 free inhabitants if this was 'consistent with the general interest of the confederacy'.

Historians have used the term *empire* to describe American territorial expansion from a wish to draw attention to U.S. violence and aggression against foreign nations and conquered peoples. But the United States in fact came closest to establishing a formal empire in the 'direct stage' of its government over the white settler population in the federal territories. Before statehood, the federal government actively shaped settlements into republics fit for incorporation in the Union. Settlers were never given 'constitutional independence' before Congress was convinced that their self-government would reflect the priorities of the American union. The federal government imposed conditions for statehood that went beyond the stipulations in the Northwest Ordinance on almost all territories seeking incorporation into the Union in the long nineteenth century. The approach was light touch in the period from 1821 to 1859, when the specific conditions on the ten states admitted to the Union were limited to regulating the status of federal land within their borders. Conditions were much more intrusive from the Civil War and onwards. This chronology confirms Hopkins's and others' interpretation that the most important outcome of the war was a northern dominated 'nation-state',[48] although it is perhaps more correct to say that increased congressional activity after the war reflects the realisation that a stable federal union could not permanently endure half slave, half free.

Both in the early decades of the republic and in the post-Civil War era, the purpose of statehood conditions was to ensure a homogeneous federal union. In James Biber's words, conditions addressed doubts that a territory could 'be assimilated as a loyal, democratic unit of government within the United States'. These doubts arose whenever settler territorial societies were 'perceived as fundamentally different from mainstream American politics and society'. Congress would then regulate civil liberties, marriage, religion, education, language, and qualification for office to make these societies conform to U.S. norms. The uncouth nature of frontier inhabitants was the impulse behind the original stipulations in the Northwest Ordinance. After the Louisiana Purchase, Louisianans had to reform their legal system and accept English as their language of government. In Utah Territory, Mormons had to abandon polygamy, promise to establish a non-sectarian public education system, and accept the division of church and state. Before incorporation, New Mexicans had to ensure English-language proficiency for all state officers and legislators, freedom of religion, and guarantees that the public education system would be non-sectarian and the language of instruction English.[49]

American Indian Nations

The Northwest Ordinance said little about the status and future of American Indians in the United States. Hopkins notes that estimates put the indigenous population at roughly 600,000 at the turn of the eighteenth century. This equals about a tenth of the total non-Indian U.S. population of 5.3 million. A century later, the U.S. Census recorded 230,000 Indians in a total U.S. population of 75.5 million.[50] By then, the American Indian population was less than a third of one percent. In the terminology of empire, the United States acted as a settler colonial state towards native peoples. It aimed to take indigenous land and eliminate the autonomy of indigenous peoples, and to people the land with white migrants as a prelude to incorporating settler colonies. North American historians have been reluctant to use the concept of *settler colonialism*, however. The term is a poor fit for post-contact North American history well into the nineteenth century. For centuries, European settlements were geographically limited, indigenous polities often stronger than settler colonies, and Indian nations more commonly perceived by imperial agents as allies and trading partners than impediments to European land grabs. Even after independence, the United States was for many decades 'an archipelago of settler islands, strung on a weak web of roads and ... aqueous spaces'.[51] But at some point – at different times in different parts of the continent – the balance between the settler colonial state and Indian polities tipped. When the nineteenth century drew to a close, it was native spaces that had been reduced to little islands in a sea of white settlement, a sea that relentlessly crashed against and eroded the remnants of indigenous territorial rights.

Yet if the term *settler colonialism* correctly characterises the broad strokes of U.S. policy, it says little about the finer details. Indigenous dispossession was neither automatic nor homogeneous, but carefully managed and shifting. The U.S. policy of Indian displacement went through three stages in the long nineteenth century: enforced retreat behind a treaty line in the decades after independence, trans-Mississippi removal beginning in the 1820s, and confinement to reservations after the Civil War.

Immediately after the War of Independence, Congress made a brief attempt to treat American Indians as conquered peoples. Faced with Indian resistance, the U.S. soon reverted to the colonial-era practice of dealing with indigenous peoples through treaties. Bethel Saler explains how the U.S. created *treaty polities* to manage Indian-settler relations and territorial cessions.[52] As the term suggests, the policy involved the creation, at least on paper, of a body politic that could become the signatory of an agreement. If land cessions were to be legitimate, the territorial claims of these indigenous bodies politic had to be recognised, or there would be no land to alienate. In addition to ratifying land cessions, early treaties established the physical separation of American Indians and European Americans by means of a treaty line, replaced commercial and political links with Britain and Spain with ties to the U.S., placed Indian nations under the protection of the United States and 'of no other sovereign' and formulated the route by which the Indians would be 'civilized' and made to conform to European-American norms of socioeconomic organisation.[53]

From the 1820s Congress moved to a policy of land exchanges, whereby Indian nations were pressed to give up their homelands for new territories west of the Mississippi River. The policy of Indian removal led Congress to create the so-called Indian Territory in 1822, located between Arkansas Territory and the Mexican state of Coahuila y Tejas, to harbour displaced peoples. Indian territory was significantly extended in 1834 to include all land between the Missouri River and the international border with Mexico and Britain, roughly the area that would become the states of Oklahoma, Kansas, Nebraska, Colorado, South and North Dakota, Montana, and Wyoming. Regardless of its size, Congress outlined neither a governmental structure for the territory nor a path for statehood. Indian nations continued to exist as autonomous polities that were self-governing with regards to their domestic affairs and beyond the pale of U.S. jurisdiction.[54]

In 1854, Indian Territory contracted to its 1822 borders when Congress laid out two new settler colonies in the territories of Kansas and Nebraska. This was part of a development that began when the Oregon Settlement in 1846 and the Mexican Cession in 1848 sparked U.S. colonisation of the Pacific coast. Frequent conflicts between migrants on the overland trails and Great Plains nations made the United States adopt the reservation system in the 1850s. In the decades after the Civil War, the federal government projected its overbearing military power onto the Great Plains in a series of 'savage wars of peace' that reduced Indian nations to captive peoples confined to reservations.[55] In contrast to the borderland region of the 1834–1854 Indian Territory, which abutted the external border of the United States, Indian reservations were located within states and territories, thereby sharply limiting indigenous autonomy.[56]

In the long nineteenth century, U.S. Indian policy can be said to have recognised indigenous nations as territorially demarcated autonomous political organisations. But whereas native peoples could be part of the loose alliance systems that made up the multiethnic composite empires of the early modern era, Indian nations were never invited to become members of the American union. This was despite the fact that the idea of an Indian state could and was imagined on repeated occasions. The very first U.S. Indian treaty, an agreement between Congress and the Delaware nation, held out the promise that the Delaware and other friendly 'tribes' could join the American union at a future date and 'form a state whereof the Delaware nation shall be the head and have representation in Congress'.[57] Facing aggression from the State of Georgia in the 1820s, the Cherokee nation crafted itself as a recognizably 'civilized' and sovereign state with a capital city having all the trappings of a white republic: a legislative building, courthouse, and bilingual newspaper.[58] On 4 July 1827, the nation adopted a constitution that was so faithfully modelled on the American republics that it even took to exclude from the 'body politic' persons 'of negro or mulatto parentage'.[59] In 1905, the Cherokee and the other 'Civilized Tribes' joined in convention in Indian Territory to write a constitution and apply for statehood for the State of Sequoyah.[60] Yet in no case did an indigenous U.S. republic materialise.[61]

Unwanted Peoples

The American template of growth by cloning also does much to explain the limits to expansion. The organisation of the United States as a homogeneous federal union of republics made it reluctant to acquire new territories encompassing large populations of ethnic 'others'. At various points in the nineteenth century, proposals to take over Mexico, Nicaragua, the Yucatan Peninsula, Cuba, Haiti, and Santo Domingo were aired.[62] A formal empire would have no problem with the principle of governing 'foreign' nations, although practical considerations may on occasion make it inadvisable. In contrast, extending rule over an alien people incapable of easy assimilation was very problematic for the United States. In 1836, in the course of a Senate debate over slavery, Senator Benjamin Leigh of Virginia made the dilemma clear. 'It is peculiar to the character of this Anglo-Saxon race of men to which we belong', said Leigh, 'that it has never been contented to live in the same country with any other distinct race, upon terms of equality; it has, invariably, when placed in that situation, proceeded to exterminate, or enslave the other race in some form or other, or, failing in that, to abandon the country'.[63] Extermination was not practicably possible in places like Mexico or Cuba. The alternatives were to rule such dominions as dependencies of non-citizens or leave them be. Some of Leigh's fellow southerners, men who had made their peace with slavery and begun to fear for its future from a northern-dominated Congress, did argue for the first option. As Hopkins notes, in the years leading up to the Civil War, the South entertained hopes of establishing 'a slave empire' in the Caribbean and Central America. 'Had the Confederacy won the war and realized its ambition, the resulting polity would have been imperial in substance as well as in intent'.[64] Instead, Lincoln rejected empire and saved the federal union.[65]

The dilemma of incorporation came to the fore in the congressional debate on the 'all-Mexico' proposal in 1848. Opponents to the proposal, such as the newly elected representative for Illinois, Abraham Lincoln, argued that the U.S. should content itself with 'the unsettled half' of Mexico, where it 'could establish land offices, sell the lands, and introduce an American population into the country'. Floridian Edward Cabell, who represented a state created a mere three years previously on territory once held by the Seminoles, agreed. Taking all of Mexico meant taking 'the *population* along with it. And shall we, by an act of Congress, convert the black, white, red, mongrel, miserable population of Mexico – the Mexicans, Indians, Mulattoes, Mestizos, Chinos, Zambos, Quinteros – into free and enlightened American citizens, entitled to all the privileges which we enjoy?'[66] In the end, Congress voted against empire and for white republics and federal homogeneity.

But even the 'unsettled half' of Mexico that would eventually become part of the United States contained significant pockets of non-white population. The federal government's handling of such problematic places shed further light on the modus operandi of American expansion. California, part of the Mexican Cession of 1848, became a state in 1850. Oregon, to which the U.S. secured title in the Oregon Settlement of 1846, became a state in 1859. With 70,000 residents in 1848, New Mexico exceeded the population threshold of the Northwest Ordinance. Yet the territory was granted statehood only in 1912. This long delay was the result of the ethnicity, language, and religion of the *neomexicanos*. Congress deemed that New Mexicans 'are not now, and for a long time to come may not be, prepared for State government'. According to the newspapers, the people were 'aliens to us in blood and language'[67] and hence 'not of us'.[68] The official report on New Mexico's statehood application from 1902 declared that it was only when the Spanish-speaking population had been diluted by an influx of English-speakers, 'who have been citizens of other States', that the people of New Mexico could form 'a credible portion of American citizenship'.[69]

Unlike modern European empires, and the twentieth century American Empire, the expanding American federal union was repelled by racial 'others'. Its rapidly growing population and its agrarian economy created an unsatiable appetite for new land, but the federal government directed expansion into the sparsely populated regions of North America. It acquired land in the first step from European and neo-European powers and in the second step from indigenous nations. Next, the federal government actively employed land distribution policies – such as the Preemption Act (1841), the Florida Armed Occupation Act (1842), the Oregon Land Donation Act (1850), the Homestead Act (1862), and the Dawes Act (1887) – to 'manufacture white majorities' on this land. By such means the 'government regulated the task of settlement by controlling its direction, pace, and scale – moving preferred populations onto contested territory in order to engineer the demography of the region in a manner that both secured and consolidated their territorial control'.[70]

The racial qualifier is important. The policy aimed to secure *white* majorities. The Dawes Act invited white settlers to acquire homesteads on Native American soil. In contrast, the Southern Homestead Act (1866), which sought to give emancipated slaves title to confiscated land in the seceding states, was repealed after a decade. Before the Civil War and after Reconstruction, Congress allowed racial discrimination and exclusion to stand in new state constitutions. Preparing for statehood Oregonians voted three to one to ban slavery, six to one to exclude blacks from their new republic. According to their state declaration of rights, 'white foreigners' were welcome to the rights of 'native-born citizens' (Sect. 32), whereas 'no free negro or mulatto, not residing in this State at the time of the adoption of this Constitution, shall come, reside or be within this State' (Sect. 36). If they tried to, public officials would remove them.[71] To the extent that the United States was more successful than contemporary empires in holding on to and incorporating new territory, it was not because it was better at 'cementing together diverse peoples over a huge geographical expanse', as Colley suggested in the quotation above, but because it managed to move the 'right' bodies onto the land in vast numbers and gave them self-government in white supremacist republics.

Concern over the impossibility of incorporating ethnic 'others' in the federal union, indigenous dispossession, and racial exclusion all came together in the history of Oklahoma statehood, which transformed Indian Territory from a native reserve to 'a white settler state in the center of the nation'.[72] From the War of 1812 to the end of the Great Plains Wars, Indian Territory served as a dumping ground for unwanted indigenous population elements from all corners of the United States. After the Civil War, around thirty nations, with a combined population of 85,000 people, resided there. Despite exceeding the population threshold for statehood, the creation of an Indian republic and its incorporation into the American union was never an alternative; nor was the continued existence of this native enclave. Congress undermined Indian autonomy and communal land ownership by adopting the Dawes General Allotment Act in 1887. Three years later it lopped off the western half of Indian Territory to create Oklahoma Territory, which was immediately opened up for white settlers in a series of land runs and lotteries. In 1900, Oklahoma Territory had 400,000 inhabitants of whom only 32,000 were classed as Indian. Meanwhile Indian Territory had also been overrun by white settlers. Of a total population of 392,000 in 1900, a minority of 90,000 were Indian.

This demographic sea-change made statehood feasible for Oklahoma Territory in the early years of the twentieth century. The five 'civilized nations' – the Cherokee, Choctaw, Chickasaw, Creek, and Seminole – left in Indian Territory petitioned Congress for separate statehood and admission to the United States as the State of Sequoyah. Named in honour of the inventor of the Cherokee syllabary, Sequoyah would have been a polity with an explicit indigenous identity. But in conformity with over a century of racially guided incorporation policies, Congress denied the application. Instead, Oklahoma Territory absorbed Indian Territory to become the State of Oklahoma in 1907.[73]

Perhaps the most important contribution of settler colonial studies lies in drawing attention to the stories settler states tell about themselves to justify indigenous dispossession.[74] Oklahoma illustrates such-story telling perfectly. On achieving statehood, the American Indian history of Oklahoma was quickly eradicated in a celebration of plucky "Boomers" and "Sooners" who brought the territory into modernity by an instant and dramatic transformation of a *terra nullius* into a flourishing agricultural economy and a white republic. The first official state song, written in 1905, described Oklahoma as 'a land whose story has just begun'.[75] It was replaced after World War II by the title song from the Rodgers and Hammerstein musical *Oklahoma!* – a quintessentially American work and one of the most popular shows ever produced in the United States. Set on the eve of statehood, *Oklahoma!* celebrates settler colonialism. In the words of the title song, 'we know we belong to the land, And the land we belong to is grand!'[76] It should come as no surprise that there are no American Indians on the role list. When the plot demands an exotic 'other', it is filled by a Persian peddler named Ali Hakim, an unlikely traveller on the North American prairie in 1907. But Indians were not the only non-whites excluded from the body politic of the new republic. In its first act as an independent republic, the Oklahoma legislature adopted Jim Crow laws. Soon after, it took away black voting rights.[77]

Empire and Internal Decolonisation

The burst of state-making in 1889–1896 when seven new republics joined the American union coincided with the declaration by the U.S. Census that the 'frontier line' between settler colonists and the indigenous population had vanished. Only two years after the admission of the State of Utah, the United States entered a new phase of territorial expansion. No longer focused on contiguous regions in North America, the federal government for the first time acquired overseas dominions. The novelty of this development lay less in their overseas location than in the formal status of the new acquisitions. National borders are the product of historical contingencies. At various points in the nineteenth-century, American expansionists had cast their eyes on Cuba and other Caribbean islands, just as others had dreamed of settling Willamette Valley and securing San Francisco Bay. For most of the century, transportation technology made the islands of the Caribbean and the rim of the Mexican Gulf far more accessible than the Pacific Coast. Rather than geographic location, the striking thing about the territories acquired after the War of 1898 is their demographic composition. Unlike the Mississippi Valley, the Midwest, and the Pacific Coast, the new territories were generally not seen as promising sites for settler colonies, but as places already densely populated by people that nineteenth-century statesmen for religious and racial reasons viewed as impossible to merge with the American nation. The unwillingness to incorporate the new dominions into the American union made overseas expansion qualitatively different from western expansion.

The Insular Cases decided in 1901 are to the American Empire of the twentieth century what the Northwest Ordinance is to nineteenth-century American expansion. The latter formulated a principle and a plan for the incorporation of new possessions on terms of full equality. It focused on a prospective population of white settler-migrants from the Eastern seaboard and tellingly skirted the question of the status of the resident indigenous population. The former, in contrast, directly addressed the status of the indigenous population in new possessions to formulate a principle of subjection and exclusion. Puerto Ricans and Filipinos were denied the 'constitutional rights' of US citizens. Their homelands were *unincorporated territories*, 'subject to the jurisdiction of the United States' but 'not of the United States'.[78] Unlike the inhabitants of the federal territories on the North American mainland, no prospect for a transition to statehood was ever held out to the subjects of America's insular empire.

Hawai'i was the exception that proves the rule. As Hopkins's analysis makes clear, the island group had a demographic resemblance to the contiguous federal territories. The rapid decline of the native population made it possible for white American settlers to overrun and dominate the islands. Admittedly, Hawai'i had a different history of engagement with the U.S. from the other conquests of 1898, but the most significant difference was that the conditions for a settler colony were in place. In contrast to Puerto Rico, the Philippines, Guam and Samoa, Hawai'i became an incorporated territory and was governed in the manner of mainland federal territories. Statehood took almost sixty years to materialise, however. Although the relative size of the indigenous population was constant, so was the 'white' population. Both, in fact, became minorities. Instead, the population majority consisted of Asian and Pacific Island immigrants, who for many decades were denied voting rights. Hawai'i never become the New Mexico of the Pacific as no white majority was ever manufactured there. Its admission to the United States in 1959 was instead preconditioned on the changing nature of American social and political ideals. Domestic reform movements and the international rivalry of the Cold War forced Congress to reconsider the legitimacy of the racial order of the American republics. Hawai'i statehood was thus part of a broader trend of an increasingly assertive federal government imposing a new kind of homogeneity on the member states of the Union, this time in favour of racial equality rather than white supremacy. In Hopkins's words, 'the admission of Hawai'i in 1959 created an irreparable hole in the wall enclosing segregation on the mainland. The succeeding Civil Rights Act, passed in 1964, took down the defenses, even if the rearguard action that followed was bitter and prolonged'.[79]

The arrière-garde is still fighting and the interpretation in this essay suggests why. From its inception the political organisation of the United States has been intimately bound up with racial inequality. The American republics realised principles of popular sovereignty, constitutional government, and representative democracy. But they and their union were also founded as a project to secure white supremacy and to extend white dominion over the North American continent. The distinction between empire and incorporation, on which Hopkins's analysis of nineteenth-century American expansion rests, helps us see that this project was not a perversion of, but central to, American founding principles. This may be a hard pill to swallow for a nation accustomed to venerating its founding and where even the struggle for inclusion has historically been organized around the unfulfilled promise issued by the pen of Thomas Jefferson in 1776. Yet if the refashioning of the American union that began in the 1950s and 1960s is to be brought to a successful conclusion, it requires that the thoughtless celebration of the founders be replaced by a critical investigation into the nation's founding ideals. Going forward, Americans should take strength from the words of Amanda Gorman, that 'being American is more than a pride we inherit. It's the past we step into and how we repair it.'[80]

Notes

1. Custer, *Boots and Saddles*, 295.
2. Twain, *Adventures of Huckleberry Finn*, 366.
3. Custer, *Boots and Saddles*, 94–114, 138–48, 216–24.
4. On the Custers, see Connell, *Son of the Morning Star* and Wert, *Custer*.
5. On settler colonialism, Ostler and Shoemaker, "Settler Colonialism."
6. Hopkins, *American Empire*, 13–15.
7. Colley, "Difficulties of Empire," 371, 382.
8. Hopkins, *American Empire*, 27.
9. Ibid., 191–207.
10. Ibid., 238.
11. Ibid., 237.
12. Ibid., 236–37.
13. Ibid., 237.
14. Belich, *Replenishing the Earth*, 166.
15. Wood, *Empire of Liberty*, 122. Wood is quoting the Northwest Ordinance, sect. 14, art. 5.
16. Pocock, "States, Republics, and Empires," 715.
17. Ibid.
18. *United States Magazine*, March 1779, cited in Onuf, *Jefferson's Empire*, 58.
19. Hamilton, "The Federalist 1," 3.
20. Hopkinson, "An Ode, Philadelphia, 4 July,"246–47.
21. Thomas Jefferson to Benjamin Chambers, 28 December 1805, in *Founders Online*, National Archives, https://founders.archives.gov/documents/Jefferson/99-01-02-2910. [This is an Early Access document from The Papers of Thomas Jeffersonhttps://founders.archives.gov/?q=%20Author%3A%22Jefferson%2C%20Thomas%22%20empire&s=1111311111&r=133].
22. Clay quoted in Frymer, *Building an American Empire*, 128.
23. Buchanan and Murtagh. *Oregon, My Oregon*.

24. Muller, "Bonds of Belonging"; Marshall, *Making and Unmaking of Empires*. See also Greene *Evaluating Empire* on contemporary British perceptions of the ethnic diversity of the Empire.
25. For example Montesquieu, *The Spirit of the Laws*, ed. Anne M. Cohler, Basia Carolyn Miller and Harold Samuel Stone. Cambridge: Cambridge University Press, 1989, 22–24. On republican thought, see Pocock, *Machiavellian Moment* and Pocock, *Virtue, Commerce and History*.
26. Guyatt, *Bind Us Apart*.
27. For example, Smith-Rosenberg, *This Violent Empire*; Parkinson, *Common Cause*.
28. Parkinson, "Friends and Enemies in the Declaration of Independence."
29. Welke, *Law and the Borders of Belonging*.
30. Act to Establish an Uniform Rule of Naturalization, March 26, 1790, ch. IV, *U.S. Statutes at Large* II, 103–4.
31. Guyatt, *Bind Us Apart*; Frymer, *Building an American Empire*, 220–62. Meinig, *Shaping of America, II: Continental America*, 296–311.
32. Keyssar, *Right to Vote*.
33. Abel, "Proposals for an Indian State"; Guyat, *Bind Us Apart*, 281–305.
34. Montesquieu, *Spirit of the Laws*, 131–33.
35. Biber, "Price of Admission," 140–50, quotation at 143 n8.
36. Josiah Quincy quoted in Biber, "Price of Admission," 135 n48.
37. Albert J. Beveridge, quoted in Frymer, *Building an American Empire*, 203–4.
38. On the post-war period, see Matson and Onuf, *Union of Interests* and Van Cleve, *We Have Not a Government*.
39. Edling, *Revolution in Favor of Government*; Edling, *Hercules in the Cradle*, 17–49; Edling, *Perfecting the Union*.
40. Hopkins, *American Empire*, 204.
41. Indigenous Digital Archives: Cessions, https://digitreaties.org/treaties/cessions/.
42. Hubbard, *American Boundaries*, 123–79, carefully accounts for the evolution of US territories and states in the long nineteenth century in no less than 38 maps. He makes no attempt to map Indian territories or land cessions, however.
43. The land ordinances and land sale policies are discussed in Berkhofer, Jr., 'Jefferson, the Ordinance of 1784, and the Origins of the American Territorial System'; Onuf, *Statehood and Union*; Saler, *Settlers' Empire*, 13–82.
44. Calloway, *Victory with No Name*.
45. Arthur St. Clair quoted in Onuf, *Statehood and Union*, 74.
46. The establishment of territorial government is discussed in Eblen, *First and Second United States Empires*, 51–171; Onuf, *Statehood and Union*, 67–87; and Saler, *Settlers' Empire*, 41–82.
47. Biber, "Price of Admission," 128.
48. Hopkins, *American Empire*, 238.
49. Biber, "Price of Admission," 120 (quotation), 132–40, 150–68.
50. Hopkins, *American Empire*, 197.
51. Truett, "Settler Colonialism," 438. A nuanced treatment of colonial expansion is Greer, *Property and Dispossession*.
52. Saler, *Settlers' Empire*, 83–120.
53. There is an extensive literature on Indian treaties and dispossession, see Sheehan, *Seeds of Extinction*; Prucha, *Great Father*; Horsman, *Expansion and American Indian Policy*; Prucha, *American Indian Treaties*; Sheehan, 'Indian Problem in the Northwest'; Deloria and Wilkins, *Tribes, Treaties, and Constitutional Tribulations*; Onuf, *Jefferson's Empire*; Banner, *How the Indians Lost Their Land*; Bergmann,

American National State; Jeffrey Ostler, "'Just and Lawful War'"; Witgen, "Nation of Settlers."

54. Gittinger, *Formation of the State of Oklahoma*, 3-56. On Indian removal in this period, see Prucha, *American Indian Policy in Formative Years*, 156–207; Prucha, *Great Father*, 179–69; Wallace, *Long Bitter Trail*; Wallace, *Jefferson and the Indians*; Banner, *How the Indians Lost Their Land*, 191–227; Ostler, *Surviving Genocide*, 247–373; Saunt, *Unworthy Republic*.
55. On the Great Plains Wars and the reservation system, see Gittinger, *Formation of the State of Oklahoma*, 96–117; Utley, *Indian Frontier*; Banner, *How the Indians Lost Their Land*, 228–56; Wooster, *American Military Frontiers*.
56. Adelman and Aron, "From Borderlands to Borders."
57. Treaty with the Delawares, Sept. 17, 1778, in Richard Peters, ed., "Treaties between the United States and the Indian Tribes", U.S. *Statutes at Large* VII (1778-1842), 13–15.
58. Young, "The Cherokee Nation"; McLoughlin, *Cherokee Renascence*.
59. Constitution of the Cherokee Nation, art. III, sect. 4, in *Cherokee Phoenix*, 21 February 1828.
60. Maxwell, "Sequoyah Convention," parts 1 and 2.
61. Abel, "Proposals for an Indian State", 89–104 and Guyatt, *Bind Us Apart*, 281–305, discuss statements and plans by U.S. politicians and reformers indicating a wish to see an indigenous state.
62. Meinig, *Shaping of America, II: Continental America*, 197–218.
63. Leigh quoted in Frymer, *Building an American Empire*, 220.
64. Hopkins, *American Empire*, 238.
65. Frymer, *Building an American Empire*, 278.
66. Lincoln and Cabell quoted in ibid., 195, 196.
67. *Cincinnati Commercial*, 3 March 1875, quoted in Larson, *New Mexico's Quest for Statehood*, 124.
68. *New York Times*, 28 October 1876, quoted in Frymer, *Building an American Empire*, 203.
69. Senator Albert J. Beveridge quoted in ibid., 204.
70. Frymer, *Building an American Empire*, 9.
71. Constitution of Oregon (1857), in Francis Newton Thorpe, ed. *The Federal and State Constitutions, Colonial Charters, and other Organic Laws of the States and Territories Now or Heretofore Forming the United States of America*, 7 vols. Washington, DC: Government Printing Office, 1909, V: 3000.
72. Frymer, *Building an American Empire*, 171.
73. Gittinger, *Formation of the State of Oklahoma*, 96-260; Frymer, *Building an American Empire*, 155-71.
74. Ostler and Shoemaker, "Introduction."
75. Camden, *Oklahoma, A Toast*.
76. *Rodgers and Hammerstein's Oklahoma!*, 45.
77. Frymer, *Building an American Empire*, 171.
78. 'Opinion by Judge Brown in *Downes v. Bidwell*', in *Opinions Delivered in the Insular Tariff Cases in the Supreme Court of the United States May 27, 1901*. Washington, DC: Government Printing Office, 1901, 66.
79. Hopkins, *American Empire*, 418, 429–30, 499, 515, 592–98, 649–52, 669–71, quotation at 671.
80. Gorman,"The Hill We Climb." .

Disclosure Statement

No potential conflict of interest was reported by the author(s).

References

Abel, Annie H. "Proposals for an Indian State, 1778-1878." In *Annual Report of the American Historical Association for the Year 1907*, 2 vols. I, edited by James Duane Doty, 89–104. Washington, DC: U.S. Government Printing Office, 1908.

Adelman, Jeremy, and Stephen Aron. "From Borderlands to Borders: Empires, Nation-States, and the Peoples in Between in North American History." *The American Historical Review* 104, no. 3 (1999): 814–841.

Anderson, Fred, and Andrew Cayton. *The Dominion of War: Empire and Liberty in North America, 1500-2000*. New York: Viking, 2005.

Banner, Stuart. *How the Indians Lost Their Land: Law and Power on the Frontier*. Cambridge, MA: Harvard University Press, 2005.

Belich, James. *Replenishing the Earth: The Settler Revolution and the Rise of the Anglo-World, 1783-1939*. Oxford: Oxford University Press, 2009.

Bergmann, William H. *The American National State and the Early West*. New York: Cambridge University Press, 2012.

Berkhofer, Jr. Robert F. "Jefferson, the Ordinance of 1784, and the Origins of the American Territorial System." *William and Mary Quarterly*, 3d. ser., 29, no. 2 (1972): 231–262.

Biber, Eric. "The Price of Admission: Causes, Effects, and Patterns of Conditions Imposed on States Entering the Union." *American Journal of Legal History* 46, no. 2 (2004): 119–208.

Buchanan, James Andrew and Henry B. Murtagh. *Oregon, My Oregon: Official Oregon State Song*. Portland, OR: s.n., 1920.

Calloway, Collin G. *The Victory with No Name: The Native American Defeat of the First American Army*. New York: Oxford University Press, 2015.

Colley, Linda. "The Difficulties of Empire: Present, Past and Future." *Historical Research* 79, no. 205 (2006): 367–382.

Camden, Harriet Parker. *Oklahoma, A Toast*. Enid, OK: Pierrat-Whitlock Music Co, 1905.

Connell, Evan S. *Son of the Morning Star: Custer and the Little Big Horn*. New York: Promontory Press, 1984.

Custer, Elizabeth B. *"Boots and Saddles": Or Life in Dakota with General Custer*. New York: Harper and Brothers, 1885.

Deloria, Jr., Vine and David E. Wilkins. *Tribes, Treaties, and Constitutional Tribulations*. Austin: University of Texas Press, 2000.

Eblen, Jack Ericson. *The First and Second United States Empires: Governors and Territorial Government, 1784-1912*. Pittsburgh, PA: University of Pittsburgh Press, 1968.

Edling, Max M. *A Revolution in Favor of Government: Origins of the US Constitution and the Making of the American State*. New York: Oxford University Press, 2003.

Edling, Max M. *A Hercules in the Cradle: War Money, and the American State, 1783-1867*. Chicago: University of Chicago Press, 2014.

Edling, Max M. *Perfecting the Union: National and State Authority in the US Constitution*. New York: Oxford University Press, 2021.

Frymer, Paul. *Building an American Empire: The Era of Territorial and Political Expansion*. Princeton, NJ: Princeton University Press, 2017.

Gittinger, Roy. *The Formation of the State of Oklahoma*. Norman: University of Oklahoma Press, 1939.

Gorman, Amanda. "The Hill We Climb." *The Guardian*, January 20, 2021.

Greene, Jack P. *Evaluating Empire and Confronting Colonialism in Eighteenth-Century Britain*. New York: Cambridge University Press, 2013.

Greer, Allan. *Property and Dispossession: Natives, Empires and Land in Early Modern North America*. New York: Cambridge University Press, 2018.

Guyatt, Nicholas. *Bind Us Apart: How Enlightened Americans Invited Racial Segregation*. New York: Basic Books, 2016.

Hamilton, Alexander. "The Federalist 1." In *The Federalist*, edited by Jacob E. Cooke, 3–7. Middletown, CT: Wesleyan University Press, 1961.

Heumann, Stefan. "The Tutelary Empire: State- and Nation Building in the Nineteenth-Century United States". Unpublished PhD dissertation: University of Pennsylvania, 2009.

Hopkins, Antony G. *American Empire: A Global History*. Princeton, NJ: Princeton University Press, 2018.

Hopkinson, Francis. "An Ode, Philadelphia, 4 July." In *The Documentary History of the Ratification of the Constitution* 34 vols. to date, edited by Merrill Jensen, John P. Kaminski and Gaspare J. Saladino, 18: 246–247. Madison: Wisconsin Historical Society Press, 1976.

Horsman, Reginald. *Expansion and American Indian Policy, 1783-1812*. Norman: University of Oklahoma Press, 1992.

Hubbard, Bill. *American Boundaries: The Nation, the States, the Rectangular Survey*. Chicago: University of Chicago Press, 2009.

Keyssar, Alexander. *The Right to Vote: The Contested History of Democracy in the United States*. New York: Basic Books, 2000.

Larson, Robert W. *New Mexico's Quest for Statehood, 1846-1912*. Albuquerque: University of New Mexico Press, 1968.

Marshall, Peter J. *The Making and Unmaking of Empires: Britain, India and America c. 1750-1783*. Oxford: Oxford University Press, 2005.

Matson, Cathy D., and Peter S. Onuf. *A Union of Interests: Political and Economic Thought in Revolutionary America*. Lawrence: University Press of Kansas, 1990.

Maxwell, Amos D. "The Sequoyah Convention', Parts 1 and 2." *The Chronicles of Oklahoma* 28, nos. 2 and 3 (1950): 161–192 and 299–340.

McLoughlin, William G. *Cherokee Renascence in the New Republic*. Princeton, NJ: Princeton University Press, 1986.

Meinig, D. W. *The Shaping of America: A Geographical Perspective on 500 Years of History. Vol II: Continental America, 1800-1867*. New Haven, CT: Yale University Press, 1993.

Muller, Hannah Weiss. "Bonds of Belonging: Subjecthood and the British Empire." *Journal of British Studies* 53, no. 1 (2014): 29–58.

Onuf, Peter S. *Statehood and Union: A History of the Northwest Ordinance*. Bloomington: Indiana University Press, 1987.

Onuf, Peter S. *Jefferson's Empire: The Language of American Nationhood*. Charlottesville: Virginia University Press, 2000.

Ostler, Jeffrey. ""Just and Lawful War" as Genocidal War in the (United States) Northwest Ordinance and Northwest Territory, 1787–1832." *Journal of Genocide Research* 18, no. 1 (2016): 1–20.

Ostler, Jeffrey. *Surviving Genocide: Native Nations and the United States from the American Revolution to Bleeding Kansas*. New Haven, CT: Yale University Press, 2019.

Ostler, Jeffrey and Nancy Shoemaker. "Settler Colonialism in Early American History: Introduction." *William and Mary Quarterly*, 3d. ser., 76, no. 3 (2019): 361–368.

Parkinson, Robert G. *The Common Cause: Creating Race and Nation in the American Revolution*. Chapel Hill: University of North Carolina Press, 2016.

Parkinson, Robert G. "Friends and Enemies in the Declaration of Independence." In *Jeffersonians in Power: The Rhetoric of Opposition Meets the Realities of Governing*,

edited by Joanne B. Freeman, and Johann N. Neem, 15–37. Charlottesville: University of Virginia Press, 2019.
Pocock, J. G. A. *Machiavellian Moment: Florentine Political Thought and the Atlantic Republican Tradition*. Princeton, NJ: Princeton University Press, 1975.
Pocock, J. G. A. *Virtue, Commerce and History: Essays on Political Thought and History, Chiefly in the Eighteenth Century*. Cambridge: Cambridge University Press, 1985.
Pocock, J. G. A. "States, Republics, and Empires: The American Founding in Early Modern Perspective." *Social Science Quarterly* 68, no. 4 (1987): 703–723.
Prucha, Francis Paul. *American Indian Policy in Formative Years: The Indian Trade and Intercourse Acts, 1790–1834*. Cambridge, MA: Harvard University Press, 1962.
Prucha, Francis Paul. *The Great Father: The United States Government and the American Indians*. Lincoln: University of Nebraska Press, 1984.
Prucha, Francis Paul. *American Indian Treaties: The History of a Political Anomaly*. Berkeley: University of California Press, 1994.
Saler, Bethel. *The Settlers' Empire: Colonialism and State Formation in America's Old Northwest*. Philadelphia: University of Pennsylvania Press, 2014.
Saunt, Claudio. *Unworthy Republic: The Dispossession of Native Americans and the Road to Indian Territory*. New York: W.W. Norton & Company, 2020.
Sheehan, Bernard W. *Seeds of Extinction: Jeffersonian Philanthropy and the American Indian*. New York: Norton, 1974.
Sheehan, Bernard W. "The Indian Problem in the Northwest: From Conquest to Philanthropy." In *Launching the "Extended Republic": The Federalist Era*, edited by Ronald Hoffman, and Peter J. Albert, 190–222. Charlottesville: University of Virginia Press, 1996.
Smith-Rosenberg, Carroll. *This Violent Empire: The Birth of an American National Identity*. Chapel Hill: University of North Carolina Press, 2010.
Truett, Samuel. "Settler Colonialism and the Borderlands of Early America." *William and Mary Quarterly*, 3d. ser., 76, no. 3 (2019): 435–442.
Twain, Mark. *The Adventures of Huckleberry Finn (Tom Sawyer's Comrade)*. New York: Charles L. Webster & Co, 1885.
Utley, Robert M. *The Indian Frontier of the American West 1846–1890*. Albuquerque: University of New Mexico Press, 1984.
Van Cleve, George William. *We Have Not a Government: The Articles of Confederation and the Road to the Constitution*. Chicago: Chicago University Press, 2017.
Wallace, Anthony F. *The Long Bitter Trail: Andrew Jackson and the Indians*. New York: Hill and Wang, 1993.
Wallace, Anthony F. *Jefferson and the Indians: The Tragic Fate of the First Americans*. Cambridge, MA: Harvard University Press, 1999.
Welke, Barbara Young. *Law and the Borders of Belonging in the Long Nineteenth Century United States*. New York: Cambridge University Press, 2010.
Wert, Jeffry D. *Custer: The Controversial Life of George Armstrong Custer*. New York: Simon & Schuster, 1996.
Witgen, Michael. 'A Nation of Settlers: The Early American Republic and the Colonization of the Northwest Territory', *William and Mary Quarterly*, 3d. ser., 76, no. 3 (2019): 391–398.
Wood, Gordon S. *Empire of Liberty: A History of the Early Republic, 1789-1815*. New York: Oxford University Press, 2009.
Wooster, Robert. *American Military Frontiers: The United States Army in the West, 1783–1900*. Albuquerque: University of New Mexico Press, 2009.
Young, Mary. "The Cherokee Nation: Mirror of the Republic." *American Quarterly* 33, no. 5 (1981): 502–524.

The British Empire after A.G. Hopkins's *American Empire*

Jay Sexton

ABSTRACT
Where does the United States fit into global histories of modern empire? This essay contends that A.G. Hopkins's depiction of nineteenth century America as the modern world's first postcolonial polity not only imaginatively advances the project of globalising U.S. history, it also reveals the ongoing significance of America to the expansion and development of the British Empire itself. Viewing the British Empire through its deep and diverse connections to postcolonial America underscores the integration, dynamism, power, and vulnerability of the British imperial system in its Victorian heyday.

A dozen or so years ago, back when I worked in a British university, I served on a search committee for a U.S. history position with several colleagues who taught British and European history. Reviewing the towering stack of applications, most of which came from American-trained U.S. historians, provided my colleagues with an involuntary crash course in the peculiarities of U.S. historiography. They were immediately struck by the specificity and depth of the scholarship.

> It is almost as if the intellectual task that these scholars set for themselves was not only to dive deeply into a single theme, in a single place, in a single decade, but also to show how their findings differed from research on similar topics in neighbouring decades,

I recall a colleague commenting in a tone that indicated both bewilderment and curiosity.

The need for U.S. historians to see the forest for the trees was by no means only voiced be foreign observers. A recurrent theme in American historiographical essays and conference round-tables at the turn of the most recent century concerned the need for a new synthesis of U.S. history, one that would replace the musty, nationalistic accounts from the Cold War.[1] But the task is easier said than done for a voluminous national historiography that has no equal in terms of scale – and, at least until recently, also stands apart in terms of its insularity and self-referentiality. Even individual U.S. states, such as Virginia,

Pennsylvania, and Texas, have historiographies that match those of European nations. A common question to a conference paper in the United States is 'what you say is interesting, but it doesn't match my research on [insert locality, state, region, ethnic group, etc.].'

This is the backstory to 2018, which witnessed the publication of not one, but two, massive, 900-plus page syntheses of U.S. history. They could hardly be more different. The first, Jill Lepore's *These Truths: A History of the United States*, was the product of America's east coast intellectual establishment.[2] Its preoccupations are the social and political processes of internal nation-making. Lepore's narrative tracks Americans' relentless, but halting and incomplete, pursuit of their nation's founding creed 'that all men are created equal.' The second synthesis of 2018, A.G. Hopkins, *American Empire: A Global History*, was the creation of a foreign interloper – a renowned British historian of empire and globalisation who happened to find himself landing in Texas to take up an academic post on 11 September 2001.[3] *American Empire* has little interest in the familiar story of Americans' unfinished (and potentially ill-fated?) attempt to construct a democracy premised on social equality and individual liberty. 'A persistent motif of the book,' Hopkins later wrote, 'is precisely the need to give prominence to themes other than liberty and democracy in understanding U.S. history.'[4]

Postcolonial America

Hopkins situates U.S. history into its global context. His objective is to probe how America fits into broader patterns of historical development, particularly the shape-shifting, cross-border processes that we now call globalisation. Grand forces, both material and cultural, drive the narrative. A strength of the book is that Hopkins avoids the Whiggish teleologies that so often structure accounts of the 'rise' of the United States, which range from simplistic narratives of national exceptionalism to darker accounts of illiberal ascendance. The objective of *American Empire* is 'not to put the United States down, but rather to put it in – to the mainstream of western history' (691). Doing so necessarily means departing from traditional, nation-based accounts of U.S. history.

Hopkins is not the first historian to place that hoary shibboleth of American exceptionalism in the middle of his cross-hairs. After all, the transnational and global turns of recent years has found much traction within the United States.[5] What most separates Hopkins's book from the pack is not simply the attempt to 'globalise' the American past, but the specific way in which he does so: focusing on the entangled evolution of empire and globalisation, Hopkins approaches U.S. history as an adjunct of the contested phases of global integration conditioned by imperial power, especially that of Britain. 'The argument that globalisation has passed through different historical phases anchors the process in time and suggests how the history of the United States can be joined to the history of Western Europe, and indeed the world' (12).

American Empire not only places U.S. history within the stages of globalisation, it also grafts the concepts of British imperial historiography onto a national historiography that has developed in a sort of 'splendid isolation' from foreign influences. The book's argument is structured by categories of analysis not often used in U.S. historiography, but ones that will be familiar to readers of this journal: fiscal-military states, Robinson and Gallagher, collaborating elites, dependent development, effective independence, free trade imperialism, invisible earnings, anticolonial nationalism, and so on. One of the strongest sections of the book, the synthetic treatment of America's post-1898 insular empire in the Pacific and Caribbean, not only integrates the experiences of the diverse island possessions of the formal U.S. empire (whose histories all too often have been siloed from one another), but also maps the U.S. empire alongside the trajectory of the British and European cases, finding that they all followed a similar rhythm of acquisition, administrative reform, consolidation, crisis, and, ultimately, de-colonisation. The similar histories of these different imperial formations, Hopkins surmises in one of the most provocative lines in a book in which there are many, all bore the imprint of macro forces of global integration, suggesting 'that there is a common explanation for the rise and fall of the Western empires as a whole in the twentieth century. National characteristics, or exceptionalism, added particularities and distinctiveness, but neither diverted nor diluted the influence of supranational forces.' (492).

The most arresting interpretation of *American Empire* to readers on the western side of the Atlantic, and the launching point for this essay, is Hopkins's depiction of nineteenth-century America as a decolonising, or postcolonial, polity that remained within the orbit of the British power. In contrast to Lepore, whose geographic horizons largely collapse once the United States becomes a sovereign, independent polity, Hopkins views nineteenth-century America through the prism of lingering imperial influence. 'Standard accounts [of the nineteenth century] pay only limited attention to the role of external relations,' Hopkins contends, 'Far from being self-contained, however, the United States felt the effects of Britain's expanding informal influence after 1783 in economic development, political choice, and forms of cultural expression' (694). The postcolonial American republic was a sort of 'honorary dominion' of the British Empire, as Hopkins elsewhere has called it.[6]

In this meaty section of the book, 'empire' most often refers to persistent British influence, not America's westward expansion. Hopkins recounts the volatile era of revolution and European warfare that lasted up to 1815, a period in which the geopolitical fortunes of the vulnerable republic hinged upon the vicissitudes of imperial conflict. The strong showing of the United States against Britain in the War of 1812 – America's 'second war of independence' – did not complete America's postcolonial phase. Indeed, far from it: British investment and cultural influence in the United States increased in the era after 1815, which witnessed a frenzied boom in transatlantic exchange that resulted in the twinning of U.S. development to British power ('dependent development'). Nineteenth-century Americans exploited British connections in order to complete their independence and stabilise their nascent nation. 'The history of the United States between 1783 and 1861 can be recast as an anticipation of what became the classic postcolonial dilemma: how to make formal independence effective' (187).

Hopkins runs with this theme, making imaginative, asynchronous comparisons with other postcolonial societies. Lines such as the following are peppered throughout the book: 'Becoming American after 1783 was no less fraught than becoming Indian was after 1947' (190); 'the obvious, though still neglected, comparison is with Britain's other colonies of white settlement, which achieved self-government but remained dependent on Britain in the political, economic, and cultural spheres' (187); 'cotton was to the South what oil was to Biafra' (35). Hopkins advances this argument with precision and range: careful not to overstate British 'neo-colonialism,' he nonetheless demonstrates pervasive British influence in early American finance, development, and culture. He recasts familiar episodes in nineteenth-century American politics and sectionalism in relation to the 'imperatives that propel all newly independent states: the quest for stability and development' (694).

British power paradoxically threatened U.S. independence while at the same time underwriting the frenetic growth and development of the expanding postcolonial republic. For all the Anglophobic harangues of American politicians in election years, there can be little question that Britain was the indispensable patron of U.S. development: British capital financed infrastructure projects like canals and railroads at lower rates of interest than were on offer to competing postcolonial polities in Latin America; British markets were the primary destination of U.S. exports, including its cash crops of cotton and wheat; peoples from the British Isles were the largest immigrant group to arrive to the United States until as late as the 1880s; British foreign policy and naval power sheltered the Yankee republic from European rivals – it was the Royal Navy that enforced the bumptious 1823 Monroe Doctrine of non-intervention in Latin America. The postcolonial connection was just as advantageous to Britain. American independence was a bitter pill to swallow, but it freed Britain from the costly overheads of imperial rule, without losing access in the long term to America's vast markets. 'Informal influence,' Hopkins writes, 'was more effective than formal rule because it was both cheaper and more acceptable to the recipients' (193–4).

The American Civil War is cast in a new light in Hopkins's paradigm: the Union triumph becomes the climax of a protracted revolutionary process, the moment in which the postcolonial struggle for political control within the United States was finally settled. The nineteenth-century American experience once again portended the age of decolonisation: 'The record of decolonisation since the Civil War has shown that newly independent states, carved from inherited imperial boundaries and often without accepted legitimacy of their own, were prime candidates for political instability' (236). The result of 1865 finally brought relative political stability to the United States. Northern power destroyed the South's slave labour regime and political power, enabling Yankee capital and industry to place it, and the booming West, under its economic control.

Here were the origins of the upstart American empire of immense potential power. But the curtain did not fall on the postcolonial phase of American history in 1865; 'effective independence' was not yet attained. The decades after the Civil War – the heyday of the steamship, telegraph, colonial expansion, and Hopkins's phase of 'modern globalisation' – witnessed another surge in the transatlantic flows of British capital, culture, and power. Indeed, the height of British investment in the United States came in this period. American nationalists responded by pursuing more assertive methods of achieving effective independence, including subjugation of Indigenous populations, measures aimed at curtailing foreign economic power within the United States, and erecting the highest tariffs in the world. Ultimately, the 'effective independence' of the United States coincided with the creation of a new overseas empire in 1898, when America defeated Spain in a short war, gobbling up in the aftermath the Philippines, Guam, Puerto Rico, as well as consolidating its grip around Cuba and, in the midst of this expansionism, annexing Hawai'i.

In sum, by foregrounding empire and globalisation, Hopkins provides an alternative to traditional accounts of nineteenth century America that highlight internal nation-making. Hopkins is not the first scholar to emphasise the postcolonial nature of nineteenth century America, but he brings it all together in a cogent narrative that ranges across the entire century (and beyond) as has no one before.[7] Of note is how he extends beyond his specialisations of economic and political history, making illuminating forays into the realms of culture, religion, and identity formation. But not all dimensions of American empire are fully integrated into the argument. Because Hopkins's interpretation of American history prioritises the global and British contexts, the on-the-ground imperial story in the American West in the nineteenth century gets shortshrift. Indigenous America, which looms ever larger in recent scholarship, receives only perfunctory treatment in the narrative (it is worth pointing out that the relative absence of Indigenous voices is also a criticism of Lepore's history).[8]

Zooming in on British power and influence places the single most important imperial formation in U.S. development under the microscope. But it risks downplaying the diverse imperial influences and legacies at work in the post-1783 United States. For example, I write this essay quarantined in the basin of the Missouri River, an historic borderland of rival imperial formations. When I repatriated to my home region several years ago as a naturalised British subject, one of my new colleagues lost no opportunity to remind me that, when moving inland from the British Atlantic seaboard, Missouri was the first U.S. territory not to have been part of the British Empire. Once the domain of the culturally versatile and politically dexterous Osage people, and further upstream under the control of the mighty Lakota, the Missouri Valley also passed through periods of French, Spanish, and Confederate control or influence.[9] The vestiges of these imperial phases remain visible today in demography, law, economy, and popular memory. Migration patterns in the Missouri basin were also diverse, including not only English-speaking settlers originating from the British Isles, but also significant waves of Germans (in the mid-nineteenth century), Italians (turn of the century), and Balkan peoples (in our current era – St. Louis has the largest Bosnian population outside of Europe).

The entangled legacies of Missouri's trans-imperial history extend beyond the United States. Next time you uncork a bottle of Bordeaux, give a toast to the 'Missouri Rhineland,' home to robust grapevines grown by German immigrants. It was the roots of these Missouri grapevines that were grafted onto the plants in France to fight off the devastating phylloxera parasite in the late-nineteenth century.[10] All should agree that here was a historic turning point, if ever there was one, in which the New World came to the rescue of the Old. After toasting the Missouri Rhineland, you can chase the French wine down with a Budweiser, also the creation of German migrants to Missouri, or a whiskey aged in casks made of Missouri's Ozark white oak, today's favoured material used by hipster distillers around the world.

The point here is not to take issue with Hopkins's interpretation that America was a postcolonial, decolonising polity subject to lingering British influence. Rather, it is to suggest that the British imperial approach that he employs can be expanded to bring into view the other imperial formations – including Indigenous ones – that conditioned the development of U.S. nation-making. Indeed, what is needed in future are studies that situate America's inchoate empire in relation to wide-ranging trans-imperial dynamics and global processes. Fortunately, recent years have seen an acceleration of research in this very area, suggesting that scholars, including American based U.S. historians, are shaking off their erstwhile insularity, in the process enriching our understanding of how the story Hopkins so ably tells fits into other imperial narratives.[11]

Turning the Tables

The rest of this essay will turn the tables by viewing the history of the British Empire in its Victorian heyday through its postcolonial connection to the

United States. What follows uses Hopkins's postcolonial interpretation of nineteenth-century America to look anew at the British Empire. Posed as a question: what characteristics of the British Empire emerge when its development is viewed through the prism of its enduring connection to postcolonial America?

Before attempting to answer that question, a few words are necessary on the historical and historiographical contexts. Even a cursory glance at the statistics reveals the centrality of postcolonial America to Britain's nineteenth-century world system. The United States was Victorian Britain's single most important trading partner, its principal source of raw materials, such as cotton, corn, and timber, as well as its largest overseas commercial market. The north Atlantic corridor, especially between the booming ports of Liverpool and New York, was the world's most plied transoceanic shipping route. The result was the creation of dense networks of exchange of all sorts – social movements, scientific collaborations, cultural productions, and on and on. More British capital went to the United States than anywhere else. As late as the 1865–1914 period, British investment in America was more than double what it was in capital markets in Canada, Argentina, and Australia. Roughly three times as much British capital went to the United States in this period than was invested in India and South Africa.[12] Perhaps the most arresting figure concerns British emigration. Of the estimated 22 million British emigrants in the 1815–1914 period, some two-thirds went to the United States.[13] Even in the late period of 1853–1920, more Britons emigrated to the United States than to the rest of the world combined.[14] Eastward migration across the Atlantic – from America to Britain – was also significant, as the recent work of Stephen Tuffnell has made clear. Though American emigrants to Britain were small in number, they left an outsized impact on the culture, commerce, and politics on both sides of the Atlantic.[15]

Contemporaries on both sides of the Atlantic were well aware that the political independence of the United States did not sever the transatlantic connection. Rather than viewing it all as a function of national exchange – as some kind of proto-'special relationship' that did not yet exist – observers more often understood these links in relation to Britain's expanding empire. Hopkins's book captures how postcolonial Americans understood themselves to be subject to ongoing British imperial influence and structured their politics around competing visions of how to complete their revolution. On the opposite side of the relationship, British observers also placed the transatlantic link within a wider imperial context. Here is *The Times* on the occasion of the 1851 Great Exhibition, which prominently featured the United States:

> For all practical purposes the United States are far more closely united with the kingdom than any one of our colonies, and keep up a perpetual interchange of the most important good offices: taking our manufactures and our surplus population and giving us in return the materials of industry, of revenue and of life.[16]

Some of the era's classic imperial texts, such as that of Charles Dilke, understood the United States to be a central component of a cosmopolitan and diverse 'Greater Britain.' 'In America,' Dilke wrote, 'the peoples of the world are being fused together, but they are into an English mould... Through America England is speaking to the world.'[17]

Late-nineteenth century talk of a British 'imperial federation' that included the United States eventually gave way to the nationally structured, but persistently racialized, alliance of 'the English-speaking peoples' that battled fascism and communism in the twentieth century. It was this process of nationally-driven alliance-making in the era of world war and global decolonisation that helps to explain the erasure of the postcolonial imperial transatlantic connection of the nineteenth century. In other words, Churchill's 'special relationship' eclipsed Dilke's 'Greater Britain,' even if elements of the latter lived on in racial consciousness and multi-lateral security systems. But in the main the imperial and global dimensions of the transatlantic connection gave way to its conception as a bilateral 'special relationship.' The change is evident in the historiography, which came to neglect America's position within a global British imperial system, instead setting itself the task of tracing the 'great rapprochement' and 'the Victorian origins of the special relationship.'[18]

But not all histories of the nineteenth century prioritised national frames over imperial ones. Of particular note was the work of Frank Thistlethwaite, whose trailblazing scholarship on the transatlantic connection should give him a stature in the field of Atlantic history akin to that enjoyed by Robinson and Gallagher in the study of the British Empire. In his precocious 1959 *The Anglo-American Connection in the Early Nineteenth Century*, Thistlethwaite approached Britain's relationship to the United States in the early nineteenth century in relation to its Latin American policy, contending that both regions were part of a British 'informal trading empire,' a point to which Robinson and Gallagher also provocatively alluded.[19]

In more recent times, it has been British imperial historians who have been most inclined to pick up where these scholars left off. The question of where to place nineteenth-century America in the British Empire has become an interesting, albeit marginal, issue in modern British imperial historiography – more of a lively after seminar pub debate than the subject of rigorous analysis. Nonetheless, the matter has attracted interest. Cain and Hopkins's 1993 *British Imperialism* was a prototype on this score in that it included the United States within its discussions of the global power wielded by 'gentlemanly capitalists,' though the authors were careful to stress the limits of Britain's imperial power in America as compared to the more effective economic control administered in the settler colonies.[20]

Studies of the British World, 'a consensual association' that was not circumscribed by the 'more familiar empire of compulsion and subordination,' were not surprisingly among those most interested in integrating the United States into their wider imperial frame.[21] For example, by foregrounding the nexus between settler sovereignty and Indigenous dispossession, Lisa Ford revealed continuities and parallel developments within Georgia and New South Wales.[22] Comparative analysis of U.S. continental imperialism and the colonisations of the 'British wests' of the settler colonies was imaginatively pursued in James Belich's 2010 *Replenishing the Earth*, a work which also contended that the economic rhythms of Anglo imperialism led to the partial economic 'recolonisation' of the United States to the British Empire in the second half of the nineteenth century.[23] Philip Magee and Andrew Thompson similarly highlighted the extent to which the United States in the late nineteenth century remained embedded within the cultural economy and social networks of the British World. Indeed, their comparative examinations of trade, capital flows, and migrations patterns demonstrated that nineteenth century America was, statistically speaking, the single most significant member of the British world. But Magee and Thompson, like Cain and Hopkins before them, cautioned against overstating America's place within the British Empire: 'The sense that America was a part of the British diaspora was real, but it was also ambivalent, open to dispute by contemporaries, and it eroded over time.'[24]

The range of perspectives on how the United States fitted within the British imperial system is illustrated by the two very different conceptions of the British Empire of Antoinette Burton and John Darwin. In his global histories, Darwin emphasises how the British-led geopolitical system of the nineteenth century, which unleashed a booming transatlantic economic complex, made 'Americans the indispensable sleeping partners of Europe's expansion into Afro-Asia.' From a geopolitical perspective, the United States came to look less like a troublesome ex-colony than a sort of 'super-dominion' of the British Empire.[25] Burton, whose study of the British Empire foregrounds 'trouble' and conflict, casts a different light on the significance of the United States. Rather than a source of imperial power, the United States appears in her book as a vital node within the global circuitry of radical anticolonialism. America's political sovereignty and freedom from colonial surveillance made it an attractive staging post for anticolonial activists, such as Irish Fenians in New York in the nineteenth century and, later on the West coast, Indian exiles Lala Lajpat Rai and Taraknath Das. 'The foundation of the Ghadar Party in California in 1913,' Burton argues, 'was a major milestone in the development of a dispersed, extra-territorial, anticolonial, radical movement that unequivocally aimed at bringing down the Raj.'[26]

The point of this whistle-stop historiographic overview is less to settle that after seminar pub debate about the best label for postcolonial America (honorary dominion? node within circuits of radical anticolonialism?), than to underscore the point that a range of historians, writing from differing perspectives, have recognised that postcolonial America was an important component of the British world. But equally significant is the fact that most historians since the mid-twentieth century, especially Americanists, have approached the nineteenth-century in national (or, more recently, transnational) terms, rather than global imperial ones. Recent scholars of the British Empire have dipped a toe into the question of how America fitted into the wider British imperial project, but are yet to dive into the matter. If we are to take the plunge that centres postcolonial America within the global story of the British Empire, what emerges?

The British Empire and Postcolonial America

The remainder of this essay contends that three characteristics of the nineteenth-century British Empire come into sharper focus. First, the inarguable significance of the United States to the British imperial system – as evidenced in its pole position in tables of capital flows, migration patterns, trading figures, shipping lines, social networks, and so on – suggests that historians should further lean into an existing trend in British imperial historiography: the move away from the assessment of forms of imperial rule (which typically entails the exclusion of the United States) toward the analysis of broader systems of imperial exchange and integration (which demands rigorous examination of America).

The power of the British Empire in the age of Victorian globalisation lay less in how it administered rule, which varied wildly from place to place in this astonishingly pluralistic empire, than it did in its 'ability to *integrate* a wide range of regions, however remote, into a single system of wealth and power,' to quote Darwin.[27] The labels we use to describe this complex and multifaceted process of imperial integration – and as an outsider I embrace blissful agnosticism on existing possibilities such as British Empire, British world, 'trouble,' imperial systems, circuits and networks, and so on – is of less significance than is the intellectual project itself. Here, an insight from the American imperial historiographer Paul Kramer is worth quoting: imperial history 'is best approached pragmatically: while debates have generally centred on questions of semantics – what the imperial 'is' – we should instead emphasise what it does.'[28] Whatever label one gives to the postcolonial United States, there can be no question that it 'did' things for the wider project of nineteenth-century British imperialism. The point here is not simply that America was statistically the most significant component of the British world system, though that is of course important; rather, the point is that the patterns and institutions of exchange with postcolonial America left their mark on Britain's global imperial project, often in diverse and unexpected ways.

An illustration of the multifaceted role postcolonial America played in the nineteenth century British imperial system can be seen in the dominant commodity of that era's global economy: cotton. It has long been recognised that the dramatic expansion of the slaveholding South went hand in glove with the industrialisation of Britain's textile sector and, in turn, the rise of British free-trade liberalism. But the 'white gold' picked by enslaved African Americans in the Deep South, which comprised roughly 80 per cent of the cotton spun in the mills of Lancashire by the mid-nineteenth century, was also an essential component of the expansion and development of the wider British imperial system. The growth of rival textile industries across Europe and the United States, many of which came to be sheltered under protective tariffs, pushed the distribution of British textiles into colonial, or informal imperial, markets, such as those in India, East Asia, and Latin America. This imperial distribution, in turn, necessitated the thickening of imperial conduits of shipping, distribution, financial services, and, not to be forgotten, importation to the Home Isles (for the ships carrying textile goods to imperial markets needed cargo for the return journey). The case of cotton underscores the diverse, even contradictory, ways in which the United States influenced British imperialism: America was at once the primary source of a raw material whose finished product comprised nearly half of all British exports in the mid nineteenth century *and* an upstart rival whose protectionism channelled British imperial expansion beyond the North Atlantic.[29]

Tracking the development of other components of the Atlantic economy similarly connects the dots between postcolonial America and the globalisation of the Victorian imperial system. Consider, for example, Anglo-American merchant banks. These entities' initial fortunes came from financing transatlantic trade, but over time they metamorphized into globe-spanning financial institutions that lubricated the grinding cross-border economic activity of Victorian globalisation. The classic case-study is Barings, whose imperial origins lay in the late-colonial boom in Atlantic exchange in the 1760s. The onset of American independence was not a threat to Barings. Far from it. It was a sort of imperial deregulation – an eighteenth century 'big bang' in transatlantic finance – that kicked the gate open to a seemingly limitless market that it was primed to exploit, not least because of its unique partnership structure which, in time, came to include both Americans and Britons in its central offices in the City. Barings expanded operations, using profits from earlier initiatives to finance new ones: its original business of underwriting trade led to ventures in U.S. public finance (the London bank famously underwrote the Louisiana Purchase), which in turn led to investment in America's metastasising infrastructure projects – forest clearing, canals, port improvements, and, most lucrative of all, railroads. The wealth Barings acquired from these American ventures spawned even more expansion, this time on a global scale. 'The world's sixth great power,' as the bank came to be called, became a player in Canadian development, where it invested in the Grand Trunk Railway in the mid-nineteenth century, as well as extending operations into markets further afield, including – disastrously, as it turned out in 1890 – Argentina and Uruguay.[30]

The connection to postcolonial America was of significance to the wider British Empire in ways beyond economics. An ideological pillar of the Victorian empire, anti-slavery, was inextricably entwined with transatlantic connections. Popular consciousness of the moral injustice of slavery within Britain took root within the milieu of the liberal ideas of the American Revolution and were institutionalised by transatlantic networks of anti-slavery agitation (including the British speaking tours of African Americans such as Frederick Douglass, who became a Victorian celebrity after his first visit to Britain and Ireland in the 1840s).[31] On the flip side, the exponential growth of the slaveholding cotton kingdom in the South provided the transatlantic antislavery movement with its greatest adversary, one which prompted uncomfortable questions about the moral legitimacy of sovereign borders.

The struggle against slavery spilled beyond the North Atlantic. Britain's campaign to suppress the transatlantic slave trade after 1807 redirected the energies of Britain's 'antislavery state' to far-flung regions of its expanding empire. Britain's ventures in Africa in the mid and late nineteenth century were a testament to the strength of Victorian antislavery, as well as manifestations of how moral sentiment could harness British power on behalf of imperial ends. 'Antislavery assumption and the slave-trade squadrons acted as bridge-builders for imperial bridgeheads,' historian Richard Huzzey concludes in his study that probes the bonds between antislavery and empire.[32] Meanwhile, the search for antislavery sources of cotton, which climaxed during the supply crisis brought on by the American Civil War, led Britain to promote alternative production in Egypt and India, which became more tightly integrated into Britain's imperial system as a result.

In sum, transatlantic connections that often dated back to the colonial era, such as trading relationships, financial institutions, and social networks, conditioned the development of the wider British imperial project, in ways direct and indirect. But the influence of postcolonial America within the British Empire was not always mediated through metropolitan institutions, such as banks and antislavery societies, nor manifested through postcolonial patterns of transatlantic exchange, like the cotton trade. As the nineteenth century progressed, decolonising America emerged as its own player within the British world system, shaping in the process the development of the British Empire. The economic dynamism, geopolitical significance, and political novelty of postcolonial America posed a formidable challenge to Britain's imperial system. The result was a trans-imperial competition that unleashed innovations in politics, economy, and culture that rippled throughout the British world.

The dynamism of the Victorian British Empire is the second characteristic that jumps out when it is viewed from the vantage of the United States. A place to begin an analysis of this sort is the British colony that was most closely connected to the United States: the provinces of British North America, whose ongoing imperial loyalty did not mean that their development occurred in isolation from their troublesome southern neighbour. Just as Hopkins situates the trajectory of the post-1898 American empire into the patterns of other empires, the nineteenth century development of the two North American polities can be seen as following a similar rhythm, at least at the macro level. Both faced political difficulties concerning land policy and the incorporation of non-English speaking territories (Quebec; former French, Spanish, and Mexican territories, as well as Native America); both underwent contentious processes of political consolidation in the 1860s; both pursued programmes of Indigenous dispossession, whose differences appear less significant when viewed from native ground; both exploited links to the City in order to finance public debt and ambitious infrastructure projects that integrated the Atlantic and Pacific coasts of North America; both pursued policies of economic nationalism in the late nineteenth century – Macdonald's 'national policy' of the 1870s mimicked U.S. political economy, even as it sought to curb American influence within Canada.

These similar patterns of development stemmed, in part, from common geography, history, and direct exchange (the mid-century U.S.-Canadian experiment in commercial reciprocity remains an understudied episode in North Atlantic history).[33] But the real explanation for the similar arcs taken by Canada and the United States can be found in the primary rule of the road in nineteenth century North America: in the continent's fast developing market economy, everything was a competition. In the scramble for advancement in North America, there was no better way to get a leg up on the competition than to plug into the circuitry of the British imperial system and pull as much power from it as possible. If you were a banker in Ontario, or a shipper in the booming port of New York, or a wheat farmer in Illinois, or a Methodist preacher in the hinterland, or an artist, novelist, or wannabe aristocrat – if you were anything like the above, there was advantage to be had from entering British networks.

There was a staggering array of such transatlantic competitions in the nineteenth century. The British provinces and the United States – including *individual* U.S. states – competed to attract capital from the City at the lowest rates, which led to new forms of political economy. They raced across the vast North American continent, battling to produce the cheapest and most abundant cash crops – the repeal of the Corn Laws in 1846 was a sort of starting gun to this race on the U.S. side of the border. They outdid one another in the 'scramble for citizens,'[34] churning out booster literature to prospective migrants that became ever more bombastic and sensational over time, as well as sending recruiting agents across the Atlantic to attract the muscle required for their labour-hungry economies. Once a successful formula had been found – state subsidies to infrastructure projects; agricultural innovations, such as the McCormick reaper; even new political technologies, such as the 'secret ballot,' which originated with the Chartists, before taking root in

Australia, then crossing the Pacific back to the United States in the late nineteenth century[35] – whenever such an innovation proved profitable, copycats quickly emerged across the British world. That sincerest form of flattery was a common feature in the Victorian British world.

Competition fuelled the frenetic colonisation of North America, and the myriad innovations that made it possible on both sides of the 49th parallel. In time, this competitive dynamic spread across the Victorian world, as the case of the secret ballot illustrates. British settler colonies in Australasia and South Africa entered the fray in the second half of the nineteenth century. The coincidence of the mid-century gold rushes in California and Victoria generated a flurry of transpacific exchange and rivalry.[36] A variation of this dynamic of imperial competition can be seen in newly independent Latin America, where British officials sparred with their upstart Yankee rivals. The prizes in this competition were trade agreements, lucrative business associations, connections with the vibrant civil society of the new republics,[37] and access to political power – always a moving target as a result of the political volatility of postcolonial Spanish America. In their race to secure a trade agreement in the 1820s, representatives from Britain and the United States sided with rival Masonic lodges in Mexico City (the British allied with the more powerful lodge); in Buenos Aires, the American and British ministers kept score of their competition by keeping tabs on attendance for the public celebrations that they sponsored, respectively, on the 4th of July and St. George's Day (the British won again!).

Latin America was the site of a century long Anglo-American imperial rivalry of this sort. But it was a structured competition: imperial rivalry was to be contained before erupting into full-blown war, and colonial annexation of new territory was off limits. These rubrics were unilaterally announced by both imperial states in the 1820s – far from a novel policy pronouncement, Monroe's non-colonisation doctrine followed on from Canning's memoranda with the French minister, the Polignac Memo, which articulated a similar policy. To be sure, there were points in which these rules were stretched to their limits, but the key take-away from the various Anglo-American war scares originating in Latin America, most famously the crisis concerning the Venezuela-Guyana border in 1895–6, was that when push came to shove, metropolitan statesmen, urged on by the barons of the Victorian economy, found a compromise solution.

This 'collaborative competition' characterised Anglo-American imperialism in regions that resembled Latin America: in places where local political power was strong enough to resist formal annexation, where Anglo settlement was minimal, and – most important of all – where lucrative markets could be exploited.[38] Such fundamentals were in place in East Asia, where Yankee merchants profited as middle-men from Britain's opium trade, British and American shipping lines integrated services, and missionaries from both nations exploited the naval and political power of whichever English-speaking imperial formation was nearest.[39] The famous U.S. 'open door' itself, which sought to maintain China's territorial integrity and inhibit imperial commercial discrimination, was less a distinctly American policy than an Anglo-American condominium.[40]

Here we arrive at our third, and final, point. Revisiting the British imperial system through its ongoing connections to postcolonial America illuminates the fundamental paradox of the Victorian British Empire: the most sophisticated imperial system that the world had yet seen was nonetheless a rickety 'unfinished empire' whose teetering imbalances and gaping vulnerabilities have become ever more apparent from our decolonising vantage. Both of these characteristics – the strength of the British Empire, as well as its persistent weaknesses – are amplified when it is viewed through the prism of its connection to postcolonial America.

The material power the postcolonial Atlantic connection generated for the wider British Empire is the headline story. North America was an immense reservoir of power – so immense that its breakneck colonisation fuelled both American and British imperialism. But America empowered the British Empire in ways beyond its role as a trading partner, investment market, and source of resources. The dynamic liberalisation that unfolded in nineteenth-century America spilled beyond its borders, sharpening Britain's imperial order in the process. For example, the social and political adjustments that stabilised the British settler colonies in the nineteenth century bore the imprint of the American experiment in federally structured empire. The formulation of white settler 'responsible government' that fostered the integration of the British diaspora, even as it devolved political sovereignty, took on board experiences from the American Revolution and federalism of Jefferson's decentralized 'empire of liberty.' 'We learnt our lesson in 1776, and have most certainly benefited from it,' Frederick Young argued in 1885.[41]

Likewise, the outcome of the American Civil War was of significance to the British Empire in ways beyond the Home Isles story of how the Union victory empowered British liberals in the run-up to the 1867 Second Reform Act.[42] The outcome of 1865, as Hopkins suggests, might have been most important on a global level not because it inaugurated an era of liberal political reform around the world, but because it gave birth to a new type of world power, the United States.[43] The Union war effort showcased the immense hard power that a democratising regime could mobilise in what Lincoln aptly called a 'people's contest' in his 4 July 1861 address to a special session of congress.[44] The pedagogic significance of the United States to the British Empire thus lay not simply in the traction of its political ideology in an age of democratisation, but also in how its liberal constitution translated into the rapid conquest of North America and its rising geopolitical power. It is revealing that the Prime Minister most attracted to Lincoln was Lloyd George, a liberal who oversaw Britain's own version of a 'people's contest.' At the unveiling of the Lincoln statue in Parliament Square in 1920, Lloyd George heralded the American leader as 'one of those giant figures, of whom there are very few in history, who lose their nationality in death.'[45] To be sure, this was an enthusiastic embrace of American political liberalism. But it was also a recognition of the global power seeded by the transformative mobilisation of Yankee power during the Civil War.

It is imperative to stress that the significance of the U.S. model to the British Empire was not uniformly progressive. If liberal ideas of self-government pulsated out of the United States, so too did sophisticated practices of Indigenous dispossession, protectionism, and racial hierarchy. Dike believed that 'the true moral of America is the vigour of the English race – the defeat of the cheaper by the dearer peoples.' He celebrated how 'the English in America are absorbing the Germans and the Celts, destroying the Red Indians, and checking the advance of the Chinese,' all of which he connected to the 'now inevitable destruction ... of the Maories [sic], and of the Australians by the English colonists.'[46] The United States played a dual role in the hardening of late-Victorian racism: the success of its imperial project buttressed racialized visions of progress, while at the same time American elites professed their buy-in to the 'white man's burden.' Meanwhile, American enterprise was sub-contracted throughout the British Empire: Yankee engineers, pharmacists, arms traders, and missionaries infiltrated the British world, entrenching trans-imperial 'Anglo-Saxonism' in the process.[47] At a geopolitical level, the U.S. colonialist outburst of 1898 was welcomed by Britain's imperialist establishment. Not only did turn of the century American imperialism provide further putative evidence of 'Anglo-Saxon' superiority, but it also – finally – transferred some of the burdens, such as enforcement of the Monroe Doctrine, away from Britain's overstretched empire towards the upstart American one.

Yet if the United States extended power and legitimacy to the British imperial project, it nonetheless constituted an existential threat to the sprawling Victorian empire. America's open borders, unregulated economy, anti-imperial politics, and unrivalled integration into British transport systems exerted a magnetic pull on discontents from around the British world. The founding of the Ghadar party in California was but one manifestation of this broader theme. The danger was noted as early as the 1839 Durham Report, which examined Canadian republicans who expatriated south of the border and threatened to make trouble thereafter. The largest and most boisterous anti-British population in the United States was of the course the Irish. The mid-century potato famine triggered the single largest immigration surge to the United States in its history (as measured by the percentage of the population). The widespread view among the Irish that the Victorian establishment had been callously indifferent to their plight helped to fuel anti-British actions launched from America: Fenian raids into Canada, funding for republican societies back in Ireland, even transatlantic shipments of arms and dynamite. Far from a Home Isles matter, the Irish question was entangled in wider imperial politics that circulated through the United States.[48]

Anti-British diasporic communities and colonial exiles intensified America's home-grown tradition of popular Anglophobia, whose roots traced back to the eighteenth-century war of independence, as well as the subsequent postcolonial struggle that Hopkins examines. It is hard to overstate the intensity of American 'Anglophobia,' a 1790s neologism that the *OED* traces to the grand-daddy of all British haters, Thomas Jefferson. Studies of American Anglophobia have tended to trace its impact on the politics and culture of the United States, but it might well be that its greatest significance lay in its circulation through the British world. Here we see how the United States most threatened Britain's imperial system. America was not a foreign rival of the British Empire that galvanised imperial loyalty, such as France or Russia. Rather, it was an intra-imperial upstart that fused frenetically growing, but haphazardly structured, power, historic resentments against the British Empire with the anticolonial institutions that they generated, and the more radical agendas of nationalists throughout the British world – many of whom began to imagine themselves as a transnational political community as they collectively read, Benedict Anderson-style, the speeches of Woodrow Wilson during the crisis of the Great War (in a revealing irony, British communications systems and print capitalism circulated Wilson's anti-imperial fourteen points throughout the British Empire).[49]

American power constituted an existential threat to Britain's world-system precisely because it emerged from within that imperial order. Ultimately, the United States hijacked Britain's imperial infrastructure, retrofitting it for the new era of the 'American century.' This transition, which unfolded over the course of decades, but mostly progressed in two massive spurts (one in the era of the Great War; the other during the British collapse of the 1940s), is beyond the scope of the essay. But it can be pointed out here that the 'special relationship' paradigm deliberately sanitised this messy and dislocating process, not least through the language used to describe it (the 'safe passage' from one English-speaking power to another; 'the passing of the baton' of global leadership).[50] In truth, America's take-over of the British Empire was a disjointed and wrenching process – less a transfer of power than a phased revolution within an imperial order.[51]

Conclusion

In conclusion, the need for a synthesis of American history attracted the focus of a British imperial historian who imaginatively placed the U.S. narrative into a global and imperial frame. Hopkins's depiction of nineteenth-century America as the modern world's first postcolonial polity not only recasts U.S. history, it also reveals the ongoing significance of America to the expansion and development of the British Empire itself. This essay has contended that viewing the British Empire through its deep and diverse connections to postcolonial America underscores the integration, dynamism, power, and vulnerability of the British imperial system in its Victorian heyday. If Hopkins's book demonstrates that British global history is central to understanding the formation of the American empire, this essay suggests that the inverse is also true: postcolonial America demands close examination in the global history of the British Empire.

Notes

1. See the discussion in Tuck, "The New American Histories."
2. Lepore, *The Truths*.
3. Hopkins, *American Empire*.
4. Hopkins response in H-Diplo Roundtable Review, Volume XX, No. 33, 22 April 2019 (https://issforum.org/roundtables/PDF/Roundtable-XX-33.pdf).
5. For the best take downs of American exceptionalism, see Tyrrell, "American Exceptionalism in an Age of International History"; Rodgers, "Exceptionalism"; Bender, *Rethinking American History in a Global Age*.
6. Hopkins, "The United States, 1783–1861."
7. Prominent examples include Yokota, *Unbecoming British*; Haynes, *Unfinished Revolution*; Sexton, "The United States in the British Empire"; Tuffnell, *Made in Britain*.
8. For an elaboration of this point, see Hoganson, "Building the Empire State". For a blistering critique of Lepore along these lines, see DeLucia, "The Vanishing Indians of 'These Truths'."
9. For the entangled history of this region, see Aron, *American Confluence*; Hamalainen, *Lakota America*; Kamphoefner, *The Westfalians*; Johnson, *The Broken Heart of America*.
10. Pinney, *A History of Wine in America*, 391–6.
11. Hoganson and Sexton, *Crossing Empires*.
12. Stone, *The Global Export of Capital from Great Britain, 1865–1914*.
13. Darwin, *Unfinished Empire*, 90.
14. Magee and Thompson, *Empire and Globalisation*, 69.
15. Tuffnell, *Made in Britain*. For the earlier period, see Flavell, *When London Was Capital of America*.
16. *The Times*, 4 July 1851.
17. Dilke, *Greater Britain*, ix.
18. Quotes come from titles of Perkins, *The Great Rapprochement*; Campbell, *Unlikely Allies*.
19. Thistlethwaite, *The Anglo-American Connection in the Early Nineteenth Century*, 4. Gallagher and Robinson, "The Imperialism of Free Trade."
20. Cain and Hopkins, *British Imperialism*; Cain and Hopkins, "The Theory and Practice of British Imperialism," 206–10.
21. Quotes from introduction of Bridge and Fedorowich, *The British World*, 8.
22. Ford, *Settler Sovereignty*.
23. Belich, *Replenishing the Earth*.
24. Magee and Thompson, *Empire and Globalisation*, 19.

25. Darwin, *After Tamerlane*, 245; Darwin, *The Empire Project*, 267.
26. Burton, *The Trouble with Empire*, 191.
27. Darwin, *Unfinished Empire*, 395.
28. Kramer, "Power and Connection."
29. Beckert, *Empire of Cotton*, 205.
30. Hidy, *The House of Baring in American Trade and Finance*; Zeigler, *The Sixth Great Power*.
31. Brown, *Moral Capital*; Blackett, *Building an Antislavery Wall*.
32. Huzzey, *Freedom Burning*, 175.
33. For political economy and trade policy in this period, see, Palen, *The 'Conspiracy' of Free Trade*.
34. Cook-Martin, *The Scramble for Citizens*.
35. For travels of the secret ballot, see Go, "Empire, Democracy, and Discipline."
36. Mountford and Tuffnell, *A Global History of Gold Rushes*.
37. Sabato, *Republics of the New World*.
38. Sexton, *The Monroe Doctrine*, 62–73.
39. Fletcher, "'Returning Kindness Received'?"
40. A point made by Hopkins, *American Empire*, 435.
41. Bell, *The Idea of Greater Britain*, 250.
42. For this story, see Biagini, *Liberty, Retrenchment and Reform*; Doyle, *The Cause of All Nations*.
43. Hopkins, *American Empire*, 234.
44. Lincoln, "Message to Congress in Special Session."
45. Carwardine and Sexton, *The Global Lincoln*, 28.
46. Dilke, *Greater Britain*, 221.
47. Kramer, "Empires, Exceptions, and Anglo-Saxons"; Tyrrell, *Reforming the World*; Tuffnell, "Crossing the Rift."
48. Sim, *A Union Forever*.
49. Manela, *The Wilsonian Moment*; Anderson, *Imagined Communities*.
50. Schake, *Safe Passage*.
51. 'The transition from British to U.S. global hegemony appears less rapid, natural, and consensual, and more gradual, coerced, and rivalrous, than the rapprochement narrative suggests … The torch of hegemony, in this telling, was not passed but seised.' Epstein, "The Conundrum of American Power in the Age of World War I." 'To describe the United States as the inheritor of Britain's hegemonic mantle is to adopt the vantage point of those who in 1908 insisted on referring to Henry Ford's Model T as a "horseless carriage." The label was not so much wrong, as vainly anachronistic. This was not a succession. This was a paradigm shift.' Tooze, *The Deluge*, 14–15.

Disclosure Statement

No potential conflict of interest was reported by the author.

References

Anderson, Benedict. *Imagined Communities: Reflections on the Origins and Spread of Nationalism*. London: Verso, 2016. rpnt from 1983.

Aron, Stephen. *American Confluence: The Missouri Frontier from Borderland to Border State*. Bloomington: University of Indiana Press, 2006.
Beckert, Sven. *Empire of Cotton: A Global History*. New York: Vintage Books, 2014.
Belich, James. *Replenishing the Earth: The Settler Revolution and the Rise of the Anglo-World, 1783–1939*. Oxford: Oxford University Press, 2009.
Bell, Duncan. *The Idea of Greater Britain: Empire and the Future of World Order, 1860–1900*. Princeton: Princeton University Press, 2007.
Bender, Thomas, ed. *Rethinking American History in a Global Age*. Berkeley: University of California Press, 2002.
Biagini, Eugenio. *Liberty, Retrenchment and Reform: Popular Liberalism in the Age of Gladstone, 1860–1880*. Cambridge: Cambridge University Press, 1992.
Blackett, R. J. M. *Building an Antislavery Wall: Black Americans in the Abolitionist Movement, 1830–1860*. Baton Rouge: Louisiana State University Press, 1983.
Bridge, Carl, and Kent Fedorowich, eds. *The British World: Diaspora, Culture and Identity*. London: Routledge, 2003.
Brown, Christopher L. *Moral Capital: Foundations of British Abolitionism*. Chapel Hill: University of North Carolina Press, 2006.
Burton, Antoinette. *The Trouble with Empire: Challenges to Modern British Imperialism*. New York: Oxford University Press, 2015.
Cain, P. J., and A. G. Hopkins. "The Theory and Practice of British Imperialism." In *Gentlemanly Capitalism and British Imperialism: The New Debate on Empire*, edited by Raymond E. Dumett, 196–220. London: Routledge, 1999.
Cain, P. J., and A. G. Hopkins. *British Imperialism: 1688–2000*. 2nd ed. London: Longman, 2001.
Campbell, Duncan Andrew. *Unlikely Allies: Britain, America and the Victorian Origins of the Special Relationship*. London: Hambledon Continuum, 2007.
Carwardine, Richard, and Jay Sexton, eds. *The Global Lincoln*. New York: Oxford University Press, 2011.
Cook-Martin, David. *The Scramble for Citizens: Dual Nationality and State Competition for Immigrants*. Stanford: Stanford University Press, 2013.
Darwin, John. *After Tamerlane: The Rise and Fall of Global Empires, 1400–2000*. London: Penguin Books, 2007.
Darwin, John. *The Empire Project: The Rise and Fall of the British World-System, 1830–1970*. Cambridge: Cambridge University Press, 2009.
Darwin, John. *Unfinished Empire: The Global Expansion of Britain*. London: Bloomsbury Press, 2012.
DeLucia, Christine. "The Vanishing Indians of 'These Truths'." *Los Angeles Review of Books*, 10 January 2019.
Dilke, Charles W. *Greater Britain: A Record of Travel in English-Speaking Countries during 1866 and 1867*. London: Macmillan and Co., 1869.
Doyle, Don. *The Cause of All Nations: An International History of the American Civil War*. New York: Basic Books, 2014.
Epstein, Kate. "The Conundrum of American Power in the Age of World War I." *Modern American History* 2 (2019): 345–365.
Flavell, Julie. *When London was Capital of America*. New Haven: Yale University Press, 2010.
Fletcher, Robert. "'Returning Kindness Received'? Missionaries, Empire and the Royal Navy in Okinawa, 1846–57." *English Historical Review* CXXV, no. 514 (June 2010): 599–641.
Ford, Lisa. *Settler Sovereignty: Jurisdiction and Indigenous People in America and Australia, 1788–1836*. Cambridge: Harvard University Press, 2010.

Gallagher, John, and Ronald Robinson. "The Imperialism of Free Trade." *The Economic History Review* VI, no. 1 (1953): 1–15.

Go, Julian. "Empire, Democracy, and Discipline: The Transimperial History of the Secret Ballot." In *Crossing Empires*, edited by Kristin Hoganson, and Jay Sexton, 93–111. Durham, NC: Duke University Press, 2020.

Hamalainen, Pekka. *Lakota America: A New History of Indigenous Power*. New Haven: Yale University Press, 2019.

Haynes, Sam. *Unfinished Revolution: The Early American Republic in a British World*. Charlottesville: University of Virginia Press, 2010.

Hidy, Ralph W. *The House of Baring in American Trade and Finance: English Merchant Bankers at Work, 1763–1861*. Cambridge: Harvard University Press, 1949.

Hoganson, Kristin, and Jay Sexton, eds. *Crossing Empires: Taking U.S. History into Transimperial Terrain*. Durham: Duke University Press, 2020.

Hoganson, Kristin. "Building the Empire State." *Diplomatic History* 43, no. 4 (September 2019): 758–762.

Hopkins, A. G. *American Empire: A Global History*. Princeton: Princeton University Press, 2018.

Hopkins, A. G. "The United States, 1783–1861: Britain's Honorary Dominion?" *Britain and the World* 4, no. 2 (2011): 232–246.

Huzzey, Richard. *Freedom Burning: Anti-Slavery and Empire in Victorian Britain*. Ithaca: Cornell University Press, 2012.

Johnson, Walter. *The Broken Heart of America: St. Louis and the Violent History of America*. New York: Basic Books, 2020.

Kamphoefner, Walter D. *The Westfalians: From Germany to Missouri*. Princeton: Princeton University Press, 1987.

Kramer, Paul. "Empires, Exceptions, and Anglo-Saxons: Race and Rule between the British and United States Empires, 1880–1910." *Journal of American History* 88, no. 4 (March 2002): 1215–1353.

Kramer, Paul. "Power and Connection: Imperial Histories of the United States in the World." *American Historical Review* 116, no. 5 (December 2011): 1348–1391.

Lepore, Jill. *These Truths: A History of the United States*. New York: Norton, 2018.

Lincoln, Abraham. "Message to Congress in Special Session." 4 July 1861. https://quod.lib.umich.edu/l/lincoln/lincoln4/1:741?rgn=div1;view=fulltext.

Magee, Gary B., and Andrew S. Thompson. *Empire and Globalisation: Networks of People, Goods and Capital in the British World, c.1850–1914*. Cambridge: Cambridge University Press, 2010.

Manela, Erez. *The Wilsonian Moment: Self-Determination and the International Origins of Anticolonial Nationalism*. New York: Oxford University Press, 2007.

Mountford, Benjamin, and Stephen Tuffnell. *A Global History of Gold Rushes*. Berkeley: University of California Press, 2018.

Palen, Marc-William. *The 'Conspiracy' of Free Trade: The Anglo-American Struggle Over Empire and Economic Globalisation, 1846–1896*. Cambridge: Cambridge University Press, 2016.

Perkins, Bradford. *The Great Rapprochement: England and the United States, 1895–1914*. New York: Antheneum, 1968.

Pinney, Thomas. *A History of Wine in America: From the Beginnings to Prohibition*. Oakland: University of California Press, 1982.

Rodgers, Daniel T. "Exceptionalism." In *Imagined Histories: American Historians Interpret the Past*, edited by Anthony Molho, and Gordon S. Wood, 21–40. Princeton: Princeton University Press, 1998.

Sabato, Hilda. *Republics of the New World: The Revolutionary Political Experiment in 19th-Century Latin America*. Princeton: Princeton University Press, 2018.

Schake, Kori. *Safe Passage: The Passage from British to American Hegemony*. Stanford: Stanford University Press, 2017.

Sexton, Jay. *A Nation Forged by Crisis: A New American History*. New York: Basic Books, 2018.

Sexton, Jay. *The Monroe Doctrine: Empire and Nation in Nineteenth-Century America*. New York: Hill and Wang, 2011.

Sexton, Jay. "The United States in the British Empire." In *Oxford History of the British Empire, Companion Series: British North American in the Seventeenth and Eighteenth Centuries*, edited by Stephen Foster, 318–348. Oxford: Oxford University Press, 2013.

Sim, David. *A Union Forever: The Irish Question and U.S. Foreign Relations in the Victorian Age*. Ithaca: Cornell University Press, 2013.

Stone, Irving. *The Global Export of Capital from Great Britain, 1865–1914: A Statistical Survey*. London: Macmillan, 1999.

Thistlethwaite, Frank. *The Anglo-American Connection in the Early Nineteenth Century*. Philadelphia: University of Pennsylvania Press, 1959.

Tooze, Adam. *The Deluge: The Great War, America and the Remaking of the Global Order, 1916–1931*. New York: Viking, 2014.

Tuck, Stephen. "The New American Histories." *Historical Journal* 48, no. 3 (2005): 811–832.

Tuffnell, Stephen. "Crossing the Rift: American Steel and Colonial Labor in Britain's East Africa Protectorate." In *Crossing Empires*, edited by Kristin Hoganson, and Jay Sexton, 46–68. Durham, NC: Duke University Press, 2020.

Tuffnell, Stephen. *Made in Britain: Nation and Emigration in Nineteenth-Century America*. Oakland: University of California Press, 2020.

Tyrrell, Ian. "American Exceptionalism in an Age of International History." *American Historical Review* 96 (October 1991): 1031–1055.

Tyrrell, Ian. *Reforming the World: The Creation of America's Moral Empire*. Princeton: Princeton University Press, 2010.

Yokota, Kariann. *Unbecoming British: How Revolutionary America Became a Postcolonial Nation*. New York: Oxford University Press, 2010.

Zeigler, Philip. *The Sixth Great Power: Barings, 1732–1929*. London: Collins, 1988.

Part III
Insular Perspectives on Empire

Cuba: Context and Consequences for the American Empire

William A. Morgan

ABSTRACT
Over the course of the twentieth century, the United States left an oversized imprint on the island of Cuba using the successful outcome of the Spanish American War to jump-start its imperial project, exert specific agendas and mandates on an otherwise sovereign nation, and make the island a testing ground for the further expansion of its empire. Yet, despite the sweep of Manifest Destiny and the heavy-handed nature of empire, local on-the-ground conditions in Cuba ensured that a tiny island, a mere 90 miles away from the mainland of America, was able to not only exercise its own autonomy but also a considerable degree of influence across an array of both small and large connections. Despite any inequities in the distribution of power, internal considerations of revolution, race and nationalism dictated the terms of Cuban history in this period and provided the rigid framework within which the United States was forced to operate. Consequently, to understand the causes and outcome of the American Empire it is necessary to place its narrative in a context that allows for a more nuanced dynamic among hegemon and subordinate. This approach calls for an examination of specific interactions occurring in distinct local conditions that maintained their own imperatives and prerogatives.

Introduction

In Antony Hopkins's *American Empire*, one rather dramatic scene in particular stands out:

> "The band of Hawaiian damsels who were to have lowered for the last time the Hawaiian flag, as the government band played for the last time officially the ponoi [the Hawaiian national anthem], would not lower it. The band refused to play ponoi, loud weeping was the only music contributed by the natives."[1]

On reading this, one cannot help but wonder about the larger context and backstory of that depiction, but not from the perspective of an 'American

Empire' or even from that of *American Empire* which simply sets it as an anecdote on the transfer of power. More critical is the vantage point of the personalities that populated a scene whose tragedy seemed to exude from every detail, and an understanding of the conditions and experiences specific to the overt recalcitrance of the damsels and band players and the visceral sorrow of those in attendance at that moment.[2] Most curious are questions related to how history had unfolded in such a manner as to place a subdued – but still clearly defiant – cast of characters alongside the agents of an American imperial project and what meant for those natives (and their nation) to be front and centre in this nascent moment of an American empire going forward. Ultimately, we are left to consider the consequences for both making and understanding empire if one fails to adequately account for local context.

To take another example, if the narrative of American empire in the context of the Spanish American War is told from the point of view represented by Washington, rather than Havana, the story behind the 'people and the politics of the moment' – as Hopkins frames it – becomes, at least from this angle, one of two American diplomats, Colonel Fitzhugh Lee, in Havana and Stewart Woodford in Madrid. Although 'undoubtedly a colorful figure' Lee, according to Hopkins, was 'never as important as he thought he was or hoped to become.' In a similar vein, Hopkins characterises Woodford as arriving on the scene woefully late and ill prepared (lacking both diplomatic experience and any knowledge of Spanish) and performing in a manner far less remarkable than his fanciful title, Envoy Extraordinary and Minister Plenipotentiary to Spain. Moreover, his signal achievement at this critical juncture seemingly only notable for carrying out President McKinley's instructions 'more or less as indicated.'[3]

This is a striking contrast with the treatment Antonio Maceo receives in the same story. Known as the Bronze Titan to Cubans and the Great Lion to many in the Spanish Army, Maceo was arguably the greatest military hero in the struggle for Cuban independence and remains a national icon today. With a backstory neither perfunctory nor filled with puffery, Maceo's life was legendary on both sides of the Atlantic. A free black who rose to prominence in the first rebellion against Spain in 1868, Maceo was one of the few patriots to reject Spain's peace treaty in 1878 (thereby securing his place in nationalist lore as an uncompromising proponent of Cuban sovereignty) and would go on to lead both a second as well as a third and final rebellion, wounded numerous times in his military career. In this last war his prowess and exploits resulted in the previously-deemed-impossible invasion of western Cuba from the eastern end of the island, a campaign that covered more than 1,000 miles in less than 100 days and involved more than two dozen enemy encounters. With these exploits, alongside numerous other victories by the insurgents, Cuba had effectively, and finally, brought Spain to the brink of defeat. Yet in the context of *American Empire*, Maceo is simply recorded as a notable 'Afro-Cuban'.[4] While this may be too narrow an example to fairly criticise a lack of detail in a nearly 800-page synthesis where Cuba plays only a bit part, it does speak to the importance of context, especially if the stated goal is to tell the story from the 'people and politics' as Hopkins intends. In this particular case, a lack of emphasis on local conditions in the lead-up to the Spanish America War suggests a different understanding than one in which the defeat of the Spanish Army – the catalyst for a new age of U.S. imperialism – arguably belongs as much to the Cubans as to the Americans.

Empirically, the gulf between these disparate lines of analysis is seen in the contrast between Teddy Roosevelt's insistence that 'we should have been better off if there had not been a single Cuban with the army ... they accomplished literally nothing' with the statement by Máximo Gómez, the military commander of Cuba's Liberation Army in 1895, in which, just a few months short of the U.S. entering Cuba, he equally insisted that the war was a 'dead war' with victory over the Spanish clearly in sight.[5] Understanding that Maceo, Gómez and their compatriots, after more than 30 years of fighting, had effectively stopped, pushed backed and were on the verge of expelling their colonial ruler challenges the idea that Cuba was effortlessly seized by a buckskin buckaroo alongside his ragtag Rough Riders. This juxtaposition also replicates the asymmetry of empire – a seemingly-default framework of both empire and of empire studies. Yet, when the traditionally asymmetrical exchanges of empire are upended, these studies produce a far different context for understanding how the history of empire unfolds.

At its heart, the debate over origins and causes of the U.S. imperial project attempts to address the question of how best to view the mission: was it a new world hegemon or classic empire, was it formal or informal? But lost in this debate is that viewpoints also matter. On a grand scale, a change in perspective from west to east forces one to consider the exceptionalism of America's imperial project more seriously. From the vantage point of London, Paris, or Madrid the United States embarked on a rather late, but well-trodden, path to maturity that was expected from any country holding pretentions of sovereignty and power; from Washington, the view inevitably must contain the full weight of a manifest destiny underlined by its providential origins as the city on a hill. On a similar but narrower scale, a shift in focus in relation to narratives of origin from the continental United States to the Caribbean before 1898 and from metropole to periphery after 1898 produces a more complex arrangement of empire. This is especially true of the question of causality, where one necessarily has to account for reciprocity accompanied by substantive, bilateral exchanges rather than unilateral dictates that more closely align with the narrative of 'a splendid little war', involving 'a lot of degenerates absolutely devoid of honor and gratitude', which led to America's rise as a new global power.[6]

As previously illustrated in the beginning of this essay, in the context of *American Empire*, a work attempting to cover three centuries of America's expanding presence on the world stage, there remains a similar need to rebalance the coloniser/colonised dynamic by granting more weight to the view of the American imperial experience from the perspective of the periphery. In the making of empire the inherent asymmetry of power that exists between external and internal actors does not inexorably translate into a similarly unequal influence in the cause and direction of the imperial project. Historically, distinct native considerations held the capacity to reset traditional balances of power. Conceptually, local context forces a necessary qualification of any arguments relying on predominantly nationalist based explanations of empire. Resetting the narrative according to a 'peripheral thesis' emphasises the usually obscured agency of people and politics on the other side of the imperial exchange. It also highlights the reality that there were consequences for both coloniser and colonised with local conditions forcing the hand of U.S. officials to variously confront, collaborate, or conform to longstanding internal traditions, values and motives (many of which predated the birth of the United States itself). That all empires are alike in that they share common attributes of power or hegemony in whatever form that may take is obvious but one important characteristic that marks them as distinct is the native touchstones within each component of the imperial sphere that individually shapes and collectively steers the course of empire. Empires may rise and fall but they are not monoliths with an unswerving trajectory. Home factors – many of which form the backbone of Hopkins' analysis – have their own effect on the path of empire but local conditions also exert their own gravitational pull, that oblige the dominant power to acknowledge and account for local conditions. Within this framework, this paper advocates for a greater recognition of internal conditions as a starting point for reorienting how best to view empire- making in this period but also, as a precondition, the need for greater insular context in understanding an insular empire.[7]

This is not to say that *American Empire* is completely devoid of any such focus. On the contrary, in an attempt at synthesising some elements of the emerging literature on the insular perspective, Hopkins is clearly attuned to the importance of understanding American involvement from the vantage of imperial reciprocities, even expressing a desire to bend the historiography to more fully consider, in the words of the African historian, John Hargreaves, these 'missing elements'. In *American Empire,* this is set out as a criticism of the current literature – which but for a few recent exceptions has tended either to ignore or diminish native personalities and politics – with the goal of bringing U.S. scholarship into a closer contact with the traditions of British and French studies. Illustrating this commitment (and criticism), Hopkins significantly notes U.S. imperialism was simultaneously 'the product of forces within the colonized societies themselves as well as of external influences.'[8]

This position reflects a long career with origins in African and imperial history in which Hopkins has accumulated a catalogue of work insisting on the centrality of the periphery and recognition of the historical actors and institutions *within* the metropole and colony dynamic. And in *American Empire*, there is a focus on the recipients of imperialism as actors not merely reacting to outside stimuli; indeed, there are places throughout this work where marked shifts in perspective to better accommodate local conditions are readily seen. Yet, despite the wink at an enlarged viewpoint – the usual cast of characters of Jose Martí and Fidel Castro (the latter of whom ranks only just ahead of *American Spelling Book* and 'Thanksgiving' in number of pages listed in the index) make their way into well-crafted introductory set pieces. Those on the other side of empire remain objects of conquest, unremarkable characters in in an 'unexceptional empire'. This is a far cry from their status as not only national heroes but ideological and revolutionary icons with a pronounced presence on the international stage.

Expanding upon the above criticism (with the full acknowledgment that the call for more context is the very first arrow all specialists reach for when assessing works on this scale), the analysis that follows attempts to identify potential places in which an adjusted perspective could better account for the people and politics that constitute a vital element in understanding just how the U.S. insular empire unfolded in this early stage. In particular, it seeks to recognise and incorporate pressure points where one can see the fits and starts of empire in flux. At its core, this essay frames empire according to the belief that native or local conditions were determinative to the extent that they could at a minimum necessitate adaptation or even force confrontation over a range of matters both big and small, effectively making any exchanges between coloniser and colonised bilateral in nature. Because Hopkins does indeed indicate the need for a peripheral perspective throughout *American Empire,* this essay is not constructed as an outright critique. Rather it is an attempt to go beyond this limited starting point to consider how a more extended treatment might alter our understanding of the causes of the war of 1898 and its consequences for Cuba.

Spain

In terms of drawing conclusions about the causes of U.S. imperialism, Hopkins begins, as many others have done, in the Caribbean and on the events surrounding 1898 in order to establish the root causes and general unfolding of how the United States set out to acquire its nascent empire. In doing so, he attempts to uncover new historiographical territory on the origins of empire that, in his view, springs from the impact of industrialisation on transitioning national economies that were experiencing an extreme period of expansion into a larger, global setting. In the case of the U.S., the imperative of uniting and consolidating the Republican party also loomed large. Yet, it is the in-depth treatment of Spain in what is perhaps a largely overlooked angle within Hopkins's work that adds particular depth to this new line of analysis and at least partly addresses the need for greater contextualisation external to Washington in any effort at identifying how the U.S. empire was made. A key beginning for reevaluating the Cuban-American-Spanish dynamic of 1898 is the revision of Spain's loss of its overseas possessions, framed largely as undergoing the same transformative crisis of modernisation that the U.S. was contemporaneously undertaking, the difference being that Spain came out on one side having failed the test, while the U.S. came out on the other side, victorious.

Starting from a position that is explicitly critical of U.S. based studies that have paid little attention to the international role of players on the other side of the Atlantic, Hopkins imbues Spain not only with a justifiable agency as a still-relevant imperial power but places it, on an equal footing as other nation states undergoing similar crises in the transition towards modern globalisation. Underlining this comparison is a necessary recalibration of the Spanish empire to reflect its position in the world more accurately at the critical moment in the late nineteenth century and not as seen from the 1600s, or even 1700s. In this view, Spain appears as a classic empire – centuries old, with considerable overseas possessions, including one of the last great slave systems in a period still largely defined by plantation commodities – and set upon by one final challenge, an unprecedented shift in geopolitical and world economic systems that would make new empires, remake old empires, and reduce still others.

Disavowing tired notions of Spain's ineptitude allows Hopkins to transcend the asymmetrical view from Washington and instead juxtapose one empire with another in an appraisal of how each attempted to consolidate political power and promote national identity in a moment of crisis. In this new narrative, Spain, much like the U.S., was wrenched into the twentieth century by processes of urbanisation and industrialisation and the pursuit of renewed relevancy through global integration. It is at this point that Hopkins rightfully pushes back against established claims of Spain as a 'passive or declining power' because the Peninsula appears to have embraced, even if tentatively, the attraction that these forces represented. Moreover, in the context of the coming war, Spain's understanding of the critical role of its overseas possessions was clear: any attempts to harness or direct a modernising economy would be heavily dependent upon the colonies because they provided the primary financial backing and ideological fulfilment of empire. And for good reason, beyond the coffee, sugar and tobacco that flowed into world markets and filled Spain's coffers it was the conspicuous hold on Cuba, the last of two remaining slave empires, that despite any moral misgivings, made Spain exceptional and still relevant in relation to its fellow imperial members. This led Spain to concentrate its attention on its overseas empire – as it had done so for the last century and a half. Moreover, industrialisation helped to make Spain a viable and at the very least a 'determined' opponent in 1898.

Yet, potential fault lines that would forewarn the loss of its empire could be found early on, as Hopkins notes. In particular, the production of substandard goods limited export opportunities while a limited capacity to absorb raw imports from its overseas possessions left Spain behind in the rapidly escalating race towards industrialisation and modernisation. Economic inadequacies in response to these tumultuous times held political ramifications as well, with Spanish imperial policies lurching between imposing restrictive measures like new taxes, inequitable commercial treaties on its territories, and limiting political representation in Madrid. These measures alternated with conciliatory actions such as administrative reform, granting new levels of autonomy for home rule, and even initiating processes of gradual emancipation to quell colonial unrest.

The issue of slavery, more specifically the end of slavery and exactly when and how that process was to be carried out, marks a significant difference between how the Spanish Empire went through the processes of modernisation and how the U.S. did, several decades earlier. Unlike the United States, abolition for Spain occurred at a separate pace and also varied within its overseas possessions. Slavery for Spain held another element that made it a more distinct problem than the U.S. faced: Cuba, Spain's most valuable colony, was precious because it possessed Spain's largest number of slaves. Maintaining or ending slavery on the island would be the fulcrum on which Spain would keep (or lose) its empire. Ultimately, Spain was caught in an unenviable position, forced on one side to address the growing abolitionist pressures both externally (from the United States, Great Britain, and other countries) as well as internally (from a rebel army that was radically multi-racial and whose aim was the overthrow of slavery on the island). At the same time, Spain was determined to keep the production of sugar flowing, which required explicit appeasement of the planter and slave-holding classes. Slavery had once made Spain's empire, but slavery's growing incompatibility with imperial directives and management would – as will be seen in the context of Cuban independence – eventually bring the empire down.

In general terms, political instability and economic uncertainty defined most of the major Western powers in this period. However, where the U.S. could see the advent of imperialism as a panacea, Spain saw Cuba and its other possessions as catalysts of additional concern and conflict. In one sense this refers to the debate over internal origins and causality of empire making, which in Hopkins's formulation lands squarely in the political realm of solidifying Republican power more than selling McCormick reapers. But the additional focus on Spain adds the benefit of seeing the U.S. experience along a parallel trajectory, yet with a different outcome, essentially a photographic negative (even if that image is not fully developed in Hopkins's account). At the heart of it all, the Spanish-American War becomes 'a conflict between powers that were attempting to manage broadly similar problems of transition, albeit under different circumstances.'[9] Yet, it is important to note the divergence between the two powers: the U.S. chose to use Cuba and the other Spanish territories to unify national identity in the aftermath of a civil war; Spain was forced to deal with a colonial uprising as a threat to imperial unity. In this view, Hopkins adroitly (and evocatively) depicts Spain in this period as 'these developments joined the Peninsula and the colonies in a marriage of inconvenience that eventually ended in divorce.'[10] But an extension of this metaphor can be applied to the U.S., so that the American imperial experience becomes a marriage of convenience that results in an extended honeymoon. (Hopkins does note that 'buyer's remorse' would set in for the U.S.). However, this perspective only hints at Spain's response to the unravelling of empire. Just as there is a need for U.S. historians to better account of Spain at the time of the Spanish American War, it is also critical to realise that there was a third entry that, like Spain, might have come out on the losing side, but nevertheless played a central role in the drama.

1868

Any attempt to place the Spanish-American War in a more local context must begin at the start of Cuba's revolutionary era several decades earlier. It is during this period that rebels fused progressive racial ideals onto a national identity. In the process of emphasising race as the primary theme through three major rebellions, the radically multi-racial army created a potent foundation for a new Cuban state. With race and nation inextricably connected, Cuba would eventually force the U.S. into a series of choices to either confront or conform to a reality that operated in direct conflict with, but still under, the auspices of America's new imperialism. The process began in 1868, when sugar plantation and slave owner Carlos Manuel de Céspedes issued what came to be known as the *Grito de Yara*, a call to arms that would spark a general uprising against Spanish rule. In what has become a signifying moment in national lore, Céspedes dramatically freed his slaves and called Cubans of all races to join the rebellion. Within months, more than 10,000 black, white, free and newly-freed Cubans fought for *Cuba Libre*. As the war progressed more slaves continued to take an active role in their own emancipation by joining the Liberation Army. Each new arrival pushed both the political and military leadership to solidify promises of total emancipation. By the end of the rebellion, nearly 20,000 newly christened *Libertos* achieved permanent freedom.

The spontaneous act of calling for independence backed by the freeing and arming of slaves not only carried immense symbolism for a singular moment but also established the central narrative that would direct the pursuit of Cuban sovereignty for the next three decades: the new nation would be explicitly free and raceless. Or, in the words of Jose Martí, 'men are more than whites, mulattos or Negroes. Cubans are more than whites, mulattos or Negroes'.[11] At the beginning of a war that would cost tens of thousands of lives, these radical ideas were immediately translated into radical measures through the establishment of a multiracial army. As the fighting progressed, the Cuban Army issued a general emancipation decree that extended new freedoms to include the opportunity not only to serve as soldiers, but also for many of the thousands of freedmen that joined its ranks, considerable opportunity and recognition, with an integrated army and free men of colour placed in positions of authority. This uprising and its embrace of freedom and equality for all was, according to the Cuban scholar Ada Ferrer, truly 'unique in the history of the Atlantic world ... a multiracial fighting force that was integrated at all ranks'.[12]

Despite its unique status, the influence of the revolutionary army does not always carry its full historiographical weight, a criticism not only applicable to the work in review here, but also to general studies of this period. With the specific demographic composition of the army as a principal foundation of rebellion, both beginning in 1865 and continuing through multiple additional conflicts over the next 30 years, the resonance for Cuban patriots was profound and sustained. Yet most accounts, at least those that focus on events external to Cuba, underestimate the reach of the first rebellion and diminish what should be an elongated chronology leading to a discussion of 1898. Moreover, in its explicit and active rejection of the racial and class hierarchies of one of the last remaining slave systems – a denunciation unalterably intertwined with the quest for independence – the Cuban Liberation Army, beginning in 1868, would fundamentally inform how the new nation would be shaped in the future, even well into the republic that was created under American occupation.

There is an important distinction to note here: this was not an acceptance of racial (black or Afro-Cuban) equality but a specific rejection of race itself. This revolutionary conceptualisation had roots in the criticism of race in the service of empire (as seen in the construct of the 'White Man's Burden') and would also extend into the period of U.S. occupation. Essentially, the first of these rebellions attempted to create the 'world's first raceless nation' and it was this context that the U.S. had to confront three decades later.[13] The U.S. was not just dealing with a native offshoot of the Spanish forces in 1898 but with a combat tested, operationally successful, insurgency with defined, progressive motivations of race that stood in stark contrast to the era of racial lynching, communal massacres, and political obscurity that marked the nadir in race relations in the U.S.A. At various points in Hopkins's account the restructuring of Cuba's labour force or an enlarged role for foreign businessmen is used to represent the long-term consequences of these developments. While the transition from slave to free labour, including increases in the numbers of Asian and Spanish workers, and a climate of opportunism among those in Cuba who sought to capitalise on market displacement and disruption are important developments, they do not explain the lead up to 1898. Rather, it is the existence of Cuba's multiracial army and its enduring legacy that is responsible for informing the conditions Americans would find when they arrived.[14]

Within this ideological context, the first rebellion promised the right for black Cuban veterans to participate in the political present and future as citizens. This was not just a promise: the rebel army populated its ranks from all segments of Cuban society and attempted to do the same (albeit with much less radical success) with leadership positions and within the government itself. Moreover, because the first rebellion embodied a true cross section of Cuban society (at least in the areas where the rebellion held sway) with an eclectic mix of urban and rural groups – artisans, merchants, planters, farmers, and sharecroppers – the potential existed for a radical expansion in entitlement to citizenship. The swelling ranks were a 'testimony to the increasingly broad appeal of anticolonial struggle' according to historian Rebecca Scott, who notes this nascent unity as 'a source of impetus for more egalitarian policies.'[15] It is this last characteristic, a progressive emphasis to accommodate a larger and more diverse set of stakeholders, that foreshadows the eventual power of black political participation when U.S. imperial ambitions confronted Cuban national considerations. By 1898, this class of veterans, based on sacrifices first earned in 1868, had earned access to political rights, learned how to speak and perform political identities, and expected, based on those considerable sacrifices, the rights and identities of citizenship to be sustained, even with the transfer in power.

1878

The first war for independence ended in 1878 with concessions that were unpalatable to both sides, which regarded Spanish overtures toward political representation and the freeing of insurrectionary slaves as half-measures. However, the initial overlay of race with independence as well as the potent combination of a multiracial army prompting greater black political participation set off a chain reaction that resulted in a second war against Spain, known as the *Guerra Chiquita*. Lasting less than a year but coming immediately on the heels of the most recent peace, this military campaign had origins in the dissatisfaction with the failed promise of Cuban sovereignty and the role black Cubans were to play in future. Accordingly, the second rebellion can be seen as an extension of 1868. However, for the purposes of how U.S. imperial policies would be implemented in 1898, the conditions it would be forced to confront, and who would be at the centre of resistance, the new war should be noted for the further emergence, and even amplification, of the role black Cubans would play in the independence movement. Buoyed by an influx of black recruits, many of them slaves who saw opportunity for freedom similar to that granted to the *Libertos*, the second rebellion filled its ranks with an extrta cadre of previously-marginalised individuals who, importantly, took additional steps towards exercising a political voice and who would become part of the citizen class by the time of Cuban nationhood.

Most importantly, the war brought to the forefront an even more conspicuous group of black leaders who stepped in to fill the void left by exiled, white leaders of the first rebellion. It is during this war that black Cubans who rose to military prominence a decade earlier, men like Guillermo Moncada, Quintín Bandera and Jose Maceo (Antonio's brother) were given the task of implementing the political policies and goals of the new revolution. The escalation in black participation and authority was notable enough for Spanish political critics and military opponents to seize upon it and effectively label it a 'blacker' more 'African' rebellion that preferred a race war to any notion of national unity. While this was an effective strategy in the short term – the threat of Haiti always loomed large as long as Cuban slavery continued to operate – Cuban rebel leadership would also learn the benefits of using the issue of race and how it could augment calls for national independence. Men like Moncada spoke of Spanish attacks on the racial composition of the army as an effort to divide and conquer the 'Cuban race' and in doing so continued to insist upon a language of independence that was dependent upon raceless nationalism. The same language would become more widespread over the next several decades, when increasing numbers of writers, newspaper editors, patriots, veterans, and workers echoed the same call, at first pushing Spain to recognise their rights and fulfil promised regulations and eventually exchanging Spain for the U.S. which would become the new foil for black Cubans to criticise and hold accountable.

Alongside the generalised calls for respecting race and nation, as conceived in the crucible of revolution, new institutions appeared to consolidate the increasing reforms and gains. Men like Martí continued to sustain the legacy of the first two revolutions as a new political party in exile, the *Partido Revolucionario Cubano* (Cuban Revolution Party or PRC) emerged in 1892. Others, like Juan Gilberto Gómez, himself an embodiment of the new class of black leadership established in the era of revolution, created the *Directorio Central de las Sociedades de Color* (Central Directory of the Societies of Color), which was dedicated to securing rights previously granted by Spanish concessions under the peace treaty but also new rights like equal access to public schools and places. Activities such as these continued to foment revolution and its characteristic of a new, raceless nation as the country moved closer and closer to a final resolution.

1895

Although the second coming of rebellion proved short-lived, its consequences, like those of its 1868 predecessor, continued to shape national political and racial discussions as the country moved closer to ending its colonial status. In 1895, these internal forces erupted when Cuban rebel forces heeded an earlier call from the PRC and took up arms under the leadership of Jose Martí, Antonio Maceo, and Máximo Gómez, each having returned from exile. With Maceo at the head of an army that was able to invade the western part of the island, the final rebellion would push Spain to the brink of defeat. The war was costly, with civilian deaths at the hands of the Spanish amounting to as many as 300,000 (nearly 10 percent of the population) as well as two of Cuba's most important and beloved icons, Martí and Maceo, who both died in battle. Yet, by 1898 the prospects of victory appeared close; Máximo Gómez at the beginning of 1898 claimed, rightly, that 'the enemy is crushed and is in complete retreat', and the Cuban leadership of the PRC began preparations for a provisional government.[16] At this moment, the leap to the arrival of U.S. forces and the advent of new American empire (by way of the USS Maine) is not a large one. However, it does require a considerable shift in perspective from one that privileges the role of a revolutionary army on the verge of finally ending their status as the 'ever faithful' island, (after more than four centuries of rule and three decades of fighting), to one that assigns Spain's loss of empire to outside actors, independent of nearly anything internal to Cuba. In assessing any grand synthesis of the U.S. imperial project, it is in this space between eventual empire and metropole that the narrative of imperial causality should be located.

For most historians of empire covering 1898, the obvious objects of attention are limited to the asymmetrical U.S. and Spain dynamic, with the more nuanced accounts willing to consider some form of Spanish agency. *American Empire* is one of these, as Hopkins centres much of his analysis around Spain's loss (rather than US seizure) of empire in Spain's inability to handle the transition from 'military fiscalism to a more open, liberal regime an orderly manner.' Specifically, Hopkins sees the conditions that presaged 1898 in an economic depression that destabilised both colonial and metropole financial systems, which in combination with a U.S. tariffs on Cuban sugar, 'destroyed Spain's slim chances of holding her empire together'.[17] While this serves as part of an explanation, at least on a macro level, it is hard to view the loss of empire, at least from the vantage point of Cuba, as anything other than resulting from a movement framed on one side by the heavily symbolic and enormously unifying words of Martí and others that provided the ideological justification for independence. On the other side, the unexpected strength, fortitude, and radical makeup of the Cuban Liberation Army, which along with its leadership, men of renown and national lore who came to represent the very thing they were fighting for, a truly free and raceless new, nation, provided the instrument for realising independence. The difference in context produces a contrast between claiming Spain lost the war because of internal forces originating in the Peninsula and other external locations and arguing that the loss of empire resulted from forces emanating from the periphery.

Three of the more important peripheral forces (or legacies of the war-time experience) include the establishment of a generation of revolutionary leaders, a newly-trained citizenry well versed in the distinct racial language of Cuban nationalism, and a unified national identity that found a ready foil in the continued crisis with Spain. That each of these are analogous to the early precedents of the American Revolution may speak to the nature of colonial conflict in the age of empires but the connections merit consideration with the arrival of the U.S. in 1898. In general terms, Cuba, which held a list of grievances as long as, and as similar to, those of the American patriots a century earlier (burdensome taxes, loss of political representation, censorship, arbitrary authoritarian displays), refused to accept the limited reforms Spain was either willing or able to offer. The island proceeded to march towards a final outcome that, like the Revolution in the mainland colonies, could result only in continued domination or freedom, much like the prelude to revolution in America. More specifically, in terms of leadership, similar to the Seven Years' War which helped train a new generation of military and political leaders like George Washington and Benjamin Franklin, the first two Cuban wars of independence witnessed the rise to prominence of men who would have a sustained involvement in the Cuban independence movement over three decades and three full rebellions.

In addition to Martí, other leading office holders within the insurgent government, like Salvador Cisneros Betancourt, would hone their organisational skills and political message as it reached a larger and more international audience, In a similar vein, soldiers such as Maceo and Calixito Garcia won renown and expertise over numerous victories and in so doing became not just individual actors in a war between nations but symbols of the nation itself. Others would provide the language of revolution that supported and justified the actions of Cuba's new leadership. Men like Juan Gilberto Gómez, who used his newspaper to promote black voices and link political rights for all Cubans to civil rights for black Cubans, was one of many writers who used this medium, much like Thomas Paine, to translate abstract thought into a weapon of resistance. A final comparison with the 1776 revolution (and one with American reverberations as well in 1898) contextualises Cuba's national struggle as built on the shared ejection of imperialism, even though Cuba differed in its foundation of a multiracial, multiclass army of liberation. That this was a unifying force fully transferable to other antagonists effectively, makes it easy to hear echoes of Patrick Henry's rejection of old signifiers in favour of a new proto-American identification: 'The distinctions between

Virginians, Pennsylvanians, New Yorkers, and New Englanders are no more. I am not a Virginian, but an American!' In Martí's assessment of the rebellion where, 'facing death, barefoot all and naked all, blacks and whites became equal: they embraced and have not separated since'.[18]

1898-1901

The literal and symbolic battleground of race and nation that was established in the revolutionary era (1868-98) and put into practice through the composition of the Liberation Army set the primary conditions that the U.S. would be forced to confront upon their entry into Cuban politics. Attention to specific, local conditions are crucial because at its base, an internal, foundational idea of a raceless nation framed nearly all the political and social context in this period and would set the stage for all future exchanges with any subsequent ruling regime. Particularly for the U.S., privileged (and resilient) views on race and nation provided a powerful antidote to the equally prevalent, external sentiment embodied by one contemporary assessment which claimed Cubans were 'little other than ... turbulent and illiterate negroes, needing the government of a stronger race, indispose to industry quite unsuited for that independence for which they have been fighting'.[19] However, this was not the case initially, as the prejudices of the U.S. seemed to carry the day, with the Liberation Army largely sidelined. Soldiers were prohibited from entering liberated towns, officials were excluded from the Spanish surrender, and its leaders barred from any discussion of peace treaties.

Yet, Martí's idea of a 'Cuba for all Cubans', backed by a national struggle for independence that saw the implementation of that idea in its fighting force, proved not only a resilient but also a formidable tool with which to resist U.S. hegemony. The language of national racelessness ensured a high floor from which black Cubans could never fall in building the new nation. That this language was supported by an active and engaged citizenry only added to the impediments the U.S faced in implementing its anti-black version of racial politics in the Cuban republic. This could be seen in the imagery of black Cubans in public portrayals and in the harsh, highly-charged racial language in the personal pronouncements of US envoys. The juxtaposition of one side operating under the paradigm of a colour line with a clear directive to erode any competing narrative that gave a high profile to black veterans on the other side ensured that this would be a contested negotiation.

In 1901, the challenge to U.S. imperial rule officially began when, after more than thirty years of fighting for independence, which saw the removal of one imperial ruler and the introduction of another, the Cuban nation was born under a new constitution. While imperial historians tend to focus on the inclusion of the infamous Platt Amendment, the new constitution also contained an equally important, and arguably more radical, clause: Article 11, which by refusing to recognise privilege of any sort for its citizens, guaranteed equality for all Cubans under the law. While black Cubans protested overt racist polices on multiple levels in terms of directly challenging official U.S. policy, Article 11 is a significant touchstone in demonstrating the high level of resistance and large degree of success black Cubans had achieved. This is especially true when compared to the 13th Amendment of the U.S. Constitution and the contrast between how the U.S. version's fared in the wake of 1877 and Cuba's iteration that went beyond a nominal equality because it translated the promises earned by black Cubans in the years of fighting into real, tangible and permanent gains.

In the previous era, members of the Liberation Army frequently used the term *ciudadano* (citizen) to describe themselves and their compatriots (regardless of rank and colour). Justified by military service, this evocation provided an early foundation for the passing of Article 11. In the following period, participation in that cornerstone of the Cuban nation, the multiracial Liberation Army, also proved to be a wellspring for translating rights earned in wartime to rights expected in peace-time. Following the precedent of both political and civil organisations, like the PRC and those headed by Juan Gilberto Gómez established in the prewar years before 1895, additional groups emerged to continue the call for legal and political equality. Some of these replicated already-established institutions such as the weekly newspaper, *El Nuevo Criollo*, published by journalist-politician Rafael Serra, one of the most vocal proponents of black equality in the new republic; others included completely new creations such as the *Instituto Booker T. Washington* in Havana, which promoted black educational goals.

Reflecting their over-representation in the previous wars, many of the new groups were led by black Cuban veterans like Generoso Campos Marquetti's Comité de Acción de Veteranos y *Sociedades de la Raza de Color* (Committee of Veterans and Associations of the race of colour) which petitioned for veteran benefits and more job placements. Through the explicit linking of veteran status with racial classification these organisations effectively pushed their government to hold the line, as much as possible against U.S. displays of martial strength and the intrusion of U.S. racial policies. As a result, black veterans would not only receive financial considerations in the new government but would also populate the civil service to a degree unfathomable in the U.S. These opportunities were not just simple gains in financial standing and class level, but rather policy decisions that confirmed the importance of contributions by veterans to the state while at the same time contradicting the negative opinions of U.S. officials who had continually scoffed at their role in fighting of 1898.

In a similar fashion, the selection of local leadership positions that the U.S. hoped (and expected) to influence proved to be another conspicuous indicator of how, despite its dominant status, the U.S. had still to confront conditions that placed its policies in conflict with the reality of a Cuban nation backed by the experience of more than three decades of a revolution dedicated to achieving a raceless nation. What transpired was the direct result of the cause and effect of local conditions and actors influencing and directing imperial processes on the ground. At the beginning of the postwar years, this meant that the imperative of a standing army motivated Cubans to choose representatives deemed fit to rule, which implied those belonging to a white, literate, property-owning class. Nevertheless, circumstances specific to the island compelled American officials to deal with a similarly potent imperative: the legacy of a multiracial army whose leadership included many prominent black Cubans. Because this reality was, even as early as 1898, so deeply ingrained in the fabric of Cuban nationhood and symbolism, U.S. measures failed to achieve the desired outcome. In Cuba, a distinct brand of nationalism acted as a bulwark against conspicuous adjustments to a colour line, which in America, was imposed with rigid and ruthless ardour. The limitations compelled by the weight of the revolution and its promise of a raceless nation spared no one. Tomás Estrada Palma, first president of the republic (and to many, especially the Fidelistas later on, a puppet of the U.S. empire), campaigned under the claim that he would guarantee public-service jobs to black Cubans and oppose U.S. imperial policies supporting segregation. Consequently, black Cubans saw an opening in society where they were able to gain membership into elite associations and integrate the professional ranks as part of a larger process of upward mobility and social progress. While limited at the top, this was a period, even under U.S. occupation, where black Cubans steadily improved their social condition through greater proportional representation in civil sector jobs, while black literacy rates also began to approach those of the white populace.

Male Suffrage

In addition to influencing the official proclamation outlined in Article 13, an omnipresent ideology of a raceless Cuba continued to shape Cuban politics. This was especially true under the U.S. occupation, where any successful opposition to the stated goals of U.S. rule was magnified by the inequity in the arrangement of power on the island that had otherwise forced Cubans into a general state of subordination. One of the more direct challenges occurred, as it usually did in this period, in the negotiation over the composition of the Cuban government and how the constitution would either further enshrine progressive racial ideals, as the revolution promised, or advance restrictive measure more in line with the desires of U.S. officials. This debate came to a head over the implementation of universal male suffrage. As a framework for understanding imperial formation, this initial encounter showed how native forces successfully navigated peripheral space within the empire. Reflecting the resonance of voting on a larger scale, the scholars Alejandro de la Fuente and Matthew Casey elevate the suffrage controversy to represent 'a cultural clash in which two different world views, informed by different experiences, expectations, and bodies of knowledge, collided'.[20]

At the outset, the issue of race was central to the deliberations with American (and some Cuban) officials who were dedicated to limiting political enfranchisement. This largely meant couching conditions respecting literacy and property to circumvent the sanctity of racelessness in the new Cuban nation. Yet, because the Liberation Army had previously won universal male suffrage from Spain (which granted it as far back as January 1898 as a concession to end the war), black Cuban veterans had considerable room to contest U.S. designs. They were instrumental in pushing for a soldier clause, guaranteeing the right to vote based on military service, that effectively negated most of these prohibitions. Consequently, universal male suffrage was granted largely behind Cuban nationalism, as conceived and established in rebellion, which allowed black Cubans to place substantial limits on both the claims of the U.S. occupiers and one of the most overtly anti-black principles in their own constitution.

As a direct challenge to U.S. authority, the unqualified stipulation of a soldier clause amounted to a concession that one historian has labelled 'an unavoidable evil' in the eyes of the U.S. provisional government.[21] Externally radical but internally justified, the advent of full male suffrage was not only 'a step ahead of other insular territories', as Hopkins notes in his own work, but an example writ large of how the U.S. imperial project unfolded according to local conditions and how traditional arrangements of power were not just contested but overcome.[22] Universal male suffrage ultimately set a powerful precedent, especially for a nation subjected to occupational rule under a 'civilizing' hegemony. On a larger scale it signified that, though the war for sovereignty was lost in 1898, the battle for autonomy was not. The precedent of revolution reinforced the conviction that claims of autonomy remained valid, despite the wishes of influential foreign powers. For those on the ground, there were substantial degrees of native autonomy to be granted and concessions to be made no matter how hegemonic outside powers deemed themselves to be.

Much as Cuban events in 1868 served as a precursor to U.S. events in 1898, these bilateral confrontations did not take place without context. They reflected deep-rooted social and political concerns that held as much influence in their final outcome as they did in the current state of affairs. In this particular case, the exchange between metropole and colony over attempts at qualifying the right to vote represented the culmination of drawn-out processes of progressive reforms that were more attuned to native, elite concerns than to direct responses to the demands of the new imperial regime. As a result, the adoption of universal male suffrage was not so much a rejection of U.S. hegemony (although it certainly was that) as the realisation of inroads, beginning nearly three decades before, of integrating educational and public spaces and expanded basic civil and political rights.

Beyond the progressive precedents that helped ensure initial success, resistance along racial lines also held long-term consequences because the assurance of universal male suffrage guaranteed that any political agenda would have to address the wishes of black Cubans. In fact, as Alejandro de la Fuente has argued, each of the presidential campaigns in the first decade of the Republic were 'fought largely over which candidate truly represented an inclusive Cubanness.' With obvious respect for the political liability of disavowing or even compromising the legacy of Cuba's Liberation Army, candidates such as Bartolome Maso explicitly appealed, with 'consideration and respect,' to the 'class of color', which represented to Cuba a 'family of heroes' and an 'essential factor of our social existence' and given the 'participation it deserves in our political character.'[23] In addition to actively shaping political discourse, black Cubans would play a vigorous role in deciding and implementing legislation. In the early republic this precedent was set on a national level, notably with Juan Gilberto Gómez and the son of a former slave, Martín Morúa Delgado. Additionally, much like the social progress many elite blacks made in this period that subsequently flowed downward, political gains at the top levels were matched from the bottom up as an increasing number of politicians of colour occupied local and provincial elected positions of power.

Cuba remained, even in the early stages of the republic, a contested site of empire marked by complex negotiations that defied traditional or unilateral outlays of power. Yet, despite the end of American active occupation and the return of sovereignty to the island in 1902, the challenges originating from the intertwining of race and nation that the U.S. would be forced to confront were not over. In 1906, disillusioned black veterans and their white political allies in the Liberal Party moved against what they deemed to be unfair elections by taking up arms in protest. This action prompted a second U.S. military intervention. Although this lasted for another three years, paradoxically it proved to be the primary vehicle for securing rights that had started the new rebellion in the first place. Largely as a means to quell future unrest, the provisional government, under command of the U.S. military governor, acknowledged many of the rebels' grievances and tried to ameliorate them by expanding the number of jobs available for black veterans. Building upon this new round of success, which again forced the U.S. to conform to a national racial reality antithetical to their own, black Cubans escalated their political mobilisation as soon as U.S. forces withdrew. Using highly-organized networks and an extensive history of mass mobilisation, black Cubans, many of whom still actively identified as veterans, consolidated various civil and political entities to form a new national organisation with widespread membership: its official newspaper, *Previsón*, would proclaim 'Cuba for the Cubans.' As a result, in 1908 black Cubans formed the *Partido Independiente de Color*

(PIC), which was the first black national political party in the Western hemisphere.

If left here, the early experience in U.S. implementation of the imperial project would remain one marked by challenge, confrontation, and at least in the context of Cuba, forced conformity at the hands of those that they supposedly had dominion over. In this story of empire, one that starts with Céspedes and the *Grito de Yara* in 1868 rather than with Teddy Roosevelt and San Juan Hill in 1898, the emergence of a true, multiracial army of independence becomes the central force in determining the outcomes for all parties involved and to which all other considerations would have to bend. Over the course of the revolutionary era, and into the beginnings of the new republic, the legacy of Cuba's Liberation Army, personified by Antonio Maceo, set off a chain reaction inextricably connecting race and nation that would force an end to one of the world's last great slave empires while fomenting another final revolution for the end of colonialism after more than 400 years of imperial rule. Upon achieving this goal, Cubans successfully challenged what would become the modern world's last great empire by imposing their own will in fully implementing universal male suffrage and creating of the first black national political party in the region. Framing the early causes of American imperialism in this way helps swing the pendulum away from Washington and provides a fuller account of Havana-based actions and actors than is given in *American Empire*.

However, simply championing a competing perspective as a means of corrective does no more to address narrative deficiencies than did the original point of contention that also favoured a singular viewpoint. The complex interplay between two long-standing nation states, both on the brink of historical epochs, produced multilayered exchanges and outcomes. In this sense, it is worth noting that the most influential scholars of Cuban history emphasise a more nuanced perspective, one insisting on both deeply-seated racial inequities preceding U.S. occupation and following U.S. rule.[24] Moreover, if race were a defining characteristic that framed revolution and republic, conditions on the ground made it a construct that both acted, and was acted upon, over the course of Cuban nationhood. This perception presents significant challenges to the unity thesis across racial (and class) lines. Within an analysis of *American Empire*, this distinction underlines a subtle view of this period by Hopkins, who rightly emphasises the sustained power of conservative elements in policy making during this period, although perhaps leaning too much toward the role of the U.S., rather than local forces in understanding its origins.[25]

And while a multitude of examples serves to undermine the myth of a raceless nation in this period, the most conspicuous and damning was the 1912 massacre of thousands of black Cubans in what amounts to one of the bloodiest race wars in the western hemisphere. Reflecting the complicated nature of race in Cuba, a multi-sided conflict emerged in the wake of the PIC being declared illegal based on prohibitions against parties formed along racial lines, as these were deemed 'racist' and unpatriotic. The reemergence of the PIC in 1912 pitted economically and socially marginalised Afro-Cubans against national forces alongside U.S. troops acting in supporting roles. After a series of violent confrontations that cost thousands of lives, including those of the leaders of the PIC, this organisation was disbanded. That such violence was perpetrated on the first black national political party in the region appears to make the story of Cuba's evolutionary era to move in reverse. This is for good reason; internally, the link between race and nation could have an adverse impact on black Cubans. As pointedly stated by Helg, 'Cuba's myth of racial equality, by denying the existence of discrimination on the basis of race, undermine the formation of a black collective consciousness.'[26] The initial need for a party like the PIC and its subsequent prohibition based on declaring such parties built around race, as adversarial (i.e. racist) to the national project, further highlights this fact. Externally, a similar argument can be made regarding race, nation, and empire: that when confronted with oppositional (and really, antithetical) policies of race, the U.S., befitting a hegemonic power, interjected its own prevailing ideologies into Cuban national politics, often with devastating consequences, even long after departing, as evidenced by the events of 1912.

In 1893 Jose Martí wrote that 'in Cuba, there will never be a racial war. The Republic cannot go backwards.'[27] He was wrong on both accounts. But this does not mean that a longer view of history does not ultimately prove him right, at least in that the revolution remained strong enough and the ideas of racial progress forceful enough, to preserve the spirit of 1868, 1887, and 1895. If the legacy of U.S. imperial process can extend to 1912 in Cuba, so too can a longer view of history reshape our understanding of *American Empire*, if the context of race and nation in Cuba is properly accounted for. Ultimately, in an age only a decade removed from abolition in one of the last great slave empires left standing and in a period defined by the violent repression of African Americans between Redemption and Jim Crow, the more remarkable exchange is the one that confronted race in Cuba and extracted from it new notions of equality and nationalism. Although the era of revolution in Cuba, when judged in 1898, can at best seem like an abject betrayal of the spirit of 1895, its legacy lies in the challenge to the very system that operated against it. Although 'that challenge was never complete and more often than not it seemed fitful and ambivalent' as Ada Ferrer contends, 'the movement, and the society from which it emerged, were changed by virtue of the challenge having been posed at all.'[28]

An even longer view of history, confirms this argument. Jumping forward to another phase when Cuba contested American imperial designs, the influence of anti-racial and anti-imperialist components in 1895, specifically in establishing the context of how they shaped U.S. policy and actions, can be seen in the revolution lead by Fidel Castro. In an interpretation shared, and conspicuously evoked by the Fidelistas themselves, the promise of a raceless and free Cuba had been denied by U.S. intervention and occupation and further inhibited by a legacy of subsequent, sustained U.S. involvement. It is only with the arrival of the victorious Barbudos out of the Sierra Maestra and into Havana in 1958, that the original goal, expressed in violent and revolutionary fashion nearly a century earlier, was realised.

Conclusion

When writing a synthesis of empire, a generally favoured position is to view the historical narrative from the outside looking in. As a rejoinder to this view *American Empire* includes, as part of its larger framework, several case studies emanating out of both the Atlantic and the Pacific that collectively form a counterweight to the traditional 'Washington' or 'outside' perspective. At their fullest, these peripheral spaces offer fertile ground for further exploration of both similarities and singularities among multiple sites of empire. Moreover, with Hopkins's appeal for diplomatic historians to look beyond Washington at the outset of his work, in the end the call for enhanced insular perspectives within *American Empire* is less of an overt criticism than a difference over which points in the push–pull continuum of the metropole and colony deserve the most emphasis.[29] Rather than a substantive disagreement on the importance of local conditions, dissent is more a question of finding a balance between metropole and periphery.

The difference is that emphasis matters. From the vantage point of Cuba, a deeper and more prominent recognition of specific, historical circumstances. like that of a multi-racial army of liberation and the subsequent development of universal male suffrage, are of critical value in demonstrating how local conditions affected, and even at times forced, U.S. imperial expansion. America's seemingly one-sided victory over the Spain, as well as the clear racial agenda it intended to install in the immediate aftermath, had the potential to place it on firm hegemonic ground. Yet, the legacy of Afro-Cuban veterans like Maceo, combined with a nationalist identity backed by a 'raceless' Cuba, served as powerful impediments to the uninterrupted sweep of American imperial history. The peripheral viewpoint offers a compelling alternative to understanding American Empire. To paraphrase one influential work on empire, race in Cuba 'was a crucible that plunged Washington's raw bureaucracy into the white heat of nationalist revolution' from which the course of empire was contested within not from without.[30] But Cuba was not singular: similar themes of race, nationalism and revolution that were central to understanding the totality of U.S. imperialism throughout the insular empire. When taken as a whole, these perspectives offer additional competing narratives and may also suggest different conclusions over the causation and characterisation of U.S. imperialism from those reached in *American Empire*.

Notes

1. Hopkins, *American Empire*, 384.
2. The example of Hawai'i has a counterpart in the treatment of the Philippines, particularly where Hopkins' description of U.S. Military tactics in 1898 is limited to: they "covered the full range of brutalities". Hopkins, *American Empire*, 415. And while it is rightfully noted that this included the use of torture and concentration camps, these are stand-ins for a multitude of inhumanity perpetuated on a civilian population the likes of which constitute one of the worst official acts within the American empire, yet one whose existence is barely recognised outside of a specialised audience. For a different, far more extensive treatment of this episode, but also in in a work devoted to American empire on a grand scale, see Immerwahr, *How to Hide an Empire*, . 97–101.
3. Hopkins, *American Empire*, 431–2.
4. Ibid., 395.
5. As quoted in, Immerwahr, *How to Hide an Empire*, 70–1.
6. As quoted in Hopkins, *American Empire*, 390.
7. Several excellent collections of this type of work can be found on the following. For an explicit focus on Latin America, see, Joseph, LeGrand, and Salvatore, *Close Encounters of Empire*. For a more recent and a wider focus, see McCoy and Scarano, *Colonial Crucible*. For a work that extends the bilateral nature of imperial power to argue for reciprocal influences and impacts, see Kaplan and Pease, *The Cultures of United States Imperialism*. Specific to Cuba, see Pérez, *On Becoming Cuban* and Utset, *A Cultural History of Cuba*.
8. Hopkins, *American Empire*, 384–85.
9. Ibid., 337.
10. Ibid., 346.
11. Martí, *My Race*.
12. Ferrer, *Race, Nation, and Revolution*, 3.
13. Ibid.
14. Hopkins, *American Empire*, 392–3.
15. Scott, *Slave Emancipation in Cuba*, 57.
16. As quoted in Perez, *Cuba Between Empires 1878-1902*, 168.
17. Hopkins, *American Empire*, 351–2.
18. Helg, *The Afro-Cuban Struggle for Equality*, 126.
19. As quoted in Helg, 93.
20. de la Fuente and Casey, "Race and the Suffrage Controversy in Cuba, 1898-1901", 221.
21. de la Fuente, "Myths of Racial Democracy: Cuba, 1900-1912", 39–73, 54.
22. Hopkins, *American Empire*, 575.
23. De la Fuente, "Myths of Racial Democracy: Cuba, 1900-1912", 56.
24. For the earlier period, Ada Ferrer argues for a host of inconsistent and outright hostile policies emerging within the Liberation Army. Following U.S. rule, Aline Helg outlines how the U.S. exacerbated racial differences while Alejandro de la Fuente suggests "ambiguity" is the best way to describe nation and race in this period.
25. Hopkins's analysis falls in line with several other recent interpretations that argue for the sustained influence of conservative elements in the upper echelon of Cuban society and politics. As examples, seede la Fuente and Casey, "Race and the Suffrage Controversy in Cuba"; Bronfman *Measures of Equality*; Utset, *A Cultural History of Cuba during the U.S. Occupation*; Pappademos, *Black Political Activism and the Cuban Republic*. For the argument of "Many Cubas" (and many Cubans)

that undermines notions of axiomatic unity, see especially, Martínez-Fernández, *Revolutionary Cuba*.
26. Helg, 16.
27. Martí, *My Race*.
28. Ferrer, 198.
29. Hopkins' starting point of Iraq lends credence to the stated emphasis on the global setting as a "reappraisal of the strong national tradition that has long formed the basis of historical studies in the United States". Hopkins, *American Empire*, 15.
30. McCoy, Scarano, and Johnson "On the Tropic of Cancer Transitions",3.

Disclosure Statement

No potential conflict of interest was reported by the author(s).

References

Bronfman, Alejandra M. *Measures of Equality: Social Science, Citizenship, and Race in Cuba, 1902-1940*. Chapel Hill, N.C.: University of North Carolina Press, 2004.

Ferrer, Ada. *Race, Nation, and Revolution, 1868-1898*. Chapel Hill, NC: University of North Carolina Press, 1999.

de la Fuente, Alejandro. "Myths of Racial Democracy: Cuba, 1900-1912." *Latin American Research Review* 34, no. 3 (1999): 39–73.

de la Fuente, Alejandro, and Matthew Casey, "Race and the Suffrage Controversy in Cuba, 1898-1901." In *Colonial Crucible: Empire in the Making of the Modern American State*, edited by McCoy and Francisco Scarano, 220–229. Madison: University of Wisconsin Press, 2009.

Helg, Aline. *The Afro-Cuban Struggle for Equality, 1886-1912*. Chapel Hill, N.C.: University of North Carolina Press, 1995.

Hopkins, A. G. *American Empire: A Global History*. Princeton: Princeton University Press, 2018.

Immerwahr, Daniel. *How to Hide an Empire*. New York: Random House, 2019.

Joseph, Gilbert M., Catherine LeGrand, and Ricardo Donato Salvatore, eds. *Close Encounters of Empire: Writing the Cultural History of U.S.-Latin American Relations*. Durham: Duke University Press, 1998.

Kaplan, Amy, and Donald E. Pease. *The Cultures of United States Imperialism*. Durham: Duke University Press, 1993.

Martí, Jose. *My Race*, Patria April 16. 1893.

Martínez-Fernández, Luis. *Revolutionary Cuba: A History*. Gainesville: University Press of Florida, 2014.

McCoy, Alfred, and Francisco Scarano, eds., *Colonial Crucible: Empire in the Making of the Modern American State*. Madison, WI: University of Wisconsin Press, 2009.

McCoy, Alfred W., Francisco A. Scarano, and Courtney Johnson "On the Tropic of Cancer Transitions and Transformations in the U.S. Imperial State". In *Colonial Crucible: Empire in the Making of the Modern American State*, edited by McCoy and Francisco Scarano, 3. Madison: University of Wisconsin Press.

Pérez, Louis. *On Becoming Cuban: Identity, Nationality, and Culture*. Chapel Hill, N.C.: University of North Carolina Press, 1999.

Pérez, Louis. *Cuba Between Empires 1878-1902*. Pittsburgh, Pa: University of Pittsburgh Press, 1983.

Pappademos, Melina. *Black Political Activism and the Cuban Republic*. Chapel Hill, N.C.: University of North Carolina Press, 2014.

Scott, Rebecca. *Slave Emancipation in Cuba*. Pittsburgh, Pa: University of Pittsburgh Press, 1985.

Utset, Marial Iglesias. *A Cultural History of Cuba During the U.S. Occupation, 1898-1902*. Chapel Hill, N.C.: University of North Carolina Press, 2011.

The Road to 1898: On American Empire and the Philippine Revolution

Reynaldo C. Ileto

ABSTRACT
'1898' marks the birth of both the American empire and the Filipino nation when the U.S. Navy joined forces with Filipino revolutionists in ending Spain's rule. The alliance ended when the Americans refused to recognise the Filipino republic and forcibly occupied the islands. Hopkins situates both the 'coming of age' of America and the rise of a Filipino nationalist elite against a wider backdrop of imperial rivalries, economic transformations, and stages of globalisation in which the British Empire looms large. The essay builds on Hopkins's account of Spanish rule leading to the Revolution. In contrast to Cuba, the Philippine interior was left relatively untouched, controlled mainly through the friar-curates who lorded it over the town centres but not their peripheries. Following upon Hopkins's discussion of the three foundational nationalists – Jose Rizal, Andres Bonifacio, and Emilio Aguinaldo – their differences can be explained by the peculiarities of the Spanish colonial system and how each of them related to their society.

A 'Wider Angle of Vision'

'By 1898, the United States had become a formidable and fully independent state; in that year, too, the Republic's newfound strength was applied to invade Cuba, Puerto Rico, and the Philippines, and to annex Hawai'i.' – A. G. Hopkins, *American Empire: A Global History*, 337.

To Filipino readers, it would be a revelation that '1898' in both American and Philippine history signifies the beginning of the nation. In the Filipino national narrative, 1898 marks the culmination of the revolt against Spain that commenced in August 1896, reached a stalemate by the end of 1897, and is quickly revived at the outbreak of the Spanish-American War. The exiled General Emilio Aguinaldo is ferried from Hong Kong back to the islands on an American warship. He declares independence from Spain in June and his revitalised army proceeds to neutralise the remaining Spanish strongholds throughout Luzon. Aguinaldo then organises the first Republican government in Malolos, north of Manila.

In this narrative, the U.S. arrives on the scene in 1898 as a fully-fledged power that, having declared its independence from Britain in 1776 and won, will now assist the Filipinos in driving out Spain. Aguinaldo expects American recognition of the republic, but the U.S. decides to 'acquire' the Philippines through a treaty with Spain. This triggers another series of events from 1899–1902 dubbed the 'Philippine insurrection.' The republic is destroyed in the aftermath of the Filipino-American War (as the event is now called). Throughout the following century, the events of 1898 will be memorialised as the 'Unfinished Revolution.'[1]

In Hopkins's monumental narrative, 1898 also signifies a beginning, but of a different sort: It marks America's attainment of full independence from the British imperial father. For the Revolution of 1775–1783 turns out to have been unfinished in Hopkins's reckoning. The fledgling American republic continues to be entangled with British power for another century at least. It remains dependent on Britain's trading networks, financial system, cultural influences, and control of the seas. Only after the Civil War and the onset of 'modern globalization,' as Hopkins puts it, will American nationalists finally break off from the British 'father.' The prowess of adulthood is demonstrated in the Spanish-American War. The ultimate proof of the United States' 'coming of age' is its defeat of Aguinaldo's army. By adopting Hopkins's 'wider angle of vision,' we arrive at the startling observation that 1898 is the culmination of both the Filipino and American struggles for independence.

Hopkins shows in detail how the moves by the U.S. in the Pacific in 1898 were an extension of the activities of the European states, all scrambling to keep the West in control of the 'new world order' that was shaping up in the 1890s. The war with Spain was part of this turmoil. Unwittingly, then, the Filipino revolutionists of the 1890s were drawn into a conflict of global proportions. Hopkins's comparative framework reveals the similarities and differences between the Philippine revolution and parallel events in Cuba, Hawai'i, and the continent (i.e. the wars with Mexico and the American Indians). The Filipino-American War emerges as the first instance in which the expansion of American power faced a real test, even though the outcome was preordained by structural forces so effectively delineated by Hopkins. The American victory would be hailed by the expansionists as 'the realization of divine will, a sign that the United States had come of age, and a mandate to proceed with the civilizing mission.' (416)[2] In the meantime, 'Filipinos were left to contemplate what they saw as a catastrophe, which left them without independence and with the challenge instead of adjusting to a new set of foreign rulers who spoke, not Spanish, but English.' (416)

Spanish Colonial Rule to 1850

The U.S. intervention that began in 1898 was an attempt to replace the lowland, Catholic, Malayo-Hispanic civilisation produced by over 300 years of Hispanisation with one imbued by Anglo-Saxon, Protestant features through the universal teaching of English— the language of the new rulers. This attempt went a long way as the Filipino elite latched on to the new American order in the expectation that independence would eventually be granted to them. Resistance at various levels, however, prevented the total displacement of the old.

One of the strengths of Hopkins's work is that the different types of Spanish colonial possessions can be compared with each other. In the Americas, the colonial setup involved conquistadors and settlers who transplanted the social order to the Americas and localised it. The Spanish colonists developed huge plantations that were worked by slaves brought in from the outside. The Philippines, as we shall see, had a different setup: Manila was intensively developed as the hub of the galleon trade, populated by merchants and clerics but few settlers. Beyond Manila and a few major cities, the Spanish presence was largely comprised of missionaries and friar curates on whom Manila depended for 'control' of the *indio* population.

According to Hopkins, Spain had staked a claim to the Philippine islands in 1521 but 'it was not until the close of the eighteenth century that a serious effort was made to turn formal possession into effective control.' (404) The colonial economy hinged upon the galleon trade that transported Mexican silver to Manila and returned to America loaded with Chinese and Southeast Asian goods. 'The entrepot trade ... left most of the interior untouched.' There was a paucity of Spanish settlers who would have engaged in plantation development, as was the case in Cuba. The friar, Hopkins then goes on to show, was 'the most visible Spanish presence outside Manila.' The religious corporations had been granted control of vast tracts of land, which were utilised for subsistence purposes and rents until the end of the eighteenth century. The Spanish administration 'employed a form of indirect rule that treated the friars as its principal agents and harnessed indigenous authorities to collect taxes and supply labor.' (404)

What kind of society was produced by this situation? The first half of this paper develops further Hopkins's picture of the largely untouched Philippine interior, which Spain controlled largely through the activities of the friars. The paper then builds on Hopkins's account of the three modern heroes, Jose Rizal, Andres Bonifacio and Emilio Aguinaldo, to show how the differences between them reveal the peculiarities of the Spanish reordering of society going back to the 'conquest' of the islands in the sixteenth and seventeenth centuries. More specifically, the contrasting careers of the three foundational heroes manifest at least three characteristics of the social ordering that was established by Spain. One of them was mentioned earlier: the divide between Manila and the hinterlands, or the metropole versus the rural pueblos. Within the pueblo lies the second characteristic: the close relationship between the friar and the local elites, which was the foundation of colonial rule. The third characteristic is the division that arose between the pueblo and the uncontrolled spaces beyond it. These characteristics made the Spanish imperial presence de facto 'indirect,' if not 'informal,' until the mid-nineteenth century. Making this possible were Madrid's distance, its minimal military presence, and the rugged topography of the larger islands.

Rather than destroying existing political entities, 'conquest' meant constructing new ones out of a relatively dispersed population. These new entities were the Filipino pueblos, the offshoots of a process called the *reducción*, the concentration and resettlement of inhabitants within hearing distance of the church bells (*bajo de las campanas*). A typical pueblo was established with the church and the priest's convent in the centre. The *datu, maguinoo*, and other important people built their houses close to the church-convento centre, while their followers and the rest of the resettled people lived a bit farther beyond the poblacion. This was the shape of the typical pueblo, or *bayan*.[3]

There is little reason to believe that the resettlement of people around the church, or the formation of towns, was the outcome of bloody conquest, enslavement, or coercion. The Philippine archipelago was at the other end of the world from Spain, whose economic and military resources simply did not allow for a bloody conquest of the islands. Certainly, there were a few armed clashes, especially in areas where the inhabitants had been converted to Islam, but these were the exception rather than the rule. The so-called conquest of the Philippines was accomplished mainly through soft power, through treaties, blood compacts, and the introduction of a new and powerful religion: Roman Catholicism.[4]

The Spanish missionaries had to prove that their religion was superior to the existing ones, and they did their best in demonstrating that superiority, while allowing Christianity to be localised or indigenised and thus easier to adopt locally. The Muslim inhabitants, of course, were not impressed; after all, Islam and Christianity belonged to the same Abrahamic family of religions, and they had clashed violently in the Iberian Peninsula. But for the pagan inhabitants, the religion of the Spaniards was quite impressive. In particular, the younger generation, the sons and daughters of the *datu* and *maguinoo*, were so taken in by this new faith that they collaborated with the missionaries in converting their elders to Christianity.

The conversion to Christianity was the first of four waves of external influences that affected mainly the youth of society over the centuries. The second was the adoption of liberal ideas by the Spanish-educated elite – the generation of Rizal – in the nineteenth century. The third was the Americanisation of the Filipino world view through the universal teaching and adoption of English, also by the youth. And the fourth was the radicalisation of more youthful generations of Filipinos in the 1930s and in the 1960s in the aftermath of the Bolshevik and Maoist revolutions.

Of these four, the conversion to Christianity has had the most profound influence in shaping what Filipinos are today as a people. This is because with religious conversion came the formation of the original towns that would form the core of the new religio-political entity called Filipinas. The concept of the *taong bayan* (lit. townspeople] arose with the formation of the original *bayan*, the Filipino pueblo or town. There are a lot of documents in the archives about the foundation of towns and their development over the centuries, but a history of the Spanish Philippines based on municipal histories alone would be a very partial one. According to Hopkins, 'limited though it was, Spanish rule was a sufficient burden on those it touched to provoke substantial resistance, which ranged from open rebellion to nativist rejection of foreign influences and included selective adaptations and syncretic syntheses aimed at fusing elements of both worlds.' (404) The hispanising pueblo seems to have been periodically afflicted with resistance, disorder, and flight.

Any substantial history of the Philippines is studded with revolts over the course of the centuries. Reduced to its most elementary feature, a revolt was about people abandoning the pueblo and moving to the peripheries and beyond, where the Spanish authorities lacked the power to impose their will upon them. As Hopkins puts it, 'in an archipelago of abundant land, dense forest, and inaccessible uplands, there was also the option of escaping to regions that lay beyond the reach of Spanish officials.' (404) Sometimes, the movement away from the town centre was due to a dissatisfaction with Christianity or its clergy and a corresponding desire to return to earlier religious practices. Or a prominent local figure, perhaps a *cabeza de barangay* (village headman) or even a *gobernadorcillo* (mayor) might get involved in a dispute with a Spanish priest or official and would run off to the hills with his followers. *Indios* abandoning the pueblo could be distancing themselves, literally, from abusive friars and colonial officials, but they could equally be running away from the law for having committed crimes in the pueblo. For whatever reason, these cases of *indios* moving away from the pueblo and re-establishing themselves outside the zones of Spanish control were usually labelled 'revolts.'

The frequent appearance of 'revolts' in the historical record is an indication that pueblo history can only give us half a picture of the past or maybe even less than that. Pueblo history, consisting of the activities of the Catholic priests, the local officials and the *taong bayan*, is only the more visible or documented part of the country's history. For every town that was established, there was another space, potentially more extensive than the pueblo, that was inhabited by apostates, heretical sects, vagabonds, bandits, and above all, the 'undocumented.' These were the *taong labas* (literally people outside [the town]).[5]

That there could be an autonomous zone beyond the pueblo was because Spanish control over the population, at least until 1800, was based mainly on the moral power of the Church-convento centre. To the local elites, there were both spiritual and material advantages to living close to the centre and working together with the Spanish establishment. If, for whatever reason, these *indios* abandoned the pueblo centre and decided to live beyond Spanish control, there was little that the friars and the local police could do to prevent it–not, at least, until the Guardia Civil and the Spanish army were reorganised and reinforced in the mid-nineteenth century so that the Spanish state could forcibly impose control over the autonomous zones beyond the pueblos.[6]

Municipal Elites and the Spanish Clergy

The pueblo (*bayan*) and the spaces beyond it (*labas*) were not entirely separate domains. There was movement back and forth, and a key interface between the two was the town mayor, who was called at various times *gobernadorcillo*, *capitan municipal*, or *presidente*. He was the point of contact between the local community and the Spanish religious and secular rulers. Once elected and proclaimed, the mayor of a pueblo had to work together with the Spanish friar during his term of office. This was his first major duty as mayor. After all, the parish priest (*cura párroco*) was no less than the representative of the Spanish monarch as well as the Pope in Rome.[7]

Was the mayor, though, merely a puppet of the friar, as most historians allege?[8] Yes, some mayors who had no guts or political will could simply be tools of friar domination. But even in such cases, how do we know what really went on behind the backs of the Spanish priest? Up to the early nineteenth century, the Spanish presence in the pueblos was minimal owing to manpower and budgetary shortages. The lone friar was thus vulnerable to manipulation by wily principales and to rumour mongering by the *taong bayan*. The ideal was for a smooth relationship to be nurtured between mayor and friar, which was crucial for the well-being of the *pueblo* at large. This relationship would provide valuable lessons for the leaders of the town in how to deal realistically with an external power personified in the friar: how to collaborate, resist, manipulate, negotiate and if necessary, yield to this power, with the survival and well-being of the community in mind.

The friars could be quite vocal in their attacks on corrupt and uncooperative mayors. Mayors, for their part, when dealing with friars who happened to be arrogant and abusive, had to be patient and crafty in handling such issues. They had to implement non-confrontational resistance. Most of the time, though, this was not necessary because the Spanish priest did a decent job of ministering to his flock, despite his parishioners belonging to a different culture and speaking a different tongue. The extremely negative image of the friar that we associate with the time of the Revolution is largely a product of anti-clerical writings from the eighteenth century onwards that were adapted to the Philippine situation by the *ilustrados*.[9]

Unlike the American teachers who were to replace them in the twentieth century, the Spanish missionaries did not teach their language to more than a tiny minority of their parishioners—the *principales* or leading citizens who lived closest to the centre. The friars had to learn the languages of their flock to deliver credible sermons and hear confession. In some cases, they became so domesticated by their adopted communities that they became drinking partners of the mayors and had intimate relationships with the local women. Once they fell into this trap, the friar could become a puppet of the mayor and the municipal elite. So, who was manipulating whom?

Aside from having to deal with the Spanish friar, the other major task of the mayor was to bring peace and order to the town by building up defences against gang attacks – *robos en cuadrilla* – by criminal elements among the *taong labas*.[10] The mayor had at his disposal his own police force called *cuadrilleros*. Armed only with bolos and other bladed weapons plus a few ancient shotguns, these local police were a pathetic bunch compared to the Guardia Civil, but with proper leadership and training they could repel a bandit attack on their town. In dealing with these gangs from the outside, the mayor had to exhibit qualities of leadership that would induce the *taong bayan*, especially those who lived in distant barrios to support the church-convento centre instead of being seduced into following those shadowy figures from the *taong labas*. A successful mayor, then, had to possess a certain amount of bravado and charisma to train and rally his police force and ordinary citizens to resist bandit attacks. They had to appear at least as tough as their rebel or bandit counterparts. Paradoxically, though, they also had to appear humble in the eyes of their followers.[11]

A big advantage that the mayor had over his Spanish partner, the friar, was his command of the local languages. The friars, even the best speakers of the vernaculars among them, were no match for mayors who could verbally appeal to their constituents in a manner that could move them emotionally. That is why, in matters of peace and order, the friar was indebted to the mayor. While a Spanish guardia civil detachment could establish peace and order by force, this was transient and unstable. Mayors could talk effectively not just to their followers but to the leaders of disgruntled *taong labas*, to engage even with tulisan chiefs, in order to neutralise their threats by making deals with them to avoid more serious damage to the community.

This was the general situation from the eighteenth to the mid-nineteenth century. After 1800, however, major changes started to take place in the economy and local politics. The British occupation of Manila (1762-64) had made evident the determination of the British Empire to put an end to the empire of their Spanish rivals. Working through masonic lodges, which were originally founded in England in 1717, literature targeting the dominance of the Catholic Church began to spread throughout the Spanish empire. The ultimate aim of the British was to cripple Spain's Pearl of the Orient, first by taking control of the external trade of the Philippine colony, and second by undermining the religio-political foundations on which the Spanish empire was built.

By the 1860s, Manila was fully integrated into the British trading and financial network centred in Hong Kong and Singapore. This was what the French Consul in Manila meant when he remarked in 1883 that 'to all intents and purposes The Philippines are a British possession.' (406) The British trading networks also became conduits for the introduction of 'subversive' literature and ideas into the Philippines.[12] The educated segments of the *principalia* class would be influenced by radical literature in the 1880s and would spread their message to the pueblos through students returning from Manila to their home provinces. Slowly this would bring about changes in the political structure of the pueblo and the sentiments of the municipal elite. Mayors and *cabezas* (village headmen) would become more assertive towards the friars.

The rising tensions between the Spanish clergy and the town elites, was paralleled by heightened efforts of the Spanish Army and Guardia Civil to control the spaces occupied by the *taong labas*. Expeditions were carried out in the 1880s to flush out the bandits and other so-called lawless elements that had 'infested' the spaces beyond the *pueblo*. It was getting more and more difficult for disgruntled *taong bayan* to simply move out to the peripheries to become *taong labas*, without getting chased and captured by the Guardia Civil. The situation came to a head with the outbreak of revolt in August 1896 by the Manila-based Katipunan secret society that developed into a major separatist rebellion involving practically all of the lowland Christian areas in the years that followed.

'In the 1890s, elements of the elite and the lower orders came together, in different degrees in different places, to produce a popular front against foreign dominance.' (351) In unpacking this statement by Hopkins, we need to be reminded that the Philippines, in stark contrast to Cuba, had not been turned into vast plantations worked by imported slaves. Furthermore, migration policies and the 'tyranny of distance' had kept the white population to a small minority mostly confined to Manila and a few other cities. In areas where a Malay aristocracy had existed, the pre-Spanish social order had been incorporated into new *pueblos*, with the old chiefs transformed into *village* headmen and town mayors, with a friar curate at the centre representing the Catholic church as well as the Spanish suzerain. The people of the pueblos consisted of the indigenous inhabitants and their social betters, with a generous sprinkling of Chinese and Spanish mestizos.[13]

Foundational Heroes: Rizal, Bonifacio, and Aguinaldo

As the nineteenth century was coming to an end, the accumulated stresses on the colony of peninsular Spain's futile attempt to play 'catch up' with its rivals, particularly Britain and France, produced a nationalist and increasingly separatist response from the Filipino elites and their constituents. Hopkins illustrates the 'evolution of this loose and shifting coalition of proto-nationalist forces' by focusing on Jose Rizal, Andres Bonifacio, and Emilio Aguinaldo, 'whose careers chart the evolution of nationalist policies as they moved from moderation to militancy.' (411-12) Rather than link the careers of these three heroic figures to the evolution of national policies, an alternative approach would be to view them as representatives of three types of Filipino elites that responded in different ways to the liberal winds of change in the late-nineteenth century. The levels of moderation or militancy in the policies they adopted reflected their varying relationships with the Spanish authorities as well as with the rank and file of their society.

The biographies of the three foundational, nationalist heroes have been the subject of controversy involving both Filipino and American scholars. This is registered in Hopkins's observations that a transition 'from veneration to admonition' has taken place in recent years and that the 'tendency toward hagiography that marked early accounts of nationalist leaders has given way to more critical appraisals.' (412) Often occluded in the debates is that, during the Filipino-American War, the U.S. Army confiscated most of the correspondence and archives of the nationalist forces and transported them to the US military archives.[14] It was not until the 1920s that selected documents were made available in translation. Furthermore, biographical writings on the heroes were circumscribed by the U.S. administration's virtual monopoly over the writing and dissemination of history through the educational system. Any discussion of nationalist historiography must include the writings of American officials and historians, which were the texts that Filipino historians often were writing against. This is easier said than done. Alfred McCoy summarily dismissed nationalist writings in the 1950s and 1960s as 'hagiography', instead of situating them in the context in which they were written: the decades of de-colonisation when Filipino historians were writing against the narratives produced by earlier generations of American scholar-officials and the Filipinos they had trained.[15]

Let us begin with Rizal, whose 'image was burnished during the period of American rule because it suited the administration to emphasise the restrained, constitutional character of his opposition to Spanish policy.' (412) Rizal was, indeed, the ideal hero to promote in the school textbooks for Filipinos in the new public schools. Conveniently, his life ends abruptly on 30 December 1896, barely four months after the start of the Katipunan uprising. His glorious career is not tainted by resistance to the U.S. occupation, and his death can be blamed squarely on Spain and, above all, on the instigation of the friars, who personify a Dark Age preceding the Revolution and the coming of the American liberators.

Furthermore, Rizal's writings could readily be subsumed into the liberal, Enlightenment ideals of the American Revolution, lending weight and legitimacy to the American promises of completing the national project initiated by Rizal, if armed resistance to its occupation were ended. Rizal's life and work readily lent themselves to the construction of a hero that stood for gradual change via education, not armed struggle, which the U.S. had spent nearly a decade (1899-1907) to neutralise and did not want repeated.[16]

Bonifacio is introduced by Hopkins as a hero 'whose standing was greatly enhanced by nationalist writers' but who 'now falls short, in some accounts, of the ambitious claims made for him.' (412) Hopkins is indebted here to historian Glenn May for having initiated 'the scholarly re-evaluation of mythology' through his book *Inventing a Hero: The Posthumous Re-Creation of Andres Bonifacio*, conveniently published in 1996, the centennial of the Katipunan uprising. 'Re-evaluation' echoes May's claim to be a scholar operating above politics, in contrast to the Filipino historians who have constructed a mythical Bonifacio to suit their nationalist and other political agendas.[17] May's stance is a variation of McCoy's claim to be writing objective accounts in contrast to hagiographies (another kind of mythology) that Filipinos end up doing because they are unable to detach themselves from personal and material interests. The positioning of these American scholars on the plane of disinterested scholarship in their attacks on Filipino writings about Rizal, Bonifacio and Aguinaldo is, I would argue, a reflection of the imperial mindset itself.

Bonifacio's 'standing' in history is not so much a matter of objectivity versus mythology as it is a reflection of broader ideological differences among his biographers, be they Filipino, American, British or Spanish.[18] Bonifacio's unbending anticlericalism and adhesion to the form and ideals of nineteenth-century masonic secret societies have to be analysed together with the texts he wrote exclusively in Tagalog, in a literary form that allowed his radical, Europe-derived, revolutionary message to be localised by his urban middle- and working-class audiences.[19] British and American writers immediately identified and constructed Bonifacio as Rizal's polar opposite.[20] Bonifacio's violent and fanatical proclivities made him unsuitable for nation-building purposes under U.S. tutelage. For militant nationalists and socialists, on the other hand, Bonifacio and his Katipunan were ideal models for labour and peasant organising and, later, the establishment of socialist and communist parties.[21] These political movements, without necessarily inventing history, interpreted Bonifacio's life to suit their goals. May's reduction of Bonifacio's historiography to one of objectivity versus mythology erases the imperial context of Bonifacio's appearance in historical writing.

Hopkins's overview of Aguinaldo, drawn from the writings of Glenn May and Rene Escalante, portrays him as having made 'seemingly contradictory decisions' that have long cast him as a controversial figure. Aguinaldo 'has suffered, too, from critical re-evaluations of his military and political leadership.' (412) The 'critical re-evaluations' of Aguinaldo's military and political leadership are not simply a sign of progress in scholarship. Even recent studies of Aguinaldo are arguably a continuation of older tensions and controversies between imperial writers and their detractors. The positive American portrayal of the leader of the Filipino forces allied to the U.S. in the war against Spain, promptly turned negative when Aguinaldo declared independence from Spain and formed a republican government.[22] His capture and capitulation to the U.S. Army in April 1901 did not terminate the resistance, which was continued by General Malvar until 1902.

Aguinaldo continued to influence the nonviolent struggle for independence throughout the American occupation. He remained a living symbol of resistance to the U.S., and thus his biographies would become entangled in the politics of independence. After 1946, Aguinaldo would figure in Cold War era histories as the model, either of a strong president and nation-builder, or a fascist leader from the ruling class that sought to suppress the aspiration of the masses from the Katipunan era to the Communist Party.

Hopkins's summation of the scholarship on the three foundational heroes of the modern republic as a 'transition from veneration to admonition' is based on the sources he utilised for his Philippines case study. These scholars, without necessarily being aware of it, are themselves situated in a struggle over historical interpretations ever since the American takeover at the beginning of the twentieth century. Nevertheless, regardless of what Hopkins has said about the evolving scholarship on the three heroes, his general argument holds: Rizal, Bonifacio and Aguinaldo emerged from the new social classes formed by economic development not just in the Philippines but throughout a world that had, by the end of the nineteenth century, been tied together by commerce. These historical figures chose to 'join the modern world' and thus oppose Spanish rule.

Agents of Modernity and Colonial Society

The question now remains: How did these modernising heroes relate to the wider Philippine society, especially the *taong bayan* and the lower orders? Let us start with Rizal, who best fits into the 'big picture' presented by Hopkins. Rizal's family was Chinese-Tagalog mestizo. It had benefited from the economic transformation of the previous half-century, gaining wealth from the agricultural produce of land rented from the Dominican religious order. The family had risen in prominence in the town, but a serious conflict with the Dominican landlords placed it at odds with the Spanish government—at least to the extent that the Archbishop had ultimate control over it. There was, however, another Spain that could provide succour to the family: liberal, republican Spain, which the talented Jose could access through education in the colonial metropolis. And so, while Rizal belonged to the municipal elite of Calamba, ever since he started his secondary schooling in Manila the pueblo ceased to be his world. Eventually, he moved from Manila to Madrid, where his involvement with the Propaganda Movement and the writing of his two novels basically 'made' his career.[23]

As Hopkins puts it, '[Rizal] was strongly influenced by the mixture of liberal, anti-clericalism, and Enlightenment thought he had absorbed when studying in Madrid in the early 1880s.' (412) His novels reflected his readings on Spanish, French, and American history. He was the best example of a Filipino *ilustrado* who had embraced the modern world that was being formed. The rural Philippines depicted in his novels are not derived from passages in a town-dweller's diary but are imagined scenarios of towns under the grip of vicious, greedy, and immoral friars and their native puppets. Towns like San Diego depicted in Rizal's first novel, *Noli me Tangere*, needed to be transformed by putting the friars in their place and allowing enlightened, forward-looking locals to take charge; this was one of the goals of the Propaganda movement.

Rizal's positioning in the social landscape enabled him to broadcast his liberal, reformist aims to fellow liberals in Spain as well as to the Spanish-educated elite in the Philippines. The vast majority of the population that could not read Spanish was largely unaware of Rizal's existence and certainly did not know what his novels were all about. Rizal's aim, in fact, was to reach out to people like himself: Spanish-literate members of the town elite who, hopefully, could be made to understand where the world was heading in the aftermath of the liberal revolutions in France and America. Wean the town elites away from the friars they had been collaborating with, place them on the path to modernity, and they would carry forward in their train the 'poor and ignorant' elements of society.[24]

When Bonifacio's Katipunan society in Manila and its environs commenced the uprising against Spain in August 1896, most municipal elites, except in the provinces adjacent to Manila, did not join in. The Franciscan friars in Tayabas province, a hundred kilometres southeast of Manila, would observe that the townspeople (*taong bayan*) who lived closest to the church-centres remained loyal to their Spanish pastors, while many in the peripheries and beyond (the *taong labas*) were being drawn to the Katipunan movement.[25]

Rizal's stature in the eyes of the people at large, and not just to the ilustrados who could read his novels, rose only after he was executed publicly on 30 December 1896. Hopkins notes this event in connection with Rizal's final work, the poem *Mi Ultimo Adios* (My Last Farewell). After Rizal's execution, 'the complete poem was smuggled out of prison, published, and circulated throughout the Hispanic world, where it gave further inspiration to the nationalist cause.' (413) Hopkins's comparative lens enables him to recognise the poem's effect in gaining sympathy throughout the Hispanic world for the uprising in distant Filipinas. But where the poem truly was an 'inspiration to the nationalist cause' was in its effect on the Filipino public that could never access Rizal in the Castilian language. Immediately after its appearance in Spanish, Bonifacio translated it into Tagalog and circulated it among the rank and file of the rebels. It was soon translated into other vernaculars as well.

The poem could be inspiring only because it accompanied the dramatic public execution of Rizal, which was widely publicised and as well as spread by word of mouth. Rizal had indicated in his letters to his friends and family that his final days would be played out at the religious register. The details of his trial, death sentence, march to the execution site, and even his final words (*Consummatum Est*! – Jesus Christ's last words on the Cross) came to be interpreted by the public as a re-enactment of Christ's suffering and death, a story well known to all lowland Christians, irrespective of region, class, and education. The Republican government of Aguinaldo would proclaim Rizal the national hero, not for his world-acclaimed novels, but for his Christ-like death and the consequent promise of redemption for his people.[26]

Now we turn to Bonifacio, who moved the 'proto-nationalist' cause a notch further by organising a secret society dedicated to a forceful separation from Mother Spain. Hopkins is correct in seeing a resemblance in 'purpose and methods' between Bonifacio and his contemporary Jose Marti. (413) Bonifacio's dream of national emancipation from Spain and obtaining it through armed resurrection was no different from Marti's. Unlike the latter, though, Bonifacio was a mestizo from the lower middle class whose family did not have the means to have him formally educated, much less sent to Europe for advanced studies. Nevertheless, Bonifacio was an avid, self-taught reader of Spanish books, although his mother tongue was Tagalog.

Marti was exiled to Spain and travelled widely to observe for himself the struggles for emancipation elsewhere, even meeting his literary idol, Victor Hugo, in France. Bonifacio had to content himself with painfully reading *Les Miserables* in Spanish. The French, American and other revolutions he learned about through books and pamphlets, provided the lenses through which he would interpret the Filipino past. His idea of revolution was derived from the radical literature of his time that valorised the ideals of the French Revolution rather than from any serious study of how a revolution could arise from the unique experience of the Spanish Philippines.[27] Bonifacio represents a type of Filipino hero who seems on the surface to be thoroughly home-grown and close to the 'masses' (as the Left likes to portray him), when in reality he was thoroughly globalised in outlook owing to the books and pamphlets that he read in his home near the commercial heart of Manila.

Being an accomplished poet and essayist in Tagalog, Bonifacio's main contribution to the revolution was to translate into the vernacular the anti-clerical and nationalist ideas that he had absorbed, however imperfectly, from the literature that was circulated by the ilustrados and fellow masons.[28] His facility with the Tagalog language enabled him to rally some from the poorer classes in Manila to join his movement. However, the leadership of the Katipunan was thoroughly middle class and well-educated. Some of them had travelled regularly to Hong Kong and Singapore for business and work, and no doubt these outposts of the British empire were conduits for the anticlerical and anticolonial writings that reached Bonifacio.[29]

Hopkins narrates that after a series of military reverses, Bonifacio lost the leadership of the revolution to Emilio Aguinaldo. The wider context of this cryptic statement is that, while the Bonifacio-led uprising in Manila and its environs began with great energy, the Spanish counter-attack and reprisals soon dislodged the supreme leader from his Manila base. Bonifacio confided to Aguinaldo, leader of the Cavite rebels, that after being trounced by the Spaniards at Balintawak and other places, his subordinates refused to obey his military orders. He expressed his gratitude to Aguinaldo for the successful uprising in Cavite that prevented further Katipunan defeats. In short, Bonifacio was pushed out of his metropolitan base and forced to seek the protection of his co-revolutionists in the pueblos of Cavite. This eventually brought him into confrontation with the municipal elites of the province, which in turn led to his demise.[30]

Hopkins introduces Aguinaldo as a scion of a wealthy Chinese-Tagalog mestizo family, just like Rizal was. But Aguinaldo moved beyond the reformist Rizal in endorsing the armed struggle 'when it became clear that Spain would not yield to moderate demands moderately expressed.' (413) He followed Bonifacio's footsteps, then, only to have Bonifacio executed for treason at a later stage of the struggle.

'Aguinaldo is a nationalist hero who made some seemingly unheroic, or at least controversial, decisions' (413) – Hopkins does not elaborate upon the controversies over Aguinaldo's stature in history, but they continue to rage even up to today.[31] One cause of misunderstanding is the tendency to locate the three main heroes of the revolution within an evolutionary series. An alternative approach is to treat these heroes in terms of their differing relationships to their society and to the changes taking place in the world beyond.

Rizal, though born in the pueblo of Calamba, found his place in history by moving out of his hometown to be educated in Manila and then in Madrid. Of the three heroes, he is the most accessible to outside observers because he easily fits into the framework of educated elites who were swept into the vortex of late nineteenth-century globalisation. Rizal fits Hopkins's template perfectly, as a mestizo from the periphery who wanted very much to be a citizen of a reinvigorated Spanish empire, but who was pushed in the direction of separatism by the onerous revenue demands placed on the colonies by a desperately modernising Spain. He insisted, though, that the people had first to be prepared through education before the act of separation.

For Bonifacio, there was no need to wait. He was similarly motivated by the achievements of the French and American revolutions but, unlike Rizal, he had never set foot outside the Philippines and hardly even outside greater Manila. His usefulness to the cause was frenetic energy as an organiser coupled with his facility with the Tagalog language, which enabled his masonic secret society to recruit from the working classes of Manila.

Aguinaldo could have been another Rizal, but he could not write a decent paragraph in Spanish because his schooling in Manila had to be terminated so that he could attend to his family's businesses upon his father's death. He had picked up liberal ideas from a masonic lodge founded by a native Filipino priest and was duly inducted into the Katipunan, but he was still a town mayor then and his duties entailed close collaboration with the parish priest, a friar. When he appeared at the head of the rebel forces in Cavite, Spanish officialdom treated him as a rogue mayor deserving of death for treachery.[32]

While Aguinaldo clearly believed that the time had come to put an end to the Spanish clergy's domination of society, he did not view the friars as a class but rather judged them on the basis of their work in their parishes. By his account, he pleaded with Bonifacio to spare the lives of two of three Spanish friars who had been taken into custody by his party (*Magdalo*) but entrusted to the rival *Magdiwang* party headed by Bonifacio. His reasoning was that the two priests were men 'of genuinely good character' (*talagang mabait*). Bonifacio scornfully rejected the pleas.[33]

In his letters and manifestos, Bonifacio comes out as categorically anti-friar. As far as he was concerned, all Spanish friars were false priests who pretended to be holy men while inflicting untold cruelties on the people. He had vowed to execute any of them who fell into his hands — in revenge, perhaps, for their collusion in the martyrdom of three reformist priests in 1872 and of Rizal in 1896. And since the rebellion was perceived by Katipunan leaders as a 'world turned upside down,' when the former friar-lords would become servants of the *indios*, Bonifacio expected deference from the subjugated foreign clerics. These were attitudes shaped by reading European history. The fact is, except in the provinces adjoining Manila, most pueblos remained loyal to their Spanish curates until 1898.

Aguinaldo's more nuanced attitude toward the friars–his willingness, even, to make peace deals brokered by a Spanish Jesuit—is indicative of his previous experience as town mayor. This is a crucial difference between both leaders. Bonifacio had been a clerk-messenger for the British firm, J.M. Fleming & Co., and supply clerk and sales agent of the German house, Carlos Fressel & Co. He had been radicalised by the writings of the Propaganda and Freemasonry that had slipped into the country via British Hong Kong and Singapore. Thrust into the rural environment of Cavite, he was in alien territory, where mayors (and friars) ruled. He addressed his Katipunan counterpart there as *Capitán* — obviously not in reference to Aguinaldo's military rank but to his reputation as *capitán municipal* of Cavite Viejo.

As we showed earlier in this essay, traditionally the mayor worked closely with the Spanish *cura párroco* in running a pueblo. A common perception was that the mayor was merely a 'puppet' of the Spanish friar. In day-to-day municipal affairs, however, both needed each other. The friar was a representative of the colonial power, possessing moral authority as well as physical backup from the local constabulary, but he could also be manipulated or even controlled by the mayor, who had his means of taming the friar, which included gossip (i.e. the *voz común*) and the women who took charge of maintaining the church and convent. In addition, the mayor had at his disposal a police force, the *cuadrilleros*, that defended the pueblo against bandit raids and could easily be transformed into a rebel force.

Such was Aguinaldo's experience prior to becoming a revolutionist. Unlike Rizal and Bonifacio, who were driven by ideology, he had learned to act in the interest of his constituents–from mediating between autocratic friars and their congregation in the 1890s to co-operating with the Japanese army in World War II, when continued resistance proved futile and self-destructive. It was easy for liberals and radicals to denigrate characters like him– another dimension of the controversy surrounding Aguinaldo. Rizal's portrayal in his novels of corrupt or friar-conniving mayors was picked up by American writers who put Aguinaldo in a bad light as a typical *cacique*, a violence-prone despot, whose control over his followers spurred them to continue resisting American rule.[34] Yet, without Aguinaldo and other nationalists with a rural background, the Katipunan would have remained an urban, middle-class movement and the armed resistance to American occupation would have fizzled out much earlier for lack of manpower.

Bonifacio's fate was sealed when he moved from metropolitan Manila, the centre of international trade and de facto satellite of the British Empire, to the pueblos of Cavite province. The municipal elites of Cavite, to be sure, had been partly radicalised by the writings of Rizal and the moving Tagalog manifestos of the Katipunan, but pueblo society continued to develop according to its own centuries-old rhythms. Bonifacio's blind hatred of the friars, his bitter rejection of an election (allegedly manipulated by pro-Aguinaldo town elites) that deprived him of power, his refusal to transform his secret society into a mass movement, and his attempt to form his own army, soon cast him and his remaining followers as *taong labas* – 'people from the outside.'

Pueblo Society and National Unification in 1898

In 1897, 'with the conflict deadlocked,' Aguinaldo 'cut a deal with the Spanish authorities that took him into voluntary exile in Hong Kong, leaving others to continue the armed struggle. At that moment, the treaty ports were in ferment, anti-Manchu nationalists were gathering, and Japan had just emerged as a major power in East Asia.' (413) In 1889, Marcelo del Pilar wrote of the

Philippines being 'bordered by British colonies and how the [Filipino] natives are making comparisons between the tranquil and prosperous life on the rugged shores of Hong Kong and Singapore, and the paltry (*raquitica*) and insecure life in the the lush abundance of the Filipino archipelago.'[35] Spanish Philippines was short on progress and freedom, and the friar orders were to blame. The British colonies not only prefigured the future Philippines but would serve as secure bases for those determined to transform their homeland. To some extent Bonifacio and Aguinaldo were pawns of the British Empire in its drive to extinguish its old rival, Spain.

The historical framework established by Hopkins enables us to pursue this alternative narrative of the road to 1898. When Aguinaldo returned to the Philippines in May of that year as an ally of the United States in the war against Spain, the municipal elites who remained loyal to their friar curates finally switched over to the nationalist cause. All over the islands, Spanish pueblo-centres and military strongholds crumbled. The friars were turned into political prisoners as Filipino secular priests took over the church-convento complexes.[36] The pueblos remained as Catholic as ever but became 'Filipino.' Having declared independence from Spain on 12 June, Aguinaldo proceeded to organise a republican government, which was proclaimed in January of the following year.

The notion that national unity from a provincial perspective 'was a prospect that threatened to install Tagalog dominance' (411) is to a great extent an artifact of American war propaganda. The official papers of the Aguinaldo government, seised by the U.S. Army in the course of the Filipino-American war, reveal a lively correspondence between the fledgling republican centre and provincial elites in Luzon, the Visayas and northern Mindanao. The scramble for representation in the Congress of 1899 reflected the extent of the Malolos Republic's influence.[37]

Clearly the recognition of Aguinaldo as president was widespread in late 1898 and early 1899. The issue remaining to be resolved was the degree to which provincial or regional interests could be preserved. A federal system would most likely have evolved, but the degree to which the national polity was grounded in a common Malayo-hispanic Christian civilisation developed over 300 years would arguably have led to a federal system even more united than what was achieved after the American Revolution. However, the war with the Americans broke out at the very moment that the Republic was beginning to function and spread its power beyond Luzon. U.S. propaganda and military victories ensured that Aguinaldo would be vilified as an oriental despot and that the broadly-based republic he presided over would be downgraded to a Tagalog insurrection.

Granted that 'national identity was scarcely formed; national unity was beyond reach,' how do we explain the fact that, again quoting Hopkins, American 'military operations in the Philippines were far more extensive than in

Cuba and also lasted much longer'? (415) The thrust of American scholarship has been to accentuate regional differences so that the revolution against Spain could be reduced to merely a 'Tagalog insurrection.' After all, a major justification for the U.S. refusal to recognise the Republic of 1898 and to forcibly acquire the Philippines was that, being localistic in outlook, Filipinos were not ready for self-government. This point is registered in Hopkins's statement that 'regional diversity remained an additional obstacle to creating a sense of national consciousness among the inhabitants of the multiplicity of diverse and poorly connected islands.' (411)

Regional diversity is certainly a given. What needs to be explored further are the civilizational implications of the Spanish Catholic ordering of society. The extraordinary attention that the Aguinaldo government gave to fostering Rizal as national hero indicates that religion was the bond that would hold the diverse regions together. The martyr, Rizal, was derived from the Christ figure familiar to all lowland Christians, from whatever region. The cultural roots of the new nation-state were to be found in the hispanised Catholic pueblos. But even beyond the *pueblo*, the so-called millenarian movements that proliferated in the late nineteenth century were not Tagalog-specific. Christ figures, such as Burgos (1872) and Rizal (1896), plus a host of martyrs of the revolutionary movement, were venerated by sects all over the archipelago.[38] Where did this nationalist layer of beliefs come from?

The evidence points to the Filipino clergy. The brightest sons of families from all the pueblos in the country travelled to seminaries in Manila to study for the priesthood. They learned not just Catholic theology but religious history as well. Ordained priests they were but competition for parishes occasioned by the influx of Spanish priests fleeing the revolutions in America relegated most of the native clergy to the status of coadjutors or assistant parish priests. Officially they played second fiddle to the friars but, just like the town mayors, they operated on a clandestine level as well. The source of religio-political content for many a so-called millenarian movement in Luzon, Visayas and northern Mindanao was often a native coadjutor.

When the Spanish friars fell from grace in late 1898 and were forced out, native and mestizo coadjutors were ready to take over their parishes. And for a brief period, they did. The Catholic faith remained intact as the changing of the guard took place. But the Filipino leadership, both secular and religious, soon faced the greatest crisis that it had ever experienced – with repercussions up to today – when the United States joined the Anglo-Saxon army of crusaders 'marching as to war,' as Hopkins so eloquently puts it, and 'treading where the saints have trod' to bring Christianity and civilisation to the world. Protestantism was 'on the march' in a campaign to create a 'world empire that has so long been waiting for it.' (366) The arrival of U.S. forces in the Philippines was to pave the way for the Protestant missionaries and teachers who would attempt to fill the void in the pueblos caused by the abrupt departure of the

Spanish friars. The meanings of 'the Philippine Revolution' would have to accommodate the clash between Anglo-Saxon Protestantism and Spanish-Filipino Catholicism that lay at the heart of the events of 1898 and the Filipino-American War that ensued.

Notes

1. 'The Unfinished Revolution in Political Discourse' (chapter 8 of Ileto, *Filipinos and their Revolution*.
2. Numbers given in brackets in the text are page references to Hopkins, *American Empire*.
3. The delineation of space in the process of pueblo formation is discussed in 'Rural Life in a Time of Revolution' (chapter 3 of Ileto, *Filipinos and their Revolution*).
4. The seminal work of Phelan, *Hispanization of the Philippines* (1967), remains an important source for this discussion of conversion to Catholicism. The discussion is raised several notches to the realm of language and translation in Rafael, *Contracting Colonialism* (1988).
5. See Ileto, Outlines of a nonlinear emplotment,' 114–9.
6. Ileto, 'Rural Life in a Time of Revolution,' 84.
7. An extensive discussion of the theory versus actual practice of the mayorship in the nineteenth-century Philippines is provided in Robles, chapter 4. However, the absence of any in-depth case study and the reliance on accounts by visiting foreigners tend to magnify the corruption and abuses by both mayors and friars. My observations about the mayor-friar relationship are derived mainly from the substantial manuscript, *Sobre queja contra el Parroco de Tiaon en Tayabas, Fr. Antonio Picayo*, in *Patronatos, 1860–1861*, Philippine National Archives. See also Ileto, *Knowledge and Pacification*, 299–302.
8. The most-thoroughly researched work arguing along these lines is May, 'Civic Ritual and Political Reality' (1989).
9. Coleman, *The Friars in the Philippines*, 37.
10. The challenge to friar and mayor alike posed by *tulisanismo* (banditry) is illustrated in detail in Isagani Medina, 'La Madre de los Ladrones' (1984). Medina's classic study is particularly germane to this article because of its focus on Cavite province, where Aguinaldo hailed from.
11. For an illustrative example of a mayor who became an exemplary revolutionary commander, see Ileto, *Knowledge and Pacification*, 30–33 and *passim*. See also Ileto, 'Rural Life.'
12. The Augustinian friar Jose Rodriguez warned against anti-Catholic pamphlets in both Spanish and Tagalog, published in Oxford and Hong Kong, illicitly entering the Philippines; *Caingat nga kayo!* (1888).
13. See Alonso (2005) and Sanchez (1991) for detailed expositions of the socio-economic features of the Filipino pueblo from the sixteenth to eighteenth centuries.
14. Ileto, *Knowledge and Pacification*, 264.
15. See McCoy's Introduction to *Lives at the Margin*.
16. Austin Craig's *Lineage, Life, and Labors of Jose Rizal* (1914) is a key text in this respect. Craig was a history professor in the newly established (1908) University of the Philippines. The 'Americanization' of Rizal was only effectively countered decades later by Guerrero's *The First Filipino* (1963).
17. 'History and Criticism: The Invention of Heroes (chapter 9 of Ileto, *Filipinos and their Revolution*, 218–37)

18. Agoncillo's *The Revolt of the Masses* (1956) is still the most stirring account of Bonifacio and the Katipunan secret society that he founded. But it also was written to legitimise the Communist-led Huk rebellion in the late 1940s. See 'The Return of Andres Bonifacio' (chapter 8 of Ileto, *Knowledge and Pacification*).
19. Although inspired by the ideals of the French Revolution, Bonifacio also inhabited the world of Tagalog metrical romances (*awit*), folk drama based on chivalric tales (*komedya*) and passion plays. See 'Bernardo Carpio: *Awit* and Revolution' (Chapter 1 of Ileto, *Filipinos and their Revolution*).
20. For a vicious and utterly dismissive portrayal of Bonifacio, see Part III of Charles Derbyshire's introduction to his translation of Rizal's *Noli me Tangere*.
21. This perspective reached its widest circulation after the publication in 1975 of Renato Constantino's *The Philippines: A Past Revisited*.
22. Saulo (1983) decries the 'American black propaganda against Aguinaldo' that began after the treacherous American refusal to allow the Filipino forces to participate in the capture of Manila in August 1898.
23. On Rizal's entrapment within the two Spains, see Sarkisyanz, *Rizal and Republican Spain*. The fracturing of Spain into liberal and conservative components sounded the death knell for the empire.
24. See Rizal's non-fictional portrayal of pueblo society from the liberal, *ilustrado* perspective in 'La verdad para todos' (31 May 1889). For a conservative, Catholic portrayal of that society, which Rizal wrote against, see Fray Miguel Lucio's *Si Tandang Basio Macunat* (1885). Though massively critiqued from anticolonial and modernist perspectives, this Franciscan narrative in Tagalog can be read against the grain to glean the sentiments of the pro-friar factions in the pueblos that were dominant prior to 1898.
25. Ileto, 'Rural Life,' 86–94.
26. 'Rizal and the Underside of Philippine History' (chapter 4 of Ileto, *Filipinos and their Revolution*)
27. For original documents on Bonifacio and the Katipunan, Richardson's *The Light of Liberty* is a treasure trove. They reveal a movement 'derived not from Catholicism or folk-Catholicism, but from masonry into which Bonifacio and many other KKK leaders had been initiated.' Richardson is particularly enthusiastic about the revelation that 'the ideals that resound loudest and clearest in the documents are the same ideals as the revolutionaries in France proclaimed in 1789 and 1848, and as were printed in large type on the certificates of the masonic lodges, the great trilogy of Liberty, Equality, and Fraternity.'
28. 'Tradition and Revolt: The Katipunan' (chapter 3 of Ileto, *Pasyon and Revolution*).
29. Font, *Filipinas: Problema Fundamental*, 12.
30. Ileto, Foreword to Angsioco (ed.), *Talang Buhay*. The same series of events is narrated elsewhere – in Agoncillo's *Revolt of the Masses*, for example – but is usually interpreted in terms of class difference or rural-urban dichotomies.
31. See Escalante, 'Collapse of the Malolos Republic' (1998) and Calairo, *Saloobin* (2019).
32. A valuable compendium of documents relating to Aguinaldo's early revolutionary career is Achutegui and Bernad, *Aguinaldo and the Revolution of 1896* (1972). It reveals, among other things, that despite a succession of Katipunan victories against Spanish forces, the Catholic Church remained intact in the pueblos of Cavite.
33. Ileto, Foreword to Angsioco (ed.), 13.
34. Anderson (1988) dismissively labels Aguinaldo and his officer corps 'caciques,' thereby emptying of meaning their resistance to American empire.
35. Del Pilar, *La Frailocracia*, 45.

36. Schumacher, *Revolutionary Clergy*, chapters 4–6. Schumacher argues that Filipino priests peacefully displaced the friars and that they represented whatever revolutionary sentiments existed among the town dwellers.
37. Corpuz, *Saga and Triumph*, chapter 12 'The Recovery of Luzon and the Revolution in the Visayas' and 13 'Self-government during the Revolution.'
38. Ileto, 'Outlines of a nonlinear emplotment,' 119–23.

Disclosure Statement

No potential conflict of interest was reported by the author(s).

References

de Achutegui, Pedro S., S. J., and Miguel A. Bernad, S. J. *Aguinaldo and the Revolution of 1896: A Documentary History*. Quezon City: Ateneo de Manila University, 1972.

Agoncillo, Teodoro A. *The Revolt of the Masses: The Story of Andres Bonifacio and the Katipunan*. Quezon City: University of the Philippines, 1956.

Alonso Alvarez, Luis. "Los señores del Barangay. La principalia indigena en las Islas Filipinas, 1565–1789: viejas evidencias y nuevas hipotesis." In *El cacicazgo en Nueva España y Filipinas*, edited by Margarita Menegus Bornemann, and Rodolfo Aguirre Salvador, 355–406. Mexico D. F.: Plaza y Valdes, S. A. de C. V., 2005.

Anderson, Benedict R. O'G. "Cacique Democracy in the Philippines: Origins and Dreams." *New Left Review* 169, no. 3 (1988): 3–31.

Angsioco, Elizabeth, ed. *Talang Buhay ng Supremo And. Bonifacio sa Kabite* (Supremo Andres Bonifacio in Cavite). Manila: National Historical Commission of the Philippines, 2020.

Calairo, Emmanuel F. *Saloobin: Mga Sagot ni Hen. Emilio Aguinaldo sa mga Paratang ng Dakilang Lumpo (Sentiments: Gen. Emilio Aguinaldo's Response to the Accusations of the Sublime Paralytic)*. Manila: National Historical Commission of the Philippines, 2019.

Coleman, Ambrose O.P. *The Friars in the Philippines*. Boston: Marlier, Callanan & Co., 1899.

Constantino, Renato. *The Philippines: A Past Revisited*. Manila: Tala Publishing Services, 1975.

Craig, Austin. *Lineage, Life, and Labors of Jose Rizal, Philippine Patriot*. Yonkers-on Hudson: World Book Company, 1914.

Corpuz, Onofre D. *Saga and Triumph: The Filipino Revolution against Spain*. Quezon City: University of the Philippines, 2002.

Del Pilar, Marcelo H. *La Frailocracia Filipina*. Barcelona: Imp. Iberica de Francisco Fossas, 1889.

Derbyshire, Charles. *The Social Cancer. A Complete English Version of Noli me Tangere from the Spanish of Jose Rizal*. Manila: Philippine Education Company, 1912.

Escalante, Rene. "Collapse of the Malolos Republic." *Philippine Studies* 46, no. 4 (1998): 452–476.

Font, Fr. Salvador O.S.A. *Filipinas: Problema Fundamental, por un Español de Larga Residencia en Aquellas Islas*. Madrid: Imp. de Don Luis Aguado.

Guerrero, Leon Maria. *The First Filipino: A Biography of Jose Rizal*. Manila: National Historical Commission, 1963.

Hopkins, A. G. *American Empire: A Global History*. Princeton University Press, 2018.

Ileto, Reynaldo Clemeña. *Filipinos and Their Revolution: Event, Discourse, and Historiography*. Quezon City: Ateneo de Manila University, 1998.

Ileto, Reynaldo Clemeña. *Knowledge and Pacification: On the U.S. Conquest and the Writing of Philippine History*. Quezon City: Ateneo de Manila University, 2017.

Ileto, Reynaldo Clemeña. "Outlines of a Nonlinear Emplotment of Philippine History." In *The Politics of Culture in the Shadow of Capital: Worlds Aligned*, edited by David Lloyd, and Lisa Lowe, 98–131. Durham, North Carolina: Duke University, 1997.

Ileto, Reynaldo Clemeña. *Pasyon and Revolution: Popular Movements in the Philippines, 1840–1910*. Quezon City: Ateneo de Manila University, 1979.

Lucio y Bustamante, Fr. Miguel O.F.M. In *Si Tandang Basio Macunat. Salitang Quinatha ni Fray Miguel Lucio y Bustamante, Religiosong Franciscano (The Elderly Basio Macunat. A Tale by Franciscan Friar Miguel Lucio y Bustamante)*. Manila: Imp. de Amigos del Pais, 1885.

May, Glenn A. "Civic Ritual and Political Reality: Municipal Elections in the Late Nineteenth Century." In *Philippine Colonial Democracy*, edited by Ruby R. Paredes, 13–40. Quezon City: Ateneo de Manila University, 1989.

May, Glenn A. *Inventing A Hero: The Posthumous Re-Creation of Andres Bonifacio*. Asian Studies: University of Wisconsin-Madison: Center for Southeast, 1997.

McCoy, Alfred W., ed. *Lives at the Margin: Biography of Filipinos Obscure, Ordinary, and Heroic*. Quezon City: Ateneo de Manila University, 2000.

Medina, Isagani R. "La Madre de los Ladrones: *Tulisanismo* in Cavite in the Nineteenth Century." *Philippine Social Sciences Review* 48, no. 1–4 (1984): 215–289.

Phelan, John L. *The Hispanization of the Philippines: Spanish Aims and Filipino Responses, 1565–1700*. Madison: The University of Wisconsin, 1967.

Rafael, Vicente L. *Contracting Colonialism: Translation and Christian Conversion in Tagalog Society under Early Spanish Rule*. Ithaca: Cornell University, 1988.

Richardson, Jim. *The Light of Liberty: Documents and Studies on the Katipunan, 1892–1897*. Quezon City: Ateneo de Manila University, 2013.

Rizal, Jose. 'La verdad para todos' (31 May 1889).. Appendix V of Marcelo Del Pilar, *La Frailocracia Filipina*, 64–72.

Robles, Eliodoro. *The Philippines in the Nineteenth Century*. Manila: Malaya Books, 1969.

Rodriguez, Fray Jose O.S.A. *Caingat Cayo! Sa mañga masasamang libro't, casulatan (All of you, Beware! Of Those Wicked Books and Pamphlets)*. Manila: Pequeña Imp. del Asilo del Huerfanos, 1888.

Saulo, Alfredo B. *Emilio Aguinaldo: Generalissimo and President of the First Philippine Republic*. Quezon City: Phoenix Press, 1983.

Sanchez Gomez, Luis Angel. *Las Principales Indigenas y La Administracion Española en Filipinas*. Madrid: Universidad Complutense de Madrid, 1991.

Sarkisyanz, Manuel. *Rizal and Republican Spain, and Other Rizalist Essays*. Manila: National Historical Institute, 1995.

Schumacher, John N., S.J. *Revolutionary Clergy; The Filipino Clergy and the Nationalist Movement, 1850–1903*. Quezon City: Ateneo de Manila University, 1981.

Restoring Asia to the Global Moment of 1898

Nicole CuUnjieng Aboitiz

ABSTRACT
This article explores the global moment surrounding 1898 to see the way in which the spectre of Japan was rapidly transforming the European imperial powers' understanding of the region and revealing to them an emerging geography of political affinity then stitching together pockets of Asia. Intra-Asian connections/affinities antedated the appearance of Western interests, were sustained during the long period of Spanish rule, and infused the anti-colonial nationalist movement that culminated in the Philippine Revolution. *American Empire: A Global History* follows most of the traditional Philippine and American literatures on the period of high imperialism in failing to acknowledge the importance of the Asian setting. While Hopkins's move to bring the larger insular American empire into a single focus is novel and deeply important, the immediate, regional Asian setting of this moment in Philippine history – and American history – should also be restored.

In 1899, the total numbers of U.S. troops in the Philippines were 40,784 enlisted men, 1412 officers, and 64 contract surgeons.[1] Karl D. White was a volunteer from Kansas in Company K of the 32nd Volunteer Infantry, which formed in response to the war. The regiment took part in the American advance of November 1899 through the main battlefields of Luzon. White's diary reveals an innocent, unconcerned attitude toward the causes for the Filipinos' fighting. The Filipinos dot White's landscape, but do not comprise it, even as he travels deep into Luzon. With the exception of the revolutionary First Philippine Republic President Emilio Aguinaldo, to whom White refers by name, the same oversight appears in White's dismissive references to the Philippine Republic's government and military. The subjectivity and interiority of White's narrative allow his account to unfold within an American worldview, consisting of American actors astride a vaguely Philippine landscape. This article seeks to fill in some of the landscape left out of view within a bilateral account of the Philippine-American encounter oriented toward the globe only through American eyes. But it also will, for a moment, linger on the singular yet emblematic diary of Karl D. White, whose unofficial, personal experience both complements traditional accounts based on the government record and allows us to experience what foreigners, particularly Americans, at times did not know and did not see, rather than merely what they did.

White's notes register no danger for the Americans. He enjoys a feeling of physical and moral security that leaves him careless and peaceful, and renders the revolutionaries who exist outside his worldview illegible and negligible. The broad categories of 'natives' and 'niggers' in which the Filipinos fit interchangeably in White's writing demonstrate the translation required for him to comprehend the Filipinos, who are undifferentiated and without their own categories. There is a certain charm to his diary, which dwells on finding 'bevs' (beverages) and catching what looks to be a catfish with an 'unsplit' tail.[2] The feeling of relative American invulnerability seems justified if one may judge as accurate his reported events of 5 November 1900: ' ... The 17th gave the niggers ned, driving them out of several towns taons [sic]. The reports of killed vary from 99 to 300 *insurrectos*. American loss 9 wounded.'[3] Taft's 1902 Statement on the 'Affairs of the Philippine Islands' would later give a similar overall confidence in American security amid confusion and uncertainty. On his visit to Samar, in the Visayas region of the archipelago, Taft wrote: 'The night before we got [to Catbalogan] ... there were shots fired into the town ... The persons who fired them disappeared, and we were not troubled when we got there, but I suppose it was a salute for us. I do not know.'[4]

Yet, the diary also offers insight into White's and his company's destabilised position in such a foreign environment. Within a string of short, blithe jottings of books read, time passed, and locations visited, the singularly long 4 April 1901 entry sits darkly and disturbingly. Deeper now in the mountains, White – as he is nowhere else in his diary – is suddenly afraid. The unfamiliar land possesses a terrifying power and incomprehensibility. White writes in hushed tones that one cannot but compare to the lucid moments of terror within the digressive, spiralling subjectivity of Marlow's narrative in Joseph Conrad's *Heart of Darkness* (1899), in which subjectivity makes impossible any stable order or morality. The points of lucid terror in White's narrative pierce false security:

> After dinner we went almost straight up an untrailbroken [sic] mountain side & then followed a slowly descending trail which crossed our forenoons line of march then turned again toward the heart of the mountains & camped that night clear back away from where there were any signs of civilization. 'The great what is it' howled till the mountains rang but we never knew what it was and those not on guard just laid still & trusted the guards & the guards just kept still and shook in their boots. During the day we passed several little shacks with new made & unfinished lug-nut boats all around them but the niggers had all left the camps before we got there. In

one place we burnt a small shack with a suspicious look to it & examined a near-by grave ... Tuesday ... Lawrence & Sharp (as with me) were awake all night & knew every move I made during my 'hours on.' They said the 'what is it' howled again but I didn't hear it.[5]

A kind of analogue of the 'great what is it' appears in Marlow's account. 'The earth seems unearthly,' Conrad writes; 'We are accustomed to look upon the shackled form of a conquered monster, but there – there you could look at a thing monstrous and free.'[6]

Are these American men 'performing acts of imperial mastery and will' in the Philippines, as Edward Said asks of the men of *Heart of Darkness*?[7] The 'great what is it' sits uncomfortably outside White's view, unincorporated and unbroken by his presence. Here, we see the flimsiness of the US's claim of immediate and absolute sovereignty, which, while enjoying the force of international law, remains alien and unproven in a foreign land the Americans have yet barely penetrated and whose contents they do not know. As Said says of Conrad, whose narrative is carefully delimited through the narrator's subjectivity in order to underscore its circularity, 'He allows us simultaneously to realize after all that imperialism, far from swallowing up its own history, was taking place in and was circumscribed by a larger history.'[8] In the light of day, in secured towns, one sees the US's potential destructive capacities in White's diary through oblique glances. This perspectival distance and unconcern mirror the easy, careless destruction it describes – casual and unremarkable: 'found "bevs" some of them got drunk & got their quarters on fire so when we got there about 1/3 of the town was in ruins.'[9] To White, Filipino violence is a minor nuisance and the sole cause of American violence, which is portrayed as retaliatory or defensive, with a presumption of American innocence.

Anthony G. Hopkins's brilliant, expansive book, *American Empire: A Global History*, panoramic as it is, manages even within such scope to register succinctly the fitful, un-masterly American imperial rule in the Philippines, of the kind that Edward Said and Joseph Conrad underline, all the while keeping alive this question of American innocence, or rather, intention. Hopkins advances still further by combining the perspectives and histories of the indigenous and imperial actors in a single frame, while at the same time stitching together the discrepant histories of the 'insular empire' to restore their legibility and visibility within a holistic understanding of American empire and its comparative place within global history. Proceeding from the perspective of the Philippines, however, the understanding of the tumultuous turn of the twentieth century, pivotal as it is for imperial and global history, lacks in Hopkins's narrative acknowledgment of the setting of Asia, as it also does in the majority of the traditional Philippine and American literatures on this period. The full realities – of a distant shore in a larger, longer, separate history – can be lost if one deracinates the Philippines as another set of islands to be plucked and abstracted onto an imperial landscape. Further, doing so leaves one unequipped to understand aspects unrecognisably outside one's known perspectives, keeping the great, howling 'what is it' ever beyond sight.

To focus on the Asian context to Philippine history runs counter to the traditional assumption of the literature: that the Filipino self-image is historically non-Asian – seeing itself as belonging, instead, to the Western hemisphere. It also runs counter to a general historiographical treatment of the Philippines within Asia as a thing apart – more like Latin America than like its Southeast Asian neighbours.[10] Indeed, internationalisation and globalisation of Philippine history has generally occurred along imperial lines, analysing it with/against the former Western imperial powers or the former colonies of Spain and the US, such as Puerto Rico.[11] While Hopkins's move to bring the larger insular American empire into a single focus is novel and deeply important, the immediate, regional Asian setting of this moment in Philippine history – and American history – should also be restored. The Philippine archipelago has long been part of the larger Malay world, and it remained so even under the Spanish crown, as well as being a participant in trade with Chinese merchants dating as far back as the second century CE. James Francis Warren has described, meanwhile, the later trading zone of *prahu* (a large native sailing ship) centred on the Sulu sultanate in Jolo in the Muslim south of the Philippines as part of the larger Malay world – until the 1870–1900 Spanish naval campaign that decimated all prahu shipping there. The Sulu sultanate had grown in wealth and power by taking advantage of the European desire to trade with China, providing the British, beginning in the late 1700s, with Malay sea and jungle products, which the British could trade for Chinese tea. The 'Sulu Zone' expanded and contracted according to the sultan's hold over outlying chiefs, but at its peak it included the east coast of Borneo (now parts of Malaysia and Indonesia), as well as the Sulu archipelago and the west and south coasts of Mindanao, in today's Philippines.[12] Indeed, by the time of the arrival of the Spanish in the sixteenth century, the archipelago had already long engaged in trade with Siam, Cambodia, India, the Moluccas, China, and Japan.

In Hopkins's history, Japan figures as a comparative 'late-start' colonial power, as an adversary in the wings in the Pacific from the interwar period until World War II, and as a combatant turned Western ally through the World War II period and into the Cold War remaking of international society. But its presence and importance in the Philippines begins earlier, and highlights the Asian setting to the dying days of the Spanish empire in the Pacific, to the imperial world stage that had swallowed the region at the turn of the twentieth century, and to the anti-colonial nationalist Propaganda Movement and Philippine Revolution, all of which have too often been understood through bilateral accounts privileging relations between Asian countries and the West. Intra-Asian connections/affinities antedated the appearance of

Western interests, were sustained during the long period of Spanish rule, and infused the anti-colonial nationalist movement that culminated in the Philippine Revolution. Hopkins alludes briefly to this when he mentions that in 1897 during the Philippine Revolution Aguinaldo:

> cut a deal with the Spanish authorities that took him into voluntary exile in Hong Kong, leaving others to continue the armed struggle. At that moment, the treaty ports were in ferment, anti-Manchu nationalists were gathering, and Japan had just emerged as a major power in East Asia. Japanese pan-Asian groups gave Aguinaldo moral, and possibly financial, support as he reorganized his supporters.[13]

Thereafter, Japan figures centrally during this pivotal turn of the century moment with regard to Hawai'i rather than to the Philippines[14] and the brief picture of a roiling, transforming Asia recedes. The Philippines's location within Asia, as opposed to only the Pacific, indirectly enters Hopkins's narrative through US government officials and strategists' alternating reluctance/need to make one or another decision due to geopolitical calculus vis-à-vis Japan[15] – but even then, this calculus is only lightly sketched.

My work has sought to restore the Philippines to the Southeast Asian and East Asian histories from which it has been historiographically separated. My book *Asian Place, Filipino Nation* charts the emplotment of 'place' in the proto-national thought and revolutionary organising of turn-of-the-twentieth-century Filipino thinkers, and how their Pan-Asian political organising and their constructions of the place of 'Asia' and of the spatial registers of race/Malayness connected them to their regional neighbours undertaking the same work. This is precisely the point that Hopkins notes regarding transnational Japanese Pan-Asian collaboration in the Philippine Revolution. Here, however, I wish to concentrate on the global moment surrounding 1898 to see the way in which, even for the established European imperial powers of the region and their on-the-ground functionaries and missionaries, the spectre of Japan, an Asian contestant to modern world power, was rapidly transforming their understanding of the region they bestrode – and revealing to them an emerging geography of political affinity then stitching together pockets of Asia. Unlike Karl D. White's ignorance, it was not only the top-level 'official minds' of the European powers that could 'see' Asia, but also their constitutive emissaries on the ground, for which reason I incorporate into this article diaries, notes, and correspondence sources that buttress accounts based largely on official government records. In this way, I seek to complement Anthony Hopkins's global account and to underscore the importance of the place of Asia therein, which has been put aside in favour of other transnational comparisons. In that way we may begin to see this imperial history alongside the 'larger history' Said mentions.

Power in the Pacific, Spanish Anxieties, and the Asian Geography of Anti-colonial Subversion

The international sphere in Asia in the late nineteenth century, as in many other parts of the world, was a 'meeting place of empires,' rather than a 'society of nations,' with the multitude of abutting empires with ever growing global interests tending towards a continuously redefined equilibrium.[16] Yet, as the imperial powers watchfully monitored this shifting status quo, the possibility of war was ever-present. The Spanish-American War of 1898 and the rise of Japan, particularly following the defeat of China in the Sino-Japanese War (1894–1895), were two such moments of challenge that redefined the Asian status quo and were of prime importance to the Philippines and all the powers who coveted the islands.

The 1868 Meiji Restoration and concomitant period of reforms had dismantled the Tokugawa shogunate and much of the country's prevailing political-economic system. The reforms included: abolishing the *han* system of 'feudal' domains; installing a centralised, unitary, bureaucratic state; reforming the tax system to stabilise the national budget; promulgating a constitution and creating a modern bureaucracy; and levelling old forms of official class privileges toward creating a modern citizenry, alongside other social and industrialising changes. Japan had also reopened full channels of foreign commerce, thereby ending the *sakoku* ('locked country') policy restrictions on Japanese travel, foreign trade, and foreign relations. These restrictions had lasted from shogun Tokugawa Iemitsu's edicts in 1633–1639 to American Commodore Matthew Perry's forced opening of Japan to wide Western trade in 1853 and 1854. Yet, Asian anti-colonial and nationalist observers, particularly in Southeast Asia, admired what they often interpreted to be Japan's selective or, even, performative modernisation – acquiring Western exterior forms while maintaining distinctive, Japanese culture and modes as foundation. In the 1880s Japan was still testing itself on the world stage; it would not be until 1899 that the country was in a position to begin revising the terms of the unequal foreign treaties it had signed with the Western imperial powers, which had symbolically designated Japan as a second-class state in the international order.

It took twenty years to regularise relations between Spain and Japan following the Meiji Restoration, with negotiations and exploratory activities leading to the opening of a Japanese Consulate in Manila in 1888; the establishment of reciprocal direct (though irregular) shipping lines between Japan and Manila;[17] the opening of a branch of the Imperial Insurance Company in Manila; and an overall increase in the low-level trade between Filipinas[18] and Japan. This trade was small, however, and on 26 November 1893, the Japanese closed the Manila Consulate and transferred its duties to the Hong Kong Consulate for three years.[19] Nevertheless, 1889–1898 saw a significant increase in Japan-Philippines trade, due to Japanese purchase of Philippine products. As

Josefa Saniel records, 'the total trade between the two countries increased at a rapid pace from 251,114 yen in 1889 to 3,409,616 yen in 1898. The yearly imports from the Philippines advanced from 227,486 yen in 1889 to 3,294,183 yen in 1898.' Yet, despite the increase, 'from 1889 to 1898, Japan's trade with the Philippines, except in 1894, remained less than 1% of Japan's total trade for each of the calendar years included.'[20]

As early as the 1880s and 1890s, some Japanese nationalists advocated territorial expansion to Filipinas as a solution to their country's geopolitical and domestic problems. Those whose gaze fixed so far south were outliers, however, with most who advocated an 'all Asian consciousness' largely working in Korea and China. Nevertheless, Asianists such as Miyazaki Tōten were already discovering how the definition of 'Asia' was extending outward, and eventually 'peripheral' Southeast Asians would effect a reconsideration of what was considered 'Asia' within the imagined 'Pan-Asia.'[21] By 1891, and with the consent of the Western Treaty Powers, Japan had successfully laid claim to various island groups, including the Bonin Islands (Ogasawarajima), the Ryūkyūs, the Kurile Islands (Chishima), and the Volcano Islands (Iwojima). While these islands were annexed under the domestic administration of Japan, without inaugurating a colonial framework of governance, this territorial expansion brought Japan physically and politically closer to the prospect of overseas colonial acquisition.[22] Indeed, the 1891 annexation of the Volcano Islands caused a momentary stir in Madrid, followed in February 1892 by the arrival of Japanese warships in Manila.[23] Japanese activities in the early 1890s in the Spanish Pacific island holdings of the Marianas and Carolinas also caused anxiety, and Japan's occupation (and eventual colonisation) of Formosa (Taiwan) following victory in the Sino-Japanese War appeared threatening to the Spanish. This was particularly perceived due to the publication of Japanese opinions in favour of expansion to Filipinas as well as Japanese attention to the challenges Spanish rule was then encountering in its Pacific colonies.[24] Fukumoto Makoto (writing under the name Fukumoto Nichinan) published articles in *Nippon* on the 1890 uprisings in the Carolinas and the retaliatory Spanish military expeditions, and on native uprisings unreported in the *Official Gazette* and other Manila newspapers, such as those in Jolo in 1890 and in Morong, Manila, and Bulacan, as well as an attack on a Franciscan church near the Pasig River in 1891.[25] A Spanish translation of Fukumoto Nichinan's article on Japan and the Southern Seas ('Nihon to nanyō') reached the Spanish Legation in Japan in May 1890; it urged the Japanese government to prevent Filipinas from falling under the possession of a powerful empire such as Germany, to the danger of Japan's southern border, and it assumed Spanish military weakness as a fact.[26]

Japan's victory in the Sino-Japanese War redrew the West's attention to the balance of power in Asia, and the Spanish press played up the 'Japanese phantom,' with dramatic editorial comments predicting 'a beautiful future of simultaneous war in Cuba, [and] Filipinas' to the effect that 'the government of the restoration may write on the ruins of the Spanish nation the historic epitaph, *Finis Hispanae*.'[27] In the wake of the Sino-Japanese War, Spain took the precaution of concluding a treaty locating the territorial boundaries between the Japanese and Spanish territories in the Pacific, constructing naval facilities in Subic Bay in Zambales, and increasing the military forces and number of Spanish cruisers in the colony.[28] By 2 October 1896, the liberal, Spanish daily newspaper *El Imparcial*'s front page featured the article 'Filipinas – Cuestión Palpitante: Lo Urgentísimo' darkly warning the Spanish public of a petition supposedly delivered to the Foreign Relations Minister of the Japanese Empire and signed by 'more than twenty thousand Filipinos' requesting Japan's annexation of Filipinas.[29] There were also rumours that a few Japanese were implicated in the outbreak of the Philippine Revolution in Manila.[30] Consul Shimizu, Chargé d'affaires in Hong Kong, was sent to Manila to verify these rumours and to consult with the German Consul in Manila, Lieutenant Spetz, whom Tokyo had requested to protect the Japanese and their interests in Manila.[31] Shimizu established over a two-week Philippine trip from 26 September to 7 October 1896 that the Japanese in Manila, who were 'all peaceful merchants,' as he recorded in his report to Vice-Minister of Foreign Affairs Komura Jutarō, were in no way involved in the Philippine Revolution, though he noted the native people's admiration for Imperial Japan.[32] The rumours of Japanese involvement in the revolution betray the peculiar power that the spectre of Japan then held, particularly given that, according to Shimizu's report, only nine Japanese were in Manila at the time.[33]

In 1896 the Catholic religious orders in the Philippines furnished the new Spanish Gobernador General del Archipielago, Camilo de Polavieja, with their notes on the lead up to the Philippine Revolution, which broke in late August 1896. Reports of Japan's looming and actual threat recur repeatedly throughout the pages. A report from 24 July 1896 described how the *indios* (natives) rejoiced at the sight of the wrappers of a tobacco company, La Batalla, which was adorned with pictures of Japanese soldiers and Japanese battleships.[34] The orders considered these a form of propaganda that strengthened both Spain's enemies in the islands and the ignorant indio masses' respect for military power – dangerously, that of Japan.[35] The head of the Guardia Civil Veterana, the urban gendarmerie force of Manila, in his 28 October 1896 notes to the Spanish representatives in Singapore, meanwhile, described the empire of Japan as grasping the 'laurels of such easy victory' against China and now attempting to 'exert its dominance in the West.'[36] He relayed the information that Andrés Bonifacio, the revolutionary leader who founded the Katipunan which began the Philippine Revolution, intended to contact the Japanese government and that the Filipinos followed the Spanish setbacks in Cuba with great interest and satisfaction, hoping Japan would play in the archipelago the role that the United States was then playing in the Antilles.[37] The reports of the Franciscan Order to Polavieja echoed these same observations, adding that many of the best known Filipino separatists moved to Yokohama after the Japanese victory in the Sino-Japanese War in 1895, while still more made frequent trips there.[38]

Though the writer Carlos Recur had remarked in 1879 that 'from the commercial point of view the Philippines is an Anglo-Chinese colony flying a Spanish flag,'[39] toward the close of the nineteenth century, Spain reimposed protectionist duties such that, 'before the final eclipse of Spanish power, the Iberian rulers ... wrested from the formidable foreign capitalists a measure of economic self-respect,' as Filomenio V. Aguilar writes in Clash of Spirits.[40] Indeed, in the 1880s, Spain had imagined itself humiliated and dismissed by foreigners observing its inability to direct its subject population and exert full rule over the islands. It was this concern that led to the new colonisation programme, *reducción de infieles*, which sought to subdue the Philippine interior, highlands, and marginal elements subverting Spanish sovereignty. The *reducción* and renewed protectionism had multiple audiences. There was a steady flow of foreigners into the 'international colony,' who seemingly needed to be reminded of Spanish sovereignty. Not only foreigners needed reminding: Josefa Saniel records that during the late 1860s to early 1870s Chancellor Otto von Bismarck entertained but ultimately refused the Sultan of Sulu's request for German protectorate status over the southern region of Filipinas as well as a second similar overture from an Austrian national, Baron von Overbeck, who owned interests in northern Borneo.[41]

Indeed, the presence of the 'international' – references to the larger, geopolitical framework of power that ordered the world – in local Visayan millenarian imaginings illustrated the transnationalised setting in which ideas of social regeneration and, later, anti-colonial revolution evolved in the Philippines. In Matuguinao, on Samar island in the Visayas region, rumours spread in 1883 that there was a new king named Conde Leynes, and that a German steamship would arrive in Catbalogan to declare that Spain did not own the Visayas Islands.[42] In 1887 in Zamboanguita in Negros Oriental, Ponciano Elopre, known as Dios Buhawi ('God Waterspout') announced himself as God, freed his followers from the obligation to pay tribute to the Spanish government, and organised an upland regime.[43] The prelude to the revolution therefore featured a double confrontation within the international colony, as Spain attempted to rearticulate its sovereignty to meet foreign capitalists' symbolic and material challenges to Spanish power[44] and as Filipino ilustrados, revolutionaries, millenarians, and southern Muslims increasingly turned toward and pinned their political protests on foreign intercession, liberal international rhetoric, and, later, transnational Asianist political support.

The reports of the religious orders and the colonial Spanish government based in Filipinas betray a long preoccupation with Japan, particularly with its allure as a model and potential ally. The Guardia Civil, the Spanish colonial civil guard, reported in 1895 that such Japan-centred Asianist thinking was fashionable in the archipelago and that its inhabitants, 'dreaming of [Japan's] protection and support' and as a 'model of culture, wealth, liberty, and strength,' 'directed their efforts uselessly to Japan,' such that 'Doroteo Cortes, with that Ramos, Basa, Español, and others' emigrated to Yokohama and established a separatist commission there in correspondence with Manila.[45] This commission was known as the Hong Kong Committee. The religious orders' and colonial government's notes were also preoccupied with Japan and Hong Kong's roles as central Asian sites enabling the safe haven and growth of anti-colonial subversion in Filipinas.

The reports incanted the place names regularly, almost as a refrain, keeping up a beat of suspicion and perceived threat. 'It is known that [Alcantara who was thought to be in Japan but actually resides in Hong Kong] fled to Hong Kong with Langay in the ship "Sum Kiang" with the money and protection of the [Free] Masons,' read one typical report from the religious orders on 7 May 1896. 'In Hong Kong he sees Doroteo Cortes daily and confers with him.'[46] Another from 17 April 1896 enjoined the colonial government to intercept the correspondence and verify the registry papers of known subversives; it read: 'Villareal is a furious Mason, he is actually in Japan. Ramos, owner of the old shop "La Gran Bretaña" is actually in Japan.'[47] The Guardia Civil asserted in an 1896 report that in Manila, Filipinos frequently embarked for Japan under 'the pretexts of recreational, instructional, or artistic trips, but that are in reality for them to conspire.'[48] Hong Kong and Japan recurred repeatedly in the reports as regular destinations of the Filipino Propagandists, Masons, and *laborantes* in their political travels, and an official 1897 report to the Ministerio de Ultramar urged its consideration of the appointment of more police agents 'in the neighbouring colonies and particularly in Hong Kong, whose consulate it may be viewed as appropriate to elevate to the level of Consulate General.'[49] Later, on 3 January 1898, a further report expounded on the importance of the foreign police and foreign intelligence: 'It should be necessary in certain points [sic], Singapore, (?), Yokohama, and Hong Kong, but in the latter it is essential, I am considering this of capital importance.'[50]

Japanese cities (particularly Yokohama, but also Kobe) and Hong Kong were crucial nodes in the region's geography of revolution – a geography whose insidious effect was imagined as covering 'the neighbouring colonies and Japan' in the religious orders' and the Spanish government's suspicions.[51] The Guardia Civil reported that the proto-revolutionary association La Liga had an important delegation in Hong Kong headed by Yldefonso Laurel.[52] A 2 May 1896 report from the religious orders to Gobernador General Polavieja recommended arranging with Spain's representative in Japan to monitor the movements of the Filipinos residing in that country and making the same recommendation to the consuls in Hong Kong, Singapore, Saigon, and Shanghai, the transit points and organising grounds where local authorities should stay abreast of the potential Filipino agitators' actions.[53] A member of the Propaganda Movement was reported in the religious orders' notes from 6 July 1896 as changing his name three times and boarding the ship the *Eleano* for Singapore and from there sailing to Saigon and Hong Kong, under the last name Lapati.[54] The notes recorded that 'while living in Hong Kong,' Lapati, who reportedly sought to reproduce in the Philippines the bloody separatist war of Cuba, 'came to know all the Filipinos there.'[55] This tone and broad generalisation demonstrate the particular suspicion reserved for Hong Kong and what it meant for Filipinos to reside there. The same presumption of suspicion applied to Japan. 'One should not forget,' warned a report from the religious orders on 2 May 1896, 'that given the way in which the aforementioned Señor [repeatedly] leaves the Archipelago for abroad, it is certain that he is going to Japan to conspire against Spain.'[56] The religious orders' notes from 1 June 1896 recorded the rumours that the Propagandists – 'Cortes, Ramos, Luna, Zamora, del Pilar, Villarroel, Agoncillo, Lecaroz (?) and other Filipinos who are in Japan' – had delivered a memorandum to the Government of Mikado requesting protection for the revolutionaries.[57] Further, it cited that the Central Junta of the Propagandists not only had established itself in Japan, but had also purchased a merchant ship to sail from Japan to Manila and Iloilo to bring the separatist cause home.[58]

The cities of Hong Kong and Yokohama were safety valves – cosmopolitan cities in which Asian subversives could act with greater political freedom as well as cities in which they imagined richer alternative lives counter to their colonial conditions. It was for this latter reason that Propagandist and future national hero José Rizal desired to set up a school for Filipinos in Hong Kong or Japan, just as the anti-colonial nationalist scholar-gentry hero Phan Bội Châu would for the Vietnamese in 1905. To the Spanish, Hong Kong was a site outside their effective surveillance and the nearest locus of subversive thought and activity for their Southeast Asian colony, which sat within a crisscrossed network of Asian revolutionary activity that also crucially included Singapore, Saigon, and Yokohama. The Subsecretario del Ministerio de Ultramar forwarded a letter from Hong Kong to the Ministerio de Estado on 21 November 1892 about the disturbing and vicious attacks in that colony's press (appearing in the *Hong Kong Telegraph* since July 1892) against the Gobernador General de Filipinas and the Catholic religious orders, as well as a piece in *Truth* on 20 October 1892 arguing in favour of Rizal following his arrest (deemed 'a disgrace to the Spanish and clerical authorities concerned').[59] Yet, on this matter, the Spanish Consul in Hong Kong could only lament that, alas 'the press is free here.'[60] Beyond Hong Kong, Gobernador General Blanco also diligently sent full accounts of the revolutionary proceedings in Cavite to the Spanish representative in Singapore. Additionally, notices and copies of the *Straits Times* articles of 30 June and 4 July 1857 on the uprising in British India, along with a detailed handwritten list of the regiments involved therein, were included in the Spanish imperial military's files on the Philippine Revolution. It seems that the relevant instances of anti-imperial subversion and its models drew from a long memory and was interpreted very widely indeed.

The religious orders' notes from 30 June 1896 alerted the Spanish government to a further twist to the purported Japanese connection, and underscored Spanish paranoia regarding the Japanese threat. This reported connection was based on a lengthy interview conducted with an indio purportedly well acquainted with the prevailing rumours and discussions in (unspecified) Masonic lodges. The leaders of the lodges were reportedly telling their members that Spain would soon have a war with Japan, and that the Japanese were already said to be building up arms to be able to attack Filipinas by land and sea.[61] Whether or not these pronouncements were actually made in the lodges, the orders' repetition of these rumours reveals Spanish fears. The religious orders also noted that the Katipunan periodical, *Kalayaan*, was published in Yokohama and smuggled from there to Manila. This was not in fact true and was a calculated ruse on the part of the Katipunan, whose revolution and society both had a strong international consciousness. The place name of 'Yokohama' conjured the spectre of transnational activism and subversion, and was used strategically to encourage membership growth through its symbolic power, as the Katipunan itself admitted. The religious orders' notes also dutifully listed indios who were discovered to own books from El Bazar Japonés, a fact noted with due suspicion, because, as the 30 April 1896 note recorded, El Bazar Japonés, situated in the Plaza del P. Moraga, seemed 'to be merely a pretext,' for 'in reality they say that it is the subversive centre where a great number of disaffected come to change impressions, sustain the propaganda, and receive letters, papers, and instructions that come from Japan and other places.'[62] The possession of literature from Hong Kong could similarly conjure conspiracies in the eyes of the Spanish state, as in the case of the April 1889 arrest of certain indios from Tondo against whom suspicion of rebellion had been 'reinforced by the seizure of printed matter from Hong Kong.'[63] The Guardia Civil similarly reported that a Japanese corvette warship, the *Kongo*, had arrived in Manila Bay in May 1895 without any explanation for its sudden appearance, and was 'mysteriously visited and entertained by a commission of Filipinos in El Bazar Japonés, where they stayed.'[64] The Guardia Civil report then qualified this notation, writing later, in a reflection on the precursors to the revolution: 'coincidences, perhaps, but alert!'[65]

Japan held the same mix of allure and subversion for the Vietnamese scholar-gentry. Several associations encouraging studies abroad, known as the Khuyến Du Học Hội, existed in the Mekong Delta area, many of which were influenced by Phan Bội Châu.[66] Phan Bội Châu's own Đông Du (Go East) Movement successfully brought Vietnamese youth to study in Japan from 1905 to 1909. Similar associations also appeared in China, following the Sino-Japanese War, sending Chinese youth to study in Japan.[67] José Rizal had also envisioned such a school in Hong Kong or Japan for Filipino youth. With regard to the Vietnamese movement, at first Châu had had a difficult time securing funding and found few applicants to his study programme in Japan; he returned to Japan in October 1905 to consult with his friend Liang Qichao for strategic advice.[68] Liang advised him to write a pamphlet; Châu penned 'Khuyến Quốc Dân Tư Trợ Du Học Văn' (Encouragement to Citizens to Contribute for Overseas Study), and Liang published 3000 copies for him for free.[69] 'In Japan we can be educated as free men,' the pamphlet declared. 'Five hundred families should put their money together and send one student.'[70] Interestingly, another pamphlet written by a Catholic priest living in Tokyo, Mai Lão Bạng, targeted Catholics in southern Vietnam. The pamphlet, 'Facitie in Dei Gloriam' (Act for the Glory of God) enjoined them to go to Japan to imitate the example of Joan of Arc, blending the symbolic power of both Japan and France in a single appeal.[71]

There is a growing body of scholarship on Japanese writings on the Philippines in this period,[72] often highlighting the dimension of fantasy and imagination involved in Japanese territorial expansion as well as in Pan-Asianism, which resonates more broadly with the literature on the role of ideology in Japanese empire building.[73] Suehiro Tetchō, a political novelist, Pan-Asianist, and, later, a member of the first House of Representatives of the Japanese Diet, famously met José Rizal aboard the SS *Belgic* in 1888. Although Suehiro Tetchō had never been to the Philippines, he wrote a book that has been studied extensively in this Pan-Asian Japanese-Philippine context: *Nanyō no Daiharan* (Storm over the South Seas). It was written in 1891, before the Philippine Revolution and before the Sino-Japanese War, and it actively constructed concepts of independence and revolution, alongside three other of his works that drew a picture of oppressed islands in revolt against the West.[74] Similarly, Bimyō Yamada translated portions of Rizal's landmark Spanish colonial critique *Noli Me Tangere* into Japanese, published as *Chino no Namida* (Bloody tears) in 1903, and published *Aguinaldo*, a novel on the Philippine Revolution, in 1902. Shunrō Oshikawa published *Bukyō no Nihon* (Japanese chivalry) and *Shin Nihontō* (New Japanese islands) in 1902 and 1906, respectively. These were adventure stories aimed at young Japanese boys that depicted a courageous Japanese samurai named Kentōji Danbara fighting alongside General Emilio Aguinaldo against Spain and the United States.[75] As Hiromu Shimizu has analysed, the discourses on Japanese expansion to the South Seas drew on phenomena such as Japanese migration to the Philippines and Filipino-Japanese intermarriage to 'solve contradictions between the Filipinos' and Japanese's interests' by imaginatively bridging imperial territorial expansion and independence through fictive kinship ties.[76] Taken together, affect, common history (against the West), and regional geography would reconstruct a broader category of race that could encompass the Filipino and Japanese under one banner. Indeed, these aspects plus that of material aid crucially comprised the Pan-Asianism of the colonised 'periphery' of Asia, outside the closely connected Sinic world.[77] Miyazaki Tōten was not only devoted to Sun Yat-sen, Kang Yu-wei, and China's revolutionary movement, but was also among the Japanese who would come to work closely with Propagandist ilustrado and later First Philippine Republic Foreign Emissary to Japan Mariano Ponce to procure arms for the First Philippine Republic. Japanese supporters would also eventually travel to the Philippines to help train the revolutionary army.[78]

All Eyes on Deck – Imperial Spectators at the Blockade of Manila Bay

'The Philippines represents a jewel which no power in the Far East would accept to see reunited with a possible rival in that part of the world,' wrote French Lieutenant Aimé-Ernest Motsch in his diary on 26 July 1898, quoting an 'English journalist.'[79] For his own part, on 17 May 1898, Motsch wrote: 'An incomparable strategic situation now exists. Manila is the key to the Far East, being the geometric center from which all places radiate where colonies are of utmost importance to the powers with interest in the Pacific.'[80] More specifically,

> With Manila as the center, having a radius equal to five days at sea, one can establish a circumference consisting of all the important commercial routes and all the trade between the north of Asia and the south of Europe, the Far East, Australia, and the United States.[81]

This was the context that drew the Western and Japanese imperial powers to Manila Bay for three months, watching while the fate of the Philippine Revolution and the subtle equilibrium of imperial power in Asia hung in limbo amid the Spanish-American War. The U.S. Navy's success in the 1 May 1898 Battle of Manila Bay, when the American Asiatic Squadron under Commodore George Dewey destroyed the Spanish Pacific Squadron under Admiral Patricio Montojo, led to the blockade of Manila Bay. The European powers present, who were materially stronger than Spain and had the luxury of observing the events unfold from a certain remove, followed the Spanish-American War with an eye to the balance of power in Europe and the Philippine Revolution with an eye to their own Asian colonies.

Motsch's diary recorded the existence of something like a pan-European imperial shield, evidenced in conversations amongst the Europeans in Manila and in Manila Bay. This shield and this idea of 'Europe' safeguarded the balance of power amongst the imperial rulers, and Motsch intimated that it was this shield, which was an uneasy mix of lust for conquest and relative gain, alongside a twin desire to direct the imperial club toward the European 'moral' and geopolitical interest, that was present there in Manila Bay aboard the naval ships. The 'most notable Frenchman in Manila,' titled 'Mr.

Commander' in Motsch's notes, apparently discussed this shield with the lieutenant. 'Do you realize that the European powers will be endangered if the Americans take possession of the Philippines?' Motsch asked him on 7 May 1898. To this 'unreasonable assumption' Mr. Commander replied, 'That's impossible! No, that will never be so. We will never permit it. I firmly believe that the Philippines is destined to rot under the Spaniards.'[82] Indeed, such a change in the balance of power seemed unthinkable to the two Frenchmen. By 21 May 1898, Motsch judged 'Europe's intervention' as 'imminent at this point.'[83] He considered England's stated impartiality and its likely support of the United States and its own interests 'at the expense of further weakening the already fragile moral unity of Europe' to be unforgivable.[84] The existence of a 'Europe' with agency and of the easy use of the pronoun 'we' when discussing the actions of its constituent members is striking in these judgments.

This pan-European imperial shield may have been more of an instrumentalised ideal than a reality, however. It was something to be invoked by those at a comparative disadvantage, but never by those with the advantage. By May 24, Motsch was already lamenting its non-existence, reflecting that there was no European moral unity nor meaningful safeguarding of European interests, at least as they were interpreted by the French. 'What naiveté in believing that the powerful nations are keeping their ships anchored around the bay in order to make sure that the interests of Europe are respected! No one sees beyond that. Policies instigated are just a matter of expediency;' he continued, 'the powerful nations are waiting for the predictable result of the struggle. Their jealousies and conflicts have merely made victory easier for the United States ... The reality is that there is no alliance.'[85] How quickly Motsch himself moved from championing moral unity on May 21 to resigning himself to the realities of the situation on May 24.

> Since Europe, torn apart by conflicting interests, can no longer control events, she then should at least try to enjoy whatever benefits are available. Under the pretext of taking the Spanish cause in hand, she should convene a political meeting and, like Hamlet, feast on the carcass and enrich herself in knowledge.[86]

This must have been a thin understanding of collective interest and concert action, indeed, or, rather, an understanding that nevertheless held at its core the premise of competitive imperial expansion.

Of this international community, in contrast to the Spanish reports, Motsch registered no immediate threat from Japan in terms of territorial interest in the Philippines. He wrote casually:

> All the economic reason which keep us on the alert in China oblige us to maintain an equal vigilance in the Philippines ... Japan, which is next door to Formosa, will merely demonstrate a mild interest, but Great Britain, which has the largest commercial involvement in the Philippines, naturally represents an element of considerable weight.[87]

Motsch repeatedly mentioned the Japanese in this tone – casually and without the fear or racial hatred exhibited in the writing of others, such as the Spanish.

> In the bay, we see the English who seem to be well positioned beside Admiral Dewey's squadron, the Germans giving the impression that they have a strategy, the Japanese who come and go, and the French who wait, observing, fully aware that their presence will not influence the coming events.

Motsch wrote on 29 May 1898 when the American blockade of Manila was a month old.[88] Despite the lack of fear or threat that Motsch interpreted the Japanese to pose, he counted them naturally and rather unremarkably as one of the powers that formed the audience for France's presence there and among which France was situated. On 6 May 1898 Motsch compared all the ships in Manila Bay against one another, cataloguing their assets and dimensions, of which the French *Bruix* he judged to be 'undeniably ... the most imposing of them all,' for 'France would not send unworthy ships to parts of the world where the strength of their fleet is weighed against that of others.'[89] He continued, 'I hope the *Bruix* stays in the Orient long enough to show its prowess in China, Japan, and other countries. For political as well as economic reasons, we should have our presence felt everywhere.'[90]

On the other side of the pan-European shield, meanwhile, 'several rumors also circulated, some of them very disconcerting to Dewey,' Luis Camara Dery notes, who noted that the Germans had come to Manila Bay in aid of the Spanish.[91] O.D. Corpuz reported that of all the spectating powers present at Manila Bay, only the Germans failed to observe the rules of the blockade, particularly the right of the blockading power to board ships, which was a right of freedom of movement in preparedness for hostile operations.[92] The German government had sent Vice-Admiral von Diedrichs's squadron to Manila Bay despite declared neutrality to pursue the viability of the three policy options – German protectorate, international partition, or joint neutralisation of the archipelago – that the German cabinet had presented to the Kaiser on 14 May 1898.[93] A few days following the conclusion of the Battle of Manila Bay, the German Consul in Manila communicated to his superiors in Berlin the possible Filipino welcome of a German protectorate status.[94] This was taken seriously enough that the German government promptly sent a ranking official, von Diedrichs, to Manila to determine the situation and sentiment there in this regard.[95] During the Germans' stay, Commodore George Dewey noted: '... Not only did the German officers frequently visit the Spanish troops and outposts, thus familiarizing themselves with the environs of Manila, but a Prince Lowenstein was taken off the *Kaiserin Augusta* by one of Aguinaldo's staff.' Moreover, 'German man-of-war boats took soundings off Malabon and the mouth of the Pasig River, and German seamen were sent to occupy the lighthouse at the mouth of the Pasig for some days.' They 'landed their men for drill at Mariveles harbour ... and took possession at the quarantine station, while Admiral Diedrichs occupied a large house which had been the quarters of the Spanish officials ... '[96]

Indeed, Dery's research shows that, in 'Senate Document No. 62' dated 18 July 1898, the American Consul in Hong Kong Rounseville Wildman attested to his superiors in Washington that the Germans approached Aguinaldo with 'tempting offers.'[97] Wildman additionally informed Washington of reported German efforts to purchase Palawan Island and of German cruisers' explorations of the island.[98] The James A. Robertson Papers also hold a letter from Mr. G. Koecke (?), Secretary to the German Consulate at Manila, to Sr. Teodoro Sandiko dated 4 January 1899, in which the Secretary appears not only to be in communication with Aguinaldo's First Philippine Republic but also offers to serve as a Filipino diplomatic agent abroad to negotiate for foreign governments' recognition of the Filipino Republic. Dery records that this was 'something which could be best obtained by a diplomatic agent who is a private person belonging to a neutral country.' The Secretary also offered: to act as agent for the Filipino Republic in future negotiations with the foreigners residing in the Philippines, particularly with those in Manila; to serve as a neutral agent for the Filipino Republic abroad to deal with authorities or persons of rank or to do other duties. When the Filipino Republic is recognised by the foreign nations as an independent nation, this German consular personnel further proposed: ... 'to serve as an assistant to the future political representative of the Filipino Government in Berlin, especially for that purpose of interesting German capital in enterprises in the Philippine Islands ... '[99] This language is not different from that which Emilio Aguinaldo claimed Dewey himself and the American Consul in Singapore would later use over April-May 1898, when the Filipino revolutionary government received promise of American assistance in defeating the Spanish and establishing the Philippine Republic under the protection of the United States, as reported in the *San Francisco Call* on 18 June 1898 in 'Agreement between Dewey and Aguinaldo.' Ultimately, however, in July, von Diedrichs was recalled as all three of his intended policy schemes fell apart. Germany's new objective was to acquire territorial concessions in the Pacific, including the Carolinas Islands and a coaling station in the Philippines.

After Dewey's victory in Manila Bay the U.S. joined with the Spanish to disarm the Philippine revolutionaries and transfer imperial sovereignty from one Western power to another. Nevertheless, imperial powers manifested private recognition of the Philippine Revolution and were ready to use its new government as a potential instrument. This intention sits alongside the genuine respect that some, such as Motsch, accorded the Philippine Revolution. 'In their manifestos and their proclamations, as well as their gatherings, it is remarkable that the Filipino leaders are haunted by the French Revolution,' Motsch noted; 'added to this is a religious undertone which recalls the American independence.'[100]

> Whether one likes it or not, these Indians are talking of a republic, of liberty, equality, fraternity, of a natural law reminiscent of western concepts. All revolutions resemble each other, based on the vindication of an ideal and of human dignity. It says a great deal for the Filipinos that this sublime symbol is recognized.[101]

This resemblance was not lost on the Filipinos. Andrés Bonifacio drew genuine inspiration from the French and American Revolutions, and Apolinario Mabini and Emilio Aguinaldo deliberately employed revolutionary rhetoric and history to make their argument recognisable and legible to the Westernised international community, whose moral backing they courted.

The British, for their part, registered Japanese imperial ambition, but did not perceive an immediate Japanese threat in the Philippines. Writing from Simla in West Bengal in 1896, Captain E. W. M. Norie of the Second Battalion Middlesex Regiment reflected Britain's attitude in his *Note on the Philippine Islands*. In the introduction to the islands, listed foremost amongst the general primer topics of essential background information was the topic 'Japan,' which was sandwiched between the topics of 'navy,' 'cultivation,' and 'trade.' It read: 'Japan is said to have long cast covetous eyes on these rich islands and the Government is always apprehensive of Japanese plots among the natives'; however, it continued, 'after her late war with China, Japan is not in a position to enter into hostilities with Spain at present.'[102] From there, he went on immediately to provide the information on cultivation and trade. Material and geopolitical realities notwithstanding, Norie attested to the increasing cultural weight of Japanese power among both the indios and the Spanish. Amongst the rumours as to the cause of the Philippine Revolution, Norie wrote, 'another version is that the Japanese are instrumental in stirring up the revolt against the Spanish and have been supplying the rebels with ammunition and arms.'[103]

As for where Japanese sympathies actually lay, though individual Japanese consistently offered assistance and empathised with the Philippine Revolution, the *official* Japanese position was to avoid all Spanish and, later, American antagonism. Yet, this did not discount Pan-Asian fantasies and possibilities. Luis Camara Dery argues that what differentiated the Japanese position from that of the other powers present at the blockade was that 'Japanese individuals gave concrete demonstrations of their sympathies for the Filipino cause with an apparent absence of any blunt request of securing a privileged position for Japanese interests in the Philippines.'[104] In this way, the lack of official support could underscore the private individuals' more *personal* support, which could be imagined to exist separately from national gain. This is indeed from where Pan-Asianism drew its persuasive force – the concepts of race and of Asia that seemingly made plausible Japanese citizens' disinterested sympathy for the Filipino cause. Growing Japanese and American strength would test this purported disinterest, as Pan-Asian solidarity increasingly abetted and overlapped with Japanese imperial ambitions, while the successful American colonisation of the Philippines and mounting global American power following

World War I increasingly redrew Filipinos' geography of political affinity away from its Asian experiments. However, Pan-Asianism was from the start multivocal, and even discrepant. What was streamlined to become the official imperial Japanese Pan-Asian ideology by the 1930s was but one thread among many that included visions as different from the Greater East Asia Co-Prosperity Sphere as that of the religious group Ōmotokyō's (Great Source Sect) Pan-Asian visions based on virtue, universal pacifism, and universal moral values.[105] Even as directly-felt American power realigned the poles of political affinity within the Philippines and Japan began to act more like the traditional Western imperial powers than an anti-colonial leader, Asianists in the Philippines and across Southeast Asia would continue to urge Japan toward its prior (perceived) purpose. They sought to keep alive the original, emancipatory spirit of Pan-Asianism, but in the end would turn to one another, instead of looking to Japan, participating in alternative and successor transnationalisms, such as Pan-Malayism and Third Worldism.

Great Britain, the largest colonial and naval power, ultimately threw its support behind the US aim of acquiring the archipelago as the solution to preserve the existing balance of power. The alternatives of dividing the archipelago between the imperial powers or joint intervention and occupation had failed to acquire consensus. Ignoring the Act of Declaration of Philippine Independence issued by Emilio Aguinaldo on June 12 1898, the U.S. Army and the Spanish forces jointly arranged the sham Battle of Manila, which enabled the Spanish to surrender to the Americans honourably on 13 August 1898 rather than to acknowledge their Filipino adversaries or risk the city falling into their possession. Following the Treaty of Paris, signed on 10 December 1898, Spain relinquished Cuba and ceded Puerto Rico, Guam, and portions of the Spanish West Indies to the US, and transferred the Philippines to the US for a sum of $20 million. Despite the formal imperial transition, the long Filipino Revolution continued. The Philippine-American War phase of the struggle formally began on 4 February 1899.

Why Asia?

What does Hopkins's narrative gain through this complementary focus? This picture of Asia is abbreviated, focusing on the imperial viewpoints and register of a shifting Asia while only gesturing toward the vernacular discourses and native perspectives. What I aimed to show was that even without radically departing from Hopkins's mainstay imperial history to chase any of the many, multivocal, related histories branching off out of sight from his own, something important had been left out of view. The globality of this history is clipped if we blot out the setting of Asia and the East-East relations that continued apace alongside East–West ones. The end of the nineteenth-century in Asia is too often apprehended through a bilateral framework that privileges relations with the West, at the expense of the broader historical regional context. Despite the treaty arrangements that France imposed upon Vietnam at the close of the century, for example, the courts of Siam and Vietnam remained deeply entrenched in their traditional interstate relations, the meanings and symbolism of which were no less vital to their conceptions and enactments of sovereignty for the presence of the West in their territory and worldviews.[106]

From an interpretive standpoint, the US became a global historical force at this moment not only because it began to act globally, which incurred global repercussions, but also because the places this imperial power went to entangled it in new stretches of the globe and *globalised* the US. This widened focus brings to the fore the longer, multiple histories at work in the places and histories of American global power, and deepens one of the great achievements of Hopkins's book – that of incorporating wide, decentralised historical agencies into a grand imperial narrative. Without incorporating the Asian setting into an account of the US's entry into the ranks of formal imperial world powers, the true stakes, nature, and consequences of this global moment and in this American history remain unacknowledged. We remain in the Philippines, as Karl D. White was, drawing from a direct, constantly evolving, bilateral account with comparative experience, but still groping for the longer history just out of sight.

The Philippine Revolution and the transition between the Spanish and American colonial powers and the rise of Japan created in the Philippines a careening moment of political possibility and societal renewal. Alternative visions of the political, or of the modern, for example, were at work during the period of transition before clear imperial footholds had been established (and indeed even afterward). Without attending to such parallel or contrarian visions we may miss the ways in which familiar insular, American, or Western global political forms, which eventually dominated the islands, bear their mark, and the ways in which they were essential dimensions of the Philippine resistance to Spain and the US.

The global imaginary that informed various Asian nationalisms at the turn of the twentieth century created various visions of 'Asia,' which were themselves central and grounding to those nationalisms. Particularly in studies of the turn of the twentieth century's new moment of globalisation, constructions of 'Asia,' Asian globalisms, and their presence in Asian nationalisms are vital. They allow us to see the globalisation of the nation-state form and attendant proliferation of nationalisms then underway as something other than merely defensive or derivative phenomena, though those aspects are also present. There was positive political imagining and material political organising involved in Asia – and beyond – and the Western imperial powers themselves recognised and responded to it.

Notes

1. Maj. Gen. Otis, "Roster of Troops Serving in the Department of the Pacific and Eight Army Corps," 25.
2. United States Army Combined Arms Center (USACAC), "Philippine Insurrection Diaries of Karl D. White, 1899-1901."
3. Ibid.
4. United States Senate Committee on the Philippines, *Affairs in the Philippine Islands, Part 1*, 34-35.
5. USACAC, "Philippine Insurrection Diaries of Karl D. White, 1899-1901."
6. Conrad, *Heart of Darkness*, 36.
7. Said, "Two Visions in Heart of Darkness," 424.
8. Ibid., 425.
9. USACAC, "Philippine Insurrection Diaries of Karl D. White, 1899-1901."
10. See: D. G. E. Hall's *A History of Southeast Asia* (1981); Victor Lieberman's *Strange Parallels: Southeast Asia in Global Context c. 800 - 1830, Vol. 1, Integration in the Mainland* (2003) and *Strange Parallels: Southeast Asia in Global Context c. 800 - 1830, Vol. 2, Mainland Mirrors* (2009).
11. See Julian Go's *American Empire and the Politics of Meaning: Elite Political Cultures in the Philippines and Puerto Rico* (2008).
12. See James Francis Warren, *The Sulu Zone 1768-1898: The Dynamics of External trade, Slavery and Ethnicity in the Transformation of a Southeast Asian Maritime State* (1981).
13. Hopkins, *American Empire: A Global History*, 413.
14. See ibid., 426-27; 429; 602-05.
15. See ibid., 416; 495; 507.
16. Iriye, *After Imperialism*, 5-6.
17. An article in *La Solidaridad* reported the tentative state of Philippines-Japan trade – 'in the Philippines, the idea of opening commercial relations with the Japanese Empire is gaining ground' – and recommended encouraging Philippine commerce by establishing 'direct commercial relations with Japan through the creation of regular shipping lines between Manila and the ports of Yokohama, Nagasaki, and Kobe.' "Filipinas en el Mercado del Japón," *La Solidaridad* 1, no. 5, April 15, 1889.
18. I use the contemporary term of 'Filipinas' to refer to the Spanish colony, as distinct from the 'Philippines' as an imagined and constructed nation and, later, nation-state.
19. Saniel, *Japan and the Philippines*, 138-37.
20. Ibid., 139.
21. See chapter 17 of Miyazaki Tōten's *My Thirty-Three Year's Dream* (Princeton: Princeton University Press, 2014).
22. Saniel, *Japan and the Philippines*, 6.
23. In July 1891 a consular agent notified the government in Madrid that an imperial ordinance was set to annex the Volcano Islands to Japan. As Josefa Saniel records, three months later the colonial government in the Philippines became responsible for verifying whether the islands were within the "jurisdictional waters of the Marianas." (Saniel, *Japan and the Philippines*, 153) Though the annexation went through, there was shortly thereafter, in February 1892, another transient moment of diplomatic anxiety due to "the suspicious circumstances surrounding the arrival of Japanese warships in Manila." (Ibid., 157) See the chapter "On Apprehensions and Intentions" in Saniel's *Japan and the Philippines* (1969) for more on this diplomatic history.

24. Saniel, *Japan and the Philippines*, 145.
25. Ibid., 17.
26. Ibid., 146.
27. Ibid., 178.
28. Ibid., 179.
29. Translation from Spanish mine, as are all to follow in this article unless otherwise stated. "Filipinas-Cuestión Palpitante: Lo Urgentísimo," *El Imparcial*, Oct. 2, 1896 (Hemeroteca Digital, Biblioteca Nacional de España).
30. Saniel, *Japan and the Philippines*, 137.
31. Ibid.
32. Ibid.
33. Three Japanese shops were established in 1889 following the opening of the Japanese Consulate. Prior to that, Japanese wares were reportedly sold through and handled by Indian shops in Manila. The direct presence of Japan in Manila was rather limited. (Ibid., 138.)
34. De Polavieja de Castillo, "Apuntos oficiales sobre los sucesos de la Insurrección Filipina facilitados por las ordenes Religiosas," July 24, 1896, Archivo de Camilo Garcia de Polavieja de Castillo, Diversos, 27, Archivo General de Indias, Seville, Spain.
35. Ibid.
36. De Polavieja de Castillo, "Antecedentes de la Insurreción y su estado en 1st Dibre 1896. Recibidos en Singapur," October 28, 1896, Archivo de Camilo Garcia de Polavieja de Castillo, Diversos, 27, Archivo General de Indias, Seville, Spain.
37. Ibid.
38. Ibid.
39. Steinberg, *The Philippines*, 61.
40. Aguilar, *Clash of Spirits*, 156.
41. Saniel, *Japan and the Philippines*, 3.
42. Cruikshank, "A History of Samar Island, The Philippines, 1768–1898," 181.
43. Sophia Marco, "Dios-Dios in the Visayas," 50.
44. Aguilar, *Clash of Spirits*, 156.
45. De Polavieja de Castillo, "Antecedentes de la Insurreción y su estado en 1st Dibre 1896. Recibidos en Singapur," October 28, 1896, Archivo de Camilo Garcia de Polavieja de Castillo, Diversos, 27, Archivo General de Indias, Seville, Spain.
46. De Polavieja de Castillo, "Apuntos oficiales sobre los sucesos de la Insurrección Filipina facilitados por las ordenes Religiosas," May 7, 1896, Archivo de Camilo Garcia de Polavieja de Castillo, Diversos, 27, Archivo General de Indias, Seville, Spain.
47. De Polavieja de Castillo, "Apuntos oficiales sobre los sucesos de la Insurrección Filipina facilitados por las ordenes Religiosas," April 17, 1896, Archivo de Camilo Garcia de Polavieja de Castillo, Diversos, 27, Archivo General de Indias, Seville, Spain.
48. De Polavieja de Castillo, "Antecedentes de la Insurreción y su estado en 1st Dibre 1896. Recibidos en Singapur," October 28, 1896, Archivo de Camilo Garcia de Polavieja de Castillo, Diversos, 27, Archivo General de Indias, Seville, Spain.
49. Ministerio de Ultramar, 1897, Ultramar, Legajo 5361, Exp. 9, No. 29, Archivo Histórico Nacional, Madrid, Spain.
50. Al Ministerio de Ultramar, January 3 1898, Ultramar, Legajo 5361, Exp. 10, No. 2, Archivo Histórico Nacional, Madrid, Spain.
51. De Polavieja de Castillo, "Apuntos oficiales sobre los sucesos de la Insurrección Filipina facilitados por las ordenes Religiosas," July 12, 1896, Archivo de Camilo Garcia de Polavieja de Castillo, Diversos, 27, Archivo General de Indias, Seville, Spain.

52. De Polavieja de Castillo, "Antecedentes de la Insurreción y su estado en 1st Dibre 1896. Recibidos en Singapur," October 28, 1896, Archivo de Camilo Garcia de Polavieja de Castillo, Diversos, 27, Archivo General de Indias, Seville, Spain.
53. De Polavieja de Castillo, "Apuntos oficiales sobre los sucesos de la Insurrección Filipina facilitados por las ordenes Religiosas," May 2, 1896, Archivo de Camilo Garcia de Polavieja de Castillo, Diversos, 27, Archivo General de Indias, Seville, Spain.
54. De Polavieja de Castillo, "Apuntos oficiales sobre los sucesos de la Insurrección Filipina facilitados por las ordenes Religiosas," July 6, 1896, Archivo de Camilo Garcia de Polavieja de Castillo, Diversos, 27, Archivo General de Indias, Seville, Spain.
55. Ibid.
56. De Polavieja de Castillo, "Apuntos oficiales sobre los sucesos de la Insurrección Filipina facilitados por las ordenes Religiosas," May 2, 1896, Archivo de Camilo Garcia de Polavieja de Castillo, Diversos, 27, Archivo General de Indias, Seville, Spain.
57. De Polavieja de Castillo, "Apuntos oficiales sobre los sucesos de la Insurrección Filipina facilitados por las ordenes Religiosas," June 1, 1896, Archivo de Camilo Garcia de Polavieja de Castillo, Diversos, 27, Archivo General de Indias, Seville, Spain.
58. Ibid.
59. Subsecretario del Ministerio de Ultramar, "Ataque de la prensa de Hong Kong contra el Gobernador General de Filipinas," November 21, 1892, Ultramar, Legajo 5329, Exp. 8, Archivo Histórico Nacional, Madrid, Spain.
60. Ibid.
61. De Polavieja de Castillo, "Apuntos oficiales sobre los sucesos de la Insurrección Filipina facilitados por las ordenes Religiosas," June 30, 1896, Archivo de Camilo Garcia de Polavieja de Castillo, Diversos, 27, Archivo General de Indias, Seville, Spain.
62. De Polavieja de Castillo, "Apuntos oficiales sobre los sucesos de la Insurrección Filipina facilitados por las ordenes Religiosas," April 30, 1896, Archivo de Camilo Garcia de Polavieja de Castillo, Diversos, 27, Archivo General de Indias, Seville, Spain.
63. Rizal, *Rizal's Correspondence with Fellow Reformists*, 312.
64. De Polavieja de Castillo, "Antecedentes de la Insurreción y su estado en 1st Dibre 1896. Recibidos en Singapur," October 28, 1896, Archivo de Camilo Garcia de Polavieja de Castillo, Diversos, 27, Archivo General de Indias, Seville, Spain.
65. Ibid.
66. Brocheux, *The Mekong Delta*, 140.
67. See Huang Fuqing, *Chinese Students in Japan in the Late Ch'ing Period* (1983).
68. Paterson, "Tenacious Texts," 77.
69. Ibid.
70. Ibid.
71. Ibid.
72. Ibid., 92.
73. Duara, "The Discourse of Civilization and Pan-Asianism," 101.
74. Paterson, "Tenacious Texts," 6.
75. Shiraishi, "Phan Boi Chau in Japan," 58.
76. Ibid., 58–59.
77. For full details see CuUnjieng Aboitiz, *Asian Place, Filipino Nation* (2020).
78. See CuUnjieng Aboitiz, "Fantasy, Affect, and Pan-Asianism."
79. Lieutenant X, *The Diary of a French Officer on the War in the Philippines 1898*, 75.
80. Ibid., 33.
81. Ibid.
82. Ibid., 17.
83. Ibid., 38.

84. Ibid., 38–39.
85. Ibid., 42.
86. Ibid.
87. Ibid., 75.
88. Ibid., 50–51.
89. Ibid., 9.
90. Ibid.
91. Dery, *The Army of the First Philippine Republic and other Historical Essays*, 89.
92. Corpuz, *Saga and Triumph*, 203.
93. Ibid., 204–05.
94. Dery, *The Army of the First Philippine Republic and other Historical Essays*, 88.
95. Ibid.
96. Ibid., 89.
97. Ibid.
98. Ibid.
99. Ibid., 91.
100. Lieutenant X, *The Diary of a French Officer on the War in the Philippines 1898*, 54.
101. Ibid.
102. Captain Norie, *Note on the Philippine Islands*, 3.
103. Ibid., 5.
104. Dery, *The Army of the First Philippine Republic and other Historical Essays*, 92.
105. See Li Narangoa, "Universal Values and Pan-Asianism: The Vision of Ōmotokyō," 52–66.
106. Both Junko Koizumi, "The 'Last' Friendship Exchanges between Siam and Vietnam, 1879–1882: Siam between Vietnam and France—and Beyond" and John Crawfurd, *Journal of an Embassy to the Courts of Siam and Cochin China* (1967) illustrate this fact.

Acknowledgments

Portions of this article are drawn from research undertaken for my dissertation, 'Constructing Political Place: The International Philippine Revolution and Transnational Pan-Asianism, 1887–1912' (PhD diss., Yale University, 2016). I wish to thank Akita Shigeru and Anthony G. Hopkins for their generous invitation for me to participate in this project as well as their patient, productive work to help me refine my contribution. I owe them both great debts, as I also do Motoe Terami-Wada, Jenifer Van Vleck, and Ben Kiernan who helped me produce and revise the thinking presented in this article. I also wish to acknowledge the Archivo General de Indias in Seville, Archivo Histórico Nacional in Madrid, and the Hemeroteca Digital, Biblioteca Nacional de España for helping to make this article possible.

Disclosure Statement

No potential conflict of interest was reported by the author(s).

References

Aguilar, Jr., Filomeno V. *Clash of Spirits: The History of Power and Sugar Planter Hegemony on a Visayan Island*. Quezon City: University of the Philippines Press, 1998.

Brocheux, Pierre. *The Mekong Delta: Ecology, Economy, and Revolution, 1860–1960*. Madison: University of Wisconsin-Madison Center for Southeast Asian Studies, 1995.

Conrad, Joseph. *Heart of Darkness: Authoritative Text, Backgrounds and Contexts, Criticism*. Edited by Paul B. Armstrong. New York: W.W. Norton & Company, 2006.

CuUnjieng Aboitiz, Nicole. *Asian Place, Filipino Nation: A Global Intellectual History of the Philippine Revolution, 1887-1912*. New York: Columbia University Press, 2020.

CuUnjieng Aboitiz, Nicole. "Fantasy, Affect, and Pan-Asianism: Mariano Ponce, the First Philippine Republic's Foreign Emissary, 1898–1912." *Philippine Studies: Historical and Ethnographic Viewpoints* 67, no. 3-4 (2019): 489–520. doi:10.1353/phs.2019.0024.

Corpuz, Onofre D. *Saga and Triumph: The Filipino Revolution Against Spain*. Manila: Philippine Centennial Commission, 1999.

Cruikshank, Robert Bruce. "A History of Samar Island, The Philippines, 1768-1898." PhD diss., University of Wisconsin-Madison, 1975.

Dery, Luis Camara. *The Army of the First Philippine Republic and Other Historical Essays*. Manila: De La Salle University Press, 1995.

Duara, Prasenjit. "The Discourse of Civilization and Pan-Asianism." *Journal of World History* 12, no. 1 (2001): 99–130. doi:10.1353/jwh.2001.0009.

Huang, Fuqing. *Chinese Students in Japan in the Late Ch'ing Period*. Tokyo: Centre for East Asian Cultural Studies, 1983.

Go, Julian. *American Empire and the Politics of Meaning: Elite Political Cultures in the Philippines and Puerto Rico*. Durham: Duke University Press, 2008.

Hall, D. G. E. *A History of Southeast Asia*. 4th ed. London: The Macmillan Press, 1981.

Hopkins, A. G. *American Empire: A Global History*. Princeton: Princeton University Press, 2018.

Iriye, Akira. *After Imperialism: The Search for a New Order in the Far East, 1921-1931, Harvard East Asian Series, 22*. Cambridge: Harvard University Press, 1965.

Koizumi, Junko. "The 'Last' Friendship Exchanges between Siam and Vietnam, 1879–1882: Siam between Vietnam and France—And Beyond." *TRaNS: Trans-Regional and -National Studies of Southeast Asia* 4, no. 1 (2016): 131–164. doi:10.1017/trn.2015.18.

Lieberman, Victor. *Strange Parallels: Southeast Asia in Global Context c. 800–1830, Vol. 1, Integration in the Mainland*. Cambridge: Cambridge University Press, 2003.

Lieberman, Victor. *Strange Parallels: Southeast Asia in Global Context c. 800–1830, Vol. 2, Mainland Mirrors*. Cambridge: Cambridge University Press, 2009.

Marco, Sophia. "Dios-Dios in the Visayas." *Philippine Studies: Historical and Ethnographic Viewpoints* 49, no. 1 (2001): 42–77.

Miyazaki, Tōten. *My Thirty-Three Year's Dream*. Edited by Marius B. Jansen and translated by Eto Shinkichi. 1982. Reprint. Princeton: Princeton University Press, 2014.

Narangoa, Li. "Universal Values and Pan-Asianism: The Vision of Ōmotokyō." In *Pan-Asianism in Modern Japanese History: Colonialism, Regionalism and Borders*, edited by Sven Saaler, and J. Victor Koschmann, 52–66. London: Routledge, 2007.

Paterson, Lorraine Marion. "Tenacious Texts: Vietnam, China, and Radical Cultural Intersections, 1890–1930." PhD diss., Yale University, 2006.

Said, Edward W. "Two Visions in Heart of Darkness." In *Heart of Darkness: Authoritative Text, Backgrounds and Contexts, Criticism*, edited by Paul B. Armstrong, 422–428. New York: W.W. Norton & Company, 2006.

Saniel, Josefa M. *Japan and the Philippines, 1868–1898*. Quezon City: University of the Philippines Press, 1969.

Shiraishi, Masaya. "Phan Boi Chau in Japan." In *Phan Boi Chau and the Dong-Du Movement*, edited by Vinh Sinh, 52–100. New Haven: Yale Southeast Asia Studies, 1988.

Steinberg, David Joel. *The Philippines: A Singular and a Plural Place*. 1988. Reprint. Boulder: Westview Press, 2000.

Warren, James Francis. *The Sulu Zone 1768 - 1898: The Dynamics of External Trade, Slavery and Ethnicity in the Transformation of a Southeast Asian Maritime State*. Singapore: NUS Press, 1981.

Part IV
The Empire in the Twentieth Century

Law Against Empire, or Law for Empire? – American Imagination and the International Legal Order in the Twentieth Century

Seiko Mimaki

ABSTRACT
This paper examines the relationship between national interest, diplomacy, and international law. It argues that, instead of hindering the development of U.S. imperial structures, international law functioned largely as a tool of U.S. empire and helped to maintain the international *status quo* during the first half of the twentieth century. Interwar American initiatives to create international arrangements that would produce a world without war were demonstrated most notably by the creation of the League of Nations (1919) and the Pact of Paris (1928). After World War II and decolonisation, international conditions changed profoundly. The U.S. retreated from international organisations and turned increasingly to unilateral action to pursue its priorities.

In his Charles R. Walgreen Foundation lecture at the University of Chicago, delivered in 1950, George F. Kennan, the American diplomat and the eminent realist who significantly contributed to shaping U.S. nascent Cold War policy and the tradition of realism in international relations theory, bitterly criticised what he called the U.S. 'legalistic-moralistic approach' to international relations. By this, he referred to an overall tendency to think about international politics in highly moralistic and legalistic terms, which he thought dominated U.S. diplomacy during the twentieth century. To survive and eventually win the Cold War, Kennan suggested, the United States should give up idealistic ventures to create a perfect world through developing international law and morality, and instead deal pragmatically with conflicts of national interest. Only through patient diplomatic efforts would some stability emerge out of chaotic conflicts among national interests.[1]

Kennan's criticism of the 'legalistic-moralistic approach' was so influential that it has been widely believed that U.S. diplomacy in the twentieth century minimised national interests and power. However, Kennan overlooked the fact that U.S. diplomatic practices and national interests were already closely intertwined with international law. Rather than hindering the development of U.S. imperial ambitions, international law functioned as a means of maintaining a *status quo* that suited U.S. interests.

This paper shows how American initiatives in creating the League of Nations (1919) and the Pact of Paris (1928) shaped the course of the American empire. Previous literature has emphasised the long-term importance of the Covenant of the League of Nations and the Pact of Paris, which had decisively influenced the development of international law toward war prohibitions.[2] Yet, neither proposed to dissolve the colonial empires. A.G. Hopkins is definitely right in pointing out that, 'World War I signified the extension of the age of empires, not the beginning of its demise'.[3] The conflict, which was fought under the banner of 'the war to make the world safe for democracy,' in U.S. President Woodrow Wilson's words, ended up 'help[ing] to make the world safe for the empires of the victors'.[4]

Though Wilson's advocacy of 'self-determination' bolstered the aspirations of the subjugated people in non-Western countries for political independence, Wilson himself never intended to apply the principle universally. Overseas colonies of Britain, France, Belgium, the Netherlands, Italy, Portugal, and the United States remained intact as a consequence of the peace settlement in 1919. The Permanent Mandates Commission was created to govern the former territories of the Ottoman Empire in the Middle East and the German colonies in Africa and the Pacific. These territories were designated by the League as 'mandates,' and were administered by France, the United Kingdom, Japan, Belgium, Australia, New Zealand, and South Africa on behalf of the League. The paternalistic notion of 'a civilising mission' penetrated the system. Article 22 of the League's Covenant, which established the mandate system, empowered Europeans, who held 'the sacred trust of civilisation,' to rule 'peoples not yet able to stand by themselves'.[5]

Nevertheless, the League and the Pact of Paris were far from being negligible influences on the history of the American Empire. This paper shows how the two organisations changed the course of the American empire thereafter. While the Covenant of the League and the Pact of Paris forbade the forcible acquisition of territory by one state at the expense of another, neither contained regulations that checked the abuse of economic power. Rather, the Covenant contained provisions on economic sanctions against a state that resorted to war in violation of the Covenant. The Pact of Paris never questioned the legality of forcible economic measures either. In a world where economic measures gained importance as a legitimate means of punishing aggressive states and of restoring the 'rule of law,' the United States, a rising economic power, increasingly saw itself as a guardian of international law.

Despite its comprehensive scope, Hopkins's book lacks an analysis of the complex ways in which the development of international law shaped the

American empire. In this respect, his study follows a route taken by other imperial historians, who are inclined to treat legal history as a separate sub-specialism. This paper helps to fill a gap in *American Empire* and aims more generally at encouraging historians of empire to show more awareness of the relevance of legal history than they have done in the past.

American International Lawyers and Empire

The projection of U.S. imperial power was not sorely the prerogative of the military but was also the job of international lawyers, especially in the first half of the twentieth century.[6] Certainly, U.S. international lawyers and the policy-makers influenced by them greatly contributed to promoting the 'rule of law' in the international arena by establishing war prohibitions in international law.[7] Nevertheless, what these 'rule of law' advocates tended to overlook was that, in the context of the interwar era, promoting 'rule of law' could mean perpetuating the unjust imperial order. In the world where 'outlawry of war' is a dominant norm, a nation that challenges the *status quo* could be recognised as an 'aggressor,' and punished by collective action for breaching international law. The U.S. government and the international lawyers supporting them never tried to observe these political functions of international law in the real world, and never questioned the existing imperial order.

During the nineteenth century, American pacifists, who had been mainly concerned with domestic peace, began to discuss the issue of international peace. In their view, the key institution should be an international court, which was expected to settle all inter-state disputes impartially.[8] They believed that the 'Supreme Court of the Nations' would produce the ultimate solution to international wars. This idea came from their observation of the domestic order in the United States, which they regarded as a paragon for the world. According to these pacifists, the United States could become the most peaceful nation in the world, because it had the Supreme Court, which successfully settled numerous interstate disputes, including difficult 'political' ones, without resorting to forcible sanctions. Early pacifists insisted that creating the 'Supreme Court of the Nations' would bring the ultimate solution to all international wars.

One of the early American advocates of an international court was William Ladd, who founded the American Peace Society in 1828, the first national non-sectarian peace organisation in the United States.[9] In his Essay on *A Congress of Nations for the Adjustment of Universal Peace*, Ladd proposed a Court of Nations whose ruling would be enforced through the 'power of public opinion,' and not through the 'power of sheriffs and vigilantes.' Ladd's ideal of a 'Supreme Court of the Nations,' whose decrees were expected to be executed through the 'moral sanctions' of public opinion, was widely shared among U.S. international lawyers and pacifists in the nineteenth century.[10]

At the turn of the twentieth century, the ideal was upheld by the leading experts on international law at the State Department, Elihu Root and James Brown Scott. Both contributed greatly to founding an American profession of international law as presidents of the American Society of International Law and government officials with legal expertise.[11] Root served as State of Secretary from 1905 to 1909; Scott served as Root's legal advisor at the State Department. They passionately promoted the creation of international courts, believing that international adjudication could eventually bring a world without wars.

The influence of the United States was also evident in the Hague Convention of 1899, which was the most comprehensive attempt made in the nineteenth century to codify the rules of war. The Convention itself built on the Lieber Code, which was enacted in 1863 to control hostilities during the U.S. Civil War. The First Hague International Peace Conference was a historic conference in the sense that the scope was extended, albeit modestly, beyond Europe with the goal of ensuring 'to all peoples the benefits of a real and lasting peace'.[12] The participants included the leaders of 26 of the world's sovereign states, and covered major European nations as well as the United States, Japan, China, Mexico, Persia and Siam. Colonies and their inhabitants, however, were excluded as participants as well as from the conference agenda.

The U.S. government was keenly interested in promoting the 'rule of law.' Before the conference, Secretary of State John M. Hay instructed the U.S. delegation to the Hague to propose the creation of a permanent international court.[13] As the result of the Conference, the Permanent Court of Arbitration was created as the world's first intergovernmental organisation dedicated to resolving international disputes. Nevertheless, its functions were by far more limited than the U.S. government originally expected.

Still, the American dream of a 'Supreme Court of the Nations' never faded. At the Second Hague Peace Conference held in 1907, the U.S. delegation was the leading proponent of a permanent international court on the model of the U.S. Supreme Court. Before the opening of the conference, Secretary of State Root instructed the delegation to work towards the creation of 'a permanent tribunal composed of judges who were judicial officers and nothing else, who are paid adequate salaries, who have no other occupation, and who will devote their entire time to the trial and decision of international cases by judicial methods and under a sense of judicial responsibility'.[14] In the instruction, Root expressed his belief that, 'If there could be a tribunal which would pass upon questions between nations with the same impartial and impersonal judgement that the Supreme Court of the United States gives to questions arising between citizens of the United States, there can be no doubt that nations would be much more ready to submit their controversies to its decision than they are now to take the chances of arbitration'.[15]

Root's belief in a permanent court was heavily influenced by James Brown Scott, who served as an adviser to the American delegation to the Second Hague Peace Conference. Scott strongly believed that a permanent court should not be backed by anything but the persuasive force of public opinion. In his article, 'The Legal Nature of International Law,' published in *American Journal of International Law*, Scott expressed his conviction that law could exist without having to be enforced by physical sanctions, emphasising that 'every-day experience shows the persuasive force of public opinion, and it is perhaps not too much to say that public opinion is more compelling in its nature than a sanction, be it never legal'.[16] Scott believed that the Permanent Court of Arbitration would eventually develop into the 'Supreme Court of the Nations,' and that the court would be able to find peaceful solutions to inter-state disputes.[17]

In 1910, the American Society for the Judicial Settlement of International Disputes was created.[18] The organisation aimed to establish 'a truly permanent court,' 'composed of judges acting under a sense of judicial responsibility' to promote the settlement of international conflicts by judicial means.[19] At their first meeting, President Scott expressed the hope that 'an international court will lessen the cause of public war, just as national courts have abolished private war',[20] and Root emphasised the need for an international court modelled after the Supreme Court of the United States. According to Root, the United States should take the initiatives toward its realisation, as American people 'have been long accustomed to the existence of a great tribunal,' 'which has no power to enforce its decrees, except the confidence of the whole people behind it.' Applying domestic legal experience to international law, Root proudly advocated a U.S. mission to spread universally the idea that 'nations, however great, and rulers, however powerful, should go before a court and submit the question whether their actions and their views accord with the principles of justice'.[21]

Other U.S. participants also advocated a 'Supreme Court of Nations' that would be supported solely by 'moral sanctions' applied by public opinion. According to these advocates, the Supreme Court in the United States had successfully settled numerous interstate disputes, including difficult political ones, such as boundary disputes, without resorting to physical sanctions. Instead, by appealing to the 'moral sanctions' of public opinion, the Supreme Court had won the voluntary adherence of the states. Applying this domestic observation to the international arena, they optimistically believed that once a 'Supreme Court of Nations' was created, international conflicts would increasingly be solved, not through military force but through judicial means, which ultimately would lead to an 'American peace' free from military power or its threats. Such tactics, they thought, represented the 'old' European way of achieving peace.[22]

In retrospect, as Martti Koskenniemi points out, a 'Supreme Court of the Nations' could be seen as an convenient ideological tool for the United States, which enabled it to keep out of European conflicts and still satisfy its sense of mission by bringing salvation to the rest of the world.[23] Nevertheless, the advocates of a 'Supreme Court of Nations' were not simply naïve utopians who optimistically believed that universal 'rule of law' could be realised through establishing an impartial judicial institution. When it came to U.S. strategic interests, they never hesitated to use their rich knowledge of international law to facilitate the exercise of U.S. power.[24]

In 1899, Root was appointed as Secretary of War by President William McKinley. The appointment bewildered Root, who saw himself as knowing nothing about war, but President McKinley, explaining the reason for his appointment, insisted that new Secretary of War should be a 'jurist' who could provide an overall intellectual framework for governing the Spanish territories won in the Spanish-American War, rather than a military man.[25]

Root's work as Secretary of War perfectly satisfied McKinley's expectations. In 1901, Root drafted a set of articles, which became later known as the Platt Amendment, outlining the rules that governed future U.S.-Cuban relations. In forming the terms of the Amendment, Root drew direct inspiration from the Britain's occupation of Egypt, which, in his words, allowed the occupiers to 'retire and still maintain her moral control'.[26] The Amendment, which included the right of the United States to interfere in Cuba's internal affairs should the island's independence be in jeopardy, became a part of the Cuban Constitution in 1902, despite considerable Cuban resistance. A large increase in foreign investment in Cuba followed the settlement. In 1906, U.S. capital invested in Cuba reached $200 million. In subsequent years, by appealing to the amendment, the United States sent troops to Cuba on several occasions to maintain friendly governments in power and protect U.S. investments.[27]

At the Second Annual Meeting of the American Society of International Law held in 1908, Root gave a presidential address titled 'Sanction of International Law,' in which he frankly admitted that the 'rule of law' had not yet been universalised because there were still many 'uncivilised' countries that failed to maintain domestic order and preferred resorting to war to solve international disputes.[28] By appealing to the logic of the dichotomised 'civilised' and 'uncivilised' countries, Root justified U.S. interventions in the Western Hemisphere and the Pacific. Root firmly believed that only by the intervention of the 'civilised' countries, with force if necessary, could countries suffering constant political instability be corrected and the 'rule of law' be enforced.[29]

World War I: A Turning Point of Law in the American Empire?

The experience of World War I, where the 'civilised' powers did not hesitate to adopt barbaric measures, such as submarine warfare and poison gas, had a profound impact on American pacifist thinking. Many pacifists could no longer maintain their optimistic belief that 'civilised' nations always preferred peaceful resolutions to conflicts, and that the 'moral sanction' of public opinion would be enough to restrain hostilities. Pacifists increasingly called for economic and military sanctions to punish defiant countries and 'enforce' peace.

In January 1918, President Woodrow Wilson outlined universal principles for future peace in his 'Fourteen Points Speech.' The principles included such commitments as open diplomacy, disarmament, free trade, and most importantly the formation of the League of Nations. Wilson regarded the pre-war international order, which relied on balancing rival powers, as being fundamentally unstable, and called instead for a 'community of nations' to provide a new security system. Wilson's idea was crystallized in Article 10 of the Covenant of the League of Nations, which stipulated territorial and political guarantees against aggression. Wilson thought that Article 10 should be the 'Heart of the Covenant'.[30] The system established by the League of Nations in 1919, expected that states would respect each other's sovereignty and territorial integrity. Peace would be maintained under League auspices by arbitration, conciliation or resort to the new Permanent Court of International Justice, while disarmament would further reduce the likelihood of war. In addition, the Covenant contained provisions on economic and military sanctions against a state which resorted to war in violation of the Covenant.

Another major American initiative for international peace in the interwar years was the Kellogg-Briand pact, or Pact of Paris, officially the General Treaty for Renunciation of War as an Instrument of National Policy. The Pact was signed in August 1928 by 15 nations including the United States, France, Germany, the United Kingdom, and Japan, which signatory states promised not to use war to resolve 'disputes or conflicts of whatever nature or of whatever origin they may be, which may arise among them'. The Pact questioned the legality of using, or threatening, military force against another country, and made annexing territory by force unlawful, though other, more indirect forms of aggression were not prohibited. Although there were no enforcement mechanisms, the treaty provided that parties failing to abide by the anti-war pledge 'should be denied of the benefits furnished by [the] treaty'. The pact was eventually signed by most of the established nations before the outbreak of World War II.

Not everyone, however, regarded the League of Nations and the Pact of Paris as turning points toward a more peaceful new world. Neither the League nor the Pact contained concrete provisions policing economic imperialism,[31] and this led to disillusion and suspicion. One of the bitterest critics was the German jurist and political philosopher, Carl Schmitt, who was widely known for his attacks on political liberalism. From Schmitt's perspectives, the League of Nations would never be regarded as an agency that could ensure world peace. Schmitt saw both logical inconsistency and hypocrisy in the Covenant of the League, particularly in Article 21, which referred to the Monroe Doctrine. Schmitt argued that the Monroe Doctrine, which was originally invented as a legitimate defense of democracy against monarchism and was confined to the Western Hemisphere, became a universal interventionist ideology by being incorporated into the Covenant. The result, by erasing the distinctions between 'war' and 'peace', would lead to a permanent state of war. 'War', as formally declared by states, would cease to exist under the Covenant, while military force exercised by the United States in the name of the Monroe Doctrine and 'sanctions' against an aggressor, would never be regarded as illegal and would never be punished by international society.

According to Schmitt, imperialism would also never diminish under the Covenant of the League of Nations. While providing collective security and thus outlawing certain wars, the Covenant made only vague reference to economic and financial questions, and thus lacked the provisions needed to protect weaker nations from economic penetration. In other words, the Covenant virtually gave unlimited scope of freedom for the imperial powers to pursue economic imperialism, unaccompanied by direct military operations and territorial acquisitions, which Schmitt saw as the dominant form of imperialism in the twentieth century. Schmitt concluded that, despite the high-sounding words of the Covenant, the real functions of the League were to introduce a set of new imperialist techniques, which would allow the major powers, especially the United States, to disguise their economic interests as the pursuit of universal values such as the 'rule of law'.[32]

Schmitt's criticism of the Pact of Paris was even harsher. Rather than preventing future wars, Schmitt claimed, the Pact of Paris gave powerful states a new rationale for waging war against any countries that they regarded as 'violating' the solemn anti-war pledge, and so break the 'peace'. The signatories put several reservations into the Pact that enabled them to wage war at their convenience. U.S. Secretary of State Frank Kellogg, one of the co-authors of the Pact, openly said that any action that the United States took under the Monroe Doctrine in the Western Hemisphere should be exempted. The signatories would continue to wage war, though they would never call it 'war'.[33]

The anxiety that the League of Nations and the Pact of Paris might function as a tool of economic imperialism was also widely shared among Japanese intellectuals. Japan was a victorious country in World War I, yet the Japanese never felt that their country was accepted as an equal partner among the great powers. At the Paris Peace Conference in 1919, Japan's proposal to insert a racial equality clause into the Covenant of the League of Nations was rejected by the United States, Britain, and Australia. Many Japanese were afraid that the territorial guarantee and sanctions clauses of the Covenant would prevent any change to the *status quo*, and that the 'peaceful' economic imperialism of the Anglo-American countries would never be punished.

Such anxiety toward the League was eloquently expressed by Japan's future Prime Minister, Fumimaro Konoe, who attended the Paris Peace Conference as an aide to Marquis Kinmochi Saionji. Before attending the conference, Konoe published an article entitled '*Eibei Honi no Heiwa-shugi wo Haisu* (Reject the

Anglo-American Centered Pacifism)' in the popular nationalistic magazine, *Nihon Oyobi Nihonjin* (Japan and the Japanese). According to Konoe, the fundamental character of international relations is a struggle between the *status quo* powers, which see benefits in maintaining the existing order, and the revisionist powers, which would benefit by destroying it. The former call for peace, and the latter cry for war. The former is not necessarily morally superior to the latter. The League of Nations, arms limitation, or whatever the Anglo-American powers propose under the name of 'peace,' are only a façade to hide their real motive - defending the *status quo* which best serves their interests.[34]

Konoe's disillusion with American idealism became deeper as U.S.-Japan relations became increasingly tense over Japan's aggressive policy toward China in the 1930s. In an article titled, '*Sekai no Genjo wo Kaizouseyo* (The Necessity of Revising the *Status Quo*)' published in 1933, Konoe justified Japan's territorial expansion into China in terms of the nation's survival. According to Konoe, the uneven distribution of land inevitably drove some nations with growing population, like Japan, to expand into other countries. Konoe served three terms as prime minister during the turbulent period of 1937–41, and in 1938 proclaimed the establishment of *Toa Shinchitsujo* (New Order in East Asia) as Japan's ultimate purpose. These developments only widened the gap between Japan and international society.[35]

Some U.S. politicians found the fundamental flaw of the League of Nations and the Pact of Paris in their silence on the issue of imperialism. In April 1917, Wisconsin progressive politician, Robert La Follette, gave a speech at the Senate that expressed his opposition to war and bitterly criticised Wilson's war slogan, a war to 'make the world safe for democracy'. La Follette questioned why, if Wilson was loyal to his ideal of supporting democracy throughout the world, he had not mentioned anything about the plights of Ireland, Egypt, or India, which had suffered under British colonial rule.[36] Towards the end of the war, La Follett insisted on the necessity of a just peace-treaty without indemnities for the vanquished, and was bitterly disappointed when the Versailles Treaty, which was signed in 1918, imposed harsh reparations and assigned war guilt for World War I sorely to Germany. In La Follette's eyes, the harsh treaty elegantly proved that the World War I was not a 'war for democracy', as President Wilson declared, but a 'war for Wall Street', which only served bankers and financiers who had loaned billions of dollars to the Allies.[37]

Regarding the Pact of Paris, another Wisconsin congressman, John J. Blaine cast the sole vote against the Pact, which was supported by a majority of 85–1. In the eyes of Blaine, a stubborn anti-imperialist, the Pact, which was silent on the issue of imperialism, could never be regarded as marking progress toward peace. Blaine's criticism of the Pact was especially directed toward Paragraph 10 of the British interpretive note on the treaty, which reserved Britain's right to send troops to 'certain regions of the world the welfare and integrity of which constitute a special and vital interest for our peace and safety'.[38] Blaine insisted that war could not be outlawed by mere words. The world could ultimately outlaw war only when the causes of war, such as protectorates, mandates, spheres of influence, foreign concessions, exploitation of natural resources, monopoly of trade routes, and increased tariff barriers were outlawed. According to Blaine, the result of the Pact would be to preserve and even strengthen the immoral *status quo* whereby colonialism and imperialism were both widespread and regarded as being lawful. Speaking at the Senate, Blaine quoted letters from Sarojini Naidu, the first Indian female president of the Indian National Congress. In her letter, Naidu demanded that the United States should oppose Britain's reservations to the treaty, showing her fear that American acceptance of the British note would unite the two largest English-speaking nations in the world behind a policy of imperialism.[39]

Concurrently with the negotiation of the Pact of Paris, the Coolidge administration was engaged in a series of military interventions in Nicaragua, which were justified by invoking the Monroe Doctrine.[40] Criticising contradictions in Kellogg's diplomatic practices, Blaine pointed out that the United States had degenerated into another 'monster of Imperialism', and no longer had the right to criticise European and Japanese imperialism. In addition to direct military interventions, Blaine criticised U.S. companies' economic penetration into Latin America, calling it the 'imperialism of the dollar', which was technically differentiated from formal imperialism, yet in reality was no less harsh.[41]

The League of Nations and the Pact of Paris were typical exercises of what Reinhold Niebuhr called America's 'innocent' imperialism. In an article entitled 'Awkward Imperialists', published in 1930, Niebuhr declared that the twentieth century would be an economic age where the dominant state would have economic rather than military power. In such an age, Niebuhr argued, it was quite easy for the United States, the wealthiest country in the world, to become a huge empire whose influence reached all over the globe. Nevertheless, Niebuhr was quite pessimistic about the future of the American Empire because it established its sway too easily without legions. Consequently, the United States had little knowledge of the intricacies of international politics and lacked political understanding of other nations. Niebuhr was particularly afraid of the combination that allied America's huge power with its innocence.[42]

At the same time, Niebuhr clearly understood that world stability could not be maintained without the exercise of American power. In the 1930s and 1940s, Niebuhr rose to prominence for his bitter opposition both to Nazism and to isolationism as an American response to the international crises, and insisted that the United States must find a way of using its great power responsibly.[43]

Empire of Economic Sanctions

After World War II, which caused widespread devastation all over the world, the United States was exceptionally well placed to become the preeminent power.[44] At the same time, the United States, with the other colonial powers, faced difficulties in handling rising anti-colonial movements. Hopkins's book gives us a clear picture of the transformation of the American Empire in the era of decolonisation.

Some political scientists have insisted that the United States played a generally benevolent role in the process of decolonisation. For example, Daniel Deudney and G. John Ikenberry argue that after World War II, the United States played a key role in the decline of empire, institutionalising free trade and multilateral cooperation, providing the infrastructure for a global economic system, thus enabling smaller and weaker states to sustain their sovereign.[45] Ikenberry describes the United States after World War II as the 'Liberal Leviathan', generating peaceful and profitable cooperation, shaping and managing a system of international institutions, norms and rules according to liberal principles. In Ikenberry's view, the United States, despite its privileged place in the global order, has been subject to the same rules as the other countries.[46]

However, Ikenberry significantly overlooks or underestimates the plain fact that far from being exceptional, the United States largely followed the European imperial powers in first trying to strengthen its grip on the insular territories.[47] The United States decolonised its own insular empire at exactly the same time as the major imperial powers did after World War II. The Philippines became independent in 1946; Puerto Rico became a 'Commonwealth', a status rather similar to that of dominion in 1952; Hawai'i was finally admitted into the Union as the fiftieth state in 1959. Despite its formal status as a sovereign state, Cuba remained a protectorate until the revolution of 1959. Moreover, the United States redoubled its efforts to retain informal influence over these territories after they gained independence.

After World War II, international law and international organisations began to cease functioning as tools of the colonial powers and began to serve the interests of the previously colonised nations. Nationalist leaders galvanised the independence movements by appealing to self-determination and human rights, which Western colonial rulers themselves had once proclaimed as the justification for their imperial mission. Certainly, these languages were not new, yet the novelty after World War II was that the ideas were adopted and applied globally. If the colonial powers accepted that the values they stood for were applicable to their colonies, they were signing up to decolonisation. If they denied these values, they risked provoking further outbursts of militant nationalism.[48] After the Bandung Conference in 1955 and the subsequent rise in the number of newly independent nations in the United Nations, the United States found it increasingly difficult to use international agreements and institutions as a convenient tool for maintaining the *status quo*.

As Hopkins warns, when we make comparisons between empires such as Rome, Britain, and the United States, we should always be aware of differences in the historical context. Though some scholars regard the United States as the heir to the British empire, Hopkins calls readers' attention to the significant differences that shaped their status and power. It is true that both were contemporaneous industrial nation-states with an acknowledged role as world powers and an unquestioned belief in the superiority of their own values. Nevertheless, Britain and the United States operated in a global context that altered significantly in the course of three centuries. The Pax Britannica was exercised in an era that either favoured or required territorial control. At that time, empires were not only a familiar part of the international scene but were also regarded as a measure of international stature. By contrast, the Pax Americana was applied in a postcolonial era where annexations were made illegal and anti-colonial movements were becoming increasingly visible. While the British Empire dealt with proto-nationalist protests, the United States had to find its way in a world of independent states founded on principles of self-determination.[49]

Today, the United States no longer even pretends to be a guardian of international law. With the collapse of the Soviet Union, the notion of the unipolar moment was born. Backed by the idea that we can do this alone, the United States has increasingly exempted itself from the treaties and important international agreements by appealing to the logic of U.S. exceptionalism: other nations should restrict their selfish behaviour by obeying international law; the United States, as an exceptionally moral state, could continue to act without external restrictions.

In 1998, the United States was among seven countries that rejected the newly created International Criminal Court, which was designed to hold individuals accountable for war crimes and genocide, which joined by Israel, Libya, China, Iraq, Qatar, and Yemen. David Scheffer, the U.S. Ambassador for War Crimes Issues, openly demanded that U.S. officials and soldiers, who shoulder the greatest responsibilities for peace, should be granted immunity from its jurisdiction.[50] U.S. disrespect for international law was also apparent in its refusal to sign the 1997 Ottawa convention prohibiting the use of anti-personnel land mines, which was supported by more than 120 countries. In 2020, the Trump administration even announced that it would reverse long-standing policies that restricted the use of anti-personnel land mines.[51]

After World War II, U.S. economic imperialism took on a new form. Certainly, the institutions formed after the agreement at Bretton Woods in 1944 have provided a secure base for currencies linked to the U.S. dollar.[52] The United State has provided a stable clearing system for financial transactions and the 'swap lines' that the U.S. Federal Reserve put in place after the global financial crisis in 2008-09, allowing foreign central banks to provide dollars to their weakened domestic financial institutions. Viewed from the opposite side, however, it means that as a custodian of the global financial system, the United States could use its privileged status in the global financial system to coerce others, in the manner Henry Farrell and Abraham Newman refer to as 'America's Financial Empire'.[53]

As globalisation has deepened during the last decade, the United States has increasingly relied on 'lawful' economic sanctions in place of 'unlawful' war as a foreign policy tool. Moreover, the ways of exercising its economic power have increasingly become subtle and informal. Instead of coercing its adversaries directly by cutting off access to U.S. firms and markets, the United States has often imposed so-called secondary sanctions, which cut off access to the global financial system itself. Because of the huge power of the U.S. dollar, even the threat of secondary sanctions prompts many companies and international banks to change their behaviour to avoid the risk of such sanctions.[54] U.S. secondary sanctions are largely implemented and enforced by the U.S. Treasury's Office of Foreign Assets Control (OFAC). Some sanctions are oriented geographically, as in the cases of Iran and Cuba; others are focused on specific individuals and entities. OFAC's Specially Designated Nationals and Blocked Persons List has approximately 6,300 names connected with sanctions targets. OFAC also maintains other sanctions lists that have different associated prohibitions.[55]

Iran has suffered economic hardship caused by U.S. economic sanctions since the Iranian Revolution in 1979. U.S. economic sanctions were intensified after the United States left the Iran nuclear deal in May 2018, when the Trump administration began ramping up economic penalties as a part of its 'maximum pressure' campaign on the Iranian regime. In January 2020, as a response to the attacks on two Iraqi military bases housing American troops, Trump decided to increase 'punishing economic sanctions on the Iranian Regime'. He also suggested possible additional sanctions if the Islamic Republic failed to change its international behaviour.[56]

Even after the deadly COVID-19 coronavirus crisis hit Iran, the Trump administration did not lift sanctions. In March 2020, Secretary of State Mike Pompeo released the statement that, 'Our sanctions will deprive the regime of critical income from its petrochemical industry and further Iran's economic and diplomatic isolation. The United States will continue to fully enforce our sanctions'.[57] Iranian officials have called the continued U.S. sanctions amid the pandemic 'medical terrorism', insisting that they would prevent the government from taking necessary measures to reduce the epidemic and its economic impact on the Iranian people, as well as increasing the difficulty of supplying daily food and medicines. The Trump administration repeatedly stated that U.S. sanctions were not designed to hurt average Iranians, just the Iranian regime, and that financial channels have been kept open for humanitarian trade. Yet, in reality, banks and companies, being fearful of U.S. penalties for circumventing sanctions, have shunned transactions with Iran for humanitarian purposes, even those permitted theoretically.

U.S. economic sanctions have also prevented Iran from securing updated information on COVID-19. Iranians have been unable to access the COVID-19 Global Cases Dashboard created by Johns Hopkins University in the United States, which is one of the most reliable virus mapping tools that tracks worldwide Covid-19 cases in real time. This source and similar services have been denied to ordinary Iranians because technical companies have had to comply with U.S. sanctions. The situation is totally contrary to what Brian Hook, the U.S. Special Representative for Iran, said in a video called 'Dispelling Myths About U.S. Sanctions on Iran', in which he tried to reassure Iranian viewers that U.S. lawmakers 'believe strongly in the free flow of communication and information'.[58]

The inhumane attitude of the U.S. toward Iran can be compared with the experience of Cuba, which has also suffered from an economic embargo, which the United States imposed after the Revolution of 1959. Despite these adverse economic conditions, Cuba has set standards of education, welfare, and medical provision that enabled exports of these services to make a major contribution to the country's balance of payment.[59] When Italy's COVID-19 death toll soared, Cuba swiftly sent medical brigades to combat COVID-19 and also deployed doctors to Venezuela, Nicaragua, Jamaica, Suriname, and Grenada.

Iran is not the only country being sanctioned by the United States. Trump has increased pressure on President Nicolás Maduro Moros, Venezuela's legitimate president, to step down. In August 2019, Trump signed an Executive Order 'Blocking Property of the Government of Venezuela', which stated that the United States would 'use every appropriate tool to end Maduro's hold on Venezuela'.[60] In fact, U.S. economic sanctions have been imposed not only on the Venezuelan government's assets in the United States, but also on the individuals, companies and countries doing business with the Venezuelan government. Though Trump justified continuing economic sanctions on Venezuela for humanitarian purposes, pointing to human rights abuses by Maduro and his aide, the report published by the Center for Economic and Policy Research shows that U.S. sanctions have inflicted very serious harm to human life and health in Venezuela. Estimates indicated more than 40,000 deaths in 2017–18, and a further 300,000 people were at risk due to lack of access to medicines. The report concluded that U.S. economic sanctions would fit the definition of 'collective punishment of the civilian population'.[61]

In recent years, however, the arbitrary use of economic coercive measures by the United States has provoked increasing international criticism. In July 2019, the Non-Aligned Movement had a ministerial conference in Caracas, Venezuela, where the delegates of 120 countries including Iran and Venezuela discussed how to confront U.S. unilateral coercive measures. Founded in 1961, the Non-Aligned Movement has historically provided a venue for formerly colonised countries to act as a unified league between the U.S. and Soviet power blocs during the Cold War. After the end of the Cold War, the Non-Aligned Movement has renewed its significance as an important multilateral framework to decrease international reliance on the U.S. dollar with alternatives to the U.S.-controlled financial system. At the conclusion of the meeting, the Non-Aligned Movement declared that the members would explore plans to sue the United States at the International Court of Justice over its arbitrary application of economic sanctions.[62]

In a speech to the U.N. Human Rights Council in September 2019, the Venezuelan Foreign Minister, Jorge Arreaza Montserrat, blasted U.S. economic sanctions, calling them 'another serious aggression' by the Trump administration. He also cited a resolution adopted by the Non-Aligned Movement urging states to refrain from applying unilateral coercive measures, adding that Venezuelan position was backed by various international institutions such as the U.N. General Assembly, the High Commissioner for Human Rights, and the Special Rapporteur on the negative impact of unilateral coercive measures. Montserrat also emphasised that it has been the poorest, most vulnerable members of the society who suffered most from the deprivation caused by U.S. economic sanctions.[63] According to the report published by the U.N. High Commissioner for Refugees in 2019, the number of Venezuelans leaving their country reached 4 million which made them one of the single largest displaced population groups.[64]

The Non-Aligned Movement held an international summit again in October 2019 to discuss ways of escaping U.S. crippling sanctions, and of challenging U.S. dollar domination. Samuel Moncada, the Venezuelan ambassador to the United Nations, denounced the imposition of sanctions by the United States as 'economic terrorism which affects a third of humanity with more than 8,000 measures in 39 countries'.[65] Responding to Moncada's accusation, Under-Secretary-General for Political and Peacebuilding Affairs of the United Nations, Rosemary A. DiCarlo, declared that 'The Non-Aligned Movement members represent two-thirds of the U.N. membership and contribute 80 percent of U.N. peacekeepers', adding that through the past years the concerns and views of the Non-Aligned Movement countries have increasingly shaped U.N. agenda, from peace and security to sustainable development and human rights.[66]

In March 2020, the U.N. Special Rapporteur on the effect of sanctions on human rights slammed the Trump administration's 'illegal and immoral forms of coercion', calling it an 'economic attack' on the Iranian people.[67] The dollar-clearing system is unlikely to collapse in near future. But the movements criticising the inhumane exercise of U.S. economic power, challenging the domination of the U.S. dollar, and creating alternative global currencies, are likely to increase, which might pose significant challenges to American financial empire.

The Rising Awareness of the Cost of Empire

One of the brilliant features of Hopkin's book is highlighting the domestic challenges to the American Empire as well as international ones. Unlike the other Western imperial powers, the decolonisation of the American insular empire after World War II proceeded in parallel with its internal decolonisation. Protests against discrimination and the denial of human rights intensified after 1945, and grew into the civil rights movements, which eventually achieved significant victories in the 1960s.[68]

Today, we are witnessing again emerging domestic challenges to the American imperial extensions. The decision to invade Iraq in 2003 sparked the same kind of debate that had been advanced in 1898; whether the assertion of U.S. primacy was an expression of the providential mission to bring liberty and democracy to the world, or just an anachronistic imposition of century-old Western imperialism.[69] After World War II, Britain and France suffered from the economic burden of maintaining colonial rule in the face of nationalist opposition.[70] Likewise, through the almost two decades of the 'war on terror', Americans are increasingly burdened by the cost of external interventions. As death, destruction, and debt caused by the war in Iraq mounted, the American public turned against the occupation. The global financial crisis in 2008, which stemmed from the collapse of the U.S. housing market and a rash of bankruptcies of financial institutions, revealed the vulnerability of U.S. economy and accelerated the inward-looking mood.[71]

According to the Cost of War Project launched by the Watson Institute at Brown University, since 2001 the 'war of terror' has expanded to more than 80 countries. So far, over 7,000 U.S. troops have died, as have approximately 8,000 contractors. Over 110,000 allied troops and national police in Iraq and Afghanistan have been killed. As of November 2019, 335,000 civilians in Iraq, Afghanistan, Yemen, Syria, and Pakistan have died as a result of the wars. The number of war refugees and displaced persons from Afghanistan, Iraq, Pakistan, Yemen, Somalia, the Philippines, Libya, and Syria is estimated at over 37 million.[72] Economically, since late 2001, the United States has appropriated and is obligated to spend an estimated $6.4 trillion on counterterrorism efforts through the end of 2020.[73]

Historically, the American empire has been backed by the belief that American values are global values that need to be universally recognised.[74] Yet, today, American citizens no longer share this optimistic belief. The 2020 Gallup poll shows that American pride reached the lowest point in the two decades measured by Gallup at a time when the country faces public health and economic crises brought on by the coronavirus pandemic and civil unrest following the death of George Floyd in May 2020. Although most U.S. adults still say they are 'extremely proud' (42%) or 'very proud' (21%) to be American, both rates are the lowest since Gallup's initial measurements in 2001.[75]

Commentators and politicians are divided between optimists who still believe that the United States will remain the world's leading power, and pessimists who expect that China will soon match the United States. However, ordinary citizens, especially young Americans, do not necessarily see American decline negatively. According to recent opinion polls, the younger generation who have grown up in the age of unsuccessful military interventions in Afghanistan, Iraq, and elsewhere, and the 2008 global financial crisis do not have a belief in the United States as an 'indispensable Nation', as described by former Secretary of State Madeleine Albright. They no longer think that the United States can and should act unilaterally. Rather, they favour a more restrained role for the United States in international affairs, and a more cooperative foreign policy that relies less on coercion and more on multilateral institutions.[76]

Here, we can see a revival of faith in international law, yet this time, not as a tool of the American empire but as a tool for international cooperation. As this paper shows, during the twentieth century, international law largely functioned as a tool to maintain the *status quo* favoured by the United States. The far-reaching changes that occurred after World War II, however, altered the attitude of the U.S. towards international organisations. Today, with the rise of a generation that has a new way of thinking, international law might acquire a new meaning in U.S. diplomatic practices and begin to function as an important base for building mutual cooperation with the other countries.

Notes

1. Kennan, *American Diplomacy, 1900–1950*, 82.
2. Hathaway and Shapiro emphasize that the League and the Pact marked a significant shift from an "Old World Order," where all states retained the right of waging war, to a new one, where aggressive war is illegal, and conflicts are solved through peaceful means. Hathaway and Shapiro, *The Internationalists*.
3. Hopkins, *American Empire*, 444.
4. Ibid., 451.
5. About the complicated legacy of the mandate system under the League of Nations, which helped prolong the era of colonialism, see Pedersen, *The Guardians*.
6. To see how international law shaped U.S. foreign policy in the first half of the 20th century, see Coates, *Legalist Empire*; Zasloff, "Law and the Shaping of American Foreign Policy". As Zasloff points out, among the nine men who served as the U.S. Secretary of State from 1905 to 1945, eight of them, with the exception of William Jennings Brian (1913-1915) were jurists, and American diplomacy during the period was significantly characterized by legalist thinking.
7. About U.S. international lawyers' contribution to establishing the core ideas of League of Nations and the Kellogg-Briand Pact, in which outlawry of war was institutionalized, see Shinohara, *US International Lawyers in the Interwar Years*.
8. Pomerance, *The United States And the World Court As A "Supreme Court of the Nations*," Chap. 1. The idea of international court has a long history. Before American pacifists began to advocate it, the idea was already proposed by European politicians

and intellectuals such as Pierre Dubois (1255-1312), an adviser of King Philip IV of France. See, Hemleben, *Plans for World Peace through Six Centuries*, Chap. 1.
9. "History of the American Peace Society and Its Work".
10. Ladd, *An Essay on a Congress of Nations for the Adjustment of International Disputes without Resort To Arms*, 6, 76–78. About the enduring impact of Ladd's ideas on American peace advocates, see, Schwarzenberger, *William Ladd*; Scott, "William Ladd's Project of a Congress and Court of Nations."
11. About the founding of the American Society of International Law, see Kirgis, *The American Society of International Law's First Century, 1906–2006*, Chap. 1.
12. "Russian Circular Note Proposing the Program of the First Conference (December 30, 1898)," in Scott, *The Hague Peace Conferences of 1899 and 1907*, Vol. 2., p. xv.
13. Hay, "Instructions to the International Peace at the Hague,1899 (April 18, 1899)," Ibid., 8.
14. Root, "Instructions to the American Delegates to the Conference of 1907 (May 31, 1907)," Ibid., 191.
15. Ibid.
16. Scott, "The Legal Nature of International Law", 844. About Scott's enduring belief in international law, see Nurnberger, "James Brown Scott: Peace through Justice"; Hepp, "James Brown Scott and the Rise of Public International Law"; Cooley and Finch, *Adventures in Internationalism*.
17. Scott, "The Proposed Court of Arbitral Justice"; Scott, "Recommendation for a Third Peace Conference at the Hague"; Scott, "Judicial Proceedings as a Substitute for War or International Self-redress"; Scott, "The Evolution of a Permanent International Judiciary".
18. "The American Society for the Judicial Settlement of International Disputes," 930–32.
19. *Proceedings of International Conference under the Auspices of American Society for Judicial Settlement of International Disputes*, x.
20. Scott, "Address of President," Ibid., 3–4.
21. Root, "The Importance of Judicial Settlement," Ibid., 13–14.
22. Ibid., 88–89, 92, 164–5, 221, 269–74, 288–90.
23. Koskenniemi, "The Ideology of International Adjudication".
24. Coate, *Legalist Empire*, passim. Landauer, "The Ambivalences of Power: Launching the American Journal of International Law in an Era of Empire and Globalization". Boyle, *Foundations of World Order*, Chap. 6.
25. Bemis ed., *American Secretaries of State and Their Diplomacy*, Vol. 9, 193.
26. Hopkins, *American Empire*, 563–4.
27. Ibid., 566–76.
28. Root, "The Sanction of International Law".
29. Root, "The Monroe Doctrine (December 22, 1904)," in Bacon and Scott, *Miscellaneous Addresses of Elihu Root*, 269. See also, Jessup, *Elihu Root*, Vol. 1, 288. Leopold, *Elihu Root and the Conservative Tradition*, 27, 37. Herman, *Eleven against War*, 33-35.
30. Wilson, "Pueblo Speech (September 25, 1919)," in Link, *Papers of Woodrow Wilson*, Vol. 63, 501–6.
31. Clavin, *Securing the World Economy*, 470.
32. Schmitt, "Form of Modern Imperialism in International Law (Völkerrechtliche Formen des modernen Imperialismus) (1933)," in Legg ed., *Spatiality, Sovereignty and Carl Schmitt*, 29–45.
33. Ibid.
34. Ito, *Konoe Ko Seidanroku*, 231–41.

35. Ibid., 242–55.
36. La Follette, "Opposition to Wilson's War Message," *U.S. Congressional Record*, 65th Cong, 1st sess., Vol. 55, Part1, 223–236.
37. Drake, *The Education of an Anti-Imperialist*, Chap. 12.
38. "Mr. Atherton to Sir Austen Chamberlain (June 23, 1928)," Avalon Project at Yale Law School.
39. Johnson, *The Peace Progressives and American Foreign Relations*, 178–9. Johnson gives a comprehensive analysis of the foreign policy perspectives of the "peace progressives," a bloc of dissenters in the U.S. Senate between 1913 and 1935 including Blaine. They were unified behind the idea that the United States should be the champion of weaker states.
40. About Kellogg's diplomacy toward Nicaragua, see Kamman, *A Search for Stability*; Ellis, *Frank B. Kellogg and American Foreign Relations, 1925–1929*, 58–85. Bryn-Jones, *Frank B. Kellogg*, 185–202.
41. Johnson, *The Peace Progressives*, 134–5.
42. Niebuhr, "Awkward Imperialists."
43. Niebuhr, "American Power and World Responsibility."
44. Hopkins, *American Empire*, 797–8.
45. Ikenberry and Deudney, "America's Impact," 15.
46. Ikenberry, *Liberal Leviathan*.
47. Hopkins, *American Empire*, 699–700. Hopkins, "Globalisation and Decolonisation," 10–11.
48. Hopkins, *American Empire*, 698–9.
49. Ibid., 734–46. In this volume, Hideki Kan's paper deals with these issues as greater length.
50. Scheffer, "Statement on Creating an International Criminal Court (August 31, 1998)," U.S. Department of State Archive.
51. Ismay and Gibbons-Neff, "160 Nations Ban These Weapons.
52. Hopkins, *American Empire*, 708.
53. Farrell and Newman, "The Twilight of America's Financial Empire."
54. Ibid.
55. U.S. Treasury Department, The Office of Foreign Assets Control.
56. Borak, "Trump Vows to Impose 'Punishing' Sanctions on Iran But Offers No Details."
57. Pompeo, "Press Statement (March 18, 2020)," U.S. Department of State.
58. Cockrell, "US Sanctions Block Iranians from Accessing Coronavirus Map."
59. Hopkins, *American Empire*, 719–20.
60. "Statement from the Press Secretary Regarding an Executive Order 'Blocking Property of the Government of Venezuela' (August 6, 2019)," U.S. Embassy in Venezuela.
61. Weisbrot and Sachs, "Economic Sanctions as Collective Punishment".
62. Parampil, "Non-Aligned Movement Gathers in Venezuela To Resist Dictatorship of Dollar".
63. Schlein, "Venezuelan Minister Calls U.S. Sanctions 'Economic Terrorism'" .
64. "Refugees and Migrants from Venezuela Top 4 Million: UNHCR and IOM (June 7, 2019)," United Nations High Commissioner for Refugees (UNHCR).
65. Zeese and Flowers, "The World Must End the U.S.' Illegal Economic War".
66. "Secretary-General's Message to the XVIII Summit of Heads of State and Government of the Non-Aligned Movement, 25–26 October (October 25, 2019)," United Nations, Secretary-General.
67. Larison, "The Inhumane and Monstrous Economic War on Iran".

68. Hopkins, "Globalisation and Decolonisation," 12–13. Hopkins, *American Empire*, 664–669.
69. Hopkins, *American Empire*, 724.
70. Ibid. 697–8.
71. Ibid. 725–6.
72. Cost of War Project, "Overview."
73. Cost of War Project (November 13. 2019).
74. Hopkins, *American Empire*, 726.
75. Brenan, "U.S. National Pride Falls to Record Low."
76. Thrall, "The Clash of Generations?". Halpin, Katulis, Juul, Agne, Gerstein, and Jain, "America Adrift."

Disclosure Statement

No potential conflict of interest was reported by the author(s).

References

Bacon, Robert, and J. B. Scott, eds. *Miscellaneous Addresses of Elihu Root*. Cambridge: Harvard University Press, 1917.
Bemis, Samuel, F., eds. *American Secretaries of State and Their Diplomacy. 10 Vols*. New York: Alfred A. Knopf Inc., 1927-1929.
Borak, Donna. "Trump Vows to Impose 'Punishing' Sanctions on Iran But Offers No Details." *CNN* (Jan 8, 2020). https://edition.cnn.com/2020/01/08/politics/trump-iran-sanctions/index.html.
Boyle, Francis A. *Foundations of World Order: The Legalist Approach to International Relations, 1898–1922*. Durham: Duke University Press, 1999.
Brenan, Megan. "U.S. National Pride Falls to Record Low." *Gallup* (June 15, 2020). https://news.gallup.com/poll/312644/national-pride-falls-record-low.aspx.
Bryn-Jones, David. *Frank B. Kellogg: A Biography*. New York: G.P. Putnam' Sons, 1937.
Clavin, Patricia. *Securing the World Economy. The Reinvention of the League of Nations, 1920-1946*. Oxford: Oxford University Press, 2013.
Coates, Benjamin Allen. *Legalist Empire: International Law and American Foreign Relations in the Early Twentieth Century*. Oxford: Oxford University Press, 2016.
Cockrell, Isobel. "U.S. Sanctions Block Iranians from Accessing Coronavirus Map." *Coda* (March 2, 2020). https://www.codastory.com/authoritarian-tech/sanctions-iran-coronavirus-map/.
Cooley, Thomas M., and G. A. Finch. *Adventures in Internationalism: A Biography of James Brown Scott*. Clark: Lawbook Exchange, 2011.
Drake, Richard. *The Education of an Anti-Imperialist: Robert La Follette and U.S. Expansion*. Madison: University of Wisconsin Press, 2013.
Ellis, Lewis E. *Frank B. Kellogg and American Foreign Relations, 1925- 1929*. New Brunswick: Rutgers University Press, 1961.
Farrell, Henry, and A. Newman. "The Twilight of America's Financial Empire: Washington's Economic Bullying Will Erode Its Power." *Foreign Affairs* (January 24, 2020). https://www.foreignaffairs.com/articles/2020-01-24/twilight-americas-financial-empire.
Halpin, John, B. Katulis, P. Juul, K. Agne, J. Gerstein, and N. Jain. "America Adrift: How the U.S. Foreign Policy Debate Misses What Voters Really Want." *Center for American Progress*

(May 5, 2019). https://www.americanprogress.org/issues/security/news/2019/10/25/476433/america-adrift-listening-americans-want-u-s-foreign-policy/.

Hathaway, Oona A., and S. J. Shapiro. *The Internationalists: How A Radical Plan to Outlaw War Remade the World*. New York: Simon and Schuster, 2017.

Hemleben, Sylvester J. *Plans for World Peace Through Six Centuries*. Chicago: University of Chicago Press, 1929.

Hepp, John. "James Brown Scott and the Rise of Public International Law." *The Journal of the Gilded Age and Progressive Era* 7, no. 2 (2008): 151–179.

Herman, Sondra R. *Eleven Against War: Studies in American Internationalist Thought, 1898–1921*. Stanford, California: Hoover Institution Press, 1969.

"History of the American Peace Society and Its Work," *The Advocate of Peace* 69, no. 1 (1907): 15–20.

Hopkins, A. G. *American Empire: A Global History*. Princeton: Princeton University Press, 2018.

Hopkins, A. G. "Globalisation and Decolonisation." *The Journal of Imperial and Commonwealth History* 45, no. 5 (2017): 729–745.

Ikenberry, G. John. *Liberal Leviathan: The Origins, Crisis, and Transformation of the American World Order*. Princeton: Princeton University Press, 2011.

Ikenberry, G. John, and D. Deudney. "America's Impact: The End of Empire and the Globalization of the Westphalian System." *Working Paper for American Political Science Association* (September, 2015): 1-60. https://scholar.princeton.edu/sites/default/files/gji3/files/am-impact-dd-gji-final-1-august-2015.pdf.

Ismay, John, and T. Gibbons-Neuf. "160 Nations Ban These Weapons. The U.S. Now Embraces Them." *New York Times* (February 7, 2020). https://www.nytimes.com/2020/02/07/us/trump-land-mines-cluster-munitions.html.

Ito, Takeshi, ed. *Konoe Ko Seidanroku*. Tokyo: Chikura Shobo, 1937.

Jessup, Philip C. *Elihu Root. 2vols*. New York: Dodd, Mead& Co., 1964 [1938].

Johnson, Robert D. *The Peace Progressives and American Foreign Relations*. Cambridge: Harvard University Press, 1995.

Kamman, William. *A Search for Stability: United States Diplomacy Toward Nicaragua, 1925-1933*. Notre Dame: University of Notre Dame Press, 1968.

Kennan, George F. *American Diplomacy, 1900 -1950*. New York: Mentor Books, 1951.

Kirgis, Frederic L. *The American Society of International Law's First Century, 1906-2006*. Leiden: Martinus Nijhoff, 2006.

Koskenniemi, Martti. "The Ideology of International Adjudication." Paper Presented at the 100th Anniversary of the Second Hague Peace Conference of 1907, The Hague Academy of International Law (September 7, 2007): 1-18.

Ladd, William. *An Essay on a Congress of Nations for the Adjustment of International Disputes Without Resort to Arms, Reprinted from the Original Edition of 1840 with an Introduction by James Brown Scott*. New York: Oxford University Press, American Branch, 1916 [1840].

Landauer, Carlo. "The Ambivalences of Power: Launching the American Journal of International Law in an Era of Empire and Globalization." *Leiden Journal of International Law* 20, no. 2 (2007): 325–358.

Larison, Daniel. "The Inhumane and Monstrous Economic War on Iran." *American Conservative* (March 18, 2020). https://www.theamericanconservative.com/larison/the-inhumane-and-monstrous-economic-war-on-iran/.

Legg, Stephen, ed. *Spatiality, Sovereignty and Carl Schmitt: Geographies of the Nomos*. Abingdon: Routledge, 2011.

Leopold, Richard W. *Elihu Root and the Conservative Tradition*. Boston: Little, Brown & Co, 1954.

Link, Arthur S. *Papers of Woodrow Wilson*. 69 Vols. Princeton: Princeton University Press, 1966-1994.

Niebuhr, Reinhold. "American Power and World Responsibility." *Christianity and Crisis* 3 (April 5, 1943): 2–4.

Niebuhr, Reinhold. "Awkward Imperialists." *Atlantic* 145, no. 5 (1930): 670–675.

Nurnberger, Ralph D. "James Brown Scott: Peace through Justice." *Ph.D. Dissertation, Georgetown University* (1975).

Parampil, Anya. "Non-Aligned Movement Gathers in Venezuela To Resist Dictatorship of Dollar." *Canadian Dimension* (August 6, 2019). https://canadiandimension.com/articles/view/non-aligned-movement-gathers-in-venezuela-to-resist-dictatorship-of-dollar.

Pedersen, Susan. *The Guardians: The League of Nations and the Crisis of Empire*. Oxford: Oxford University Press, 2015.

Pomerance, Michla. *The United States And the World Court As A "Supreme Court of The Nations: Dreams, Illusions and Disillusion*. The Hague: Martinus Nijhoff, 1996.

Proceedings of International Conference under the Auspices of American Society for Judicial Settlement of International Disputes, December, 15-17, 1910, Washington, D.C. Baltimore: Waverly Press, 1911.

Root, Elihu. "The Sanction of International Law." *American Journal of International Law* 2, no. 3 (1908): 451–457.

Schlein, Lisa. "Venezuelan Minister Calls US Sanctions 'Economic Terrorism'." Vox (September 12, 2019). https://www.voanews.com/americas/venezuelan-minister-calls-us-sanctions-economic-terrorism.

Schwarzenberger, Georg. *William Ladd: An Examination of an American Proposal for an International Equity Tribunal*. London: Constable, 1935.

Scott, James. "Judicial Proceedings as a Substitute for War or International Self-Redress." *Maryland Peace Society Quarterly* 1 (1910): 3–16.

Scott, James. "Recommendation for a Third Peace Conference at the Hague." *American Journal of International Law* 2, no. 4 (1908): 815–822.

Scott, James. "The Evolution of a Permanent International Judiciary." *American Journal of International Law* 6, no. 2 (1912): 316–358.

Scott, James. "The Legal Nature of International Law." *American Journal of International Law* 1, no. 4 (1907): 831–866.

Scott, James. "The Proposed Court of Arbitral Justice." *American Journal of International Law* 2, no. 4 (1908): 772–810.

Scott, James. "William Ladd's Project of a Congress and Court of Nations." *The Advocate of Peace* 70, no. 8 (1908): 196–200.

Scott, James. *The Hague Peace Conferences of 1899 and 1907: A Series of Lectures Delivered Before the Johns Hopkins University in the Year of 1908*. 2 Vols. New York: Garland Pub., 1972 [1909].

Shinohara, Hatsue. *US International Lawyers in the Interwar Years: A. Forgotten Crusade*. Cambridge: Cambridge University Press, 2012.

"The American Society for the Judicial Settlement of International Disputes," *The American Journal of International Law* 4, no. 4 (1910): 930-932.

Thrall, Trevor. "The Clash of Generations? Intergenerational Change and American Foreign Policy Views." *Chicago Council on Global Affairs* (June 25, 2018). https://www.thechicagocouncil.org/publication/clash-generations-intergenerational-change-and-american-foreign-policy-views.

U.S. Congressional Record, 65th Cong, 1st sess., Vol. 55, Part 1.

Weisbrot, Mark, and Jeffrey Sachs. "Economic Sanctions as Collective Punishment: The Case of Venezuela." *Center for Economic and Policy Research* (April, 2019). https://cepr.net/images/stories/reports/venezuela-sanctions-2019-04.pdf.

Zasloff, Jonathan. "Law and the Shaping of American Foreign Policy: The Twenty Years' Crisis." *Southern California Law Review* 77, no. 3 (2003-2004): 583–682.

Zeese, Kavin, and M. Flowers. "The World Must End the U.S.' Illegal Economic War." *Popular Resistance* (January 12, 2020). https://popularresistance.org/illegal-us-economic-war/.

Website

Avalon Project at Yale Law School. https://avalon.law.yale.edu

United Nations High Commissioner for Refugees (UNHCR). https://www.unhcr.org/

United Nations, Secretary-General. https://www.un.org/sg

U.S. Department of States. https://www.state.gov/

U.S. Department of State Archive. https://1997-2001.state.gov//index.htm

U.S. Embassy in Venezuela. https://ve.usembassy.gov/

U.S. Treasury Department, The Office of Foreign Assets Control (OFAC). https://www.treasury.gov/resource-center/sanctions/Pages/default.aspx

Cost of War Project, Watson Institute at Brown University. https://watson.brown.edu/costsofwar/costs

Informal Empire and the Cold War

Hideki Kan

ABSTRACT

Hopkins's *American Empire* is quite illuminating in his comparative analysis and detailed account of the dependent territories in the Caribbean and the Pacific. He convincingly demonstrates that the American empire was not exceptional, though distinct, and that it shared more commonalities than differences with other Western colonial powers. This essay attempts to shed light on some other aspects that Hopkins's analysis of the 'insular empire' did not fully cover in his work. It employs the term 'informal empire' rather than hegemony to grasp the distinct characteristics of American empire-building and highlights the dialectical process of interaction between America's anti-colonial tradition, on the one hand, and the imperial impulses, on the other. In contrast with Hopkins's portrayal of the United States as 'an aspiring hegemon,' it argues that the interwar years were a transitional stage of U.S. empire-building that subsequently transformed itself into a fully-fledged informal empire during the Cold War years. The article shows that the Cold War order was hierarchical and coercive, and similar to the old imperial order embodied by the European colonial powers. It shares Hopkins's view that the first signs of the decline of U.S. power appeared in the 1970s but disagrees about the rate the trend developed. It contends that the decline was rather gradual and winding, though cumulative, and that the United States managed to remain an informal empire for some time after the ending of the Cold War.

'The Insular Empire' in *American Empire*

An orthodox or traditional interpretation of the American empire by Americanists generally denies that the United States is an empire. They assert that the acquiring of Guam, Hawai'i and the Philippines was an aberration in American history.[1] The aberration argument is no longer common among U.S. historians because it was effectively challenged by William A. Williams's work, *The Tragedy of American Diplomacy* (1959). Williams's theory of American empire is known as 'Open Door imperialism'.

He argued that the ideas expressed in John Hay's Open Door notes became 'the basic strategy and tactics of America's secular and imperial expansion in the twentieth century'.[2] The Wisconsin School's reputation experienced ups and downs, reaching its height in the 1960s and early 1970s. The fact that Williams was elected the president of the Organization of American Historians (OAH) in 1980 shows that his 'Open Door imperialism' had acquired a kind of 'citizenship' in the profession, if not among policy-makers in Washington.[3]

Novel and stimulating as it was, Williams's pioneering work, as well as those of his students, was not a comparative study of empires. The Wisconsin School showed little interest in the formal empire. Williams's 'Open Door imperialism' emphasised the continuity of overseas expansion in the twentieth century but did not explore changing features of empire-building at different stages of capitalist development. On the other hand, Hopkins's *American Empire* is illuminating and path-breaking in a number of respects. He rediscovered the 'insular empire' in American history and placed it in a comparative perspective. His portrayal of the dependent territories in the Caribbean and the Pacific is detailed and very informative, shedding light on the interactions between the coloniser and the colonised as well as the various mechanisms of U.S. colonial rule. 'No one before him has analyzed the administration of the American dependencies,' commented the authoritative historian of the British empire, Roger Louis, 'on such a scale and with such exactitude'.[4] This monumental work brilliantly uncovered 'the most neglected topics' in the U.S. historiography of modern empires.

Hopkins also provides the reader with a broad, long-term perspective to understand a global history of empires. Particularly impressive is the author's attempt to place the Cold War in a long-term history of decolonisation. He views the Cold War as 'part of the wider process of decolonization' and proposes that 'instead of fitting decolonization into the Cold War, the Cold War needs to be fitted into decolonization'.[5] Most striking of all is his insight that decolonisation is 'the product of the shift from modern to postcolonial globalization' and therefore 'needs to be placed in the wider context of the global transformation of power, interests, and values in the postwar era'.[6] According to *American Empire*, the era of 'postcolonial globalization' witnessed structural changes in international trade and the diversification of the global economy, the moral revolution as seen in the rise of human rights, and the change in the composition of nationalist movements in the colonies into mass movements. These new developments in turn combined to raise the cost of empires to unbearably high levels, eventually sounding the death-knell of territorial empires in the late 1950s and early 1960s.

The term post-colonial globalisation so defined in *American Empire* brilliantly explains why territorial empires could not survive longer than they did. But to what extent did the new phase of the post-war world influence the status of the United States? This question needs further examination, given America's unprecedented geopolitical and financial role during and after World War II.

Patrick O'Brien, writing in 2002, stated that World War II 'marked a fundamental discontinuity in geopolitics which renders comparisons between the Pax Britannica and American hegemony anachronistic'.[7] America's unique arsenal 'continues to afford the United States a position of formal and informal supremacy over the North Atlantic Treaty Organization and over its relations (through its "mutual" security treaties) with an evolving range of other non-communist states'.[8]

O'Brien's observation raises the following questions. What kind of international order emerged in the postwar world? Was the Cold War order imperial or not? How do we explain the semi-sovereign status of East European countries in the socialist camp led by Moscow? Were NATO members and Japan able to exercise effective independence vis-à-vis the United States? How do we define their status within the 'free world' led by Washington?

American Empire emphasises that the United States had an empire just like other Western colonial powers from 1898 to 1959. The author also contends that, after 1945, the United States ceased to be an empire, instead becoming 'an aspiring hegemon' or a world power.[9] He does not explain, however, why both the 'insular empire' and a hegemonic state coexisted from 1945 to 1959 in the American state. The juxtaposition of 'the insular empire' with a hegemon in his scheme of *American Empire* implies that both formal and informal empire-building are part of the same movement and could take place concurrently.[10] This dual phenomenon suggests the transitional nature of U.S. empire-building during the inter-war years. The main current of America's overseas expansion in the twentieth century, one could argue, was running in the direction of 'imperialism without colonies'.[11] Viewed in this light, the inter-war years can be regarded as a transition from the 'insular empire' to informal empire.[12] It also implies the newly emerging imperial status of the United States in the postwar years. The Cold War order was more akin to the old imperial order as shown, for example, by the collaborative relationships between the United States and European empires in the Cold War struggle against the Soviet Union.[13]

Hopkins's exclusive focus on the 'insular empire' is liable to minimise another important aspect of U.S. empire-building. One of the distinct historical developments of U.S. empire-building is the dialectical process of anti-colonialism and imperialism that William's notions of 'imperial anticolonialism' and the 'imperialism of idealism' suggest.[14] Missing from Hopkins's portrayal of the post-war United States as a hegemon rather than an informal empire is the analysis of the juxtaposition of anti-colonial nationalism and imperialism in U.S. empire-building. Its anti-colonial process cannot be separated from American imperialism.[15] Both aspects need to be more closely examined.

The American system of informal empire that exercises power through indirect influence was more congenial to the consciousness of its own colonial past. It also accords with the 'Open Door' principles of equal opportunities in commerce and respect for the territorial integrity of nation-states (or respect for nominal state sovereignty). Given that it was characterised by loose U.S. spheres of influence in the Western Hemisphere as well as its insistence on non-interference in the area by the European powers, the Monroe Doctrine of 1823 can be considered in line with the anti-colonial tradition of the United States.

Hopkins observes that the United States reached the peak of its power relative to its rivals in the 1970s and that by the 1980s, the economic supremacy was faltering.[16] In his evaluation of American power and influence in the mid-1970s, however, he does not place sufficient weight on the role of military power and how it functioned in the Cold War years. Neither does he take into due consideration other means of informal influence that were available to the United States, such as the CIA's covert and overt operations to overthrow anti-American nationalist and communist regimes, and its support for regimes of U.S. collaborators through economic and military assistance.

Given the debate between American declinists and anti-declinists about America's status in world affairs during the Cold War years, it is worth-while examining this question more closely. This article will argue that the United States was not only an informal empire but also able to weather the tumultuous years of the 1970s and 1980s and managed to maintain its status for a while after the end of the Cold War.

Formal Empire, Informal Empire, and Hegemon

I agree with the main thrust of the argument in *American Empire* that the United States became a colonial power (formal, territorial empire) in the Pacific and Caribbean in the wake of the 'Spanish-American War' of 1898 by acquiring the insular possessions. However, I will also argue that the United States, following John Hay's 'Notes', initiated an 'Open Door' policy toward China, and subsequently endeavoured to globalise the principle. The Truman Doctrine of March 1947 and the Marshall Plan of June 1947 were post-war manifestations of the globalisation of both the Monroe Doctrine and Hay's 'Open Door' policy or informal empire, while the United States gradually relinquished its territorial possessions during the post-World War II years.[17]

Largely adapting Hopkins's definition of empire, I will define the term informal empire as follows. Empires (formal empires) have overseas territories, while informal empires do not possess foreign territories. Their methods of political control over dependencies or semi-sovereign states are different. Formal empires exercise direct, territorial power over dependencies. As opposed to the techniques of direct political control by formal empires, informal empires employ more indirect methods of control, such as the protection of national security and/or 'informal techniques of free trade'.[18] It does not imply, however, that they refrain from resorting to coercion or military means. Most important of all, from my perspective, informal empires respect the nominal sovereignty of other nations. Therefore, they are more resilient in the face of the growing challenges associated with the postwar anti-colonial nationalist movements and the development of norms such as national self-determination and human rights, while territorial empires are more vulnerable to these pressures. Their respect for the formal sovereignty of other nations obliges them to exercise power indirectly. But informal influence is not always less effective in controlling the foreign policies of other states. Informal empires have the power to create loose spheres of influence, as the Monroe Doctrine did, through techniques of economic dependence, material rewards and mutual good-feelings, security protection, and military intervention, when needed. Both territorial empires and informal empires have collaborators, whilst the latter without them would not have been able to exercise power long enough to control the external behaviour of other states.[19] It follows, therefore, that informal empires, in addition to supplying 'international public goods', need to complement and reinforce their power by providing various material rewards, political support, and security protection to local elites to recognise their loyalty and collaboration.

Given the above definition of informal empire, the term has some advantages in describing the characteristics of U.S. empire-building. One of these is the juxtaposition of anti-colonialism and imperialism. As his support for the Monroe Doctrine shows, President Woodrow Wilson was ambivalent toward independence, self-determination, and self-government for colonial people.[20] Though not always faithful to these norms in terms of policy and action in the face of security threats, U.S. policy-makers nonetheless found it difficult to abandon them, and these principles, together with freedom and democracy, formed the character of the American state. After all, the United States is a nation of immigrants with various ethnic, religious, linguistic, and cultural backgrounds. American ideals, such as freedom, democracy and self-determination, have long continued to constitute the intellectual and psychological foundation that can integrate the nation as one, while upholding the diversity of society.[21]

Second, principles and ideals work both ways. Historically, American empire-builders employed these principles as political weapons to expand U.S. spheres of influence. Decolonisation in North America, in the words of one noted U.S. diplomatic historian, Walter LaFeber, was 'a device for conquering a continental empire'.[22] The United States first decolonised regions in North America that were claimed by several other European empires and, with decolonisation, pulled these regions into its own Union.

This method of decolonising and its anti-imperial rhetoric were later repeated during the Cold War period. Washington's approach toward the question of colonialism and de-colonisation in the Cold War years was at best ambivalent. Notwithstanding Washington's public support for national self-determination, U.S. policymakers did not hesitate to suppress nationalist movements in the Third World when and where they were supported by or aligned with Moscow. Likewise, the United States exploited its anti-colonial ideology as a political weapon to undermine European colonial empires and gain support from leaders of the Third World, where U.S. officials felt the colonial powers were unable to maintain domestic order in the face of anti-colonial nationalist movements.[23]

Third, the term which suggests, according to Hopkins, 'parity with the status of empire,' helps to highlight the unprecedented financial and military power that the United States came to possess in the post-World War II era. The huge power of the United States was unrivalled in the global history of empires and justifies the use of the term 'informal empire' rather than 'an aspiring hegemon'.

The Interwar Years as a Transition to Informal Empire

The disappearance of the 'insular empire' after 1898 is an omission unparalleled in the historiography of modern empires. Hopkins's rediscovery of 'the insular empire' is a major contribution in this sense. Yet, his emphasis on the 'the insular empire' applies to the United States from the late nineteenth century to the end of World War II. The period between World War I and World War II can more appropriately be considered a transition in which the United States transformed the insular empire into an empire of a different kind. After the end of World War II, the United States emerged as an informal empire without overseas territories, while gradually phasing out its existing imperial possessions.

The development of the Monroe Doctrine in the twentieth century shows the growing power of the United States. The Doctrine was a unilateral declaration of non-intervention. However, as time passed, other states came to tacitly submit themselves to a loose U.S. sphere of influence in the Western Hemisphere. As the historian Jay Sexton points out, the fusion of anti-colonialism and imperialism was characteristic of the first century of the Monroe Doctrine.[24] The anticolonial process of nation-building and empire-building went hand in hand.

Furthermore, upon Woodrow Wilson's insistence, the Monroe Doctrine was incorporated into Article 21 of the League of Nations Covenant. Its reference to the Doctrine in Article 21 as an 'understanding' meant that it did not contradict the League Covenant. According to Carl Schmitt, the kind of power exercised by the United States is 'typical of every true and great imperialism'.[25] Hay's declaration of the 'Open Door' policy was also a unilateral act on the part of the U.S. government. However, it was eventually written into the Nine-Power Treaty, which was signed by the four powers (the United States,

Japan, Britain, and France), plus Italy, China, Belgium, the Netherlands, and Portugal in 1922. Taken together, as Walter LaFeber points out, they 'put the open-door principles into international law'.[26] Not only Tokyo but also the other imperial powers accepted the open-door principles Washington insisted upon at the conference. In this sense, the conference was 'a success' from Washington's point of view.[27] It marks a very important phase in the historical development of the United States as an informal empire. If the contents of a political treaty, as E. H. Carr states, 'reflect in some degree the relative strength of the contracting parties',[28] then the event illustrates the growing power and influence of the United States in the inter-war years.

The conclusion of the Nine-Power Treaty was made possible because a compromise over the difficult issue of conflicting approaches to China (open door vs spheres of influence) had been worked out among the powers concerned before the conference was convened. In October 1918, Woodrow Wilson resurrected a new consortium policy for China after the failure of his unilateral attempt to penetrate the China market through a group of the consortium of American bankers. Wilson's new proposal to Tokyo, London and Paris aimed at opening the Chinese market to the United States by preventing any other powers, Japan and Great Britain in particular, from expanding their spheres of influence or interfering in China through unilateral loans. During the negotiations, the American bankers, notably Thomas Lamont and J. P. Morgan, made it clear that they would participate on condition that the consortium members would be given priority for investments and loans in China. The attached condition was intended to contain further expansion of spheres of influence by the imperial powers with vested interests in China. Japan, however, insisted that its special rights in Manchuria and Inner Mongolia had to be recognised by the participating parties, a demand that the other powers refused. In the end, they worked out a compromise in which the other three parties would recognise Japan's special interests specifically guaranteed by the previous agreements. By limiting Japan's right to defined economic interests, such as the construction of the South Manchurian railway, rather than its exclusive sphere of influence in the region, the consortium practically contributed to 'substantiating the open-door principles in China'.[29]

To put a double lock on Japan, U.S. Secretary of State Charles Evans Hughes used the power of the dollar to pressure Japan to abide by the open-door pledge. Hughes intended to make Japan dependent on the New York City money market. Japan needed capital in the wake of a severe postwar economic downturn, the 'Taisho Depression', that Japan experienced in April 1920. New York banker Thomas Lamont agreed to extend huge loans to the Japanese. In return, the Japanese government agreed to respect open-door principles in China.

By 1926, Japan had borrowed $ 200 million. Nearly 40 per cent of its foreign loans came from the United States. The Japanese also bought more goods from the United States. In return, Americans imported more than 40 per cent of

Japan's exports in the 1920s.[30] Unfortunately, however, the Depression of 1929 dashed Hughes's hope of bringing Japan under control through the Washington treaties and Tokyo's dependence on the U.S. money. Japan then invaded northern China following the Manchurian Incident in September 1931, and expanded further into China in 1937, when the Sino-Japanese war began. All these efforts by Washington officials to control Japan did not work.

The Washington treaty system collapsed under the shocks of the World Depression and the subsequent arms race among the powers. However, the Washington conference was significant in revealing U.S. policymakers' attempt to build an informal empire during the inter-war years. The outbreak of World War II provided an opportunity to renew the effort to establish an informal empire. The United States played a pivotal role as the arsenal of democracy and the source of financing the war through the lend-lease agreements with U.S. allies.

Hopkins's treatment of 'isolationism' in America also needs reconsideration. As *American Empire* aptly points out, Williams's 'Open Door' thesis emphasised the overseas expansion of the United States while glossing over the structural changes accompanied by different stages of its capitalist development. In this context, Hopkins contends that Williams's argument needs modifying because it downplayed the isolationist impulses of the inter-war period. Hopkins stresses that the isolationist sentiments reinforced by the Depression significantly curbed Washington's interventionist policies. However, Seiko Mimaki's paper in this volume shows that American lawyers and U.S. policymakers were active in promoting the international order in favour of the status quo powers such as Great Britain and the United States. The Kellogg-Briand pact of 1928 gave the status quo powers a rationale for punishing any country that tried to change the existing order by force. Fumimaro Konoe, who would later serve as prime minister of Japan during 1937–41, criticised the international order in the inter-war period as being 'Anglo-American centered'.[31] In 1933, two years after the Manchurian Incident, Konoe published an article that advocated the need to revise the status quo and led to the proclamation of the 'New Order in East Asia' in 1938 as being Japan's ultimate purpose.

It is true that the 1929 Depression reinforced isolationist sentiments and the Franklin D. Roosevelt administration pursued inward-looking, nationalist policies in the first term. In giving priority to fighting the deflationary pressures of the U.S. economy, for example, the President refused to go along with the other participants' calls to stabilise exchange rates at the World Economic Conference in 1933. However, Roosevelt soon realised that his domestic recovery policies were failing. Thus, he turned around and embarked upon trade expansion, beginning with the Reciprocal Trade Agreement Act of 1934, which was a victory for the internationalists or advocates of equal access and freer trade.[32] The Roosevelt administration also grappled with another obstacle: lack of money for financing exports. Roosevelt created the first Export-Import Bank originally to handle applications for financing exports to the Soviet Union. After Japan's full-scale war with China in July 1937, the Export-Import Bank extended credits to China in 1938. Furthermore, in 1934, Congress passed the Gold Reserve Act, creating a Stabilization Fund under the control of the Secretary of the Treasury. The Stabilization Fund became a vehicle for the administration to coordinate monetary policy with other nations to try to regulate the international economy.

Reviving an old World War I statute, the Trading with the Enemy Act of 1917, gave President Roosevelt broad powers over foreign economic policy. Invoking a clause in this Act and the Banking Act of 1933, Roosevelt extended controls over foreign-exchange transactions in 1933 and froze transfers of funds to countries under German control in April 1940. The freeze on assets was extended to Japan in July 1941. In the same year, the President persuaded Congress to pass the Lend-Lease Act, which allowed the United States to sell, lend, or lease any article to any country whose defense the President considered vital to national security.

Given the strong domestic opposition to foreign involvement as seen, for example, in the isolationists' obstinate resistance to revising the Neutrality Acts, the Roosevelt administration carefully avoided military entanglements and/or military commitments during the 1930s. At the same time, however, the administration developed new tools of economic diplomacy that became a precursor to the 'postwar regulatory state' characterised by the IMF, World Bank and GATT.[33]

Conventional wisdom is that American diplomacy in the inter-war years was seriously constrained under the strong influence of 'isolationism'. However, the 1930s should be more aptly characterised as a period of 'independent internationalism'.[34] The Depression temporarily slowed U.S. overseas expansion. Yet, Washington's efforts to engage and expand internationally continued after the first term of the Roosevelt administration. Moreover, it should be noted that Washington's failure to lead in the inter-war years was due not so much to lack of power and influence as to the lack of political will on the part of policy-makers. The outbreak of World War II eventually helped overcome these inward-looking sentiments. Likewise, the Cold War enabled the United States to overcome 'isolationism' and act as the leader of the 'free world'.

The Cold War, Informal Empire, and Collaboration

American Empire emphasises that the United States had an empire just like the other Western colonial powers from 1898 to 1959. But Hopkins contends that, after 1945, the United States became 'an aspiring hegemon' or a world power, suggesting that Washington policy-makers maintained their aspiration to control and lead until the end of the 1980s. He has no explanation, however, about the overlapping time-period (1945-1959) during which both the 'insular empire' and a hegemonic state coexisted in the American state. But the coexistence between them from 1945 to 1959 shows that formal empire-building and informal empire-building could take place concurrently and were not necessarily in antithetical and incompatible relationships. It also shows that the Cold War order was hierarchical and often coercive. Furthermore, it was even imperial at least until 1959.

The hierarchical, coercive, and imperial nature of the Cold War order was globalised in the post-war years. Hopkins's insight that empires are 'agents of globalization' or 'globalizing forces'[35] is in line with my argument that the Truman Doctrine of March 1947 and the Marshall Plan of June 1947 were post-war manifestations of the globalisation of both the Monroe Doctrine and Hay's 'Open Door' imperialism (informal empire). The Cold War promoted globalisation in the following sense. The two superpowers tried to integrate other nation-states into their own spheres of influence, respectively called the Washington–led Western blocs and the Moscow-led Eastern blocs. Given that the Cold War was fought on a global scale, its impact was also global.

The existence of the non-aligned movement shows that there were limits to integration during the Cold War.[36] Nevertheless, the United States tried to organise, in varying degrees, both industrialised and developing nations into a 'liberal international order' by establishing the IMF/World Bank/GATT regimes. A weighted voting system in the IMF and the World Bank ensured that Washington would have veto power over their decisions. In addition, the NATO in Europe, and the bilateral networks of alliances called the 'hub and spokes' led by the United States in the Asia-Pacific region, were helpful in integrating allies and friends into accepting its loose, informal spheres of influence by assuring security. Similarly, the Soviet Union organised the communist countries into a more tightly-knit informal empire under the Moscow-led COMECON and the Warsaw Pact regimes. The Warsaw Pact allowed Soviet troops to be stationed in Eastern European countries. The members of the Soviet bloc shared an anti-imperialist and anti-capitalist ideology as well as a centralised economic and political system. In an attempt to integrate Eastern European regimes more firmly into the Soviet orbit, the Kremlin relied not only on military coercion but also on subsidising their economies by supplying them with cheap oil and raw materials in exchange for imports of their finished products.[37]

Moreover, Washington policy-makers often cooperated with European colonial powers in the Cold War struggle against Moscow. The 'liberal international order' that the United States pursued in the Cold War era retained a degree of congeniality with the colonial order under European empires.[38] In other words, the Cold War logic giving priority to the U.S. containment of the Soviet Union and communism prevailed over its support for anti-colonial nationalism in the Third World, when and where it suited U.S. national interests.

In this connection, we need to re-examine Roger Louis's somewhat exaggerated assertion that emphasises American anti-colonialism as 'amounting to an article of faith'. Louis argued American anti-colonialism was 'a force in itself which helped to shape the substance of defense, economic, and foreign policy' and that it was 'a set of principles that most Americans upheld'.[39] Louis's treatment of this subject needs to be qualified.

Like President Wilson, U.S. policy toward self-determination, self-government, and anti-colonialism, was ambiguous and often rhetorical. Anti-colonial ideology often gave way to U.S. security needs and anti-communism in the post-World War II years as well. The sources of this ambiguity came from the complex interactions of major trends during the early Cold War period: colonialism, anti-colonial nationalism in the Third World, and the U.S. logic of the Cold War (the primacy of anti-communism in the U.S. Cold War strategy) as well as American skepticism of the ability of dependent peoples to govern themselves effectively.[40]

In this context, a question arises as to which of the two is the 'real' American empire in the twentieth century: the territorial empire (the 'insular empire') or the non-territorial informal empire. A search for an answer needs to bear in mind the concurrence of two types of polity in the American state between 1945 and 1959 that Hopkins addresses. My view of the U.S. status in the Cold War years is that of informal empire characterised by the following features.

First, despite the huge power the United States acquired after World War II, its predominant mode of rule was not that of a formal empire with territorial acquisitions. Washington policy-makers tried to pay varying degrees of respect to nominal state sovereignty, even though they often intervened into the internal affairs of other countries or resorted to force to contain Moscow and communism in various parts of the world.

Second, the United States accordingly exercised its power to achieve its post-war objectives through indirect influence and by establishing collaborative ties with ruling elites in other countries. Washington policymakers tried to control or manage the foreign policies of other countries through a system of collaboration, though they were not always successful. When and where a collaborative system of control broke down, the U.S. militarily intervened or supported *coups d'état* to protect its interests. On the other hand, the American government provided collaborating regimes with security and prosperity. For this purpose, the United States built a world-wide network of military alliances, including a huge nuclear arsenal. The United States not only took over the responsibility as manager of the global economy through the IMF/GATT system but also provided military and economic assistance to reward collaborating regimes for their allegiance and cooperation.

Third, the premise of Washington's Cold War strategy was that local ruling elites would defer to U.S. imperial leadership by submitting to the liberal rules and norms required for the functioning of the global capitalist economy, as well as following the Cold War 'rules of the game' laid down by Washington. The pattern of responses, however, ranged from acceptance, cooperation, and adaptation to resistance, depending upon the recipients' perception of the security needs and material benefits they expected from Washington.[41] To the extent that collaborating regimes followed U.S. leadership in world affairs, they were willing to accept varying degrees of constraint on state sovereignty and autonomy in return for security and material rewards.[42]

Fourth, there were limits to the power and influence of the United States. Thus, Washington policy-makers were not always successful in controlling or managing the foreign policies of other countries. In this context, it is important to bear in mind Hopkins's concept of 'postcolonial globalization' which imposed considerable constraints on the exercise of U.S. power. However, it should also be said that, of the three main features of 'postcolonial globalization' mentioned by Hopkins, the power of the moral revolution as seen in the rise of human rights in international relations began to gain momentum and influence in policy-making circles in the mid-1970s. Hopkins also recognises that these declarations of ideals 'lacked political heft' in the short run.[43] A second feature, the change in the composition of nationalist movements into mass movements, certainly raised the costs of imperial rule, but the power of the Third World movements should not be exaggerated, given what happened to the U.N. General Assembly resolution of April 1974 calling for the establishment of a New International Economic Order (NIEO). By the time the G-7 Cancun summit was held in Mexico in 1981, the frustration of the NIEOs was evident. The campaign against the NIEOs was led by Henry Kissinger, Secretary of State in the Ford administration in the latter half of the 1970s.[44] Besides, anti-colonial nationalist movements had a more devastating impact upon European empires that exercised direct rule over foreign territories and people than upon the United States, which respected nominal state sovereignty. A third feature, structural changes in international trade and the diversification of the global economy, also gained momentum much later than 1945. Trade liberalisation was initiated by the Kennedy Round negotiations in the 1960s. Economic and financial liberalisation was further accelerated by the oil shocks in the 1970s and then with the neo-liberal turn initiated by the Reagan administration in the early 1980s. Therefore, granted that the era of 'postcolonial globalization' imposed considerable constraints on the exercise of power, it is not appropriate to treat its impact upon the United States and the European empires on an equal footing, given the huge gap in the power and influence between them that emerged in the postwar years. As Hopkins aptly points out elsewhere, our avoidance of the concept of informal empire leaves us 'with the problem of how to treat countries that retained their formal independence but were clearly subordinated to an external power'.[45]

To ascertain the above features of informal empire, I have examined U.S. interactions and negotiations with the Chiang-Kai-shek regime in China, the Ngo Din Diem regime in South Vietnam, the Shigeru Yoshida regime in Japan, the regimes of Pakistan from 1954 to the second Indo-Pakistan border war of 1965, Jawaharlal Nehru's India, South Korea under Rhee Syngman and Park Chun-hee, and the Suharto regime in Indonesia.[46] To summarise the findings of the above cases, Washington's efforts to maintain Chiang-Kai-shek and Ngo Din Diem as collaborators did not last very long. Washington managed to maintain the collaborative relationships with Lee and Park who behaved as U.S. collaborators despite occasional wrangling over their differing approaches to North Korea. To obtain economic and military assistance, the Pakistani leaders invited themselves into a bilateral alliance relationship with Washington in May 1954 and SEATO in October of the same year. The relationship turned sour during the second Indo-Pakistan War of September 1965, which eventually put an end to the bilateral alliance in December of the same year. As for India and Indonesia, the leading members of the non-aligned movement, the Nehru government kept its distance from Washington, while Suharto and his cohorts worked out a collaborative relationship with the U.S. government.[47]

These cases show that the United States during the Cold War years was both successful and unsuccessful in establishing collaborative ties with local elites. The latter cases indicate the limits to informal influence exercised by the United States which paid varying degrees of respect for the nominal sovereignty of nation states, as compared with a system of rule under territorial empire that could wield direct territorial power. Informal empire exercises power through indirect means. The way the United States exercised power fits in with the reality of the post-World War II world. In the era of 'postcolonial globalization' characterised by powerful anti-colonial nationalism in the Third World, the growing strength of international norms (mutual respect for state sovereignty and human rights), and the 'retreat of the state' in deepening globalisation, the United States with its anti-colonial tradition tried to observe those principles and norms, including non-intervention in internal affairs of other countries. These considerations imposed constraints on the exercise of U.S. structural power during the Cold War years. Nevertheless, the overwhelming preponderance of power the United States possessed was able to offset these constraints to a substantial degree. Japan is an example of a successful case of a collaborating regime that deserves further attention here.

In the introduction to the Japanese edition of his study of the Cold War, published in 2010, the Cold War historian Arne Westad described postwar Japan as follows. 'Japan surrendered and was occupied. The Japanese elites, to remain in power, had to submit to the U.S. objectives in Asia. Owing to the Allied occupation and the Japan-U.S. security treaty that came into existence during the occupation, Japan lost the status as an independent player in world affairs, and played the role of contributing to the U.S. role in the Cold War'.[48] Bruce Cumings in 1993 described the mechanism of U.S. control over postwar Japan more succinctly. The American architects of the postwar order 'wished to situate Japan structurally in a world system shaped by the United States so that Japan would do what it should without having to be told. In so doing they placed distinct outer limits on Japan's behavior, and these limits persist today'.[49] John Dower aptly described the Japanese attitude as 'embracing defeat'.[50]

What kind of post-war structure built during the occupation period made Japanese governments behave as U.S. collaborators? The Japanese 'post-war regime' (sengo taisei)[51] was structured by the mutually contradictory combination of Article 9 of the Japanese Constitution of 1947 and the Japan-U.S. security treaty signed on September 8, 1951, the same day that the San Francisco Peace Treaty was signed with the victors of World War II. The so-called war renunciation clause of Article 9 prohibited Japan from rearming, which left the Japanese government no choice but to sign the security treaty with the United States. The treaty allowed U.S. troops to be stationed in Japan and was further buttressed by America's continued administration of the Ryukyu Islands, which were strategically located in the Southwestern Pacific.

From Washington's standpoint, the treaty had two purposes. One was to use the U.S. bases not only to 'deter armed attack upon Japan' but also to contain Soviet encroachments in Asia. The other was to control the possible revival of Japan's militarism that might threaten the United States in future. The latter objective of 'double containment' was publicly hidden but was clearly in the mind of the American architects of the post-war East Asian order and was partly embodied in the so-called 'anti-subversion clause' of the 1951 treaty (later to be abolished in the revised security treaty of 1960). The provision gave the United States the right to mobilise U.S. troops to suppress demonstrations against the U.S.-supported regime should they get out of control.[52]

The ruling political elite, including Shigeru Yoshida, then Foreign Minister who would become prime minister in May 1946, initially objected bitterly to the war-renunciation clause. However, the General Headquarters (GHQ) under General Douglas MacArthur linked the retention of Japan's imperial system of government, which was supported by the ruling elite, with acceptance of Article 9. Article 1 of the Constitution identified the emperor as the symbol of the Japanese state. It was an ingenious device of MacArthur's GHQ to evade the possible indictment of Emperor Hirohito as a war criminal at the approaching Tokyo Trial. Its insertion was made conditional on Japan's acceptance of the war-renunciation clause. On February 13, 1946, Japan's political elites were shown the GHQ's Constitutional draft by Lt. General Courtney Whitney, then director of the civil affairs section of the GHQ. They were all flabbergasted and reacted negatively to the war-renunciation clause. Whitney then advised them that General MacArthur was 'determined to protect the Emperor from the pressures by other countries to investigate him as a war criminal' and that 'if the clauses of the new constitutional draft had been accepted, the emperor would be safe as a matter of fact'. Whitney also added that whether the current elite could remain in power depended upon their acceptance of the draft.[53] Consequently, the ruling elites reluctantly accepted it. Afterwards, Prime Minister Yoshida publicly defended Article 9.

The institutional structure of the 'post-war regime' was internationally sanctioned by the San Francisco Peace Treaty. Article 3 assured the U.S. administration of the Ryukyu Islands and other southern Japanese islands. Given that 74 per cent of the U.S. forces stationed in Japan are concentrated on the Ryukyu Islands today, the significance of Article 3 in terms of U.S. objectives is beyond question. Article 6, in anticipation of a conclusion of the ongoing negotiation on the Japan-U.S. security treaty, enabled Tokyo and Washington to enter a bilateral agreement that allowed 'the stationing or retention of foreign armed forces in Japanese territory'. Article 11 mentions Japan's acceptance of the judgments of the Tokyo Trial, which avoided the indictment of the Emperor as a war criminal.

Washington policy-makers tried to control and influence Japan's external behaviour by integrating Japan into the U.S.-led 'liberal international order' through the IMF/GATT system and by assisting Japan's economic advance into Southeast Asia as the substitute for the lost Chinese market for imports of raw materials and exports of manufactured goods.[54] Washington policy-makers supported Japan in joining the IMF and the World Bank in 1952, followed by her membership in the Colombo Plan in October 1954.[55] Japan was then admitted to the GATT in September 1955. Japan also benefited from the extension of the Japan-U.S. Reciprocal Trade Acts of 1953, 1954, and 1955.

Washington's strategy was to influence Japan's external behaviour to ensure that it served U.S. containment policy in Asia. George F. Kennan remarked in October 1949 that this could be done by 'controlling the overseas sources of supply and the naval power and air power without which it cannot become again aggressive'. Kennan added that the United States ought to 'have power over what Japan imports in the way of oil and such other things as she has got to get from overseas' so that 'we would have veto power on what she does need in the military and industrial field'.[56]

The Japan-U.S. security treaty functioned as an essential mechanism of Washington's control over Japanese foreign policy. In addition, with the Japanese economy having been firmly integrated into the IMF/GATT system as well as into the triangular economic relations between Washington, Tokyo and Southeast Asia, Japan remained economically dependent on the United States. The American architects of the postwar order thus set outer limits within which Japan would continue to do what it should without having to be told. A National Security Council document dated June 11, 1960 states that 'Because Japan continues to be almost dependent on the United States for military security and heavily dependent on the United States economically, the United States is in a position to have a critical impact on Japan's international orientation'.[57] Richard Sneider, State Department Country Director for Japan, in his memorandum to William Bundy, Assistant Secretary of State for East Asian and Pacific Affairs, reported on April 26, 1968 as follows. Japanese 'brooding about the need for an "independent" Japanese foreign policy' is 'not new'. It is 'a theme which has reoccurred periodically throughout the post-occupation era'. But 'the hard fact is that Japan cannot escape from its economic and military dependence on the United States without a fundamental and costly policy change'. 'This change, the Government of Japan and the vast majority of Japanese are unprepared to undertake'.[58] As they had predicted, the Japanese governments under the Liberal Democratic Party continued to behave as U.S. collaborators in a global system of informal empire. This situation continues even after the end of the Cold War now that the Soviet threat is being replaced by the rise of Communist China, which is being seen by a growing number of Japanese as an increasing potential security threat and keeps Japan reliant on the United States for its security.

Informal Empire and the Role of U.S. Military Power

Hopkins points out that informal empire suggests 'parity with the status of empire' and is a stronger term than the concept of hegemony.[59] Given the various constraints that the features of 'postcolonial globalization' imposed upon the power and influence of post-war America, he prefers to view the United States after World War II as an 'aspiring hegemon', rather than an informal empire. In other words, the difference between *American Empire* and my paper is one of emphasis. However, I am inclined to think that the post-war United States qualifies for the status of informal empire and that it is not appropriate to minimise the enormous gap in the power and influence between the United States and the European imperial powers in the post-war years. In calculating informal influence, not only do we need to pay attention to the huge financial power of the United States but also put more weight on the role of the military and other dimensions of U.S. power in the post-war years than *American Empire* does. In particular, the political role of military power needs to be taken into due consideration in America's imperial project.

The inquiry concerns two kinds of power, that is, 'relational power' and 'structural power'. According to Susan Strange, structural power is 'the power to shape and determine the structures of the global political economy within which other states, their political institutions, their economic enterprises and (not least) their scientists and other professional people have to operate'. Four sources of structural power are security, production, finance, and knowledge.[60] Structural power is less visible and more indirect in the way it is exercised.

As for structural power and informal influence, a good historical example can be observed in *American Empire*'s description of the relationship between the British Empire and post-colonial America.[61] Making a distinction between formal independence and effective independence (chapters 4, 5, 6 and 7), Hopkins noted that Britain exercised structural power over post-colonial America and that its influence on the latter was 'profound', thereby setting the rules of the game, and shaping the options open to the leaders of the American Revolution.[62] He pointed out that 'informal influence was more effective than formal rule because it was both cheaper and more acceptable to the recipients'.[63] He further stated that, because Britain's continued informal influence was so profound and enduring, post-colonial America did not achieve effective and real independence until 1898, suggesting that the young Republic remained part of the globalising British imperial system.

Hopkins's portrayal of power that the British empire exercised over post-colonial America is analogous to that of U.S. informal empire in the post-World War II era. In this kind of power relationship, the newly independent Republic was an outpost in Britain's informal empire.[64] In the same vein, the structural power exercised by the United States during the Cold War period was similar to the one exercised by the nineteenth-century British empire over post-colonial America.

Another point to be considered is relational power.[65] In my view, *American Empire* does not take into due enough account U.S. military power and how it functioned during the Cold War. Washington policy-makers built a world-wide network of military alliances and stationed U.S. troops on overseas bases. Chalmers Johnson points out that the United States maintained approximately 1,700 military installations in about one hundred countries during the Cold War period.[66] Many of them had varying degrees of clientelist ties to the United States.[67]

It should be noted in this connection that the U.S. informal empire exercised military power for foreign policy objectives but not for territorial acquisitions, as territorial empires did. It employed military power for policing actions or for disciplinary purposes to maintain stability and order in other countries. Most of all, U.S. military bases overseas served foreign policy objectives by functioning as an 'unconscious' aspect of structural power to exercise control over external behaviours of other nation states. It is a kind of influence that 'need(s) not be confined to outcomes consciously or deliberately sought for'. In other words, power can be 'effectively exercised by "being there," without intending the creation or exploitation of privilege or the transfer of cost or risks from oneself to others'.[68]

Johnson's 'empire of bases' states that its purpose was to maintain 'absolute military preponderance over the rest of the world, a task that included imperial policing to ensure that no part of the empire slips the leash'.[69] The U.S. military arsenal, constantly augmented and updated, ensured such a position not only in the 'Free World' but also over other regimes in developing nations. In addition to its global network of military bases overseas, the United States had other resources of influence, such as resort to the CIA's overt and covert operations to support collaborators or overthrow antagonistic regimes, including communist governments. It suffices to mention, for example, U.S. military intervention in the Dominican Republic (1965), Grenada (1983), Panama (1989), and support for or engineering of coups d'état in Brazil (1964), Bolivia (1971), Uruguay (1973), Chili (1973), and Argentine (1976).[70]

The debate between American declinists and anti-declinists continues into the post-Cold War era. *American Empire* mentions that the United States reached the peak of its power relative to its rivals in the 1970s, and by the 1980s, its economic supremacy was faltering, and that it ceased to be a hegemon by the 1980s.[71] Although *American Empire* is very careful not to embrace a 'declinist' argument,[72] the fundamental asymmetry in the security structure of the United States and many other countries except China and Russia remains unchanged. Always in the background, there remains the contrast between the provision of security by the U.S. defense forces and the dependence of its partners upon them.

Given the overwhelming military power of the United States, Washington policy-makers often intervened militarily into internal affairs of other countries to protect U.S. interests when and where the collaborative system of informal empire broke down. According to the study by Blechman and Kaplan, the United States resorted to military measures to achieve political purposes on no fewer than 215 occasions between January 1, 1946 and December 31, 1975.[73] Such demonstrations of force had a psychological and political impact upon defiant political leaders in other countries.

In the decade after the end of the Cold War, American attitudes toward the role of military power changed profoundly. A respected diplomatic historian, Andrew Bacevich, commented that 'the military component of U.S. policy became more not less important'. It became 'a central element in what little remained of an American identity'.[74] Samuel R. Berger, Assistant to the President for National Security Affairs during the Clinton administration, made the following remarks at the Council of Foreign Relations in Washington, D.C. in October 1999. 'Our military expenditures now are larger than those of all other countries combined; our weaponry is a generation ahead of our nearest potential rival'. 'Because we are the only nation on earth able to project power in every region on earth,' he went on to say, 'others look to us to deliver decisive influence' where it is needed.[75] In fact, the U.S. military expenditures for the year 2012 amounted to more than $ 685 billion, followed by China which spent $ 166 billion. The U.S. military expenditures were larger than those of the next top nine countries combined (China, Russia, Great Britain, Japan, France, Saudi Arabia, India, Germany, and Italy).[76]

'Even if the direct use of force were banned among a group of countries,' states Joseph Nye, military force 'is a factor not mentioned openly but present in the back of statesmen's minds'.[77] Such is the function of U.S. military forces and overseas bases in the post-war world. The past record of U.S. military interventions is telling not only in the eyes of its partners but also to other countries which need security protection.

The Status of Informal Empire in the Post-Cold War World

The first visible signs of the decline of U.S. power appeared in the early 1970s following the collapse of the Bretton Woods system. The huge military costs of the Vietnam War added to this trend, followed by the two oil shocks of 1973 and 1979 that brought economic crises to the industrialised countries and the world economy. Therefore, I share Hopkins's observation that the first signs of decline appeared in the 1970s but disagree about the rate the trend developed. The decline was rather gradual and winding, though cumulative. Washington policy-makers tried to hold the line after the Bretton Woods system collapsed. The 'exorbitant privilege' derived from the U.S. dollar as the key international currency has persisted, and the international monetary system has continued to function as a kind of 'a taxation regime' for financing U.S. leadership.[78] Consequently, the United States managed to remain an informal empire for a while after the Cold War.

After the end of the Cold War, the administration of President George H. W. Bush expressed its intention to build a 'new international order'. Following the Iraqi invasion of Kuwait in August 1990, President Bush declared to Congress that the United States would embark on this post-Cold War project. The Gulf War in January 1991 provided such an opportunity. President Bush announced that the pursuit of a new international order was one of the purposes of the war. Even though the Bush administration succeeded in expelling the Iraqi troops from Kuwait, thereby burying the 'Vietnam syndrome' in the sand of the Arabian desert, the first Gulf War demonstrated not only the overwhelming military power of the United States but also its need for support from other states. It was the first time that the United States had asked its allies (Saudi Arabia, Kuwait, Japan, and Germany) to share the financial costs of the multi-national force. Under strong U.S. pressure, the Japanese government contributed $13 billion for the war effort. Vice Minister of Foreign Affairs, Takakazu Kuriyama, mused later that this new way of fighting the war, financed by the collaborating regimes, foreshadowed the decline of Pax Americana.[79]

The George H. W. Bush administration wisely stopped short of overthrowing Saddam Hussein's regime in the first Gulf War. However, when the second

Gulf War (or the war in Iraq) began on March 20, 2003, President George W. Bush's administration went further, by aiming to overthrow the Hussein regime by force. The Bush administration's use of military power to enforce regime change in Iraq showed that 'imperialism on the cheap'[80] was not working and that it was a sign of weakness rather than its strength. 'The international system breaks down,' states David Calleo, 'not only because unbalanced and aggressive new powers seek to dominate their neighbors, but also because declining old powers, rather than adjusting and accommodating, try to convert their slipping preeminence into an exploitative hegemony'.[81]

No less striking and important was the fact that various new interventionist ideologies had been in circulation for some time after the end of the Cold War. The new interventionist ideologues advocated the 'just war doctrine' and the doctrine of humanitarian intervention. Before the U.S. invasion of Iraq in 2003, they had forged an American version of the Brezhnev Doctrine, advocating in favour of and justifying the limitation of state sovereignty. Richard Haass, Director of Policy Planning for the Department of State in the Bush administration, revealed the doctrine in the spring of 2002. He justified the right to intervene in other countries when governments fail to fulfil their obligations to protect their own people or by supporting terrorism.[82] This rationale led to the Bush Doctrine that President Bush had announced in a speech at West Point on June 1, 2002. The war in Iraq was a disaster for the United States. It cost the lives of nearly 4,500 U.S. soldiers and more than 58,000 casualties. The war expenditures of the United States in Iraq and Afghanistan exceeded $ 1 trillion.

The difference between the first Gulf War and the war in Iraq was that President Bush (senior) and his senior advisors refrained from overthrowing the Hussein government, despite the neo-conservatives' clamour for regime-change. On the other hand, President Bush (junior), influenced by Vice-President Dick Cheney, Secretary of Defense Donald Rumsfeld and neo-conservatives like Under Secretary of Defense Paul Wolfowitz, decided not only to overthrow Hussein but also to occupy Iraq. These measures changed the Iraqi people's view of the United States from that of a liberator to that of an occupying authority. The ensuing resistance to the occupation led to chaos and confusion during the attempted post-war reconstruction of Iraq.[83] In other words, the United States behaved as informal empire in the first Gulf War, while it acted in the Iraqi war as if it were a colonial power, which made the crucial difference in the consequences.

Next came the financial crisis ('Lehman shocks') of 2007-2008. Many analysts had predicted that such a crisis would trigger a collapse of foreign confidence in the U.S. currency. On the contrary, however, the crisis highlighted the enduring nature of U.S. structural power in global finance.

American declinists rest their arguments heavily on the fall in the U.S. share of world output (from 40 per cent to 22 per cent), and the decline of the U.S.

share of world exports of manufactures (from 30 per cent to 13 per cent) in the thirty years from the early 1950s to the early 1980s. However, as Hopkins cogently observes, the economic crisis of 2008 shows the importance of finance rather than industry in the world economy.[84] Thus, it offers a good indication of the power and influence of the United States in the post-Cold War world.

The most important initiative for managing the 2008 financial crisis came from the U.S. Federal Reserve Bank (FRB), which provided massive sums of dollar liquidity through a series of swap agreements with foreign central banks to help their firms and markets in distress.[85] According to Eric Helleiner, the FRB's decisions concerning which countries to support 'were made only after consultation with the highest levels of the State Department and Treasury'. FRB chairman Benjamin Bernanke, and Secretary of the Treasury Henry Paulson and Secretary of State Condoleeza Rice, for example, agreed that Mexico, Brazil, Singapore, and Korea were 'the countries that among emerging markets are the most important from its financial and economic perspective and a diplomatic perspective'. On the other hand, India, Indonesia, and South Africa were considered not worthy of swaps.[86]

When the bubbles in emerging markets burst in the Asian economic crisis in 1997, foreign and domestic investors withdrew their funds quickly, thereby causing exchange-rate crises in these countries. However, these unwelcome scenarios did not come to pass in the U.S. case, even though the country had large external debts and growing current account deficits. The difference can be attributed to U.S. structural power. The U.S. Treasury market was not only the largest in the world but also could inject liquidity into the market. Moreover, it was buttressed by the world's dominant military and economic power. Given the unique attributes of the United States as an international lender of last resort as well as world policeman, government officials and private investors regarded other countries as riskier than the United States.

China was no exception. China was the largest holder of foreign reserves in U.S. dollars at the time. As one Chinese official quipped in early 2009, 'U.S. Treasuries are the safe-haven. Selling U.S. Treasury bonds will invite depreciation of the dollar'. In other words, China as well as other countries holding U.S. dollars in reserve was in the 'entrapment' situation in which they would incur losses through the depreciation of the dollar. In addition, China did not want the renminbi to appreciate because it would damage export-oriented Chinese firms.[87]

Concerning the 2008 crisis, Eichengreen points out that the dollar, contrary to many expectations, 'strengthened against the euro and other currencies'. We were reminded again that the dollar was 'still the ultimate safe-haven for frightened investors around the world'.[88] The 2008 crisis demonstrated the enduring nature of U.S. structural power in the global financial system. It should be added that the 'exorbitant privilege' enjoyed by the United States was backed by its military power and world-wide alliance networks, which provided assurance to investors and banks as well as to government officials the world over.

However, its long-term impact on American power remains to be seen. The experience of the 2008 crisis does not necessary mean that the dollar's singular status would be secure in the future. Eichengreen warns that it is 'the fundamental fallacy' to believe that 'there is room for only one international currency'. History indicates that there has always been more than one international currency. He suggests, therefore, that we need to prepare for 'a world of several international currencies'.[89] Serious economic and financial mismanagements by the United States could increase dissatisfaction among other nations with the existing operation of the international monetary system and precipitate a flight from the dollar.

Concluding Remarks

Hopkins's work is illuminating in his comparative analysis and detailed account of the dependent territories in the Caribbean and the Pacific. He convincingly demonstrates that the American empire was not exceptional, though distinctive, and that it shared more commonalities than differences with other Western colonial powers. This essay has tried to shed light on some other aspects that his insightful analysis of the 'insular empire' did not fully cover in *American Empire*. For my interpretative framework, I used the term informal empire rather than hegemon for the following reasons.

First, rather than Hopkins's distinction between the 'insular empire' and 'an aspiring hegemon', the intermediate concept of informal empire is more useful in capturing what I regard as the transitional stage of U.S. empire-building in the inter-war years before it transformed itself into a fully-fledged informal empire during the Cold War years. The term also highlights the unprecedented structural power of the United States and its relationships with those countries that retained their formal independence but were subordinated to it. Second, it has an advantage in grasping the dialectical process of interaction between America's anti-colonial tradition, on the one hand, and the imperial impulses, on the other, in the history of U.S. empire-building. Third, the term informal empire can better explain the nature of the Cold War order, which was hierarchical and coercive, and more akin to the old imperial order embodied by European colonial powers. As Westad observes, the Cold War, especially seen from the Third World, 'was a continuation of colonialism through slightly different means'. The two historical projects that 'were genuinely anticolonial in their origin became part of a much older pattern of domination'.[90]

Lastly, as Hopkins points out, the decline of the power and influence exercised by the United States began in the early 1970s. However, its process was rather gradual and irregular, though cumulative, and not a linear trend. It is difficult to determine exactly when the United States ceased to be an informal empire (as it is in the case of a hegemon). However, the United States continued to demonstrate its will to lead the world until the advent of the Obama administration. At the same time, it has become apparent that the United States under the Trump administration abandoned its global leadership, as his slogan, 'America First', showed.

Notes

1. The aberration argument was popularised by Bemis, *A Diplomatic History of the United States*.
2. Williams, *The Tragedy of American Diplomacy*, 18–19, 45. Most of the Japanese historians who treated U.S. foreign policy as that of an empire were Marxist historians. But some of the Japanese works on the U.S. empire such as those of Takahashi and Shimizu were clearly influenced by Williams' works as they studied with him at the University of Wisconsin. Most influential was Shimizu, *Amerika Teikoku*. Shimizu, Takahashi and Tomita, *Amerika Shi Kenkyu Nyumon* treats the American history as that of an empire from the start of the American Revolution. The authors of *Amerika Shi Kenkyu Nyumon* described the entire American history as that of making an empire. The book divides the history of the American empire into stages of development: the making of the American empire (1770s~1820s), the establishment of the American empire (1828~1877), the road to a global empire (roughly 1898~WWI) and the completion and unraveling of the global empire (WWII~1960s).Takahashi, *Amerika Teikokushugi Seiritsu Shi Kenkyu* is more focused, covering the Spanish-American War (Takahashi referred to it as 'the Spanish-American-Cuban-Philippine War'), Cuba's protectorate status, 'Open Door imperialism', and Taft's 'dollar diplomacy'. The book tries to place the making of the American empire at the turn of the twentieth century in the world-system framework of analysis.
3. For the ebb and flow of the Wisconsin School's reputation, see Gardner and McCormick, "Walter LaFeber: The Making of a Wisconsin School Revisionist," 623–4. "William Appleman Williams: A Roundtable," 275–316. For the post-Cold War revival of the debate on American empire involving the 'neo-conservative' ideologues, realists and the left, see Kan, "Amerika Teikokuron no Genjo to Sekai Chitsujo no Yukue," 45–62.
4. Louis, "Review---Books".
5. Hopkins, *American Empire*, 700.
6. Hopkins, *American Empire*, 640–1. See also Iriye's view that the Cold War should be placed in the longer history of decolonisation, internationalism, human rights, economic globalisation and environmentalism. His suggestion to place the Cold War history in the longer story of decolonisation is similar to Hopkins's perspective from which to view the Cold War in the larger context of post-colonial globalisation. Akira Iriye, "Historicizing the Cold War," 18–31.
7. O'Brien and Clesse, eds. *Two Hegemonies Britain 1846–1914 and the United States 1941–2001*, 44, 46.
8. Ibid.
9. Hopkins, *American Empire*, 31–2, 41, 707–21.
10. Yamamuro's view on the relationship between nation-state and empire is relevant here. His concept of 'kokumin teikoku' (nation-state empire) notes the duality of

empire-building. Nation-states compete for power in the nation-state system. In the process for power struggle, some nation-states increase their power to dominate weaker states and construct an empire characterised by the relationship between the metropole and dependent territories. Located in the center of empires are the nation-states, and both are inseparably linked with each other in the age of imperialism and empire. Yamamuro, "Teikokuron no Shatei," 88–125

11. For this term and discussions, see Magdoff, *imperialism without colonies*, chapter 4.
12. For a similar view, see Reynolds' article. 'For the most part', he points out, 'American imperialism was informal rather than formal-a web of trade and investment, bases and alliances that spread out from the Western Hemisphere during the course of the twentieth century'. Reynolds, "American Globalism," 251. Duara also describes the United States during the Cold War period as 'the imperialism of nation-states' or 'the new imperialism', which is similar to the term informal empire. Duara, "The Cold War as a historical period," 8–13. Idem, "The Cold War and the Imperialism of Nation-States," 86–104.
13. For a view that the Cold War order is an extension in a new configuration of interest, enlightenment, and military violence, see Duara's article. 'With the Cold War', he argues, 'the US developed a global empire', and that 'the post-war United States represented the apogee of the imperialism of nation-state'. Duara, "The Cold War as a historical period," 12. Louis and Robinson argue that 'the new African informal empire' after 1957 'would be increasingly Anglo-American rather than British'. Louis and Robinson, "Empire Preserv'd," 158–61. See also, Louis and Robinson, "The Imperialism of Decolonization," 468, 493–5.
14. For these terms, see *The Tragedy of American Diplomacy,* chapters 1 and 2.
15. In the historical development of the Monroe Doctrine, Sexton points out, the U.S. anticolonial struggle to consolidate its independence from the British empire was impossible to separate from America's imperial expansion in the nineteenth century. His insight can also be applied to the history of U.S. empire-building in the twentieth century. Sexton, *The Monroe Doctrine,* 6–7. I am indebted to Hopkins for reminding me of Sexton's work.
16. Hopkins, *American Empire*, 707, 728.
17. Akimoto and Kan, *Amerika 20-seiki Shi*, 4–7.
18. The term in the parenthesis is Gallaher's and Robinson's usage. Gallagher and Robinson, "The Imperialism of Free Trade," 6.
19. Robinson, "Non-European Foundation of European Imperialism," 130.
20. Manela shows that Wilson distinguished colonial people's right to self-determination in theory but was pessimistic in practice. Manela, "'Peoples of Many Races,'" 198. Such feature of the Monroe Doctrine was expressed by President Woodrow Wilson. Proposing that 'the nations should with one accord adopt the doctrine of President Monroe as the doctrine of the world', Wilson emphasized that 'no nation should seek to extend its polity over any other nation or people, but that every people should be left to determine its own polity · · · '. Woodrow Wilson's Address to the Senate, 22 January, 1917, 444. Given that the Doctrine established a loose sphere of influence in the Western hemisphere, Wilson's remarks are self-deceiving.
21. Kohn, *American Nationalism*. Schlesinger, *The Disuniting of America*.
22. LaFeber, "The American View of Decolonization, 1776–1920," 29, 31.
23. For this argument, see Kan, "The Making of the 'American Empire' and US Response to Decolonization in the early Cold War Years," 147–80.
24. Sexton, *The Monroe Doctrine,* 5, 243.

25. Schmitt, "Forms of Modern Imperialism in International Law," (1933), Leg, ed., *Spatiality, Sovereignty and Carl Schmitt*, 35.
26. LaFeber, *The American Age*, 322.
27. For discussions of the following paragraphs, see Kan, "'Pakusu Amerikaana' no Sekai," 241–302.
28. Carr, *The Twenty Years' Crisis, 1919–1939*, 190.
29. Mitani, *Wooru Sutoriito to Kyokuto*, 78–83.
30. Ibid., 152–3. LaFeber, *The American Age*, 334.
31. Konoe, "Eibei Honi no Heiwashugi wo Haisu," 47–52. Konoe's statements on the 'New Order in East Asia' were announced twice, respectively on 3 November and 22 December, 1938, in Gaimusho, *Nihon Gaiko Nenpyo narabini Shuyo Bunsho, 1984–1945*, Vol. 2, 401, 407.
32. For my interpretation of the Reciprocal Trade Agreement Act of 1935, see *Amerika 20-seiki Shi*, 102–4. The Act was an example typical of 'independent internationalism'.
33. Rosenberg, *Spreading the American Dream*, 186–8. The usage is Rosenberg's. See also, Gardner, *Economic Aspects of New Deal Diplomacy*. For a detailed analysis of Roosevelt's endeavour, though unsuccessful, to revise the Neutrality Acts in preparation for the coming war, see Kennedy, *Freedom from Fear*.
34. Hoff, "The American Century," 185.
35. Hopkins, *American Empire*, 6, 12, 37.
36. For further discussion of the Cold War integration and its limits, see Kan, "Haken Sisutemu to shiteno Reisen to Guroobaru Gabanansu no Henyo," 104–26,
37. For a similar argument, see Darwin, *After Tamerlane*, 468–79.
38. By employing the concept of 'the Cold War integration' (reisen togo), the following article highlights the imperial and often coercive nature of the orders organised and promoted respectively by Washington and Moscow. Kan, "Haken Sisutemu to shiteno Reisen to Guroobaru Gabanansu no Henyo," 104–26.
39. Louis, "American Anti-Colonialism and the Dissolution of the British Empire," 263–73.
40. Kan, "The Making of 'an American Empire' and US Responses to Decolonization in the early Cold War Years," 147–80.
41. For this formulation, see Howe, *Empire*, 94–103.
42. 'Imperialism,' Hopkins notes, 'Involves the Diminution of Sovereignty through the Exercise of Power.' Hopkins, "Informal Empire in Argentina," 476.
43. Hopkins, *American Empire*, 646.
44. For details, see Sargent, *A Superpower Transformed*, 178–82.
45. Hopkins, "Globalisation and Decolonisation," *JICH*, 8.
46. Kan, *Reisen to 'Amerika no Seiki' Ajia ni okeru 'Hi-koshiki Teikoku' no Chitsujo Keisei*. For the case study of South Korea, see chapter 5, Kan, *Reisenki Amerika no Ajia Seisaku 'Jiyushugiteki Kokusai Chitsujo' no Henyo to 'Nichibei Kyouryoku,'* 212–64.
47. Ibid.
48. "Introduction" to the Japanese edition, Westad, *Guroobaru Reisen Shi*, 6.
49. Bruce Cumings, "Japan's Position in the World System," 34.
50. The phrase is adopted from Dower's book. Dower, *Embracing Defeat*.
51. For the ongoing struggle between liberals and conservatives over the Japanese postwar regime (sengo taisei), see Kan, "Challengers to the 'Postwar Regime' and the 'History Problem' in the Asia-Pacific," 37–43.
52. Article 1 of the security treaty states that the U.S. troops could be utilised not only to maintain 'international peace and security in the Far East and to the security of Japan

against armed attack from without' but also to assist 'to put down large-scale internal riots and disturbances in Japan'.
53. Quoted in Kan, *Reisen to 'Amerika no Seiki,'* 84–5.
54. America's effort to economically and commercially integrate Japan and Southeast Asia, see Kan, "Amerika no Sengo Chitsujo Koso to Ajia no Chiiki Togo, 1945~1950," 109–25.
55. For Washington's support for Japanese membership in the Colombo Plan, see my article. "US Cold War policy and the Colombo Plan," 177–98. As for 'the Japan-U.S. cooperation' and the establishment of the Asian Development Bank, see my article. "U.S.-Japan Relations in the 1960s and U.S. Policy toward the Emerging Regionalism in Asia," 41–59.
56. Kennan's remarks are from 'Transcripts of Roundtable Discussion on American Foreign Policy toward China,' U.S. State Department, 6–8 Oct. 1949, quoted in Cumings, "Japan's Position in the World System," 40. See also, 'The Position of the United States with respect to Asia,' NSC 48/1, 23 December, 1949, 225–72.
57. NSC 6008/1 'United States Policy Toward Japan,' 11 June, 1960, Lot File 63 D 351 'NSC 6008,' NA.
58. Memorandum from Sneider to Bundy, 26 April, 1968, *FRUS*, 273.
59. Hopkins, "The American 'Empire' in the 'American Century,'" 5.
60. Strange, *States and Markets*, 24–32. The first edition was published in 1988. She believed her concept of structural power remained applicable at least until 1996. See Strange, *The Retreat of the State*, 26–7. The important point here is not the year of the publication but whether the concept is still applicable in grasping the U.S. power and influence in the post-Cold War era.
61. Hopkins also argues that the British-Argentine relation from the late nineteenth century to 1914 was that of an informal empire. Hopkins, "Informal Empire in Argentina," 469–83.
62. Hopkins, *American Empire*, 143–4.
63. Ibid., 193–4.
64. Akita applies the concept of 'teikokuteki kozokenryoku' (imperial structural power) to his analysis of the British empire in the interwar years. Akita, "Teikokuteki na Kozoteki Kenryoku, " in Yamamoto, ed. *Teikoku no Kenkyu,* 257–90. It is interesting to note that probably because he draws on Strange's concept of structural power and emphasizes the role of finance capital and services, Akita highlights aspects of an 'informal empire' rather than those of a territorial empire in his analysis of the British empire.
65. Relational power is more conventional and is defined by realists as 'the power of A to get to B to do something that they would not otherwise do.' Strange, *States and Markets,* 24.
66. Johnson, *The Sorrows of Empire,* 32.
67. For a detailed analysis of the United States as 'an empire of client states,' see Sylvan and Majeski, *U.S. Foreign Policy in Perspectives*.
68. Strange, *The Retreat of the State,* 26.
69. Johnson, *The Sorrows of Empire*, chapter 6, esp. 151. Cumings, noting the significant role of U.S. overseas bases, calls the United States during the Cold War period as the 'archipelago of empire'. Cumings, *Dominion from Sea to Sea,* 388–423.
70. Sylvan and Majeski, *U.S. Foreign Policy in Perspectives*, chapters 5 and 6. Grow, *U.S. Presidents and Latin American Interventions Pursuing Regime Change in the Cold War*. Weiner, *Legacies of Ashes*.
71. Hopkins, *American Empire*, 707, 728.

72. Ibid., 722–9.
73. Blechman and Kaplan, *Force without War*, 23, 33.
74. Bacevich, *American Empire*, 122.
75. Berger, 'American Power: Hegemony, Isolationism or Engagement,' 21 October, 1999.
76. SIPRI, *SIPRI Yearbook 2013*, 183–7.
77. Nye, *Bound to Lead*, 31.
78. Calleo, "Introduction Decline," xv.
79. Kuriyama, *Nichibei Domei Hyoryu kara no Dakkyaku*, 34.
80. Gallagher and Robinson, "The Imperialism of Free Trade," 13.
81. Calleo, *Beyond American Hegemony*, 142. For a similar analysis, see Arrighi and Silver, *Chaos and Governance in the Modern World System*, 288–9.
82. Lemann, "The Next World Order," 4–5.
83. Kan, *Amerika no Sekai Senryaku*, chapters 7~11.
84. Hopkins, *American Empire*, 726. Similarly, Strange emphasized the growing importance of the U.S. share of the world market for services and finance, 'much more profitable and much more powerful sources of influence over others.' *States and Markets*, 238.
85. Convincing arguments on U.S. authorities' responses to the crisis are made by Helleiner, "Still an Extraordinary Power after All These Years" (June 2004), 1–21. Through bilateral swap agreements, the FRB provided massive sums of dollar liquidity to the European Central Bank, Swiss National Bank, Bank of England, the Bank of Japan, and the other central banks of Brazil, Mexico, Singapore, South Korea, Australia, Canada, Sweden, Denmark, Norway, and New Zealand. Strange also argued in 1988 that 'on balance American structural power may actually have increased in recent decades.' See also, Strange, "The Future of the American Empire," 13–14.
86. Helleiner, "Still an Extraordinary Power after All These Years," 4–5.
87. Ibid., 10–11.
88. Eichengreen, *Exorbitant Privilege*, 98.
89. Ibid., 8.
90. Westad, *The Global Cold War*, 396–7.

Acknowledgements

I would like to express my deep appreciation to Professors A. G. Hopkins and Shigeru Akita for their very useful comments on my draft. I am also very grateful to Professor Hopkins for his kind suggestions for stylistic changes in writing.

Disclosure Statement

No potential conflict of interest was reported by the author(s).

References

Akimoto, Eiich, and Hideki Kan. *Amerika 20-seiki Shi [The Twentieth Century History of the United States]*. Tokyo: Tokyo University Press, 2003.

Akita, Shigeru. "Teikokuteki na Kozoteki kenryoku-Igirisu Teikoku to Kokusai Chitsujo," [Imperial Structural Power-The British Empire and International Order]." In *Teikoku Kenkyu*, edited by Yuzo Yamamoto, 257–290. Nagoya: Nagoya University Press, 2003.

Arrighi, Giovanni, and Beverly J. Silver. *Chaos and Governance in the Modern World System*. Minneapolis: University of Minneapolis Press, 1999.

Bacevich, Andrew J. *American Empire The Realities & Consequences of U.S. Diplomacy*. Cambridge, Massachusetts: Harvard University Press, 2002.

Bemis, Samuel F. *A Diplomatic History of the United States*. New York: Henry Holt & Co., 1936.

Berger, Samuel R. *American Power: Hegemony, Isolationism or Engagement*. Washington, D. C.: The Council of Foreign Relations, 21 October, 1999. Accessed June 26, 2020. https://1997-2001. state.gov/. State.gov/global/arms/speeches/berger_19991021.html

Blechman, B. M., and S. S. Kaplan. *Force without War*. Washington, D. C.: The Brookings Institution, 1978.

Calleo, David P. *Beyond American Hegemony The Future of the Western Alliance*. New York: Basic Books, 1987.

Calleo, David P. "Introduction Decline: American Style." In *Is the West in Decline?*, edited by Benjyamin M. Rowland, vii–xix. Lanham/Boulder: Lexington Books, 2016.

Carr, E. H. *The Twenty Years' Crisis, 1919–1939*. New York: Perennial, 2001.

Cumings, Bruce. *Dominion from Sea to Sea Pacific Ascendancy and American Power*. New Haven: Yale University Press, 2009.

Cumings, Bruce. "Japan's Position in the World System." In *Postwar Japan as History*, edited by Andrew Gordon, 34–63. Berkley, California: University of California Press, 1993.

Darwin, John. *After Tamerlane The Rise and Fall of Global Empires, 1400-2000*. New York: Bloomsbury Press, 2008.

Dower, John W. *Embracing Defeat Japan in the Wake of World War II*. New York: W. W. Norton & Co./The New Press, 1999.

Duara, Prasenjit. "The Cold War and the Imperialism of Nation-States." In *The Oxford Handbook of the Cold War*, edited by Richard H. Immerman, and Petra Goedde, 86–104. Oxford: Oxford University Press, 2013.

Duara, Prasenjit. "The Cold War as a Historical Period: An Interpretative Essay." *Journal of Global History* 6, no. 3 (2011): 1–42. Accessed June 20, 2020. https//www.researchgate.net/publication/22740888.

Eichengreen, Barry. *Exorbitant Privilege The Rise and Fall of the Dollar and the Future of the International Monetary System*. Oxford: Oxford University Press, 2011.

Gaimusho, ed. *Nihon Gaiko Nenpyo narabini Shuyo Bunsho [A Chronology of Japanese Diplomacy and Major Documents]*, Vol. 2. Tokyo: Hara Shobo, 1969.

Gallagher, John, and Ronald Robinson. "The Imperialism of Free Trade." *The Economic History Review* 6, no. 1 (1953): 1–15.

Gardner, C. Lloyd. *Economic Aspects of New Deal Diplomacy*. Madison: University of Wisconsin Press, 1964.

Gardner, C. Lloyd, and Thomas J. McCormick. "Walter LaFeber: The Making of a Wisconsin School Revisionist." *Diplomatic History* 28, no. 5 (2004): 613–624.

Grow, Michael. *U.S. Presidents and Latin American Interventions Pursuing Regime Change in the Cold War*. Lawrence, Kansas: The University of Kansas, 2008.

Helleiner, Eric. "Still an Extraordinary Power after All These Years: US and the Global Financial Crisis of 2008." (2004): 1-21. Accessed July 2, 2020. http://web.isanet.org/Web/Conferences/FLACSOISA%20BuenosAires%202014/Archive/4e0e0a9b-2dfb-4f6f-814e-8e85e7bb78b0.pdf.

Hopkins, A. G. *American Empire A Global History*. Princeton: Princeton University Press, 2018.

Hopkins, A. G. "American 'Empire' in the 'American Century'." A paper originally prepared for the 70th Annual Conference of the Japanese Association of Western History, 16th-17th May 2020, revised 10 June, 2020. The Japanese version of the paper "'Amerika no Seiki' ni okeru Amerika 'Teikoku'" appeared in *Shiso* [Thought] no. 1161 (2021): 62–81.

Hopkins, A. G. "Informal Empire in Argentina: An Alternative View." *Journal of Latin American Studies* 26, no. 2 (1994): 496–484.

Hopkins, A. G. "Globalisation and Decolonisation." *The Journal of Imperial and Commonwealth History* 45, no. 5 (2017): 1–17.

Howe, Stephen. *Empire: A Very Short Introduction*. Oxford: Oxford University Press, 2002.

Hoff, Joan. "The American Century: From Sarajevo to Sarajevo." In *The Ambiguous Legacy U.S. Foreign Relations in the 'American Century'*, edited by Michael J. Hogan, 183–213. Cambridge: Cambridge University Press, 1999.

Iriye, Akira. "Historicizing the Cold War." In *The Oxford Handbook of the Cold War*, edited by Richard H. Immerman, and Petra Goedde, 18–31. Oxford: Oxford University Press, 2013.

Johnson, Chalmers. *The Sorrows of Empire Militarism, Secrecy, and the End of the Republic*. New York: Metropolitan Books, Henry Holt and Co, 2004.

Kan, Hideki. *Amerika no Sekai Senryaku [U.S. Global Strategy]*. Tokyo: Chuo Koron Shin-sha, 2008.

Kan, Hideki. ""Amerika no Sengo Chitsujo Koso to Ajia no Chiiki Togo, 1945–1950" [America's Design for Postwar Order and Regional Integration in Asia, 1945–1950]." *Kokusai Seiji [International Relations]* 89 (1988): 109–125.

Kan, Hideki. ""Amerika Teikokuron no Genjo to Sekai Chitsujo no Yukue" [The State of the Art on American Empire and A Prospect for the World Order]." In *Sekai Seifu no Tembo [A Prospect for World Government]*, edited by Nihon Heiwa Gakkai, 45–62. Tokyo: Waseda University Press, 2003.

Kan, Hideki. "Challengers to the 'Postwar Regime' and the 'History Problem' in the Asia-Pacific." *COSMICA* 47 (2018): 37–43.

Kan, Hideki. ""Haken Sisutemu to shiteno Reisen to Guroobaru Gabananasu no Henyoo" [The Cold War as the Hegemonic System and the Transformation of Global Governance]." In *Guroobaru Gabananasu Gaku I [Global Governance Studies I Theory, History, and Norm]*, edited by The Japan Association of Global Governance, 104–126. Kyoto: Horitsu Bunka Sha, 2018.

Kan, Hideki. ""Pakusu Amerikaana" no Sekai [The World of 'Pax Americana']." In *Guroobaru-ka no Sekai Shi [The World History of Globalisation]*, edited by Shigeru Akita, 241–302. Kyoto: Minerva Shobo, 2019.

Kan, Hideki. *Reisen to 'Amerika no Seiki' Ajia ni okeru 'Hi-koshiki Teikoku' no Chitsujo Keisei [The Cold War and the 'American Century' 'An Informal Empire''s Order-making in Asia]*. Tokyo: Iwanami Shoten, 2016.

Kan, Hideki. *Reisenki Amerika no Ajia Seisaku 'Jiyushugiteki Kokusai Chitsujo' no Henyo to 'Nichibei Kyouryoku' [American Policy toward Asia during the Cold War Years: The Transformation of 'Liberal International Order' and 'Japan-U.S. Cooperation']*. Kyoto: Koyo Shobo, 2019.

Kan, Hideki. "The Making of the 'American Empire' and US Response to Decolonization in the Early Cold War Years." In *Comparing Modern Empires Imperial Rule and Decolonization in the Changing World Order*, edited by Tomohiko Uyama, 147–180. Sapporo: Slavic-Eurasian Research Center, Hokkaido University Press.

Kan, Hideki. "US Cold War Policy and the Colombo Plan A Continuing Search for Regional Cooperation in Asia in the 1950s." In *The Transformation of the International Order of Asia Decolonization, the Cold War, and the Colombo Plan*, edited by Shigeru Akita, Gerold Krozewski, and Shoichi Watanabe, 177–198. New York: Routledge, 2015.

Kan, Hideki. "U.S.-Japan Relations in the 1960s and U.S. Policy toward the Emerging Regionalism in Asia: Nationalism, Regionalism, and Collective Security." *Hosei Kenkyu [Journal of Law and Politics]* 66, no. 2 (July 1989): 41–59.

Kennedy, David M. *Freedom from Fear: The American People in Depression and War, 1929-1945*. Oxford: Oxford University Press, 1999.

Kohn, Hans. *American Nationalism*. New York: Macmillan, 1957.

Konoe, Fumimaro. "'Eibei Honi no Heiwashugi wo Haisu,' [Reject Anglo-American Centered Pacifism]." In *Sengo Nihon Gaiko Ronshu [A Compilation of Essays on Postwar Japanese Diplomacy]*, edited by Shinichi Kitaoka, 47–67. Tokyo: Chuo Koron Sha, 1995.

Kuriyama, Takakazu. *Nichibei Domei Hyoryu kara no Dakkyaku [The Japan-U.S. Alliance Overcoming the Drifting of the Alliance]*. Tokyo: Nihon Keizai Shinbun Sha, 1997.

LaFeber, Walter. *The American Age United States Foreign Policy at Home and Abroad Since 1750*. New York: W. W. Norton, 1989.

LaFeber, Walter. "The American View of Decolonization, 1776-1920: an Ironic Legacy." In *The United States and Decolonization Power and Freedom*, edited by David Ryan, and Victor Pungong, 24–40. New York: St. Martin's Press, Inc., 2000.

Lemann, Nicholas. "The Next World Order: The Bush Administration may have a brand-new doctrine of power." *The New Yorker*, 1 April, 2002. Accessed June 29, 2020. https://www.newyorker.com/magazine/2002/04/01/the-next-world-order.

Louis, Wm Roger. "American Anti-Colonialism and the Dissolution of the British Empire." In *The 'Special Relationship': Anglo-American Relations Since 1945*, edited by William Roger Louis, and Hedley Bull, 261–283. Oxford: Oxford University Press, 1986.

Louis, Wm Roger. "Review—Books: Signing Up for the Imperial Club." *The Wall Street Journal*, 23 March, 2018.

Louis, Wm Roger, and Ronald Robinson. "Empire Preserv'd How the Americans put Anti-Communism Before Anti-Imperialism." In *Decolonization Perspectives from Now and Then*, edited by Prasenjit Duara, 152–161. London: Routledge, 2004.

Louis, Wm Roger, and Ronald Robinson. "The Imperialism of Decolonization." *The Journal of Imperial and Commonwealth History* 22, no. 3 (1994): 462–511.

Manela, Ereza. "'Peoples of Many Races': The World beyond Europe in the Wilsonian Imagination." In *Jefferson, Lincoln and Wilson The American Dilemma of Race and Democracy*, edited by John M. Cooper, Jr. and Thomas J. Knock, 184–208. Charlottesville: University of Virginia Press, 2010.

Memorandum from Sneider to Bundy, *Foreign Relations of the United States, 1964–1968* (*FRUS*), XXIX, pt. 2, Japan. Washington D.C.: USGPO, 2006, 1968, 26 April.

Mitani, Taichiro. *Wooru Sutoriito to Kyokuto: Seiji ni okeru Kokusai Kinyuu Shihon [Wall Street and the Far East: International Financial Capital in Politics]*. Tokyo: Tokyo University Press, 2009.

NSC 6008/1 "United States Policy Toward Japan". Lot File 63 D 351, NSC 6008. National Archives, College Park, Maryland, U.S.A, 11 June, 1960.

Nye, S. Joseph, Jr. *Bound to Lead The Changing Nature of American Power*. New York: Basic Books, 1990.

O'Brien, Patrick Karl, and Armand Clesse, eds. *Two Hegemonies Britain 1846–1914 and the United States 1941–2001*. Aldershot: Ashugate, 2002.

Reynolds, David. "American Globalism: Mass, Motion, and the Multiplier Effect." In *Globalization in World History*, edited by A. G. Hopkins, 144–263. New York: W. W. Norton & Co., 2002.

Robinson, Ronald. "Non-European Foundation of European Imperialism: Sketch for a Theory of Collaboration." In *Studies in the Theory of Imperialism*, edited by Roger Owen, and Bob Sutciffe, 117–142. London: Longman, 1972.

Rosenberg, Emily S. *Spreading the American Dream American Economic and Cultural Expansion 1890–1945*. New York: Hill & Wang, 1982.

Sargent, Daniel J. *A Superpower Transformed The Making of American Foreign Relations in the 1970s*. Oxford: Oxford University Press, 2015.

Schlesinger, Arthur, Jr. *The Disuniting of America: Reflections on a Multicultural Society*. New York: W. W. Norton & Co., 1998.

Schmitt, Carl. ""Forms of Modern Imperialism in International law" (1933)." In *Spatiality, Sovereignty and Carl Schmitt: Geographies of the Nomos*, edited by Stephen Leg, 29–45. Abingdon: Routledge, 2011.

Sexton, Jay. *The Monroe Doctrine: Empire and Nation in Nineteenth-Century America*. New York: Hill and Wang, 2011.

Shimizu, Tomohisa. *Amerika Teikoku [American Empire]*. Tokyo: Akishobo, 1968.

Shimizu, Tomohisa, Akira Takahashi, and Torao Tomita. *Americashi Kenkyu Nyumon [Introduction to American History]*. Tokyo: Yamakawa Shuppan Sha, 1974.

Stockholm International Peace Research Institute. *SIPRI Yearbook 2013*. Oxford: Oxford University Press, 2013.

Strange, Susan. *States and Markets*. London: Continuum, 1994. 2nd ed. The first edition was published in 1988.

Strange, Susan. "The Future of the American Empire." *Journal of International Affairs* 42, no. 1 (1988): 1–17.

Strange, Susan. "The Persistent Myth of Lost Hegemony." *International Organization* 41, no. 4 (1987): 551–574.

Strange, Susan. *The Retreat of the State The Diffusion of Power in the World Economy*. Cambridge: Cambridge University Press, 1996.

Sylvan, David, and Stephen Majeski. *U.S. Foreign Policy in Perspectives Clients, Enemies and Empire*. London/New York: Routledge, 2009.

Takahashi, Akira. *Amerika Teikokushugi Seiritsu Shi Kenkyu [The Study of the Making of the History of American Empire]*. Nagoya: Nagoya University Press, 1999.

"The Position of the United States with respect to Asia," NSC 48/1. In *U.S.-Vietnam Relations 1945-1967: Study Prepared by the Department of Defense*, Book 8 of 12, 225-272. Washington D. C.: USGPO, 1971, 23 December, 1949.

Weiner, Tim. *Legacies of Ashes The History of the CIA*. New York: Doubleday, 2007.

Westad, O. Arne. "Josho" [Introduction] of the Japanese translation of *The Global Cold War* (2005), 1-10. Nagoya: Nagoya University Press, 2010.

Westad, O. Arne. *The Global Cold War Third World Intervention and the Making of Our Modern Times*. Cambridge: Cambridge University Press, 2005.

Williams, A. William. *The Tragedy of American Diplomacy*. New York: Delta Book, 1962.

"William Appleman Williams: A Roundtable." *Diplomatic History* 25, no. 2 (2001): 275–316.

Woodrow Wilson's Address to the Senate. In *Ideas and Diplomacy Readings in the Intellectual Tradition of American Foreign Policy*, edited by Norman A. Graebner, 441-445. New York: Oxford University Press, 1962, 22 January, 1917.

Yamamuro, Shinichi. ""Teikokuron no Shatei" [A Range of the Theory of Empire]." In *Teikoku no Kenkyu [The Study of Empire]*, edited by Yuzo Yamamoto, 88–15. Nagoya: Nagoya University Press, 2003.

Part V
Response

Imperial Puzzles

A. G. Hopkins

ABSTRACT
This essay reflects on the contributions to the symposium on American Empire. In discussing the previous commentaries, the 'Response' acknowledges some of the book's limits and defends some of its interpretations. Its main purpose, however, is to endorse the various lines of enquiry the contributors have set out because they suggest ways of opening a subject that has long been confined by national borders and separated by regional specialisations. In doing so, the authors of the essays presented here have begun to assemble an agenda for writing a connected, global history to fit an age of globalisation.

Reflections on Criticism

The death of scholarship is not criticism: it is neglect. If this aphorism is indeed true, it is a relief to be able to report that I am still alive. The few books I have written have had the good fortune of being discussed and, invariably, criticised. Much of the criticism has been justified: interpretations have been modified; cryptic examples have been amplified and refined. Most reviewers, having struggled with their own publications, are inclined towards generosity. Occasionally, however the experience of reading my work has exasperated a critic to the point where truth prevails over scholarly courtesies. In climbing to the apex of his 50-page essay on my first book, published in 1974, one authority declared that 'the power of the mind to screen out evidence that is not in favour of one's own ego-laden interpretation, is staggering.'[1] A reviewer of a subsequent book was inspired to invent a colourful analogy to express his dissent. In referring to the concept of 'gentlemanly capitalism', he commented that 'the number of historians who agree with this thesis can be fitted inside the confines of a London telephone box.'[2] While the claim was not strictly true, it was sufficiently memorable to be repeated by others.

The list of adverse judgments could be greatly extended, though doing so might turn an autocritique into a suicide mission. My own reaction to criticism has evolved with my career. I admit to being rattled by the demolition the reviewer quoted above undertook on my first book. Despite other favourable reviews, I could not erase the thought that, after a decade of hard labour, I had succeeded in so alienating a senior scholar that he felt compelled to dedicate a considerable amount of time to preventing my many errors from gaining circulation. I saw my career ending just as I thought it was beginning. In the event, my luck held. A few years later, I was able to look back and deduce an abiding moral from the episode: established scholars should reflect on their own stumbling past before treating their acquired certainties as a licence to demolish apprentices to the profession. Twenty years on, the assertion that only 12 people agreed with an argument developed to illuminate the causes of British imperialism was disappointing, to say the least, and at the time mildly irritating too, but the light touch and clever humour of the criticism was aimed at the interpretation and only indirectly at the author.[3] Today, after nearly another 30 years have passed, I am almost concerned, though also relieved, to find that criticism of *American Empire* has not, or not yet, galvanised critics either to reach for their guns or to dip their pens in strong acid.[4]

My reaction to criticism is probably typical. Young scholars need support for their endeavours and can be deflated quickly if it is not forthcoming. As time passes, the measure of confidence that accompanies survival provides an antidote to wounds inflicted by the 'slings and arrows' of outrageous commentary. A more important development is also at work: time brings engagement with both the subject and other historians and produces a more refined appreciation of the purpose of scholarship and the limits placed on mortals who reach for its unattainable requirements. Right, wrong, and even truth are not part of the formula, except at a commonplace level. For me, at least, the aim of historical work is to deliver illumination with plausibility. Illumination means seeing a familiar problem from a fresh angle; plausibility requires that evidence be sufficiently robust for the interpretation to be taken seriously. Success means only that other scholars feel obliged to engage with the work in question. The merit of this approach is that it allows for a range of error, providing the basic principles remain sufficiently sturdy to keep the structure upright. All historical studies can be stripped of mistakes, improved, and extended. It is a comfort to realise, finally, that historical scholarship, like politics, is the art of the possible.

The authors of the previous articles are well equipped to see where art has exceeded science. They wear a badge of authority that raises their work to levels that an outsider cannot reach. The range and depth of the citations they have mobilised stand like centurions guarding the gates to the ivory tower. Although the citations in my book extend to almost 200 pages, they fall far short of the entry requirements. Jay Sexton puts the point very well at the outset of his contribution, where he refers to the 'voluminous national historiography that has no equal in terms of scale – and, at least until recently, also stands apart in terms of its insularity and self-referentiality.'[5] Had a mixture of ignorance and residual innocence not guided me at the outset, I doubt that I would have had the temerity to attempt to cross the border. By the time the full implications of the undertaking had become apparent, it was too late to turn back.

Part I: The American Revolution and the Post-colonial Order

The contributions to this section of the symposium form a triptych portraying the imperial continuities that joined colonial America to the United States. The authors discard the over-general application of the term 'empire' that is commonly applied to the United States during this period in favour of a definition that reflects contemporary understanding. Between them, the three articles explore the meaning of revolution and independence, the character and extent of informal influence after the constitutional break with Britain in 1783, and the sub-imperialism that carried the independent republic across the continent through the agency of white settlers.

Patrick Griffin's starting point is the recent literature that depicts the new state after 1783 as being not only strong but also imperial. The Revolution was a departure that gave the United States the power to achieve sovereignty and reconcile it with liberty. This literature, as he points out, misses a dimension of the story because it is largely self-contained. The purpose of his article is to identify the missing link. The dimension Griffin uncovers is found not by accentuating the differences between the colonial regime and the post-colonial order, but by examining the continuities, especially the enduring bonds with the former colonial power. This claim produces an illuminating paradox: dependence supported sovereignty; western expansion allowed liberty to flourish by providing an outlet for settlers who might otherwise have posed problems of social control and civil order. The vision was of ending empire; the reality was the growth of the settler state through territorial acquisition at the expense of Native Americans. In summary: 'America could act imperially because it was part of another empire.'[6] Imperialism, however, did not mean creating an empire; its aim and its ultimate result was to strengthen and expand a sovereign nation state.

This is a stimulating argument that places current research on the transition from colony to republic in the much older context of the Age of Revolutions – and revises both approaches. Two key terms, 'empire' and 'revolution', merit further reflection. With notable exceptions, historians of the United States tend to use 'empire' as an all-purpose label that can be fixed to a broad range of cases, places, and periods. During the eighteenth century, however, 'empire' was deployed principally to refer to an expanding sovereign state, even one that had spread overseas. The issue need not be elaborated here because Max Endling deals with it concisely and convincingly in his article. To 'act imperially' was to act assertively in annexing land and dislodging indigenous people for the purpose of expanding the settler state. It was not until the mid-nineteenth century that the accumulation of exceptions (notably India) enlarged the term so that it became synonymous with colonies that were separate and subordinate. Evidently, if the definition applicable to one period is transferred to another it will produce misunderstanding rather than enlightenment. The term 'revolution' also has as many quills as a porcupine. If it is taken to refer to a fundamental social revolution, as in France in 1789 or Russia in 1917, it is a poor fit for the events of 1776 and 1783 in Britain's mainland colonies. The constitutional break should not of course be underestimated, but the broad outcome is more accurately understood as being a secession rather than a revolution.

These observations underline the force of Griffin's argument. If 'empire' is understood as contemporaries understood it, the story of westward expansion is one of an expanding settler state. Griffin is surely right to emphasise the importance of space (or, more exactly, productive space) in explaining the success of the American experiment. Productive space, when politicised through the device of federalism, enabled a strong state to cohabit with liberty.[7] This approach, which Sexton also advocates, draws attention to the merits of connecting the U.S. literature on the 'settler state' to long-established work on other white settler societies, prominent among them being Britain's dominions and the neighbouring territories that became Canada in particular.[8]

If 'secession' is preferred to 'revolution', the continuities joining the mainland colonies to the post-colonial state become far more visible. The junction ought not to be surprising. Even successful revolutions are hampered by the undertow of inherited institutions and mentalities. Nevertheless, an interpretation that emphasises continuities prompts the question of how and when effective independence was achieved. The answer lies in tracing the course of dependent development to the point where the economy was able to support diversification, a sizeable domestic market, and the tax revenues needed to expand the capacity of the state. The process was inevitably evolutionary rather than revolutionary. Like the emergence of a sense of nationality, it was not the 'growth of a night'.[9] My own suggestion placed the date at the end of the nineteenth century rather than at its beginning, but the main purpose of the speculation was to alert better qualified scholars to the need to take the question seriously.

As Sexton's contribution correctly points out, my book tended to amalgamate diversity and provided only limited treatment of westward expansion and the history of Native Americans. As if in response to the omission, Max Edling sends Colonel Custer and his cavalry to claim territory that I had seen only through binoculars. His article reappraises the 'westward surge' and its consequences for the political geography of the United States in the nineteenth century. He departs from honoured traditions, such as the 'story of democracy' and dissents from the unreflective use of honorary terms, such as 'empire', which have been deployed for 'rhetorical effect more than for analytical insight.' He offers instead a bold and refreshing interpretation based on an understanding of the structural differences between states and empires.

Edling shares the view expressed by Jefferson and his contemporaries, endorsed by Griffin and followed in *American Empire*, that the term 'empire' refers to an expanding sovereign state. Sovereign states, and especially embryonic nation states, aim for homogeneity, even though they are obliged to tolerate degrees of difference arising from provincialism and other affiliations. Empires, however, are multi-ethnic polities that depend for their longevity on upholding heterogeneity. The rulers of both types of state are involved in a perpetual balancing act to ensure that differences do not develop to the point where they undermine the unity made possible by homogeneity or allow heterogeneity to promote separatism. Montesquieu had warned that the expansion of sovereign states could lead to the development of autocracy. The solution, which made his work so popular in the United States after 1783, was to introduce a federal system that would maintain the authority of the centre, allow 'liberty' to flourish by dispersing it, and avoid 'despotism' of the kind that George III was accused of exercising.

Edling illustrates these propositions by contrasting the growth of the British Empire with the expansion of the new U.S. state. British policy sought to manage the different ethnicities that affected its interests in the mainland colonies. The new U.S. state expanded westwards and southwards by reproducing itself in newly-acquired territories. The process of incorporation took time. A period of controlled development was required before territories could become states. Although the period of transition exhibited some of the characteristics of colonial rule, it fails to qualify for the designation 'empire' because the aim, and the result, was the creation of an expanded nation state. The key criterion for achieving incorporation, as Edling demonstrates, was race: the successful cloning of federal states depended on the dominance of white settlers; non-whites were denied equality. The priority given to the white population explains much of the chronology of the transition from territory to state: Oklahoma was admitted to the Union only in 1907, when the white population there had finally become the majority.

This analysis sharpens the distinction between continental and overseas expansion. The Supreme Court had to tie itself in knots to reconcile the acquisition of overseas possessions with constitutional theory and practice. It did so by distinguishing between territories that could hope to be incorporated at some point and those that would remain unincorporated.[10] Race remained the determining consideration and explains why Hawai'i, which had otherwise been well qualified for decades, did not become a state until 1959, when other pressures finally compelled Washington to breach long-held principles of racial discrimination.[11]

It is worth pausing at this point to explain why, as Sexton noted, my treatment of westward expansion was attenuated.[12] One of the difficulties in writing a spacious synthesis of a large subject is knowing when to stop. Authors who hack their way through to one frontier find that another, even more distant, lies ahead. The aim of *American Empire* at this point was to underline Britain's continuing influence on its former colonies without being drawn into writing a history of the United States, a task that would have carried me far beyond my purpose and competence. The judgement made in this case stemmed from the proposition that the United States was not creating a territorial empire but extending a sovereign state. Edling extends this analysis in ways that I had either not seen or lacked the authority to pursue.

Nevertheless, Edling's assessment suggests that, on this occasion, I might have been on the right trail. A related clarification, prompted by his remarks on the way the term 'empire' has been used, concerns the consequences of viewing westward expansion as being the product of a sovereign state. The aim is not to give empires a free pass, but to show that neither the potential for subordination nor its consequences are neatly correlated with one type of state rather than another. It is salutary to remember that unitary and federal states with effective central governments are well placed to discriminate against minorities and entrench social inequalities, and have a long record of doing so, as the history of Native Americans, among others, clearly shows.

Jay Sexton's article begins with an admirable summary of my interpretation of the period between 1783 and 1861, which argued that impulses transmitted by Britain had a strong influence on the United States after it had achieved formal independence. Sexton adds his own deft illustrations to the analysis, including some inviting reflections on how the world might look if seen from Missouri rather than London. Such thoughts are a salutary reminder that one person's centre is another's periphery, and that perspective can transmit bias as well as insight.

Sexton then inverts the analysis to reveal how a return trade from the United States affected not only the former 'mother country' but also the wider British world.[13] Britain's massive investments in the United States generated profits that were reinvested elsewhere; cotton exports from the South were turned into textiles that were sold throughout the world; protectionist policies in the United States helped to drive British exports into other markets, sometimes by imperialist means. Trans-Atlantic networks also spread an assortment of political and social programmes, ranging from the anti-slavery movement and republicanism to ideas of racism and models of segregation, all of which were re-exported to other parts of the British world. Evidence of increasing harmony, as the War of 1812 slipped into memory, was partly offset by a continuing strain of popular Anglophobia, which could be mobilised when votes were needed. Sexton's enlarged view of the trans-Atlantic connection indicates that specialists on the United States can benefit from incorporating the literature on the British world into their own research. This thought complements Griffin's in underlining the need to place studies of the westward movement in the context of settler societies elsewhere. Sexton cites the Canadian example as one that seems obvious but has been undervalued by specialists whose work, unlike the settlers themselves, halts at the border between the two countries.

Sexton's contribution also helps to amplify the notion of dependent development referred to earlier. The return trade and its wider consequences are evidence of increasing integration in a world that was becoming globalised. The most telling of his examples occurred during the second half of the century, when the United States combined a renewed sense of national unity after the Civil War with rapid industrialisation. This phase of 'collaborative competition', as Sexton terms it, was evidence of the rising power of the former colony. Britain's plan for an imperial federation that would include the United States was too grandiose to be practical, but it indicated that by the last quarter of the century London regarded the former colonies, by then successfully reunited, as partners rather than as subordinates. The willingness of the United States to confront Britain during the Venezuela Crisis of 1895 and offer financial support to the City of London during the Anglo-South African War confirmed the increasing weight of its presence in international affairs. In 1898, following the Spanish-American War, Britain welcomed the United States into the imperial club. Whether or not this date is a reasonable approximation for the attainment of effective independence, it undoubted marked a shift from dependent development to a point of parity between the two nations.

Andrew Carnegie's vision of a union of the 'Anglo-Saxon race' remained a fantasy. Parity between the United States and Britain was followed by the 'special relationship', a bilateral formula used by successive British governments to disguise the growing imbalance between the two countries. The two World Wars, when Britain became heavily dependent on U. S. financial and military power, were large and irreversible steps on the uneven road towards inequality. It has been said that empire ends when the periphery takes over the centre. With the arrival of G.I.s at the end of the Second World War, the British public was treated to the marvels of everyday affluence. At one remove, Hollywood's inviting representations of American life and values inspired awe, some imitation, and even more aspiration. Nevertheless, the pretensions embodied in the special relationship survived. Great powers thrive on a diet of nostalgia. Unrealistic hopes of recapturing the assumed greatness of the past continue to resonate in Britain, inhibiting necessary adjustments to reality. It remains to be seen whether the United States faces the same problem and how it will react if it does.

Griffin, Edling, and Sexton all emphasise the importance of setting the westward movement in the context of the advancing frontier of Anglo-settlement in other parts of the world. Griffin and Edling refer explicitly to 'settler colonialism'; Sexton underlines the value of making use of comparative examples. The approach has the great merit of lifting the subject out of its insularity. Nevertheless, like the concept of 'empire', the term 'settler colonialism' needs careful handling. The original Greek meaning of colonies referred to movements of settlers from their homeland. Later, the term was applied to emigrants who left Britain for parts of the world that became, like Canada, dominions. In this sense, 'settler colonialism' was a form of sub-imperialism occurring with the framework of a territorial empire. If, however, the United States is thought of as an emerging nation state rather than an empire, the term 'settler colonialism' is, strictly speaking, anachronistic. An alternative, 'settler imperialism' would be consistent with an expansive sovereign state because imperialist impulses can arise in different types of polity. Leaving pedantry aside, an awareness of the terminological issue might help to prevent the devaluation of the wider currency circulating under the imperial crown, 'empire'.

Part II: Insular Perspectives on Empire

The three articles in this section shift the focus from the centre to what used to be called, without qualification, the periphery. The changed perspective accords with the view that explanations of imperialism need to incorporate evidence from both sides of the frontier. The approach is now uncontroversial and follows from an awareness of the research on Area Studies undertaken since the 1960s. Nevertheless, the advance of knowledge presents historians of empire-building with formidable difficulties in trying to incorporate detailed research from different parts of the world. If they say too little, regional specialists will be disappointed; if they say too much, the central theme will be lost in the details of diversity. *American Empire* adopted a centrist position but recognised the importance of insular perspectives by including detailed studies of Cuba, Puerto Rico, the Philippines, and Hawai'i. As the contributions to this section show, however, it is not easy to strike a balance that meets the needs of competing priorities.

The war with Spain that ended by making the United States an imperial power with possessions in the Caribbean and Pacific began in Cuba, which is also the starting point of this section of my Response. William Morgan provides a clear and powerful account of the nationalist movement that underlines its causal relationship not only to the Revolution of 1895 but also to the defeat of Spain in 1898. The United States arrived as the contest had almost been decided. Theodore Roosevelt's highly-publicised charge up San Juan Hill disguised the reality that the Cuban army had already brought Spain to the point of defeat. As Morgan shows, the success of Cuban opposition to Spanish rule stemmed from a long history of preparation that went back to the Ten Years' War of 1868–78. Military experience was allied to fundamental social change: the ending of slavery made the prospect of a new civic order based on equality a political possibility; an accompanying commitment to creating an inclusive, 'raceless nation' gave political activists a unifying ideology. By focusing on developments within Cuba, Morgan produces an interpretation that both extends the lines causation leading from Madrid and Washington and reverses their direction: Cuban nationalists ended Spanish rule; the United States arrived in time to collect the spoils of their victory.

This interpretation is a valuable and necessary extension of American Empire, which touched on these themes but did not explore them fully. By taking my argument seriously while also dissenting from the emphasis it places on external causes, Morgan opens an important discussion and one that many regional specialists will approve. Morgan's position is associated with what used to be called the 'peripheral thesis', which was a reaction to traditional views that saw imperialism as an imposition from a distant but powerful centre. As noted earlier, the peripheral thesis has now been absorbed to the extent that historians of empire are aware of the important research completed on former colonial territories during the last half century. My purpose on this occasion, however, was to fit the United States into the story of Western expansion during the last three centuries. I signalled the importance of developments beyond the frontiers established by the Western powers by including a chapter on imperial expansion that was deliberately entitled 'Insular Perspectives on an Intrusive World'.[14] I did not set out to provide a full account of the role of indigenous societies in opposing or assisting the advance of imperialist forces. That aim could not have been achieved without writing a different and even larger book.

This response evades the key question of cause that Morgan rightly identifies in shifting its direction to forces within Cuba. I was aware of the supporting evidence he cites regarding Cuban military success and the unifying power of a multiracial ideology. The difficulty, however, is that both points are open to qualification. Other research suggests that the Cuban army was short of weapons and that the concessions Spain offered in 1897 were prompted mainly by fears of U.S. intervention. The ideal of multiracial unity also needs to be treated cautiously, given the presence of cross-currents of wealth and status. These manifested themselves dramatically in the rapid alienation of Afro-Cubans that led to the formation of a separate political party in 1908 and to a substantial armed rebellion in 1912.[15] Although Morgan acknowledges these qualifications, he does not use them to modify his main thesis. Evidently, there is a balance to be struck here, but it requires not only a mastery of the fine details of the case but also an awareness that specialists themselves are divided on the issue. My own knowledge extended far enough for me to realise that it would be unwise to pronounce on the matter and that the best course was to indicate the complexities involved in arriving at a judgment.

The difficulty with the peripheral thesis from the standpoint adopted in *American Empire* is that there were many peripheries, and each had its own agents who made their contributions to the stack of necessary causes. The central point, however, is that the series of crises that erupted on peripheries across the world in the late nineteenth century cannot be explained by focusing on events unfolding on individual frontiers, unless, improbably, they are treated as coincidences. Accordingly, and consistent with my purpose, I looked for causes that were common to all four of the different islands that fell under U.S. rule or control. The widespread depression in international trade in the late nineteenth century was one of the most prominent. All the islands experienced falling net incomes; the three Spanish islands also suffered from increased taxation as Madrid tried to solve its own acute fiscal problems. Cuba, which was heavily depended on sugar exports, faced a major crisis as prices for cane sugar collapsed and competition from beet destroyed its European market. It is hard to separate the discontent that fuelled the nationalist movements from these developments, which had direct and adverse consequences for colonial subjects in the Caribbean and Pacific, and other parts of the world too.

Reynaldo Ileto's article also reveals complexities in the story of anti-colonial nationalism in the Philippines that outsiders writing at a high level of generalisation are likely to miss or over-compress. *American Empire* located the three most famous nationalist leaders, José Rizal, Andrés Bonifacio, and Emilio Aguinaldo, in the context of the far-reaching changes taking place in the nineteenth century and viewed them as a following a sequential transition from reformist hopes to revolutionary imperatives. The sequence not only reflected the findings of the accessible literature on the Philippines but also fitted the evolution of anti-colonial nationalist movements elsewhere. However, my assessment was also limited: it signalled the importance of incorporating insular perspectives but is open to the criticism that it did not go far enough to include key features of the revolution that erupted in 1896.

Ileto shows that a longer historical perspective reveals the enduring importance of three political fields of force: Manila, the administrative and commercial centre; the pueblos, the village communities under the control of the friars, who acted on behalf the Spanish state as well as the Church; and the large, predominately rural spaces that lay beyond the pueblos. The relationship between these arenas and the nationalist leaders, Ileto suggests, is the key to understanding the aims and outcomes of the revolutionary movement. Rizal was a highly educated, cosmopolitan mestizo based in Manila who aimed to unite likeminded ilustrados (the educated, 'enlightened' elite) behind a programme of reform. Bonifacio was also based in Manila, where he was open to cosmopolitan political and intellectual influences, but was self-educated, used Tagalog rather than Spanish, and wanted to spread the opposition to Spain beyond a narrow band of urban ilustrados. Aguinaldo stood apart because he came from a provincial town and had only a limited education, but his experience included being a town mayor and the ability to speak for, as well as to, the wider population. Rizal was not committed to expanding the resistance beyond the middle class; Bonifacio lacked the necessary technique and connections to do so; Aguinaldo, the rural provincial, know how to deal with the friars, municipal elites, and villagers, and had the capacity to transform the opposition to Spain into a national movement.

Ileto provides a fresh, stimulating, and authoritative analysis of the three most famous leaders of the Revolution of 1896. This is a considerable achievement, given that their reputations have been anatomised in forensic detail by several generations of historians. As Ileto is the leading authority on the subject, it is comforting as well as instructive to learn that the revisions he suggests adjust some of his own thinking as well as confirm his dissent from interpretations he departs from. His central contention that Aguinaldo's claim to national leadership was far more effective outside Luzon than has generally been acknowledged will compel other scholars to rebalance the weight they have attached to the influence of the three leaders. Ileto provides other insights that deserve attention when space allows. Britain's commitment to its interests in the archipelago was even greater than has been assumed; the British Empire, represented by Hong Kong and Singapore, was a source of refuge and radicalism for Filipino nationalists – a theme elaborated by Nicole CuUnjieng Aboitiz in the article that follows.

Fools should not rush in where national historians have already trodden the ground flat. To interpret the role of the nationalist leaders is also to examine the soul of the nation. Because the past lives on in the present, it is hard for historians to avoid measuring famous men against tests derived from the state of the nation today. An enduring question is whether, and if so why, the Revolution remained incomplete. Answers often accompany normative assumptions about what the Revolution ought to have achieved. Competing assumptions and different appraisals of the current state of the nation inspire varying interpretations of history. Reputations rise and fall. Rizal, lauded by American-sponsored historiography, has been reduced in size by nationalist historians. Approval of the more radical Bonifacio, who initiated the Revolution, is now tempered by an awareness of his limited leadership qualities. Uncertainty over Aguinaldo's role can be resolved by underlining his success in turning opposition to Spain into a national cause. The cascade of possibilities, far from being unusual, characterises the historiography of most former colonial states. In the case of the American Empire, moderates like Rizal, had counterparts in the leaders in Puerto Rico; revolutionaries like Bonifacio and Aguinaldo had their equivalents in Cuba. Similar debates over the identification of leaders who pursued the 'true' path and those who departed from it are equally familiar from studies of other parts of the colonial world.

Ileto amplifies and greatly advances our understanding of the attributes of each phase of the development of the national movement. Nevertheless, the sequence that began with moderate claims and ended with revolutionary ambitions retains its value. Rizal began the process of raising the national consciousness; Bonifacio turned reform into revolution; Aguinaldo made the programme a reality. The progression is a common feature of the history of anti-colonial movements. Colonial policy is equally predictable: decisions to suppress moderates typically provoke more radical claims. Some lessons of history can be learned but rarely are.

Ileto focusses on the internal developments that shaped the Revolution; Nicole CuUnjieng Aboitiz examines its Asian context. She criticises standard approaches, which relate the Philippines mainly or even solely to Western powers, principally Spain and the United States, and underlines the importance of connections with Southeast and East Asia instead. This is a valuable revision and fully in accord with the current priority of seeing the world from the perspective of the 'Rest' rather than the 'West'.[16] As she suggests, *American Empire* is limited in this respect. One response is to say that it was not the purpose of the book to reach beyond its already capacious main theme. Honesty, however, must sometimes overcome the instinct for self-defence. The answer, as Dr. Johnson said when questioned about an error in his famous dictionary, is: 'ignorance, madam, pure ignorance.' Had I known more about the Asian context, I would have amplified my highly-compressed reference to it. CuUnjieng Aboitiz's work will enable future studies to do exactly that.

Western globalisation spread into Southeast and East Asia via the Suez Canal, the advance of imperialism, the modernisation of Japan, and the diffusion of anti-colonial ideologies. The Philippines already had extensive and long-standing cosmopolitan ties with the region. Malaya and China had supplied immigrants; China was a source of trade; Vietnam provided a contemporary example of opposition to Western imperialism. It was Japan, however, that captured the eye and the imagination. It offered a route out of subordination through political reform and rapid industrialisation. Japan's victories over China and Russia within the space of ten years boosted its prestige and elevated it to the leadership of countries in the region that wished to overthrow or avert colonial subordination. Unsurprisingly, opposition leaders in the Philippines turned to Japan for sanctuary and support. The Japanese government was anxious to avoid alienating the major Western powers, but private groups provided places of refuge and material aid. Subsidiary centres also contributed: Hong Kong and Singapore were exemplary cases that showed how colonialism incubated its own opposition. Ironically, Hong Kong is currently trying to preserve freedoms that its liberation from colonial rule has jeopardised.

In the event, material support was far exceeded by ideological support, which was expressed in ideas of pan-Asian solidarity. This was an evolving and ambiguous concept. It offered qualities of equality and unity that could defeat

Western imperialism, but also contained the possibility that uneven development would produce an Asian hierarchy dominated by Japan. The Western powers were in no doubt that pan-Asian unity would be a threat rather than a promise. The fake news of the day, spread mainly by rumour, stoked by Western racial prejudices and heightened by fears of the 'Yellow peril', led the great powers to exaggerate the danger they faced. Asian unity was a currency that had limited circulation in international affairs; Japan's priorities lay elsewhere than in the Philippines. Nevertheless, as CuUnjieng Aboitiz shows, ideas that linked racial unity to resistance not only inspired nationalist leaders in the Philippines but also helped to create a febrile atmosphere among the Western powers.

As a result of CuUnjieng Aboitiz's research, we now know that the Philippines was integrated with Southeast and East Asia far more closely than its previous status as a regional 'outlier' assumed. The emphasis on Japan is well founded, but it is interesting to find that Malaya and China appear to have had relatively little influence on the nationalist ideas and organisation, despite the antiquity of their relations with the Philippines. The self-strengthening movement in China, had much in common with reformers in the Philippines, yet appears to have had few connections and slight influence there. A future study could also amplify the brief treatment of the 'alternative vision' of modernity that pan-Asianists formulated to show far it departed from the Japanese model, which was strongly imitative of the Western example. An even larger question concerns the relative weight to be attributed to Asian and Western influences as causes of imperial actions and resistance to them. The great merit of CuUnjieng Aboitiz's study is that future studies will be obliged to deal with questions that have not been seen so clearly before.

Part III: The Empire in the Twentieth Century

This section of the symposium spans two contrasting periods: the first half of the century, when the United States possessed a formal territorial empire that was comparable in structure and function, though not in size, to the other Western empires, and the second half down to the present, when, following decolonisation, power in international relations was exercised by other means. The difference raises the question, discussed previously with reference to the nineteenth century, as to whether the United States should continue to be described as an empire after the 1950s, when its period of formal colonial rule ended.

Seiko Mimaki provides a timely reminder of the importance of international law in historical studies. My neglect of the subject deserves more than her mild admonition because I was already aware of pioneering studies by Lauren Benton and others.[17] I can now see how I might have incorporated the subject into the way I framed the three phases of globalisation that formed the analytical basis of *American Empire*. Once again, hindsight reveals all. Fortunately, Mimaki fills a gap in my own work and in doing so alerts other imperial historians who, as she remarks, 'are inclined to treat legal history as a separate sub-specialism', to the relevance of the subject to their own work.

Mimaki's article is in two sections. The first section, which deals with the period of formal colonial rule, shows that that U.S. policy was instrumental in promoting international organisations that were committed to finding peaceful solutions to global problems. Initiatives taken by the United States included the Hague Conferences of 1898 and 1907, the foundation of the League of Nations in 1920, and the Kellog-Briand Pact (also known as the Pact of Paris) in 1928. The priority attached to cooperative efforts to secure peace stemmed from a combination of internal experience and international calculation. The Civil War produced the innovative Lieber Code of 1863, which set out comprehensive rules for the conduct of war. The emergence of the United States as an international power at the start of the twentieth century posed the problem of how a country with a small regular army could best defend its increasing external obligations. Mimaki illustrates the point by referring to President William McKinley's choice of a lawyer, Elihu Root, as Secretary for War in 1899. McKinley's explicit purpose was to allocate authority to an appointee who had the expertise to devise a constitutional and legal framework for governing the new U. S. overseas territories.

This decision was only a beginning. Mimaki goes on to show that the 'pitch for peace' supported subsequent U.S. expansion, which continued through largely informal means. Moreover, international law, though ostensibly framed to preserve peace, permitted assertive action in ways that fitted U.S. interests. The League of Nations excluded existing empires from its remit, left the Monroe Doctrine untouched, and failed to condemn racial inequality. Consequently, as critics such as the German jurist, Carl Schmidt, pointed out in the 1930s, military intervention continued without formal declarations of war, while other means of domination, through economic penetration and sanctions, were allowed and even encouraged.

The position changed after the Second World War with the foundation of the United Nations and decolonisation. The Cold War was fought with lofty rhetoric and proclaimed ideals, but also by means of economic coercion and overt and covert military intervention in the internal affairs of other sovereign states. Following the collapse of the Soviet Empire, the United States declared that the 'unipolar moment' had arrived and with it full disclosure of the right to unilateral action in international affairs. The most dramatic expression of the new policy occurred in 2003, when the United States invaded Iraq as a prelude to the aim of remaking the Middle East.

Mimaki's contribution adds a valuable dimension to the interpretation advanced in *American Empire*. Her analysis could be given even greater weight at the point of transition after the Second World War. *American*

Empire argued that this was a defining moment in the history of globalisation because it initiated a new phase that brought an end to the conditions that had underpinned the Western empires since the nineteenth century. The structure and orientation of world trade began to change; anti-colonial nationalist movements acquired mass membership and greater power; the United Nations and associated international organisations promoted a programme of human rights and racial equality. As decolonisation progressed, criticism of Western dominance became increasingly vociferous. These developments were not what the victorious allies intended or anticipated. The reaction of the United States, as Mimaki shows, was to modify or even abandon its previous support for international organisations that no longer served its interests and move towards a policy of unilateralism. The trend continued under President Donald Trump, not with fresh military adventures, but with an 'America First' policy marked by withdrawing from or bypassing international organisations, including those that the U.S. had been instrumental in establishing.

Hideki Kan's article expands my compressed final chapter and provides a robust challenge to its main argument. *American Empire* questioned the predominant view that the United States was an imperial power after 1945 and treated it instead as an aspiring hegemon whose ambitions were marked by some striking setbacks. The idea that the US had achieved imperial status originated during the Cold War. It imported the ideologies of the time and adopted a generally unreflective understanding of the term 'empire', which became a shorthand reference for a great power that pursued dubious policies. As noted in *American Empire* and confirmed in previous articles in this symposium, the term is one that that needs careful handling.

Kan argues that the United States is best seen as managing an informal empire, which was an alternative means of continuing and extending the formal territorial empire that spanned the period 1898–1959. He supports his case with copious examples of U.S. influence and intervention across the world throughout the twentieth century and includes particularly interesting samples of his own research on Asia. In sum, Kan provides a stimulating restatement of the continuity thesis, which at its fullest extent joins the expansion occurring in the twentieth century to the westward movement that gathered pace after 1783. His article is especially welcome because should it help to reopen a debate that has lost impetus in recent years. I will focus here on an alternative position so that readers can explore both.

Most of the examples Kan cites are not in dispute and appear in *American Empire*. Similarly, we are agreed on the importance of U.S. military and financial power in the world after 1945. The key issue is one of interpretation, and here we take different positions. Two sets of problems arise from the emphasis on continuity. The first is methodological and occurs when historians read into the past rather than out of it. Theories that view the 'American Century' as a period of supreme U.S. peak power are tempted to treat distant events as part of a cumulative trend leading to the present instead of relating them to the different priorities of their own times. My interpretation was formed not when U.S. supremacy was at its height but when it was being questioned. It was easier for me to envisage a world in which the purpose of history was not to account for the origins and onward march of U.S. dominance.

An additional methodological point follows from the continuity thesis. If the United States is regarded as an empire, even an informal empire, after 1945, the claim implies that it can be compared to previous empires, most obviously those that immediately preceded it. This step involves a categorical error: the United States was indeed a great power but not all great powers are empires. The empires that flourished before the Second World War, including the insular empire of the United States, were products of different circumstances, notably the shift from dynastic to nation states, the transition from agricultural to industrial economies, and the formulation of justificatory theories of racial supremacy. Their aim was to control and integrate parts of the world so that they could serve nation-building and industrialising strategies. Informal influence was part of this strategy. The United States had different priorities. Ends and means had changed fundamentally. After 1945, the principal aim of the US was to build an international security system. This involved establishing military bases throughout the world and interfering freely in the affairs of other states. It did not, however, require other states to be integrated or governed directly for the purpose of reshaping basic social institutions. On the contrary, the aim was to keep them at arm's length. After 1945, informal influence was not an adjunct to formal empire; it was its main characteristic.

The second set of problems is substantive and empirical. An emphasis on continuity makes it necessary either to minimise the changes that reshaped the global order after 1945 or to show that they had little influence on the distribution of power in the world. As suggested in *American Empire*, the case for underlining the far-reaching changes that reshaped world trade, mobilised anti-colonial nationalism, and transformed the concept of human rights is a powerful one. It amounted to a shift in the character of globalisation that in turn transformed international relations. None of these developments occurred instantly; hence the overlap between formal and informal means of control that Kan refers to immediately after the Second World War. Nevertheless, the cumulative consequences were linked not only to decolonisation in Africa and Asia, but also to the achievement of effective independence elsewhere, including the former British dominions. They continue to remake the world today.[18]

An extension of this observation suggests that there is room to doubt that the 'informal empire' was as effective as Kan claims. As argued in *American Empire*, European states began to reassert their independence once they had recovered from the Second World War; the Soviet Union was beyond reach; India established itself as a neutral, independent nation; the outcome of the Korean War favoured China; the war in Vietnam was a catastrophic defeat for the United States; interventions in the Middle East, Africa, and Latin America had some short-term success in overturing governments but long-term costs that generated powerful nationalist reactions. Moreover, even after the collapse of the Soviet Union, the United States was unable to capitalise on the 'unipolar moment', as the disasters in Iraq and Afghanistan demonstrated. The U.S. undoubtedly had the most powerful military force ever known. It was no longer fighting the Second World War, however, but engaging with a world in which other people had accepted self-determination as a civic right and were prepared to see that it was implemented.

Empires – of any kind – have lost moral authority and relevance and face unprecedented resistance to invasion and occupation. Post-war globalisation changed the world. President Joseph Biden appears to have reached a similar conclusion: 'We will not promote democracy through costly military interventions or by attempting to overthrow authoritarian regimes by force. We have tried these measures in the past. However well intentioned, they haven't worked well.'[19]

Imperial Puzzles Pursued

It is impossible for this Special Issue, or any single book, to solve the puzzles arising from the study of imperial history. Nevertheless, the contributions made here indicate how some of the key issues can be pursued. The main message sent by the preceding articles is that U.S. history has much to gain from being drawn out of its insularity and joined to the wider world. The recommendation is by no means novel but has usually been received with formal acceptance rather than realised through commitment to empirical research. The previous articles have demonstrated that the imperial connection has the potential to reinvigorate familiar themes in U.S. history. If this is to happen, historians of the United States will need to show greater familiarity with imperial history, and historians of empire will need to revise their custom of abandoning the United States between 1783 and 1941.

Evidence presented in the first three articles demonstrates how a comparative approach produces fresh interpretations of empire, revolution, and imperialism during the first century of independence. The three articles that follow advertise the depth and quality of research on the insular empire and make a case for granting the islands greater prominence in studies of imperialism than they have been allowed. The third section of the symposium shows that, despite the mountain of studies on the twentieth century, there is still scope for revising imperial history by exploring new approaches and reappraising established debates. Looked at as a whole, the Special Issue has planted some large signposts to guide future research. Terms such as 'empire' are shifting products of their times and not the reassuring fixtures that much of the literature on U.S. history tends to assume; knowledge of settler imperialism elsewhere has much to contribute to studies of the United States that treat the moving frontier as a regional or national phenomenon; the history of islands far exceeds their boundaries and can be appreciated fully only if single cases are related through intra- and inter-imperial studies. Put at its simplest, empires were globalising forces and require a global perspective if their role in history is to be understood.

My Response has tried to add to the comments on *American Empire* in a spirit that matches the constructive approach taken by the contributors and the need to accept that, despite years of labour, an author cannot move beyond his limits and may not always realise what they are. The preceding commentaries have overlooked many shortcomings that could easily have been elaborated and instead have extended, adjusted, and contested my interpretation by opening new lines of enquiry. While I have felt justified in defending my position at several points, I hope I have also acknowledged at least some of the weaknesses in my book and shown respect for the scholarship of authors whose authority exceeds my own. Differences that remain should not be allowed to cloud my deep appreciation of the time and expertise my colleagues have devoted to appraising my work.

Notes

1. Hopkins, *Economic History of West Africa*. The reviewer was George Dalton, a prominent economic anthropologist.
2. Cain and Hopkins, *British Imperialism*. The reviewer was Peter Burroughs, a noted specialist on the history of the dominions.
3. The world record for fitting humans into London telephone boxes was set by a German team in 1997 and stands at 12. In 2003, a team from Northern Ireland squeezed in 14 people, but because two of them were children the feat did not entitle them to the record. Nevertheless, we can be confident that the number of those who agree that 'gentlemanly capitalists' were the driving force behind British imperialism is at least in double figures, if only by a small margin.
4. Hopkins, *American Empire*.
5. Sexton, "The British Empire", in this volume. And this is without including the extensive and diverse literature on the insular components of the American Empire.
6. Griffin, "Imperial Confusion", above.
7. Even so, 'success' was qualified. It was built on compromises that (among other matters) excluded slaves, and it broke down in 1861.
8. See also Hopkins, *American Empire*, 191–208.
9. *North American Review*, 1864. Quoted in Hopkins, *American Empire*, 211.
10. Hopkins, *American Empire*, 514–16.
11. Ibid. 669–71.
12. William Morgan makes a similar criticism in his article on Cuba in this volume.
13. Sexton, "The United States and the British Empire".
14. The theme is also followed in subsequent articles.
15. Hopkins, *American Empire*, 568–76.

16. This is also a major theme in Hopkins, *Globalisation in World History*.
17. Benton, *A Search for Sovereignty*; Benton and Ford, *Rage for Order*.
18. Hopkins, "Rethinking Decolonisation"; idem, "Globalisation and Decolonisation".
19. Quoted in the *Financial Times*, 4 March 2021, 17.

Disclosure Statement

No potential conflict of interest was reported by the author(s).

References

Benton, Laura. *A Search for Sovereignty: Law and Geography in European Empires, 1400-1900*. Cambridge: Cambridge University Press, 2010.

Benton, Laura, and Lisa Ford. *Rage for Order: The British Empire and the Origins of International Law, 1800-1850*. Cambridge, MA: Harvard University Press, 2016.

Cain, P. J., and A. G. Hopkins. *British Imperialism, 1688-2015*. 3rd ed. London: Routledge, 2016.

Hopkins, A. G. *An Economic History of West Africa*. London: Longman, 1973; 2nd ed, London: Routledge, 2019.

Hopkins, A. G. *American Empire: A Global History*. Princeton: Princeton University Press, 2018.

Hopkins, A. G. ed., *Globalisation in World History*. London: Pimlico; New York: Norton, 2002.

Hopkins, A. G. "Globalisation and Decolonisation." *Journal of Imperial & Commonwealth History* 45 (2017): 729–745.

Hopkins, A. G. "Rethinking Globalisation." *Past & Present* 200 (2008): 211–247.

Sexton, Jay. "The United States and the British Empire since 1783." In *The Oxford History of the British Empire, Companion Volume on the American Colonies*, edited by Stephen Foster, 318–348. Oxford: Oxford University Press, 2013.

Index

Note: Folios followed by "n" indicate endnotes.

Act of Declaration of Philippine Independence 153
Adventures of Huckleberry Finn (Twain) 37
Afghanistan 178–9, 205, 235
Africa 39, 44, 70, 75, 77, 164, 206, 234–5
African American Maroon 45
African Americans 39, 43–5, 74–5, 108
Afro-Asia 72
Afro-Cuban 91, 97, 108–9, 227
Agoncillo, Teodoro A.: *Revolt of the Masses, The* 132n18
Aguilar, Filomenio V.: *Clash of Spirits* 143
Aguinaldo, Emilio 10, 113–15, 121–3, 126–30, 132n22, 132n32, 132n34, 135, 139, 147, 150–3, 228–30
Aguinaldo and the Revolution of 1896 (de Achutegui and Bernad) 132n32
Alleghany Mountains 37
American Empire: A Global History (Hopkins) 3–4, 6–7, 9, 11–13, 20, 36, 38, 40, 64–81, 89–90, 92–3, 100, 107–9, 113, 137, 165, 186–8, 194, 201–3, 220, 224, 226, 228, 232–6
American Indian(s) 39–40, 42–4, 47–8, 50, 51–2, 56, 114
American Indian Nations 51–3
American Revolution 5, 10, 22, 25, 42, 75, 78, 101, 122, 127, 129, 152, 202, 208n2, 221–6
American Society for the Judicial Settlement of International Disputes 167
American Society of International Law 166
American Spelling Book 93
American West 26, 68
Anderson, Fred 22; *Dominion of War: Empire and Liberty in North America, 1500–2000, The* 38
Anglo-American 8, 74, 77–8, 170–1, 193, 209n13
Anglo-American Connection in the Early Nineteenth Century (Thistlethwaite) 71
Anglophobia 80, 224
Anglo-Saxon 53, 79, 115, 130–1, 225
Anglo-South African War 225

anti-colonial: nationalism/nationalist 138–9, 145, 188, 190–1, 195–8, 228, 233; subversion 140–8
Appalachian Mountains 46
area studies 8–11, 226
Argentina 70, 74
Arizona 47
Arkansas Territory 52
Article 11, 102–3, 200
Article 13, 104
Articles of Confederation 45–6
Asia 4, 139, 140–8, 153–4, 198–9, 233–4; *see also* Global Moment of 1898
Asian Place, Filipino Nation 139
Atlantic 8–9, 19, 21–3, 26–7, 36, 42, 46, 48, 66, 70–1, 74, 76, 78, 90, 94, 97, 109
Australasia 77
Australia 3, 70, 77, 79, 148, 164, 170
awareness 165, 178–9, 226–7, 229

Bacon, Elizabeth Clift 37
Bailyn, Bernard 21; *Ideological Origins of the American Revolution* 19
Balogh, Brian 25
Bandera, Quintín 99
Battle of Manila 148, 150, 153
Belgium 164, 192
Belich, James 40, 72
Berger, Samuel R. 203
Bernad, S. J.: *Aguinaldo and the Revolution of 1896* 132n32
Bernanke, Benjamin 206
Betancourt, Salvador Cisneros 101
bilateral special relationship 71
Bimyō Yamada 147
Bolivar, Simon 30
Bonifacio, Andrés 113, 115, 121–9, 132n27, 132n18–19, 142, 152, 228–30
Boomers 56
Boots and Saddles (Custer) 36–7
Breen, T. H. 22
British Atlantic 22, 69

British Crown 44
British Empire 38, 42, 44, 64–81, 119, 128; history 69–73; Postcolonial America 65–9, 73–80
British Imperialism 71
British Isles 69
British North America 75
British occupation of Manila 119–20
Building an American Empire (Frymer) 38
Bundy, William 201
Burgos 130
Burton, Antoinette 72
Bush, George H. W. 204–5

Cabell, Edward 54
Cain, P. J. 71
California 54, 77
Calleo, David 205
Cambodia 138
Canada 70, 76, 79
Caribbean 6, 44, 53, 56, 66, 91, 93, 186–7, 189, 207, 226, 228
Carlos Fressel & Co. 127
Carr, E. H. 192
Casey, Matthew 105
Castro, Fidel 93, 108
Catch-22 31
Catholic Church 10, 120, 132n32
Catholic faith 130
Cayton, Andrew: *Dominion of War: Empire and Liberty in North America,1500–2000, The* 38
Central America 53
Central Asia 39
Charles R. Walgreen Foundation 163
Cheney, Dick 205
Cherokee nation 53
China 3, 78, 138, 140–1, 166, 179, 192–3, 230, 235
Chinese-Tagalog mestizo 123
Chippewa 44, 48
Christianity 116
Civil Rights Act 57
Civil War 5, 29, 36, 40, 45, 50–3, 55, 67, 68, 75, 78–9, 114, 166, 232
Clash of Spirits (Aguilar) 143
Clay, Henry 41
Coahuila y Tejas 52
Cogliano, Frank 25
cohabitation 43
Cold War 57, 64, 123, 138, 163, 194–201, 209n13, 210n38, 232
collaboration 3, 10, 12–13, 70, 127, 139, 190, 194–201
collaborative competition 8, 77, 225
collaborators 11–12, 189–90, 198–9, 201, 203
Colley, Linda 38, 55
Colombia 27
colonial continuities 22
colonial society 123–8

colonization/colonisation 28, 44–5, 52, 77–8, 121, 141, 143, 152, 190; *see also* decolonisation/decolonization
Colorado 52
COMECON 195
Communist Party 123
Congress 3, 46–9, 51–2, 54–5, 57, 204
Congress of Nations for the Adjustment of Universal Peace, A (Ladd) 165
Connecticut 37
Conrad, Joseph: *Heart of Darkness* 136–7
Constitution of 1787 47
Conway, Stephen 22
Corn Laws in 1846 76
Corpuz, O. D. 150
Cost of War Project 178
Covenant 11, 164, 169–70, 191
COVID-19 3, 175–6
Craig, Austin: *Lineage, Life, and Labors of Jose Rizal* 131n16
creole(s): North American 27; rebellion 27; revolutionaries 29–30; societies 29
criticism 92–3, 97, 109, 219–21, 233
Cuba 53, 56, 89–109, 114, 168; (1868) 96–8; (1878) 98–9; (1895) 100–2; (1898–1901) 102–4; male suffrage 104–9; Spain 93–6
Cuba Libre 96
Cuban Liberation Army 91, 97, 100
Cumings, Bruce 199
Custer, Elizabeth Bacon 37–8; *Boots and Saddles* 36–7
Custer, George 37–8

Dakota 37
Darwin, John 72–3
Das, Taraknath 72
Dawes Act (1887) 54
Dawes General Allotment Act in 1887 55
de Achutegui, Pedro S., S. J.: *Aguinaldo and the Revolution of1896* 132n32
de Céspedes, Carlos Manuel 96
Declaration of Independence 43
decolonisation/decolonization 6–8, 173, 178, 187, 190, 208n6, 232–3; global 71; internal 56–8; *see also* colonization/colonisation
Deep South 74
de la Fuente, Alejandro 104, 106
Delaware 43, 48, 52
Delgado, Martín Morúa 106
del Pilar, Marcelo 128
democratization 44, 78
dependent colony 49
de Polavieja, Camilo 142
Depression (1929) 193
Dery, Luis Camara 150–2
de San Martin, Jose 30
Deudney, Daniel 173
Dewey, George 148
DiCarlo, Rosemary A. 177

Dilke, Charles 71
Directorio Central de las Sociedades de Color (Central Directory of the Societies of Color) 99
Dominion of War: Empire and Liberty in North America,1500-2000, The (Anderson and Cayton) 38
double containment 199
Douglass, Frederick 75
Dower, John 199
Durham Report (1839) 79

East Asia 3, 74, 77, 128
East Coast 36
economic sanctions 164, 172-7
Edling, Max 25
effective independence 7, 66, 68, 188, 202, 222, 225, 234
Egypt 30, 75, 168
El Nuevo Criollo 103
empire 39-42, 56-8; case against 21-4; case for 24-6; formal 39-40, 189-91; insular perspectives on 226-31; of and for liberty 25, 30-1; in twentieth century 231-5; *see also* formal empire; informal empire
Empire of Liberty (Wood) 38
Escalante, Rene 123
Eurasia 4, 9
Europe 3-5
European Americans 43, 52
expansion and incorporation nineteenth century 36-58; American Indian Nations 51-3; empire 39-42, 56-8; federal union of republics 42-6; internal decolonisation 56-8; organising 46-51; unwanted peoples 53-6
Export-Import Bank 193-4

Far East 148
Farrell, Henry 175
Federalist, The 41
Federal Reserve Bank (FRB) 206, 212n85
federal union of republics 42-6
Ferrer, Ada 97, 108, 110n24
Filipino-American War 114, 121, 129, 131
Finis Hispanae (epitaph) 142
Florida 42
Florida Armed Occupation Act (1842) 54
Floyd, George 178
Ford, Lisa 72
formal empire 39-40, 189-91; *see also* empire; informal empire
France 26, 80, 150, 154, 164, 169, 178
Franklin, Benjamin 101
French Revolution 125, 132n19, 151
Frymer, Paul: *Building an American Empire* 38

Gallagher, John 66, 71
Garcia, Calixito 101
George, Lloyd 78-9

George III 43
Georgia 53, 72
Germany 141, 169
globalisation 4-6, 12-13, 65-6, 68, 73-4, 126, 138, 174-5, 195, 198, 230
Global Moment of 1898 135-54; anti-colonial subversion 140-8; Asia 140-8, 153-4; imperial spectators 148-53; Manila Bay 148-53; Pacific 140-8; Spain 140-8
Godechot, Jacques 21
Gold Reserve Act 194
Gómez, Juan Gilberto 99, 101, 103, 106
Gómez, Máximo 91, 100
Gould, Eliga 22, 25
Grand Trunk Railway 74
Great Britain 3-5, 22, 40-2, 52, 66, 70, 73, 75, 80, 114, 153, 164, 168, 178, 192-3, 202, 225
Greater East Asia Co-Prosperity Sphere 153
Great Exhibition (1851) 70
Great Plains Wars 37, 55
Great War 80
Greene, Jack 22
Grenada 42
Grito de Yara 96, 107
Guam 57, 68, 186
Guardia Civil 118, 120, 142-3
Guerra Chiquita 98
Gulf War 204
Guyatt, Nicholas 43

Haiti 27, 53
Hakim, Ali 56
Hamilton, Alexander 41
Hargreaves, John 92
Hathaway, Oona A. 179n2
Havana 90
Hawai'i 57, 68, 110n2, 114, 186
Hay, John M. 166
Heart of Darkness (Conrad) 136-7
Hegemon 189-91
Helleiner, Eric 206
Henry, Patrick 101
Heumann, Stefan: 'Tutelary Empire, The' 38
Hiromu Shimizu 147
Hispanization of the Philippines (Phelan) 131n4
Homestead Act (1862) 54
homogeneity 8, 45-6, 54, 57, 223
Hong Kong 120, 126, 144, 230
Hopkins, Antony G. 22-3, 38, 110n25, 111n29; *American Empire: A Global History* 3-4, 6-7, 9, 11-13, 20, 36, 38, 40, 64-81, 89-90, 92-3, 100, 107-9, 113, 137, 165, 186-8, 194, 201-3, 220, 224, 226, 228, 232-6
Hugo, Victor 125
Hussein, Saddam 204
Huzzey, Richard 75

Iberian Peninsula 116
Ideological Origins of the American Revolution (Bailyn) 19

Ikenberry, G. John 173
imperial anticolonialism 188
imperial federation 71
imperialism 4, 209n12, 221, 226; anti-colonial nationalism and 188; assertive 5; causes 93; collaboration with 10; colonialism and 172; continental 72; economic 170; free trade 66; of idealism 188
Imperial Japan 142
imperial state 19–31; case against empire 21–4; case for empire 24–6; empire of and for liberty 30–1; post-colonial state 26–30; post-revolutionary state 26–30
imperial structural power 211n64
India 3, 74–5, 138, 198, 234
Indiana Territory 47
Indian Savages 43
Indian Territory 48, 52, 55
Indigenous America 68
Indigenous Digital Archives 47
Indonesia 198
Indo-Pakistan War of September 1965 198
industrialisation 5–6, 74, 93–5, 225, 230
informal empire 11–12, 40, 186–218; Cold War 194–201; collaboration 194–201; formal empire 189–91; Hegemon 189–91; insular empire 186–9; in Post-Cold War World 204–7; U.S. military power 201–4
informal trading empire 71; *see also* empire
Inner Mongolia 192
Institute for Open and Transdisciplinary Research Initiatives (OTRI) 3
Instituto Booker T. Washington 103
Insular Cases 57
insular empire 137, 186–9
internal decolonisation 56–8
internationalisation 138
international lawyers and empire 165–8
intra-imperial relationship 6–8
Inventing a Hero: The Posthumous Re-Creation of Andres Bonifacio (May) 122
Iran 176
Iranian Revolution in 1979 175
Iraq 235
Ireland 79
Islam 116
Italy 164, 192

Japan 128, 138–41, 144, 164, 166, 192, 230
Jefferson, Thomas 23, 30, 38, 41, 58
Jim Crow 56, 108
J.M. Fleming & Co. 127
Johns Hopkins University 176
Jutarō, Komura 142

Kang Yu-wei 148
Kansas 52
Kellog-Briand Pact 169, 179n7, 193, 232
Kennan, George F. 163, 200
Kentōji Danbara 147

Kissinger, Henry 197
Konoe, Fumimaro 171, 193
Korea 3, 141
Korean War 234
Koskenniemi, Martti 167
Kramer, Paul 73

Ladd, William: *Congress of Nations for the Adjustment of Universal Peace, A* 165
LaFeber, Walter 190, 192
La Follette, Robert 171
Lakota Sioux 37
Lamont, Thomas 192
Lancashire 74
La Solidaridad 155n17
Latin America 27, 67, 74, 77, 235
Laurel, Yldefonso 144
law/regulation 163–79; Act of Declaration of Philippine Independence 153; awareness 178–9; Civil Rights Act 57; Dawes Act (1887) 54; Dawes General Allotment Act in 1887 55; economic sanctions 172–7; Florida Armed Occupation Act (1842) 54; Gold Reserve Act 194; Homestead Act (1862) 54; international lawyers and empire 165–8; Kellog-Briand Pact 169, 179n7, 193, 232; Lend-Lease Act 194; Oregon Land Donation Act (1850) 54; Pact of Paris 164, 169; Preemption Act (1841) 54; Reciprocal Trade Agreement Act of 1934 193; Southern Homestead Act (1866) 54–5; Warsaw Pact 195; World War I 168–72
League of Nations 164
Lee, Fitzhugh 90
legalistic-moralistic approach 163
Lend-Lease Act 194
Lepore, Jill 68; *These Truths: A History of the United States* 65
Les Miserables 125
Leynes, Conde 143
Liang Qichao 147
Liberal Democratic Party 201
liberal international order 195, 200
Liberal Leviathan 173
Liberation Army 102, 103, 105, 107
Lieber Code of 1863 232
Light of Liberty, The (Richardson) 132n27
Lincoln, Abraham 53
Lineage, Life, and Labors of Jose Rizal (Craig) 131n16
Little Bighorn River 37
Liverpool 70
Louis, Roger 196
Louisiana 46
Louisiana Purchase 29, 38, 41, 50
Louverture, Toussaint 30

Mabini, Apolinario 152
MacArthur, Douglas 199–200
Maceo, Antonio 90, 100, 107

Maceo, Jose 99
Madrid 116, 124, 126, 141
Magee, Philip 72
Mai Lão Bạng 147
Makoto, Fukumoto 141
Malayo-Hispanic civilisation 115
male suffrage 104–9
Manchuria 192
Manila 115, 124, 126, 141, 144
Manila Bay 148
Manila Consulate 140
Marquetti, Campos 103
Marshall Plan of June 1947 195
Martí, Jose 93, 97, 100–1
Maryland 37–8
Maso, Bartolome 106
May, Glenn 123; *Inventing a Hero: The Posthumous Re-Creation of Andres Bonifacio* 122
McConville, Brendan 22
McCoy, Alfred 121–2
McCoy, Drew 29
McKinley, William 91, 168
Medina, Isagani 131n10
Meiji Restoration (1868) 140
Mesoamerica 44
Mexican Cession of 1848 54
Mexico 27, 40, 52–4, 166
Mexico City 77
Miami 44, 48
Michigan 38
Michigan Territory 47
Middle East 164, 235
Mississippi River 46, 52
Mississippi Valley 56
Missouri Rhineland 69
Missouri River 52, 69
Missouri Territory 47
Mi Ultimo Adios (My Last Farewell) (Rizal) 124
Miyazaki Tōten 148
modernity 56, 123–8, 231
Moluccas 138
Moncada, Guillermo 99
Moncada, Samuel 177
Monroe County 37
Monroe Doctrine 67, 79, 169, 172, 189, 209n15, 209n20
Montana 52
Montesquieu: *Spirit of the Laws* 45
Montojo, Patricio 148
Montserrat, Jorge Arreaza 177
Morgan, J. P. 192
Moros, Nicolás Maduro 176
Motsch, Aimé-Ernest 148, 150
municipal elites 118–20
Murrin, John 22

Naidu, Sarojini 172
Napoleon 26, 30

Napoleonic Wars 29
National Archives 47
national identity 94, 96, 101, 109, 129
National Security Council 201
national unification 128–31
nation-state 5, 7, 9, 25, 29, 40, 50, 154, 174, 189, 195
Native America 40
Nazism 172
Nebraska 52
Negroes 97
neo-colonialism 40, 67; *see also* colonization/ colonisation
Netherlands 164, 192
New International Economic Order (NIEO) 197
Newman, Abraham 175
New Mexico 46–7, 50, 54, 57
New South Wales 72
New World 29
New York 37, 70
New York City 192
New Zealand 164
Nicaragua 53
Niebuhr, Reinhold 172
Nine-Power Treaty 192
Noli me Tangere (Rizal) 124
Non-Aligned Movement 176–7
Norie, E. W. M.: *Note on the Philippine Islands* 152
North America 26–7, 42, 54, 56–7, 76–8, 190
North Atlantic 74–5
North Atlantic Treaty Organization 188
North Dakota 52
Northern Great Plains 36
Northern Ireland 236n3
Northwest Ordinance 41, 43–5, 47–51, 54, 57
Northwest Territory 37, 49–50
Note on the Philippine Islands (Norie) 152
Nye, Joseph 204

O'Brien, Patrick 188
Office of Foreign Assets Control (OFAC) 175
Ohio 37–8
Ohio River 46, 48
Oklahoma 52, 55–6
Ontario 76
Onuf, Peter 24–5
Open Door imperialism 11–12, 186–7, 195
Oregon 41–2
Oregon Land Donation Act (1850) 54
Oregon Settlement (1846) 52, 54
Oregon Territory 47
organising expansion 46–51
Organization of American Historians (OAH) 187
Osaka University: Institute for Open and Transdisciplinary Research Initiatives (OTRI) 3
O'Shaughnessy, Andrew 22
Ottoman Empire 164

Pacific 57, 77, 114, 140–8
Pact of Paris 11, 163–4, 169–72, 232
Palma, Tomás Estrada 104
Palmer, R. R. 21
Partido Independiente de Color (PIC) 106–7
Partido RevolucionarioCubano (PRC) (Cuban Revolution Party) 99
Pax Americana 4, 174
Pax Britannica 23, 174, 188
Peace of Paris (1783) 46
Pennsylvania 65
peripheral approaches 8–11
peripheral thesis 227
Perpetual Union 41, 45–6, 50
Perry, Matthew 140
Persia 166
Phan Bội Châu 145
Phelan, John L.: *Hispanization of the Philippines* 131n4
Philadelphia 26, 37
Philippine-American War 153
Philippine Revolution (1898) 113–31, 138–9, 142, 146, 148, 151–2, 154; Aguinaldo, Emilio 121–3; Bonifacio, Andres 121–3; colonial society 123–8; modernity 123–8; municipal elites 118–20; national unification 128–31; Pueblo society 128–31; Rizal, Jose 121–3; Spanish clergy 118–20; Spanish Colonial Rule to 1850 115–18
Philippines 57, 68, 117, 186
Pincus, Steven 22
Pocock, J. G. A. 45
political instability 68
political stability 68
politicisation 25, 27–8
Ponce, Mariano 148
Portugal 164, 192
Post-Cold War World 204–7
post-colonial America 65–9, 73–80
post-colonial globalization 197
post-coloniality 28
post-colonial order 221–6
post-colonial society 21
post-colonial state 26–30
post-revolutionary state 21, 26–30
post-World War II 198
Preemption Act (1841) 54
Previsón 106
Proclamation Line 42
Propaganda Movement 124, 138, 145
Protestants 115, 130–1
proto-globalisation 4; *see also* globalisation
Pueblo society 128–31
Puerto Rico 57, 68, 138

Quebec 42

Rai, Lala Lajpat 72
Rao, Gautham 19–20
Reciprocal Trade Agreement Act of 1934 193

Recur, Carlos 143
reducción 116
regions 8–11
regulation *see* law/regulation
Replenishing the Earth 72
Revolt of the Masses, The (Agoncillo) 132n18
Revolutionary Clergy (Schumacher) 133n36
Rice, Condoleeza 206
Richardson, Jim: *Light of Liberty, The* 132n27
Rizal, Jose 115, 121–3, 124, 132n23–4, 145, 147; *Mi Ultimo Adios* (My Last Farewell) 124; *Noli me Tangere* 124
Robinson, Ronald 66, 71
Roman Catholicism 116
Roosevelt, Franklin D. 193–4
Roosevelt, Teddy 91
Root, Elihu 166, 168
Royal Navy 67
Rule of Warfare 43
Rumsfeld, Donald 205
Russia 80, 230
Russian Empire 39
Ryukyu Islands 199

Said, Edward 137
Saint-Domingue 27, 30
Saler, Bethel 51; *Settlers' Empire, The* 38
Samoa 57
San Francisco Bay 56
San Francisco Peace Treaty 199–200
Saniel, Josefa 141, 155n23
Santo Domingo 53
Sauk 44, 48
Saulo, Alfredo B. 132n22
Scheffer, David 174
Schmidt, Carl 232
Schmitt, Carl 169, 191
Schumacher, John N.: *Revolutionary Clergy* 133n36
Scott, James Brown 166–7
Scott, Rebecca 98
secession 222
Serra, Rafael 103
settler colonialism 6–8, 20, 38, 51, 226
settler imperialism 226, 236
Settlers' Empire, The (Saler) 38
Seven Ranges 48
Seven Years' War 22, 27, 42, 101
Sexton, Jay 191
Shapiro, S. J. 179n2
Shawnee 43, 48
Shimizu 142
Shunrō Oshikawa 147
Siam 138, 154, 166
Siberia 39
Singapore 120, 126, 230
Sino-Japanese War (1894–1895) 140–3
Sneider, Richard 201
social revolution 24
Sooners 56

South Africa 77, 164
South Dakota 52
Southeast Asia 153
Southern Homestead Act (1866) 54–5
Soviet Union 188, 195, 234–5
Spain 52, 68, 93–6, 138, 140–8
Spanish-American War 20, 89–91, 113, 140, 148, 168, 189, 225
Spanish Army 90–1, 120
Spanish clergy 118–20
Spanish Colonial Rule to 1850 115–18
Spanish Philippines 117, 125
special relationship 71, 80
Spirit of the Laws (Montesquieu) 45
State of Sequoyah 55
structural power 198, 201–2, 205–7, 211n60, 211n64, 212n85
Suehiro Tetchō 147
Sulu sultanate in Jolo 138
Sumner, Charles 46
Sun Yat-sen 148
Supreme Court of the Nations 165

Tagalog insurrection 130
Taisho Depression 192
taong labas 119
technology of destruction 5
Territory of Louisiana 47
Texas 65
These Truths: A History of the United States (Lepore) 65
Third World 207
Thistlethwaite, Frank: *Anglo-American Connection in the Early Nineteenth Century* 71
Thompson, Andrew 72
Tōten, Miyazaki 141
Tragedy of American Diplomacy, The (Williams) 186, 208n2
Treaty of Paris 29, 153
treaty polities 51
Trump, Donald 233
Tuffnell, Stephen 70
Turner, Frederick Jackson 28
'Tutelary Empire, The' (Heumann) 38
Twain, Mark: *Adventures of Huckleberry Finn* 37

unexceptional empire 93; *see also* empire
Unfinished Revolution 114
unincorporated territories 57
unitary state 40
United Nations (UN) 6, 232; General Assembly 177, 197; Special Rapporteur 177
United States (US) 3–5; expansion 6; invasion of Iraq 205; military power 201–4

United States Magazine 41
unwanted peoples 53–6
Uruguay 74
U.S. Army 123, 129
U.S. Cavalry (7th) 36
U.S. Census 51, 56
U.S. Constitution 103
U.S. Federal Reserve 174
U.S. Navy 113
U.S. Treasury 206
Utah 47, 56
Utah Territory 47

Venezuela 176
Venezuela Crisis of 1895 225
Versailles Treaty 171
Victoria 77
Victorian British Empire 78
Vietnam 154, 235
Vietnam War 204
Virginia 64
von Bismarck, Otto 143
von Overbeck, Baron 143

War of 1812 55
War of 1898 56
War of Independence 51
Warren, James Francis 138
Warsaw Pact 195
Washington, George 40, 90–1, 94, 101, 188, 190–2, 197, 200, 202–3
Weaver, John 40
Westad, Arne 198
West Africa 44
Western Treaty Powers 141
White, Karl D. 135–6, 139, 154
Willamette Valley 56
William and Mary Quarterly 19
Williams, William A.: *Tragedy of American Diplomacy, The* 186, 208n2
Wilson, Woodrow 169, 191
Wolfowitz, Paul 205
Wood, Gordon 25, 41; *Empire of Liberty* 38
Woodford, Stewart 90
World Economic Conference in 1933 193
World War I 168–72, 191
World War II 5, 38, 128, 138, 172–4, 178–9, 188, 191, 193–4, 199, 201, 225, 232, 234
Wyandot 43, 48
Wyoming 52

Yamamuro 208–9n10
Yokohama 143–4
Yucatan Peninsula 53

Zasloff, Jonathan 179n6